D0938711

# Airlines in a Post-Pandemic World

The COVID-19 pandemic represents an extraordinary inflection point that caught airlines worldwide unprepared, causing CEOs to recalibrate their business models. This book expounds upon why this unprecedented pandemic is different from the past disruptions experienced by the airline industry during the past 50 years, and what airlines and related businesses now can do to adapt to the dramatically changed marketplace.

This book presents two future scenarios: continuous improvements and elastic supply. These are considered in four specific contexts for the rebuilding of the airline business. These contexts, *in the order of urgency* with respect to change from the status quo, are the following. The first context is for airlines to become better prepared to deal with frequent and deeper disruptions that could be localized or globalized relating to such areas as climate change, geopolitics, and cybersecurity. The second context is to collaborate and integrate within the much broader and dynamic travel ecosystem, possibly using platforms to innovate on new value systems and share risk. The third context, which has always been the case but now needs a much greater focus, is for airlines to offer real solutions to people's travel needs, solutions developed with imagination and turbocharged innovation, even as we contemplate new technology airplanes and mobility as service solutions. The fourth context is to refocus on the need to improve the experience, the development, and the enablement of employees at all levels within the organizations.

This book is recommended reading for all senior-level practitioners of airlines and related businesses, as well as aviation policy makers worldwide.

**Nawal K. Taneja** has five decades of experience in the airline industry and is a published author. He is currently Executive-in-Residence at Fisher College of Business, The Ohio State University, USA.

# Airlines in a Post-Pandemic World

## Preparing for Constant Turbulence Ahead

Nawal K. Taneja

Routledge
Taylor & Francis Group

LONDON AND NEW YORK

First published 2021
by Routledge
2 Park Square, Milton Park, Abingdon, Oxon OX14 4RN

and by Routledge
52 Vanderbilt Avenue, New York, NY 10017

*Routledge is an imprint of the Taylor & Francis Group, an informa business*

© 2021 Nawal K. Taneja

The right of Nawal K. Taneja to be identified as author of this work has been
asserted by him in accordance with sections 77 and 78 of the Copyright,
Designs and Patents Act 1988.

*British Library Cataloguing-in-Publication Data*
A catalogue record for this book is available from the British Library

*Library of Congress Cataloging-in-Publication Data*
Names: Taneja, Nawal K., author.
Title: Airlines in a post-pandemic world: preparing for
constant turbulence ahead / Nawal K. Taneja.
Description: Abingdon, Oxon; New York, NY: Routledge, 2021. |
Includes bibliographical references and index.
Identifiers: LCCN 2020052596 (print) | LCCN 2020052597 (ebook)
Subjects: LCSH: Airlines–Management. | Aeronautics, Commercial. |
COVID-19 (Disease)–Economic aspects. | Disasters–Economic aspects.
Classification: LCC HE9780 .T3596 2021 (print) |
LCC HE9780 (ebook) | DDC 387.7068–dc23
LC record available at https://lccn.loc.gov/2020052596
LC ebook record available at https://lccn.loc.gov/2020052597

ISBN: 978-0-367-71582-3 (hbk)
ISBN: 978-0-367-71584-7 (pbk)
ISBN: 978-1-003-15270-5 (ebk)

Typeset in Bembo
by Newgen Publishing UK

Dedicated to Angela, Matthew, Sophia, and Ravi

# Contents

# Figures

# Tables

# Acknowledgments

I would like to express my appreciation for all those who contributed in different ways, especially Angela Taneja (my business research analyst), Peeter Kivestu (formerly with Teradata and now a Principal with Oplytix), Dietmar Kirchner (formerly a SVP at Lufthansa and now Senior Aviation Advisor and co-Chairman of the International Airline Symposium Planning Committee), Zhihang Chi (Vice President and General Manager of North America for Air China), and Nico Buchholz (formerly a senior executive with Lufthansa, Bombardier, and Airbus) for discussions on challenges and opportunities facing the global airline industry and related businesses.

The second group of individuals that I would like to recognize include, at:

Airbus—Lukas Bratt Lejring;
APEX—Joe Leader;
Aviation Strategy—James Halstead and Keith McMullan;
Boeing Commercial Airplanes—Craig Auestad and Adam Kohorn;
Delta Air Lines—Chul Lee (formerly with);
Fraport AG—Michaela Schultheiss-Münch;
HaCon (a Siemens Company)—Michael Frankenberg and Svenja Katharina Weiss;
heyworld (a subsidiary of Lufthansa Cargo)—Timo Schamber;
HyperloopTT—Robert Miller;
IATA—Eric Leopold (formerly with) and Brian Pearce;
Lufthansa German Airlines—Karl Echtermeyer;
Lufthansa German Airlines Cargo—Jorga Ahlborn;
MKmetric GmbH—Benedikt Mandel;
OAG—John Grant;
Ohio State University—Sean To;
Predicio—Adam Ejsmont;
Salesforce—Antoine de Kerviler and Taimur Khan;
Siemens—Nicolas Petrovic;
Southwest Airlines—John Jamotta (formerly with); and
Travel Daily—Mark Ross-Smith.

Third, there are a number of other people who provided significant help: at Routledge of the Taylor & Francis Group (Guy Loft, Senior Editor, Aviation/ Health & Safety; Julia Pollacco, Editorial Assistant, Business and Management; and Peter Hall, Production Editor); and at Newgen Publishing UK (Liz Davey, Project Manager, as well as Copy Editor Gillian Bourn).

Finally, I would also like to thank my family for their support and patience.

# Foreword

*Fariba E. Alamdari*

*Former Vice President Marketing Strategy, Boeing Commercial Airplane, USA.*
*Former Professor of Air Transport Management and Dean of Engineering,*
*Manufacturing and Science, Cranfield University, UK*

The aviation industry is currently experiencing one of the most challenging periods of its history due to the Coronavirus pandemic. Companies in the travel industry are being forced to be more innovative than ever in order to serve their customers and keep their employees engaged.

Undoubtedly, the aviation industry has gone through significant transformation in the last two decades due to innovative products, business models and services. However, given the frequency of turbulences impacting aviation there is an urgent need for rethinking and innovative ideas to get the industry out of this current challenging situation. For sure, the urgency of the situation calls for innovations in every segment of the industry.

Numerous studies have produced evidence highlighting the importance of culture on organizational performance and effectiveness. As discussed in *Best Practice: Process Innovation Management*, the most innovative companies of the future will be dominated by those that do not simply focus energies upon product and technical innovation, but have managed to build enduring environments of human communities striving towards innovation through the creation of appropriate cultures and climate.[1]

Dr. Taneja in his book also emphasizes that one of the key requirements for the acceleration of the scale and scope of innovation is a significant change of corporate culture in aviation companies to create and capture value during much more uncertain times. This clearly requires the replacement of old assumptions and practices with more dynamic and innovative processes.

Challenging times with all their painful moments provide opportunity for change. Responding to crises often requires behavioral change at a company level. Although such a change requires everyone's involvement, from the bottom of the organization to the top, strong leadership is critical to a company's ability to overcome the adverse impact of disruptions.

Leaders should ask themselves how much effort they are putting into creating a culture of innovation, and what are the fundamental drivers for creating it? I believe the foundation for an innovation culture is the level of trust, candor and emotional safety that employees experience in their work place. Such a foundation is necessary for employees to air their ideas without the fear of being judged.

Organizations need to pay attention to cultural resistance as one of the barriers to achieving such a goal, so that ideas do not get dismissed outright because they are a departure from the norm. Innovation does not come from rigid thinking but rather from the freedom to think differently, communicate our thoughts, disagree, debate and challenge the status quo (all in a constructive manner)! There needs to be a healthy balance between conformity and diversity of thoughts.

Courageous leaders know how to create the right kind of environment for success, an environment in which innovation is seen as a way of life and an opportunity, In such an environment leaders inspire their team to achieve high goals and objectives. Team members are empowered to meaningfully contribute, they are engaged in the purpose as well as the vision of the organization, learn collectively from both positive lessons and mistakes, are not afraid of being wrong, and work collaboratively not hierarchically. Innovative ideas can come from inside the company as well as outside to feed the company's strategy. Speed is important and paralysis by analysis is not the norm, company politics do not play a role in recognizing good ideas. Information does not flow upwards while directive flows downwards. Such organizations do not continue drinking from their own bath water but they are interested in successful ideas and business models outside their own industry. Innovation is not viewed as a "one-off" kind of activity that only happens during tough times. Instead, it is a continuous part of normal, healthy business processes, during good times as well as bad times. Expectation is set that innovation is part of everyone's job.

In such an environment excuses such as "But this is the way we've always done it" or "Yes but we're a big company, we'll be fine" or "If it isn't broken why fix it?" or "Don't mess with success!" are used to reject good ideas. As John Maynard Keynes stated, "The real difficulty in changing any enterprise lies not in developing new ideas, but in escaping from the old ones."

Obviously, creating such an environment is a tall order. It requires open, constant "all-way" communication and sharing of information. It means everyone understands the vision and plans in ways that allow team members to specifically identify their role as contributing effectively and innovatively in the short and long term. Perhaps most important, it demands a collective belief that innovation is inevitable in the business in order to prepare, adapt and prevail in the aviation industry that frequently faces crises.

If these characteristics are difficult to be woven in the fabric of the company, a separate and safe place for innovation outside the company standards and procedures could be established.

While we cannot always know exactly what every disruption will look like, we do know that these new challenges are more complex and unfold more rapidly than ever before. Staying successful will only work if innovation truly becomes a vital part of the aviation corporation life.

In this book Dr. Taneja proposes innovative and thought-provoking techniques about managing airlines' passenger demand based on a flexible and agile planning process. He also offers several examples of innovative ideas from companies outside the aviation industry that could have applications for organizations in this industry. Dr. Taneja calls for leaders to ensure their corporate culture is able to flourish and recognize innovative ideas. The leaders in this industry are encouraged to ponder these ideas and adapt accordingly.

The aviation industry is currently facing an unprecedented challenge that requires all the key players including airlines, airports and manufacturers not only to work collaboratively but consider innovation in their corporate culture as well as their products and services! Clearly the aviation industry is very interdependent, and innovation is needed in all sectors in order to effectively and rapidly overcome the adverse impact of unpredictable crises the industry periodically faces.

*Bellevue, Washington, USA*

## Note

1 Mohamed Zairi, *Best Practice: Process Innovation Management* (Routledge, 2011).

# Foreword

*Kimberly J. Becker*

*President and CEO, San Diego County Regional Airport Authority*

The COVID-19 pandemic created a greater understanding of the importance of the aviation industry to the socio-economic well-being of the world. In the calendar year 2019, US airlines generated $13.9 billion in profit. The previous year generated $12.7 billion in profit. Those profits plummeted due to the global disruption caused by the Coronavirus pandemic as business travel came to a standstill and leisure traffic diminished overnight, international service effectively ceased, and conventions and meetings were cancelled. The aviation industry had never before experienced a sustained decline in traffic at this extraordinary level.

## Settling into a new norm

Six months after the onset of COVID-19, most US airports' passenger volumes leveled out to 65–75% of the previous year's passenger volumes. The aviation industry continued to grapple with significant financial shortfalls. Airports Council International (ACI) World forecasted that airports would lose $97 billion in revenues in 2020. For the aviation industry that provides roughly 11 million direct jobs and 65.5 million indirect jobs globally, the economic impact has been staggering. Forecasts for recovery range anywhere from late 2023 to 2025. It remains to be seen what full recovery might look like in a post-pandemic world.

As described in Mr. Taneja's book, *Airlines in a Post-Pandemic World: Preparing for Constant Turbulence Ahead*, long-term strategies for airports and airlines must constantly evolve. The industry has always been dynamic, but COVID-19 has intensified and quickened the pace of change. In many ways COVID-19 will be a reset to the way the industry conducts business.

## Changing airport business models

Passenger concerns about health and safety measures and the uncertainty of air travel require a significant shift in the way airports conduct business. Many passengers are indicating they will not return to the skies until a vaccine for COVID-19 is in place. As a result, enhancing the customer experience will become increasingly important to the airport's bottom line, necessitating that many of the immediate changes initiated by the industry for the health and safety of the traveling public remain a part of the future flight experience. Additionally, core business strategies for airports must be revisited with a laser focus on financial sustainability.

Even before the COVID pandemic, disruption at airports was not uncommon. In a dynamic environment with changing circumstances and many unknowns, the continuous improvement scenario, as suggested in Mr. Taneja's book, is a critical component of an airport's success. For example, with the introduction of rideshare services such as Uber and Lyft, airport parking models had to be adjusted to compensate for the impacts of fewer vehicles parking at the airports. Roadways were impacted with a significant increase in the number of vehicles and a new fee structure had to be established to account for the newly emerging technology. Much like the introduction of transportation network companies (TNCs), COVID-19 has also impacted the way passengers are arriving at the airport, causing airport operators to shift parking business models once again. Airport operators must review parking rates and models to create new demand and recover lost revenue. Some airports have transitioned to dynamic parking models that allow rates to fluctuate dependent upon demand. Many airports will have to upgrade parking systems to accommodate passengers who will expect cashless transactions and more automated services such as self-payment kiosks. Health and safety measures are now a priority for the traveling public and a necessary component of any airport business models.

Another example of a business model that has been significantly impacted by the pandemic is the traditional airport concession model. In the United States, most concession fees are based on a minimum annual guarantee or MAG. A MAG is usually established using a percentage of the previous year's sales or a percentage of gross sales receipts and is typically no lower than the value of the space rented. With many concessions making little to no revenue for nearly eight months and no end in sight, airport operators will inevitably have to determine a new approach to the concession model as most airport contracts with tenants did not anticipate an event with such devastating and long-lasting impacts as the COVID pandemic.

Mr. Taneja's second scenario of linear thinking is apparent in longer-term changes required at the airport such as the master planning process, to include the design of a terminal. Similar to the changes that were implemented as a result of September 11, the pandemic requires changes to enhance the health and safety measures returning passengers will demand. After September 11, with the creation of the TSA, new security screening equipment and procedures required complete overhauls of existing security checkpoints causing significant disruption to terminal layouts. Now, as new facilities are built, designs have been modified to include the TSA requirements. Similarly, COVID-19 will have long-lasting impacts on terminal design. Terminals must be modified to include social distancing measures and other health and safety considerations such as modified holdroom and restroom designs to allow for additional personal space, or allocation of additional space for new services such as temperature checking or COVID-19 testing. Airline fleet mixes may change as their business strategies adjust to fewer passenger levels having significant implications for the way the terminal operates, and consequently requiring operators to revisit gate layouts or even design standards. There may even be fewer airlines in the market possibly influencing overall space allocations. What is still unknown is the duration of the changes. Are the impacts of the pandemic here to stay and will the industry rebound to what it once was? Will the same airlines be flying as the financial impact continues to stress the industry in unprecedented ways? Only time will provide the answers to those unknowns.

The considerations for terminal design are far-reaching and most airports are not in the position to build new facilities, therefore requiring operators to make costly and time-consuming modifications to existing facilities. The biggest factor still to be determined is how the customer will react to the post-COVID environment and whether the changes made by airports or airlines will provide enough security for passengers to return to air travel at pre-COVID levels.

## Hope for the future

The aviation industry is in survival mode and it will be some time until we have a better indication of what our future holds. Until then, airports must modify business models and continuously adapt to changing requirements in an effort to attract passengers back to the airport and gain some level of financial stability for their operations. Airports must continue to work with their industry partners to face the many challenges COVID-19 has created, together, to ensure they are prepared for the return of their mutual passengers.

There are two certainties as the industry goes forward. Just as the industry rebounded after September 11, we will also rebound from the effects of the pandemic. And, because airports are dynamic, complex operations, there will be another disruption around the corner—whether it is through aerial ridesharing networks or unmanned aerial systems or a new regulatory requirement—and the industry will respond positively, as a team, working together, resulting in a better travel experience for everyone.

*San Diego, California, USA*

# Foreword

*Sir Tim Clark*

*President, Emirates Airline*

This book is published at a time when the airline industry deals with the greatest disruption in its history, characterised by unprecedented demand destruction, business failures and the global economy shifting into reverse. It proposes a number of pathways through the disruption's aftermath and at the same time addresses the need for a reassessment and adaptation of airline business models to ensure they are fit for purpose once the pandemic has run its course. This will happen sooner rather than later and there is no doubt that demand will return at pace in a robust and substantive manner.

*Dubai, United Arab Emirates*

# Foreword

*Pradeep Fernandes*

*Vice President of Strategy, Boeing Commercial Airplanes*

One year before the time of writing, none of us envisioned we would now be in the deepest downturn in commercial aviation history. While no part of the aviation ecosystem has been spared, some have fared worse than others, some have been lucky, and some were better prepared to weather the current situation.

Being better prepared is an ambition we all share as we look toward an uncertain "new normal" coming out of the downturn as well as the potential for new paradigms and additional forms of disruption in the future. This discipline—scenario planning—applied to our current situation and future prospects is the focus of Professor Taneja's research and writings in this book.

Gradually recovering air traffic—led by short-haul and followed by long-haul, with business and leisure travel returning to long-term trends—represents, for many, the current forecast of what we think "will" happen. We have built our operational plans around this future state and it serves as a reasonable baseline scenario. But we must recognize the adjustments needed to our analytical frameworks and algorithms during the transition period ahead. Consider, for a moment, that important facets may not materialize as expected. We could see permanent structural shifts with material impact to our plans. As Professor Taneja outlines, this falls into several categories:

**Recovery**: Will the resumption of air travel follow a predictable path, or will it be volatile and inconsistent country to country? How will this affect approaches to staffing, fleet management, and network planning?

**Mobility**: With the rapid shift to virtual work, enabled by technology such as Zoom and Microsoft Teams, will expensive business travel return to the same levels? Will virtual work be a catalyst encouraging the desire for greater face-to-face engagements? Or will people travel as a result of choosing to work remotely from new and interesting locations?

**Geopolitics**: Will nationalism grow? What happens if international trade agreements become more parochial? What does this mean for open skies agreements versus more conservative bilateral agreements? What will be the future of foreign ownership and investment in cash-strapped airlines? Will the future of national carriers versus sixth-freedom carriers shift course?

**Social**: With increased dependence on government support to weather the downturn, does this strengthen the voice and influence of different political and non-governmental entities? Will this alter the course of legislation and regulation? Could it alter or accelerate environmental causes? Could it shift labor laws?

**Business models**: With a disparity of weak versus strong players in the ecosystem, how will consolidation, partnerships, and acquisitions play out? Beyond airline versus airline, what about well-positioned non-aviation players that may stand to benefit from greater access to passengers as consumers? In these new relationships, who will be commoditized and who will be positioned to harvest the most value? Whether it is ticket prices, onboard ancillaries, airport retail, or adjacent services, will these business models shift spending streams or share of wallet? Where will supply base concentration shift power?

The sheer range of unknowns and uncertainties is overwhelming. Beyond the baseline scenario of the expected outlook, logical groupings such as a scenario built around the high likelihood and high impact outcomes as well as low probability scenarios that pose high or higher impact outcomes help focus these discussions. As Professor Taneja points out, other scenarios framed around future pandemics, cyber terrorism, and accelerated climate change are valuable to assess beyond our necessary attention to the current pandemic. The importance of these scenarios is not embodied in their elegance, but as a pathway leading us to actions to consider:

**"No regrets"** actions that yield benefit no matter which scenario of outcomes materializes.

Presumably, rationalizing cost structures, improving planning flexibility, simplifying systems, and digitizing processes yield benefits in most, if not all, scenarios.

**"Reactive"** actions that can be implemented quickly and yield benefit only in one or a few scenarios.

By their nature, these actions can be collected and archived in a "playbook"—held at the ready and implemented as specific outcomes become clear.

There are a number of "levers" that can quickly be implemented, if helpful: adjusting frequencies, streamlining route structures, fine-tuning aircraft utilization, parking or retiring aircraft, shifting network flows, outsourcing functions (baggage handling, maintenance), furloughs, utilizing lines of credit. These playbooks may be global, regional, or aligned to specific situations.

**"Pre-emptive"** actions that take a long time to implement or are no longer available as options once the situation of need arises.

Most critical to consider in scenario planning are pre-emptive actions to "prepare" for defined unknowns and uncertainties. They may drive non-trivial cost or burden in any other situation, but represent deliberate "resilience" to specific facets of the unknown.

Fleet flexibility focused on types with more versatile capabilities versus those optimized for a narrow set of missions and traffic volumes. Airport slot utilization. Strategic and marketing alliances. Capital structure and financial reserves. Insurance and hedging portfolios. Proportion of operating leases. Government relationship cultivation. Take or pay versus consumption-based vendor agreements.

Decisions on topics such as these merit deep analysis and debate. Is the cost worth the potential benefit? Which scenarios would see these choices yield benefits and how likely are those scenarios to materialize? Would some of these choices, beyond the cost burden, represent a material disadvantage in other scenarios?

Professor Taneja's book delves into these topics, considerations, and tradeoffs for those of us in and around the commercial aviation ecosystem. Looking forward thoughtfully at the uncertainties of the "new normal" affords us the opportunity to better position ourselves and our industry to not only survive, but thrive.

*Seattle, Washington, USA*

# Foreword

*Michael Frankenberg*

*Chief Executive Officer, HaCon, and Head Intermodal Solutions at Siemens Mobility*

## From intermodal travel to mobility as a service: opportunities and challenges

People love to be on the road and are constantly moving between different places. However, they are not exactly interested in traveling from airport to airport, but rather from their home to their vacation destination or from a business appointment to their home.

Due to the typical location of airports, the first and last miles are usually covered by at least one other mean of transportation—such as cab, rental car, suburban train or long-distance train. These modes are the so-called "feeders" and "fetchers" to the main connection. This type of travel is not a new development, as trips including a flight have always been intermodal.

But what has changed is that there are a plethora of new possibilities for intermodal travel and the ability to digitally map these potentially complex travel chains makes these trips more pleasant and attractive for the passenger.

This is where Mobility as a Service (MaaS) comes into play: MaaS refers to a holistic mobility approach to transportation: One that seeks the best possible interlinking of available modes of transportation services. The overall aim is to offer passengers a tailored mobility experience—as seamless, comfortable and hassle-free as possible. Simplification through digitalization is the key to making this possible.

The MaaS concept is human centered and thus puts the customer at the center of the equation. All the components required to serve the customer's individual preferences are bundled into one simple service. In addition to improving the passenger experience, MaaS platforms help to balance the unique needs of travelers with the revenue interests of transport providers and public interests such as $CO_2$ reduction. This can be achieved, for example, through appropriate routing or pricing strategies.

Seamless integration into intermodal travel chains is also becoming increasingly important for the aviation industry as it is likely that the public debate on the ecological aspects of air travel will lead some travelers to be more selective and conscious about their travel patterns. We anticipate seeing an increase in comparing and combining different modes of transport, which will affect short- and medium-haul flights in particular. Furthermore, especially carriers and airports have a strong interest in improving the integration into mobility chains, as accessibility to an airport has a bearing on how comfortable and attractive a connection is perceived.

## What are the implications?

Travelers need a single place to go to that supports them throughout all steps of the passenger journey—a tool that consolidates the necessary processes and information flows.

They only want to enter their connection and contact details once, prefer one payment transaction over several and want to have one channel for communication and updates that affect their specific travel itinerary. All relevant transport modes should therefore be bundled in a central mobility platform, as also discussed by Nawal Taneja in this book. The most user-friendly way to provide this would be with a traveler app.

While this may seem relatively straightforward, there are several challenges that have to be addressed in the implementation process:

For one, higher security requirements are necessary for flights in comparison to train or bus travel. This complicates the booking processes as particularly sensitive information such as visa and ID data must be requested. While this may be business-as-usual for airlines, it must be kept in mind when creating the security and privacy concept for a digital mobility platform—especially when it comes to how user data is synchronized between the individual transport providers. Additionally, time allotments for security checks and the check-in processes at the airport (which may differ according to departure and destination airports) must be taken into account in intermodal connection planning—in a customer- and travel-specific manner.

Another aspect is the impact that deviations from the planned itinerary may have: If a delay occurs in a "bus, train, and rental car" travel chain, this is less problematic than if, for example, a "feeder" train to the flight is cancelled. Rebooking delayed passengers is much more complex and cost-intensive in air travel because there is less flexibility in capacity planning, longer intervals between connections and higher logistical and bureaucratic costs.

Therefore it is essential to incorporate appropriate parameters for time buffers in connection planning and to pass on real-time delay data from the feeders to the airlines so that they can adequately plan and calculate whether it is reasonable, for example, to make a plane wait for delayed passengers coming in by train.

It is also important to consider that legal regulations in air and passenger rights generally provide for different tolerance limits for delays/cancellations. If the travel chain is offered as a whole, it must be determined which provisions apply and how the mobility providers want to allocate the responsibilities among them. Additionally, to counter fears passengers should also be clearly informed on what happens in the event of a delay or cancellation and who bears the risk.

Many of these (and many more) challenges can be solved with technology. In the background, however, large amounts of data—of the most varied formats and from different stakeholders—must be brought together and then processed intelligently. The use of big-data technology, smart algorithms and a well-thought-out platform architecture is just as critical to a platform's success as the trustworthiness and cooperative interactions between the various stakeholders. This is a point that Nawal Taneja emphasizes throughout the book.

It is fundamental that different means of transport do not see each other as competitors, but rather complements of one another in their qualities and thus strengthen one another by working together. Successfully realizing Mobility as a Service is always a team effort.

The future of the aviation industry depends on the willingness to see itself as an integral part of a much more complex transport system and to act accordingly—by always putting the passenger's needs first and by cooperating closely with other players.

*Hannover, Germany*

# Foreword

*Bob Lange*

*Senior Vice President, Business Analysis and Market Forecast, Airbus*

This book comes at a critical moment for commercial aviation. Some 35% by value of all international trade is carried by air. Close to 60% of international tourists travel by air. The commercial aviation industry supports around 88 million jobs worldwide and contributes up to $3.5 trillion of world GDP, or 4.1% of world economic activity.[1]

Air transport offers a vital lifeline to remote communities and islands and helps develop closer relationships between people and between states. The global aerospace sector will play a powerful role in the economic recovery as an engine of employment, innovation and prosperity.

A year ago we were debating whether or not commercial aviation had become a less cyclical industry. Data supporting predictions that "the cycle had peaked" were balanced by data supporting continued growth. If challenged, we reminded ourselves how quickly our industry had recovered from previous shocks. Then came COVID-19, the most severe crisis ever to hit air transport. As a result of the pandemic, worldwide air traffic fell by more than 90% from its peak. By April more than two-thirds of the 21,000 airliners in the world fleet were idle. The byword for the whole industry was "Cash containment"—cancelling or deferring any expense not critical for business continuity. How to survive in order to thrive later?

As we set about understanding the situation and modelling how the future might look, our approach leverages data analytics and machine learning applied to huge volumes of data that were simply unavailable in previous crises, notably those from Airbus' Skywise data platform. Mark Twain reputedly said: "History never repeats itself, but it rhymes." We can see patterns in SARS (health-related travel restrictions), the post 9/11 fear of flying and of course the economic consequences of previous recessions. Recovery of traffic to 2019 levels will likely take between 3 and 5 years, with domestic markets recovering first, followed by intra-regional markets, with long-haul intercontinental travel trailing.

As the health and fear factors are resolved, through vaccines and confidence-building via sharing of data, the long tail of the recovery will be driven by socio-economic factors and potentially by behavioural changes that have pre-COVID roots. There will be some reduction of business and corporate travel in the short to medium term as the world discovered the practical application of widespread virtual interactions and societal attitudes to air travel that were already emerging are likely to be reinforced.

Airlines have managed their fixed costs down to a minimum and have been operating effectively in "hibernation mode." Restarting operations is fraught with risk, and therefore tentative. Yet it is precisely at this time that management teams have the opportunity to review their strategies from the starting point of an enforced, smaller, footprint and re-orient their business models and the axes of their future growth. Legacy choices carry a different weight now than they did before and are open to question.

Nawal Taneja comments and challenges some of our industry's "sacred cows" such as the relationship between travel demand and GDP, and the price elasticity of demand which is historically largely based on data heading only in one direction: lower pricing stimulating demand. His two scenarios of *Continuous Improvements* and *Elastic Supply* are compelling as they provide a useful stimulus for strategic thinking and also a framing of potential outcomes. The latter scenario has consequences for all companies in the commercial aviation supply chain.

His arguments go beyond the obvious conclusions of a deep crisis such as the management imperative for an even greater focus on agility, robustness and resilience in their businesses: The ability to use the insights from the deep, rich seams of data in revenue management systems to leverage even more efficient use of physical assets such as aircraft will be a real differentiator. It will drive the more efficient use of the whole aircraft volume for passengers and cargo, and the efficient use of airspace and airport infrastructure. Not least it should stimulate large airline groupings and alliances to progress further on the flexibility and rapidity of re-allocating capacity between different operating units and may shape future asset pooling and even equity structures involving smaller players.

Our industry has always been exemplary in its focus on safety, which as we know can never be taken for granted or be the subject of time-saving short cuts. We have developed a deserved reputation for efficiency and reliability. Now we must include sustainability, which in future will become our licence to operate. The pandemic has brought the social and environmental agendas for business into the spotlight as never before. At the same time as we manage through this crisis, we must oversee the most important transition in our industry's history: the decarbonisation and digital transformation of the air transport sector.

At Airbus, we want to rise to the climate change challenge, and we are conscious of the growing expectation from society too. We are convinced that carbon-neutral aviation is not only possible, but achievable within our lifetime. This conviction is reinforced in a post-pandemic world.

Working alongside our aviation industry partners, Airbus has committed with the Air Transport Action Group (ATAG) to ambitious industry-wide decarbonisation targets. To achieve this ambition we had already started exploring disruptive technologies and concepts long before the current crisis. Our objective is to develop technology demonstrators to be able to make technology choices by the late 2020s and have an entry into service of an aircraft in the following decade.

But we're looking more broadly than the aircraft itself. We are also examining the energy sources and carriers needed for zero-emissions aviation. We believe hydrogen holds exceptional promise. It is already in use in various sectors. When generated from renewable energy sources, hydrogen can be a zero-emission fuel. It can be combusted through modified gas-turbine engines or converted into electric power via fuel cells. In addition hydrogen can be used to make sustainable synthetic "e-Fuels" such as "power-to-liquid" fuels which can be used directly in our existing aircraft, so important in the future for long-range aircraft. So hydrogen holds rich potential. The question is how to develop that potential on an industrial scale.

But there's intense pressure on commercial aviation to make progress today. And to ensure our projected growth as a sector is carbon neutral. That calls for rapid action on several fronts:

- Replacing older aircraft with the latest generation of aircraft can reduce emissions by 20–25%.
- Improving operational efficiency. For example, our "Fello'fly" project for aircraft wake trailing has the potential to reduce fuel burn and emissions from 5 to 10%.
- Scaling up the availability of affordable sustainable aviation fuels, which can reduce aircraft $CO_2$ emissions by up to 80% on a life cycle basis.
- Market-based measures such as carbon offsetting or carbon capture, for which we have CORSIA (the Carbon Offsetting and Reduction Scheme for International Aviation), a viable global offsetting scheme to ensure the industry's growth is carbon neutral.

Each of these measures poses challenges. But, together, they can drive a significant reduction in $CO_2$ emissions over the next decade and are the first stage in a credible global roadmap towards net-zero emissions in our sector.

The COVID pandemic has heavily impacted our industry and our economies. We must not let it derail our plans to meet our ambitious climate targets. This will require deep collaboration between industry, government and civil society. Improving the environmental performance of commercial aviation will also require global policies and regulations that apply to all players around the world in a uniform way.

The path to sustainability, and the disruption caused by the pandemic will act as catalysts for change, and this book will nourish reflection and debate among airline and aerospace executives whose decisions will chart the industry's future course.

*Toulouse, France*

## Note

1  2018 estimates, source: ATAG "Aviation Beyond Borders", September 2020.

# Foreword

## Joe Leader

*Chief Executive Officer, APEX (Airline Passenger Experience Association)/IFSA (International Flight Services Association)*

As the CEO of the second-largest global airline association in the world, I have witnessed first-hand the devastation COVID-19 has wrought upon our global aviation industry. Our future success depends upon learning from our past and innovating with incredible speed. I cited Nawal Taneja's books a half-dozen times in my PhD research on accelerating aviation innovations. When he asked me to write a foreword to his newest book, *Airlines in a Post-Pandemic World*, I responded, yes, immediately with a profound sense of honor and respect.

How can our airlines best respond to a post-pandemic world? Two central themes align strongly with the approach that Nawal has taken in this book. First, airline resilience embedded in our industry's evolutionary DNA has formed the initial protective response. Next, embracing the future travel experience will propel our industry past the Coronavirus crisis into a more agile and customer-centric future.

## The evolutionary resilience of airlines

We will see our industry survive and once again thrive, but it will never again be the same. Remember how quickly airline security procedures worldwide shifted after 9/11? The aftershocks of COVID-19 will be stronger as health and safety becomes a permanent fixture of air travel.

Much like COVID-19 most severely affects those with pre-existing conditions, the pandemic's ramifications have most hurt airlines in weaker economic health. Just as governments backed their financial institutions during the Great Recession, countries must offer their airlines similar backstops to support their future aviation infrastructure. Governments must also embrace minimal aviation taxation to encourage faster economic recovery after the Coronavirus-triggered downturn.

We are social, traveling creatures craving to explore our world and connect with others. Air travel will survive COVID-19, but the ramifications of health and safety awareness will remain. Customers accustomed to frequently interacting with their devices will grow accustomed to more automated, artificial intelligence-driven passenger service. Self-serve baggage drops will become as commonplace as self-check-in kiosks over the next decade. At the gate, boarding in sequential numbered order will be more logical than gate crowding. Selecting beverages and food from a smartphone connected to in-flight connectivity reduces face-to-face time while enhancing service. Just as customers subconsciously judge restaurant food by bathroom cleanliness, passengers will likewise subconsciously rank a portion of airline quality by health and safety practices. The "winners" of health and safety will be the airlines that provide a greater sense of certainty and consistency to their customers.

In one of the only silver linings to the dark COVID-19 cloud, the pandemic triggered aviation to accelerate environmental sustainability. Older, less fuel-efficient aircraft have been retired at the fastest rate in aviation history. The remaining aircraft will advance our industry permanently towards cleaner, more sustainable skies. The newer aircraft have the technological edge most enjoyed by passengers with lighter in-seat entertainment screens, next-generation seating comfort ergonomics, improved connectivity, enhanced lighting, and customer-centric onboard enhancements. Aviation environmental awareness is not a fad. Genuine sustainability will remain a game-changing trend. While aviation may only represent 2% of global greenhouse gas emissions, we have a higher calling to set a positive example for other industries to follow. Relating to sustainability, here is one quote from the book (p. 134):

> Airlines need to think about the environment in broader terms than just compliance. Sustainability aspects need to be part of the strategy, not just a compliance requirement to deal with the next inflection point.

Environmental evolution will also tie into end-to-end transportation solutions in alignment with air travel. Passengers do not want to simply fly on a route from New York to Los Angeles. They have beginning points at their homes and endpoints at their end destinations that may require many additional travel hours. Autonomous vehicles, next-generation air taxis, and new end-to-end transportation solutions will trigger an evolutionary change in airlines towards complete journey management.

## The revolutionary future travel experience

To correctly predict the future travel experience, we must first fully embrace current reality. When thinking about the future, people often expect a dramatic change over the next 5 to 10 years. Change typically occurs incrementally driven by overarching trends. These "megatrends" reach far beyond air travel and into our everyday lives. Environmental sustainability will remain a long-term megatrend alongside airline health and safety. Smartphones and connected voice assistants demonstrate future paths for airline technological upgrades. The FAANG companies of Facebook, Amazon, Apple, Netflix, and Google highlight the megatrend of providing the right content based on each individual's unique preferences. Learning from missteps of data management, airlines will have to embrace passenger ownership of their identity while enabling next-generation loyalty platforms. We will witness customers embracing artificial intelligence to serve their journey better. For example, Uber shines as a megatrend beacon for simplicity in journey management from point A to point B.

Driven by technology from smartphone screens, the seatback screen in front of passengers at the end of this decade will be a dynamic screen nearly as thin and light as seatback plastic. First, screens this light and efficient will drive a new renaissance of screens. Airlines driven away from screens by weight or logistics will no longer feel restricted. In addition to the airlines' onboard entertainment content servers, these next-generation seatback screens will seamlessly synchronize to smartphones for enhanced additional permission. For example, a customer's Disney+ account may enable a broader range of licensed content from the server when possible or via connectivity when needed. Having next-generation seatback screen surfaces serve as an extension of customer devices broadens possibilities. A business traveler may have the additional screen act as a second screen for their notebook computer. A relaxing passenger may use their phone for social media while watching a movie.

Passenger devices will serve as the gatekeeper of the passenger's personally identifiable information and preferences. Airlines may not want the data liability issues of unnecessarily storing customer preferences. Customers will have to grant explicit opt-in permissions that engage preferred individual preferences in-flight. With device-based customer opt-in approvals, the boundaries between airport and airline experience will blur. The passenger owns their identity. They may temporarily share it with the airport, their airline, and service providers along the journey. Customers will only share data with airlines along their journey in exchange for utility and value. The most significant area for airline integration stems from the expansive reach of their loyalty programs. In the decade ahead, airline loyalty programs may become a more widely leveraged currency available for use far beyond travel. Nawal talks about airlines developing digital assets that can be leveraged to maximize the value of physical assets. He lists loyalty as an example of a digital asset, along with brand and cross-border equities, as two other digital assets.

Just as the smartphone expedited in-flight entertainment touchscreens, future smartphones will encourage artificial intelligent (AI) surfaces. Already, customers are growing more accustomed to "talking to" smart assistants at home and on-the-go. By the end of this decade, customers will be able to speak to their airline in-seat entertainment. Whispering a command like "Show me a romantic comedy we haven't seen that my wife and I would both enjoy" would trigger a complex, multistep interaction. Your phone would calculate your viewing history preferences, your wife's linked history preferences, and cross-reference to the catalog of movies provided by the airline. This orchestra of artificial intelligence interaction will be automatic and effortless, triggering additional AI-driven steps to serve the customers. The wireless earbuds used with your phone would automatically connect to the screen. The movie would start and stop simultaneously for both customers.

Even today, self-driving cars are continually becoming more intelligent with software upgrades that better leverage onboard camera hardware. On aircraft, screens and smart surfaces will follow a similar trajectory. With only a lifespan of a decade, screens must continuously evolve. For example, some in-flight screens already have cameras, even though those cameras have no current use. With passenger permission, screens could allow touchless gesture control or even control by a customer's eyes. Again with explicit consent, these same types of cameras can monitor passenger health and well-being. As an example, existing cameras could monitor heart rate or signs of dehydration. They could encourage passenger movement to prevent deep-vein thrombosis (DVT). The health possibilities of permission-based health monitoring extend to future use cases to provide greater passenger certainty in a post-pandemic world.

In summary, airlines need to embrace a combination of their resilience with evolutionary change alongside a vision for flying at best speed towards the future travel experience. As Nawal suggests, airlines must (1) market passenger-centric solutions rather than itineraries, and (2) work within an elastic supply framework to deal with the unprecedented uncertainty. Airlines must also prepare to be their own revolutionary disrupters in building the future travel experience. Like Apple, airlines should become a trusted brand worthy of tremendous loyalty. For sustainability, airlines should become beacons of self-imposed environmental stewardship. Post-pandemic airlines will continuously provide customer-enhanced health and safety for continuous well-being. Technological advancements on aircraft will maintain pace with the best of consumer electronics technology. Leading the charge for customer information protection, airlines will set the example of explicit opt-in permission-based services. The approach will build confidence in expanded airline loyalty programs and integrated end-to-end journey management. Every step in this post-pandemic air travel journey climbs towards the end-to-end travel experience of our skyward dreams.

*Atlanta, Georgia, USA*

# Foreword

*Andres de Leon*

*Chief Executive Officer, HyperloopTT*

When we started HyperloopTT, we wanted to create a new mode of transportation that could become a creative disruption for the whole industry of moving people and moving freight.

HyperloopTT could revolutionize the way we travel today creating a mode of transportation system that is profitable, sustainable and passenger-centric.

The HyperloopTT system will solve the problem governments have of subsidizing their rail systems, because studies have shown that hyperloop could be profitable and financially viable itself without the help of public subsidies. Based on peer-reviewed feasibility studies, hyperloop lines can have a return on investment period of less than 25 years allowing the private initiative to lead the market and allowing less developed countries to have access to the model.

The HyperloopTT system is fully sustainable and a zero-emissions operation system. We have the potential to generate more energy than we consume with alternative energy systems like solar, wind and kinetic energy. This will change the status quo and is a great opportunity for the whole industry to fight climate change.

The HyperloopTT system is passenger-centric, putting the user at the center and focused on creating a seamless experience for travel. We have developed the concept of the "Naked Passenger," an entire ecosystem of technologies and interactions that will reduce the friction of travel and will improve dramatically comfort and the overall travel experience.

More than 5 years ago when we decided to start developing hyperloop, we had one clear idea in our mind at HyperloopTT. The idea that we could not do it alone and we could not do it against everyone in the transportation industry.

We are not only implementing the most efficient, sustainable and passenger-oriented mode of transport, we are doing it together with the transportation industry and giving a chance to visionaries to work together to arrive at our final goal.

At HyperloopTT, we work in a completely unique way. We started the project in our crowd-sourcing platform and we immediately had more than 200 people that wanted to collaborate in exchange of equity. Today we have more than 800 scientists, engineers and professionals and more than 50 companies collaborating under the same organizational model.

It is there, in the collaboration, where we developed our strength. This type of collaboration within the ecosystem is a point that Nawal Taneja makes throughout this book.

In Toulouse, the center of the aerospace industry in Europe and the home of Airbus, we developed our first full-scale test and certification bench for hyperloop in the world. And in Toulouse we partnered with the whole ecosystem and created more than 15 collaborative projects in different areas with some of the largest names in the aeronautics industry.

That way of working, that radical collaboration, has allowed us to develop technology in years that would have taken decades following normal corporate practices and restrictive scenarios.

And this is just the beginning. We, as a network orchestrator, want to utilize the same strategy for the commercial deployment of hyperloop systems worldwide. We have already demonstrated that the model works for reducing the time to develop the technology.

Now is the time to demonstrate to the world and to the entire infrastructure operators within the aviation industry that we can reduce dramatically time to market using the same methodology for the commercial implementation of hyperloop systems.

We are not a competitor. We are a future partner. We can partner with the infrastructure operators managing the airports, with the airlines managing the planes and crews and with the large original equipment manufacturers (OEMs) and the tier 1 and 2 industries behind them.

We are not a threat. We are an opportunity. We are a creative disruption that can change the way this industry has been operating and that can be an amazing solution for governments, users and the community. A transportation system that is more sustainable, more efficient and more passenger-centric.

We are an opportunity for the airport operators (private or public) to become the Hyperloop System Infrastructure Operator (HSIO) and design, build and manage the linear infrastructure. They will have the same chance as the rail infrastructure operators to be the future equity partners and operators of hyperloop stations and hyperloop systems.

We are also an opportunity for the airlines to become hyperloop transportation operators and manage the traffic of the hyperloop capsules, buying slots from the HSIO and creating a competitive and open environment that will benefit the final user. And that opportunity will allow them to change dramatically the passenger experience, getting rid of legacy practices and putting the passenger in the center to compete.

Nine of the ten most important passenger routes are in the Middle East and Asia Pacific region. Examples like Jeddah to Riyadh, Sydney to Melbourne or Beijing to Shanghai could be great opportunities for hyperloop routes from city center to city center. But we cannot forget about the United States. The US is a market that could change dramatically when large cities are connected with a hyperloop network. This is a great opportunity for the aviation industry to change its focus and rebuild on sustainability and passenger comfort.

We, again, are an opportunity for the aeronautics OEM to become the future assemblers and OEM of hyperloop capsules around the world. Companies like Airbus, Boeing, Embraer and others can compete in a new industry. And along with them their network of partners and suppliers can benefit.

Naturally, we are also an opportunity for all the auxiliary industries, like baggage handling, the maintenance teams, and others, to innovate and improve operational efficiency to make a system that is oriented to create value, comfort and reliability.

All of these opportunities are in a financial environment that will force companies to vary costs and to transform capital expenses into operating expenses and the investment in assets in hours of service and performance. The time to purchase planes and trains for operators is over. In the future, hyperloop OEMs will have to be prepared not to sell capsules but sell hours of the capsule working. The maintenance companies will not sell services but hours of availability of the assets that they maintain. Mobility as a Service (MaaS) is here to stay.

Of course, all of this is happening in the middle of a pandemic crisis that will force us to rethink the way we travel, putting passenger health and safety in the middle of each simple interaction and adapting our operational procedures to a world that perhaps will never be the same. COVID-19 or future similar pandemics will be much easier to fight with a transportation system that has been designed taking into consideration new technologies that can help to fight the virus. Biometric sensors with real-time health-monitoring, advanced air purification systems, UV-C disinfecting robots and contactless ticket systems are part of a solution developed with the latest technologies available and that does not have the disadvantage of legacy systems and processes. And a system that carries a maximum of 50 passengers in each capsule reduces the risk of contagious and overcrowded environments.

Governments around the world need to lead the economic recovery helping the private sector to invest in sustainable infrastructures that help to fight climate change and in safe and healthy modes of transport that will take care of their citizens.

Hyperloop is all of this and more, representing a new era and a blank page where the future of the transportation industry can be rewritten. Hyperloop is here. It has arrived as a radical improvement that is here to stay.

As Nawal Taneja discusses in this book, we have an opportunity to reinvent travel and logistics together. Let's do it.

*Dubai, United Arab Emirates*

# Foreword

*Andrew Lobbenberg*

*European Aviation Equity Research Analysts, HSBC*

I have had the pleasure of reading Nawal's many books on the airline industry over the years. I have sometimes been sceptical of his visions for the industry, seeing his envisioned changes as too radical to come to pass. They did not happen at first but then, very often, they did. This probably reflects the myopic manner with which capital markets (through whose eyes I observe the industry as an equity research analyst) make judgements on aviation. Nawal is normally right. It is an honour to offer a foreword to Nawal's latest book, seeking to understand what happens to the aviation sector through and after the pandemic.

On this occasion, mid-pandemic, there can be no doubt that change, very big change, is coming to the aviation industry. The debate is whether the aviation industry can come back as a better industry. It will be particularly interesting to see how aviation's sustainability develops and also how the relationships between different participants in the value chain evolve.

The pandemic has illustrated very clearly that aviation matters to society. As aviation was grounded across large parts of the world in spring 2020, we saw many governments, of widely varying political orientations, provide significant support to the airline industry. Where health security rules have allowed for travel, we have seen demand for air travel for leisure and visiting friends and relations recover surprisingly brightly, as the Chinese domestic market, flying at 2019 capacity levels in summer 2020, illustrated. For governments and for consumers, aviation really matters.

Will aviation build back better? Some commentators might argue that the airline industry was in good shape prior to the pandemic: from 2015 to 2019 International Air Transport Association (IATA) data shows the global airline industry consistently created economic value earning a return on capital above its cost of capital. This was for the first time ever since Orville and Wilbur flew. Yet once the pandemic hit, even the most profitable airlines in the pre-pandemic world—the US airlines—needed government aid to survive. The high levels of profitability from the industry had been used to deliver strong shareholder cash returns which left the companies no better placed for the challenges of the virus than less profitable peers around the world. Capital markets tend to take a short-term approach to this industry, even though the assets like aircraft can fly for 25 years and airport infrastructure can last 50 years or more.

Some airlines, pre-pandemic, focused very specifically on delivering for all stakeholders, seeing quality jobs and highly valued travel products for consumers as the best path to sustainable performance for shareholders. As aviation businesses restructure through the pandemic, seeking financially sustainable employment structures, networks and products, we watch to see if companies will balance the interests of all stakeholders and if the providers of capital will evolve to be more long-term oriented.

Environmental sustainability was surging onto the aviation industry's agenda prior to the pandemic. In the short run, the retirement of old and even midlife aircraft will see environmental performance improve. The shrinking of premium cabins on long-haul aircraft will also improve environmental key performance indicators (KPIs): the slower recovery of corporate travel will lead to smaller premium cabins, higher numbers of seats on long-haul aircraft and hence lower emissions per seat. Yet after these changes play out, many airlines globally will stamp on the capex brakes in an effort to repair their balance sheets. As demand will thus likely soften for current generation jets, it may become a catalyst for a step change in technology, be it towards Airbus's vision of hydrogen powered flight, the industrialisation of sustainable aviation fuels or more radical aircraft designs, such as KLM and Delft University's flying V.

In addition to watching how the stakeholder balance within the industry evolves, we will watch with great interest how the balance of power evolves within the broad supply chain of air transport. The airline industry's historic gripe—that everyone makes money out of aviation except airlines—was becoming less true as the airline sector delivered its record profits in the 5 years before the pandemic. Yet in this period airports, aircraft manufacturers, lessors, maintenance providers, in-flight caterers and airports all benefitted. Consolidation within the airline industry did support stronger financial returns from 2015 to 2019, but these other sectors remained less competitive, more consolidated and generated very strong financial performance.

We see the balance of power changing across the value chain. As the airline industry shrinks, and further consolidates through the pandemic, we expect to see the surviving airlines' balance of power with companies in the supply chain improve.

For example, we expect to see secondary airports needing to compete with even more vigour than before to attract footloose low-cost carrier capacity. Major hubs will face traffic shortfalls as flag carriers restructure. Yet for regulated airports, the basic principle of utility regulation, setting tariffs to allow return on capital to equal the cost of capital, will not be sustainable. Such maths would imply airport charges increases which are not sustainable post-pandemic.

Pre-pandemic, aircraft manufacturers benefitted from record backlogs of orders. Through the pandemic, they have known only deferrals and order cancellations. Those rare airlines that are in expansive mode will benefit from pricing opportunities for new or used aircraft that were not even seen in the aftermath of the 9/11 terror attacks.

Consumers want to travel. Governments want the global connectivity that aviation offers for global economies. We expect travel for leisure and visiting friends and relations to rebound ahead of business travel. But we think that corporate travel will return too: business is about people and relationships. These relationships have the same need for meeting physically as relationships with family and friends. The pace of the recovery from the pandemic is unknowable, resting as it does on wholly unpredictable developments in health and pharmaceutical innovation and also critically on government policies and collaboration around biosecurity.

As the recovery plays out, we will watch for stakeholder balance, for step changes in technology to deliver green aviation and for changes to the balance of power across the supply chain. The old gripe of airlines being the only part of the supply chain to not make money from aviation was getting weak. It may become wholly redundant—and not, before you wonder, because no one will be able to make money from aviation. In due course, distant though it may seem now, there is the chance of a world where people will fly, the aviation industry will grow sustainably, and airlines will have the chance to make money alongside other businesses in the supply chain.

*London, England*

# Foreword

*Nicolas Petrovic*

*Chief Executive Officer, Siemens for France and Belgium*

How far will the COVID crisis transform the transport industry? Given the scale of the impact on the airline sector, it seems that nothing will ever be the same again... but like many times before, airlines will find ways to adapt themselves and prosper again. Long-distance transportation, airlines and trains, have become a driver of prosperity and an integral element of many people's personal lives. As such, the demand for air travel will come back, the question is in what volume and with what customer expectation?

How will air travel evolve to bounce back in a post-COVID world? It is obviously impossible to forecast the future while we are still in the middle of a major crisis, but some scenarios can be plausibly explored, based on the acceleration of pre-existing trends.

The first trend to explore is towards more digital and customer-focused business models. As Amazon or Uber have shown, offering a simple and intuitive offer built on customers' expectations is a winning business model. Even before COVID, airlines were trying to move their offerings in that direction with better e-commerce, loyalty programmes or digitally enhanced customer experience.

Yet, their business model is still mostly an offer-led model, offering capacity (the network) and trying to capture an ever-expanding demand. But the COVID pandemic will affect the level of demand for a long time (some airlines say 3 to 5 years) and being closer to the customer will be even more important than in the past. How to convince customers to board planes? How to know them better and be able to adapt the offer to their needs rather than the opposite?

It could be argued that the "youngest" airlines, having fewer legacy IT systems, will be in a better position to adapt themselves fast. It could even be argued that a brand-new airline based on the latest technologies and therefore benefitting from a lower and more agile cost base could benefit from the current situation! Will we see a new actor offering door-to-door travel, seamlessly integrating different modes of transport at a simple and attractive price? Like any time of crisis, the possibilities are endless and exciting.

A second trend which I think will be accelerated is the move towards low-emission aircrafts. More and more influential voices are taking the opportunity of the COVID crisis and its associated lockdowns to challenge the need for "carbonated" transportation, mainly by car but also by plane. At a time when airlines are already suffering a deep crisis, they now have to find a way to demonstrate how they can lower their $CO_2$ emissions and join the fight against global warming.

On their side, aircraft manufacturers are facing a life-threatening crisis, with a collapse in orders and a lack of positive perspectives while so many jets are grounded, idle.

This is why the acceleration of the development of a "clean" aircraft will be the way to overcome the current crisis. Not only would it address a key concern of passengers and governments, but it would also be a reason for airlines to invest in new fleets. Airbus has already announced its ambition to create a hydrogen-fuelled plane by 2035. Others will certainly follow with an array of different technologies.

Last but not least, this crisis might accelerate the shift of traffic from planes to trains, especially high-speed trains on short distances. Up to 500 to 600 km, high-speed trains are able to compete very effectively against airlines and eventually reach a commanding market share. This has been the case in Europe and Asia where investments in new high-speed lines have shrunk journey times. For instance London is only two-and-a-half hours away from Paris or Brussels and three hours from the Netherlands. Chinese trains run at speeds of up to 350 kph and Japan boasts a high-speed train network that links major cities with unparalleled punctuality. Over the past few years, this shift from short-haul air trips to high-speed trains has gathered even more momentum as congestion in airports and environmental concerns have made the train option even more appealing.

As governments and the EU prioritize investments in infrastructures, especially new high-speed lines, we should see more and more short-haul trips transferring from air to rail. Air France has for instance recently announced they would abandon all liaisons where a competing high-speed train journey takes less than two hours. And if we look at the EU in particular, the coming deregulation of the rail market in 2022 will create competition between operators, leading to an increase in passenger numbers. By opening markets which are today national monopolies, the EU regulation will encourage rail operators to compete against each other all over Europe. This will lead to lower prices and better customer experience as the operators fight to gain market share. This has already happened in Italy where a private operator was created by a group of entrepreneurs to compete against the National State Operator. And as a result of this new competition, the number of passengers choosing to travel by train has increased very significantly.

Train manufacturers are already preparing the next generation of high-speed trains to benefit from these opportunities, adding better Wi-Fi connections, enhanced automation of train driving, better comfort on board. The step change from one generation of train to the other can be spectacular as I experienced first-hand when I was the CEO of Eurostar (the high-speed train operator linking London to France, Belgium and the Netherlands). When we rolled out a new fleet a few years ago, the technology allowed us to run trains at a higher frequency, for more miles with lower maintenance costs. Passengers benefitted from better seat pitch even though more seats were available on the train. In the next generations of trains, these trends will continue with potentially completely autonomous trains, a technology which is already popular for metro systems and at seat services that will allow passengers to literally feel at home (or in their offices): catering, Wi-Fi connection, privacy, and so on.

In conclusion, the COVID pandemic opens many possible scenarios for the airline industry, some of those being the emergence of customer-focused and digitally driven door-to-door travel operators, the rapid development of $CO_2$-free aircrafts and the shift of short-haul traffic from plane to rail.

Only time will tell, but as in any crisis situation, the future winners will be those who innovate and read the future trends before others. This is why this book, by Nawal Taneja, will provide much needed insight in how the different actors of the airline world see the future. A great read at the right moment: enjoy!

*Paris, France*

# Foreword

*Sébastien Rigoigne*

*Co-Founder, Chief Executive & Data Privacy Officer, Predicio*

Data is now the most valuable currency on earth. More precious than gold, data runs our lives day in and day out. From managing city expansion, urban planning to ad personalization. Data is being created, collected, and categorized around the clock. Our economies and businesses are reliant on high-quality data to help decision-makers improve their business performance, increase their market penetration, and gain a competitive edge against market rivals. The aviation industry is no different. Now more than ever, airlines need to make sense of data to cut costs, predict travel demand, enhance revenue, improve customer experience, and plan for future growth. The future of air travel depends on how companies will leverage the data around them to create optimal growth opportunities. In this book, Nawal explains how location and movement data can be used in innovative ways by the airline and the airport sectors as alternative sources for network and marketing planning.

The aviation industry was unfamiliar territory not only to Predicio, but also to the location data space. It was time to come up with innovative solutions in order to help market leaders leverage alternative data in their future planning.

So what is location data and how is it relevant to solving the unforeseen challenges in aviation? Location data is essentially information processed on an electronic communications network and includes geographic information on where a certain device is located. Location data relates to the GPS (latitude and longitude) information of a device, the direction of travel, and the time record of the registered point.

Some of the use cases discussed in this book will help in many spheres. Such examples include traffic analysis and demand forecasting for understanding trends of air travelers. To achieve this, airlines can look at the distance a customer traveled to arrive at an airport, time spent at airports, frequency of visits, where the customer started, had a connecting flight, and their final destination. These insights not only help them understand global air flight trends, but also help in more effective network planning and marketing and sales initiatives. Essentially, this will help airlines get a holistic view of trends to plan better routes and to maximize coordination, efficiency, and customer experience.

In a fast-paced world, consumers expect to have a one-to-one, personalized experience when shopping, dining, and traveling. As such, marketing interactions, customer knowledge, and preferences have become a primary focus across industries. Airlines are looking for new solutions to ensure their passengers' expectations are met or exceeded throughout transit. Mobile location data can be used to do just that. Airlines can use this information to enhance their user segmentation efforts, discover location-based audiences, and deliver higher quality marketing offers at the right time and in the right place to receptive user segments. Moreover, they can develop and sustain strong relationships with loyal customers. What we have been helping countless companies with is to ingest geolocation data to enrich their customer relationship management (CRM) platforms. Airlines are no exception to this practice. Based on frequent flyer memberships and loyalty programs, companies like Predicio can help airlines to match their frequent flyers to their data panel and return the geographic information with a list of marketing segments those flyers belong to in order to understand where they shop and where they spend their free time. Understanding consumer preferences and behaviors allows airlines to provide a more enjoyable and personalized user experience at scale.

Throughout the COVID-19 pandemic, Predicio was (and as of the time I write this foreword still is) helping companies to find themselves in this new reality with the help of data. One way we are helping organizations to recuperate from losses and to minimize crisis-related vulnerabilities is by offering mobile location data to uncover insights based on the behavior of mobile users in the real world. In times of crisis like the pandemic outbreak we are experiencing in 2020 and 2021, data-driven solutions can be the light at the end of the tunnel for businesses that are scrambling to recover from the disruption.

We believe that there is still a lot more that can be done to ensure the airline industry bounces back as it has many times before. We're certain that alternative datasets including location data will be game changers in this effort, and we're ready to play our part. Nawal is determined to prove the value of alternative data in rebuilding the aviation industry during periods of great uncertainty. With this book, he puts the ball in your court and asks, what are you waiting for?

*Paris, France*

# Foreword

*Timo Schamber*

*Managing Director, heyworld GmbH, a subsidiary of Lufthansa Cargo*

How can an airline modify its business model to adapt to, and even benefit from, the new realities in times of the Coronavirus pandemic? This is the theme of this book by Nawal Taneja. I believe that eCommerce is an opportunity for airlines, especially during this time of a pandemic.

## eCommerce: An opportunity for airlines—especially in times of a pandemic

While the Corona pandemic has presented disruptions and unprecedented challenges to countless industries, including the aviation sector, some industries have benefitted from the pandemic. This is especially true for eCommerce. COVID-19 has deeply impacted consumers' behavior and affected almost all aspects of everyday life. Most of us are working from home and business travel has almost come to a complete halt. We rarely attend events or visit bars and restaurants. But we are shopping online—much more than before the pandemic. It has become commonplace to order everyday items, such as groceries, stationery or drugstore items on the internet. Even in niche segments like fitness equipment, online vendors have profited from changing behaviors in times of Corona. In 2020, the eCommerce industry remained on its growth trajectory globally. Although consumers have less disposable income, it is expected that the revenues of the December 2020 holiday season will match or exceed those generated in 2019.

At the same time, the pandemic has presented eCommerce logistics with new challenges. Reduced capacities, especially in air cargo, have resulted in rising costs, squeezing the already tight margins of online retailers. In addition, bottlenecks in air freight and last mile services have negatively impacted delivery times—a stark departure from the trend towards ever-faster delivery of previous years. New ideas for global transportation of rising numbers of parcels are needed. This presents airlines with large opportunities—if they can meet the specific requirements of the eCommerce industry. This is also a view presented in this book.

## Characteristics of the eCommerce industry

Digital forwarders, such as heyworld, can contribute to airlines' adaptation to the changing market environment and help them diversify in two ways: (1) by achieving a high degree of digitization in our own processes, and (2) through the power of data. Before elaborating on the opportunities created by these two factors for airlines, it is worthwhile to examine the specific characteristics of the eCommerce industry.

To serve our target industry, it is absolutely imperative to digitize processes. Reliably offering cross-border eCommerce logistics with a very high standard of quality requires digitization of the entire transport chain. Today's consumers demand integrated end-to-end tracking. To meet this requirement, visibility throughout the transport chain must be achieved at the parcel level—on land and in the air. This degree of visibility and an exemplary level of data quality is also required to ensure smooth export and import customs clearance. The information on each and every parcel must be available immediately at any time.

Moving on to the physical processes of cross-border transportation of eCommerce shipments, these differ significantly from those of general cargo. eCommerce processes must be designed to enable the handling of large numbers of packages. To meet the extreme peaks of eCommerce, such as spikes of volumes around Black Friday and Double Eleven (Chinese unofficial holiday), processes must be highly scalable. Meeting these requirements is aided by the small size of parcels and their typical maximum weight of 31.5 kg. These characteristics of eCommerce shipments allow for a much higher degree of standardization and more efficient processes than those required for general cargo.

For an airline, this means that the transport of eCommerce goods can reduce the complexity of physical handling, but large volumes of data and transparency requirements drive complexity in documentation.

### *Opportunities for airlines*

With their small size and weight, eCommerce shipments are the perfect cargo to fill underutilized belly capacities. Low-cost carriers frequently do not carry any cargo, whereas traditional airlines oftentimes close certain flights for cargo. These unused capacities present a large potential—in times of pandemic and beyond. As continuous growth of cross-border eCommerce is expected for years to come, the demand for airfreight capacity from this industry will continue to grow. eCommerce has the potential to fill bellies even once the global capacity offer returns to pre-pandemic levels. An investment into enabling the transport of eCommerce shipments will therefore pay off not only in the short term, but also in the medium and long term.

One reason why airlines restrict the transport of cargo in their bellies is the complexity of cargo operations on the one hand, and loadability issues on non-containerized narrow-body and regional aircraft on the other hand. Both concerns are mitigated by the parcel structure of cross-border eCommerce:

1. Unit load devices (ULDs) are not a necessity for eCommerce shipments. Instead of using containers or pallets, loading accessories such as (reusable) bags can be used. Due to their light weight and small volume, these bags can easily be loaded and they require minimal securing on board. Even regional airliners or the bulk compartment on larger aircraft can thus hold a large number of shipments.
2. As mentioned above, the parcel structure of eCommerce significantly reduces the complexity of handling and ground operations. In fact, many processes of baggage handling can also be used to handle eCommerce shipments. The standardized dimensions of parcels allow for simple handling processes that are easily deployable across multiple locations. Space requirements to build-up and break-down are minimal. Because fast delivery times are the key, eCommerce shipments do not require interim storage—this further reduces space requirements in warehouses. There is a much lower need for handling equipment than in general cargo, and the equipment that is needed can be of a smaller size. As an example, X-ray machines, comparable in size to those used for carry-on baggage screening, are sufficient to screen bags containing eCommerce parcels.

A second reason why bellies are closed is that many flights operate on lanes with little demand for air cargo. Cross-border eCommerce is quickly becoming a global phenomenon, with demand on the export and import side rising in ever more countries. In an attempt to reduce labor cost, online retailers specifically seek out areas with weak economies to establish their fulfillment centers. Likewise, last mile carriers typically have hubs in various locations around any given country. This means typically unattractive flights between secondary airports can be just as viable to the eCommerce industry as those operating between major economic centers.

The challenge for airlines in participating in global eCommerce logistics is the requirement for comprehensive and complete data. Larger transport units must be linked to each parcel they contain to enable piece-level tracking. Data is the key, not only to digitizing operational processes and increasing efficiency, but also to meeting consumer demands.

heyworld's application programming interface (API)-first approach enables airlines to meet those requirements. Digital forwarders like heyworld must be able to gather shipment data directly from the shop software or enterprise resource planning (ERP) systems of their customers. This data must then be distributed to all actors along the global transport chain, including airlines, in a transparent manner. Airlines need to establish their own APIs to receive this data and enrich it with tracking information at the piece level. The ability to receive this wealth of data will enable airlines to optimize their own processes. Complete transparency on expected volumes, dimensions and weight can, for example, contribute to optimized load planning. Furthermore, the large volume of data available can be used to develop forecasting models to anticipate peaks. In times of geopolitical developments towards a higher degree of protectionism, such as Brexit, the availability of fully accurate shipment data is also imperative to enable airlines to file accurate manifests and comply with more stringent requirements in terms of customs.

To summarize, transparent data flows and a digitization of airline processes are important preconditions for airlines to participate in eCommerce logistics. Utilizing data presents an opportunity for airlines to improve their services in terms of physical and digital processes. As a digital forwarder, we are important enablers because we hold the required data in our systems and can provide it to airlines. The foundation has thus been laid—now it must be built upon.

*Frankfurt, Germany*

# Foreword

*Stefan Schulte*

*Executive Board Chairman of Fraport AG Frankfurt Airport Services Worldwide*

Nawal K. Taneja is renowned for continuously and comprehensively analyzing the powerful forces driving the aviation business, with a view to customers, regulators and other factors. He frequently pointed to the disruptive changes that were to come from inside and outside the industry. At the time of writing, in 2020, aviation—like many other industries—has to face the disruptive forces of the Coronavirus pandemic, slashing the business to an unprecedented extent and with yet no clear picture on future recovery.

Airports and airlines have extensive experience in dealing with major crises, gained from previous disruptions such as SARS, the 9/11 attacks or the financial crisis. In the past, aviation always recovered more quickly than other industries after such turbulences. This is because the global division of labor requires people to stay mobile. And because people love sun holidays or exploring foreign cultures. Could it be different this time? Even in the long run? With the pandemic spreading globally and affecting everybody, will health and safety measures adopted worldwide lead to a change in our beliefs and behavior? Will the new "Corona spirit" that emerged during lockdown join the demands for increased sustainability? Will the benefits of staycation win over the drive to explore foreign countries? And can digital formats truly replace in-person networking and humans' desire to socially interact? We simply do not know yet if the awareness of the pandemic will fade away in people's minds or if we somehow will learn to live with the Coronavirus. We do not even know if previous normality will return once people have been vaccinated against the virus or there is medicine to cure it. Or, otherwise, if the pandemic will change our basic needs in an even more fundamental way.

In his new book, Nawal K. Taneja suggests and elaborates on two different types of business strategy scenarios for an industry in disruption: one of continuous improvement based on linear thinking and the other one of elastic supply based on non-linear thinking. Switching immediately to a non-linear approach would be hard, if not unrealistic, for established aviation companies, since it would require them to implement a major cultural, organizational and procedural change within a still linear-thinking environment.

Fraport therefore takes a two-way approach. We apply linear thinking when it comes to adapting and further developing our current business model. This is due to the characteristics of airports and their infrastructure, which require long-term planning and building processes, entail high overhead costs, and have only limited flexibility to adapt to disruptive events. These factors place clear limits to the variability of the existing business model.

Nevertheless, we continuously evaluate the suitability of our business model by applying various scenarios. In doing so, we have specifically recognized the need for improved intermodal transportation and an even more seamless passenger journey. The call is not just for smooth train-to-air connections but also refers to the so-called "last mile" covering services such as door-to-door deliveries. Frankfurt Airport has the advantage of being one of the world's largest traffic hubs. To cement this position for the future, we are cooperating with both established and new players in the market. An essential success factor will be the integration of data from all business partners, including from government agencies. Moreover, we will need strategies to attract passengers from incoming markets to our hub, thus actively fostering the appeal of our region.

Simultaneously, however, we also need to prepare for the possibility that air traffic might not rebound to the previous growth path. Factors such as new political frameworks, enforced environmental measures, the rise of new airlines and changed business models of other industry partners could make it necessary to develop a completely revised airport business model. To face this kind of "brave new aviation world" we need to build and look at scenarios also by applying non-linear thinking. Any new business model will have to be derived from market and customer requirements. Its implementation will depend on the close cooperation not just with known partners in the field of aviation but also with new players from outside. And it will need to be based on low-value chains allowing sufficient flexibility, plus an infrastructure suitable for multi-purposes.

A different approach is also required when looking at airports' future capacity situation, including the assignment of take-off and landing slots. For some years to come, these slots might be widely available because airports are no longer facing constraints. Less demand for air travel—not just because of the crisis—hence less flight offerings, as well as airline consolidation measures and environmental concerns might be some of the factors leading to such a scenario. Moreover, people may switch to train services for short-haul routes, with new options available that enable the smooth integration of rail and air services. Yet another scenario suggests that point-to-point air services could see unexpected growth due to the availability of new aircraft models, such as the Airbus A321 XLR. Other new, smaller aircraft, which are both economically viable and environmentally friendly, might also be developed. Business people, in particular, may prefer these services to avoid the hassle of transfer flights. In the past, however, "point-to-point" proved to be less efficient and sustainable than the hub-and-spoke system—which brings us to the next issue.

Airports and airlines are challenged to come up with appropriate solutions for climate protection and increased sustainability. Fraport is committed to green electricity. Major initiatives in this field include the planned use of offshore wind energy at Frankfurt Airport and a photovoltaic system to be installed on the parking garage of the future Terminal 3. In addition, more and more apron vehicles have already been equipped with electric drives.

To save costs and cushion the expected decline in profit margins, it will be vital for the industry to further automate airport and airline processes—also by using artificial intelligence in the future. Collaboration will be key to success.

Last but not least, cargo is an important business factor with large potential for automation. Frankfurt Airport will continue to foster automated processes along the supply chain, both for traditional cargo and in the area of eCommerce.

So, how can we manage these changes and challenges within an established organization like Fraport and its deeply rooted corporate DNA? We believe it requires an "organization within the organization", i.e. an agile project organization able to embrace different skills from different departments and partners. For this purpose, we have launched our Digital Factory. One of the main functions of the Digital Factory will be to work on given tasks and deliver a minimum viable product (MVP) in short time. This will allow us to better and more flexibly react to the changing requirements of our business.

In his new book, Nawal K. Taneja provides comprehensive guidelines on how to build non-conventional scenarios, strategies and how to manage operational changes. It is therefore a compelling read in these turbulent times for the aviation industry.

*Frankfurt, Germany*

# Foreword

*Thomas Wittmann*

*Managing Director, Lufthansa Systems, GmbH*

While this book is published, the aviation industry is experiencing the biggest disruption ever, not through its own faults but through a pandemic that stops people from travelling, either because of the anticipated health risks or by governments significantly restricting travel. How will our industry cope with this unprecedented situation? How will the industry recover? In order to explore this, Nawal Taneja offers two scenarios to think about the future of aviation: a linear extrapolation of what happened in the past in one scenario and an alternative scenario (elastic supply) with more erratic demand patterns and new ways of thinking in airline management in order to cope with these difficult circumstances.

The COVID-19 pandemic changed our world in many ways, and we have to be prepared that some of these changes will last. Therefore, the new normal of aviation will be significantly different from what we know today. Thinking in scenarios is a good way to explore what the future may hold. The point is not to prepare for a specific scenario but to understand the space of possible futures we have to be prepared for.

The COVID pandemic acts as an accelerator of change in many areas. One example: 20 years ago with common availability of the internet, futurists predicted that working from home would be the future of work for many. Now, triggered through the pandemic (and after increases in network bandwidth and with the availability of user-friendly communications tools in the cloud such as Zoom or Teams), this change happened overnight. It will not only change commuter traffic significantly but also business air travel, and airlines will lose an important part of the demand and source of revenue. There is a lot of change that was imminent and that now is accelerated through the pandemic. Therefore, we will have to cope with significant disruption to our industry.

Fortunately, there will still be a deep desire to meet a person I am doing business with, or who is part of my extended family, or to see, with my own eyes, the places I have read about. Therefore, there will still be a demand for air travel, and the airlines that will survive this crisis are the ones that are best in adapting to change quickly.

What does it take to survive in changing conditions with a lot of uncertainty and with very limited economic flexibility? I think intelligent and pragmatic use of technology to be fast and flexible, experimentation and iteration, and using data intelligently to understand the customer needs and to spot opportunities are key capabilities. That sounds more like the key capabilities of an internet startup than typical airline skills. Indeed this is the right time to forget typical airline thinking and copy the startup way of working.

I am confident that information technology will play an important role to accelerate core airline processes so that the old silos relating to schedule planning, revenue management, and operations control can converge into an integrated planning and control process that considers operational constraints to maximize economic outcome. The tools to do this are already around and computing power is now abundant and flexibly available from the cloud. With cloud storage and new abilities in data science and AI we will be able to solve the airlines' planning and operations challenges and to adapt quickly to changing demand.

Technology is also available to move customer interaction and customer understanding to the digital and contactless space: airlines have already invested a lot to move booking, check-in and boarding to digital. Now it is important to close the gaps in digital customer interaction (e.g. on board) and to create a consistent picture of customers and their interactions with the airline, linking the different channels travelers use for interaction with the airline: (online) travel agents, airline websites and apps, frequent flyer websites and apps, airline staff, and so on. This way we can create a consistent picture of the customer's needs and to provide always the right information or offer at the right time.

Taneja forces us to apply fresh thinking by proposing a second scenario (elastic supply) that differs from the linear extrapolation base scenario by assuming widely fluctuating demand and forcing us to think in new approaches. In this scenario an airline can only be successful by applying new ways of thinking and acting. Let's accept the invitation to think along these lines to make airlines better at managing current and upcoming challenges.

*Frankfurt, Germany*

# 1 Introduction

## Background

Toward the end of 2019, while there were some discussions of a possible recession in the US, there were also indications that the expansion in the economy, which began 12 years back, might continue. Then, having made profits for 10 consecutive years, and with almost no end in sight, airlines began to struggle for their survival in the beginning of 2020 with the arrival of the Coronavirus pandemic. And in a matter of months, their primary focus changed from riding the revenue and profit growth curves to surviving by maintaining liquidity, managing cash flows, and restarting operations, in some cases, from ground zero. During 2020, it began to appear that this unprecedented disruption of the global airline industry, brought about by the global spread of the Coronavirus, followed by the global recession, would likely change the fundamental structure of the airline industry, not to mention the structure of other sectors in the broader aviation industry. Airports have also experienced an extensive reduction in revenue and are beginning to be concerned about how they would pay, going forward, for their planned expansions, relating to terminals and runways, not to mention the expected airport-related regulatory changes. Similarly, not only did aircraft manufacturers begin to see postponement and cancellation of some orders, but some analysts even began to question the continuation of the dominance of the two global manufacturers, not to mention a potential reduction in R&D for totally new products.[1]

Next, there is a concern that airlines may decide to transfer more of the risk in the value chain, to airports and aircraft manufacturers, for instance. Given the breadth and depth of the impact of this virus-led disruption, there is even a thought of "creative destruction" of the civil aviation industry, based on the thought leadership of the world-renowned economist, Joseph Schumpeter. He is credited as the author of this term that relates to the replacement of old assumptions and practices with more dynamic and innovative processes. If this were to be the case, then this disruption may become a catalyst for an innovative transformation not only of the airline industry, but also other sectors of the civil aviation industry.

The manuscript of the book *Transforming Airlines: A Flight Plan for Navigating Structural Changes*, was completed in December 2019, just as the news about the Coronavirus was being reported. As such, it did not discuss either the potential breadth or the depth of this disruption, or its implications for different sectors of the aviation industry. That book, however, did discuss some examples of megatrends as well as the emergence of some inflection, or turning, points that could lead to various degrees of structural changes in the airline industry and the need for building flexibility and agility into the planning processes to mitigate threats and seize timely and powerful opportunities. Coronavirus is now one example of an inflection point that has already taken place. Going forward, there could be other inflection points, such as the result of significant changes in the climate around the globe (with seismic shifts in society and businesses), geopolitical upheavals, cybersecurity (affecting private and sensitive information worldwide or affecting the GPS system), or disruptive transportation technology (such as the hyperloop capsules). Such disruptions could occur individually or in some combination.

While riding the revenue and profit growth curves during the past decade, different airlines had been fine-tuning, to different extents, their business models, as exemplified throughout this book. From now on, however, airlines need to accelerate the change to their business models to adapt to this unprecedented disruption, as well as to future potential disruptions. These fast-track changes by airlines will also cause other business sectors of the aviation industry, in particular airports, aircraft manufacturers, aircraft lessors, maintenance, repair, and overhaul organizations (MROs), and third-party distributors, to realign their business models. Even some government policy makers will need to rethink their aviation-related policies, not to mention the speed of change relating to these policies, to protect the environment and to continue the contribution of aviation sectors to the social and economic development of nations. However, in changing their business models, airlines are coming to the conclusion that strategies that worked in the past may not work in the future to deal not only with the intensity of the current disruption, but also with future potential disruptions, whether they might be local or global, and whether they might relate to health, or to geopolitics, or the climate, or cybersecurity, or new forms of transportation, such as aerial urban mobility and the hyperloop capsules that provide airplane speed with travel "on the ground." Consequently, this Coronavirus-led disruption has:

- forced airlines to think fast about how to restart the business, in many areas, from ground zero,
- forced airlines to find meaningful ways to reduce their operating costs significantly, particularly their fixed costs,
- accelerated the need to transform the airline business not only through innovation and digital transformation, but also through collaboration and coordination, inside and outside their organizations, for example, relating to labor and government policy makers,

- underlined the need to not only speed up the decision-making process, but also make decisions more proactively, and within a bottom-up framework, and
- highlighted the need for leading airlines to think differently—non-linearly, or tangentially—to recreate value not just for their customers, but also for other stakeholders, including employees, communities, and public policy makers.

And, since dramatic changes in the business models of airlines will also impact the models of other sectors in the aviation industry, the need for interconnectivity among different sectors of the aviation industry has resurfaced, creating, in turn, a need to collaborate much more broadly and proactively within the travel ecosystem. If an airline is to build up from ground zero, an airline could ask itself, for example, the following question: Do I want to continue to be a provider of schedule services from airports to airports, or do I want to be a provider of convenient mobility services?

Admitted, disruption is hardly a new concept in the airline industry that has experienced numerous external interruptions and disorders, as well as numerous internal developments, in the past. Examples of external interruptions include oil shocks, Gulf wars, financial crises, terrorist attacks, viruses (such as Ebola, MERS, and SARS) and an eruption of a volcano in Iceland. Examples of internal developments include the introduction of new aircraft, new regulatory policies, new types of competitors, and new marketing initiatives (new products, new revenue management systems, and new distribution systems). This industry has been very good at managing disruptions. It succeeded in adapting to each one of the aforementioned external disruptions and internal developments with viable strategies, using evolving systems and processes.

Figure 1.1 shows the actual growth in global passenger traffic during the past five decades, between 1970 and 2019, and an estimated exponential growth curve (suggested by the Excel program). It shows that while traffic did decline during each disruption (for example, the September 11 disruption in 2001 and the financial crisis in 2008) by different amounts, the level of traffic returned to its base fairly quickly. In the case of the 2001 disruption, the time to return to the normal base was about 3 years, even when this event was followed by three other events in the next 2 years: a recession, the second Gulf War, and SARS. In the case of the 2008 financial crisis, the recovery period was about 2 years. Another way of looking at the historical growth in traffic is the length of time between peak-to-peak cycles: It was 9 years between 1970 and 1979, 11 years between 1979 and 1990, 10 years between 1990 and 2000, 8 years between 2000 and 2008, and 11 years between 2008 and 2019. Although each disruption did cause a decline in passenger traffic, in each case traffic returned to its previous level and the long-term exponential growth trend continued, as shown in Figure 1.1. It is also worth noting that while the reduction in traffic in 2020 will be much larger than the reductions caused by the previous disruptions, traffic at

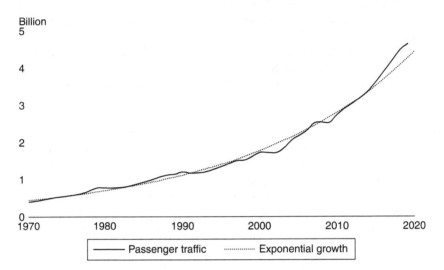

*Figure 1.1* Actual airline passenger growth between 1970 and 2019
Source: Constructed from the data provided by the Economics Department of IATA.

the end of 2019 was at the highest level, well above the projected growth level, shown by the dotted line in Figure 1.1.

The current disruption is, however, quite different from the previous disruptions, displayed in Figure 1.1, for a combination of the following reasons.

- It has affected economies, people's health, social patterns in all societies, and global supply chains.
- This disruption is global in scope and has created not just a few contact-free businesses (for example, tele-medicine and tele-health care), but according to some, it is beginning to create "contact-free economies."
- According to experts, this is the first virus to (1) infect humans in a sustained manner, (2) transmit quickly from one person to another, and (3) have a high level of mortality.[2]
- According to the International Air Transport Association (IATA), based on forecasts made at the end of November 2020, the airline industry is expected to lose $118 billion for the year 2020, instead of the $30 billion profit for 2020 that was forecasted at the end of 2019. Moreover, the industry is expected to lose $38 billion in 2021. The expected losses in 2021are much higher than the losses experienced in 2001 as a result of the terrorist attacks ($13 billion) and in 2008 as a result of the financial crisis ($26 billion).
- Whereas after the previous disruptions, for example in 2001 and 2008, the world still continued to become more globalized and more connected, now there is concern about the direction of the globalization movement,

not just in light of the changing geopolitics, but also changes in technologies and the increasing focus on sustainability.

- Some developing countries not only are expected to experience a significant reduction in their economies and problems relating to having taken on a substantial amount of debt, but could also face uncertainty relating to the stability of their political systems.
- Some countries may lose connectivity from time to time, depending on government-implemented policies relating to health. International borders can become open or closed at very short notice.
- This disruption is reportedly having a greater effect on the lower-income segments of the populations.
- Inequality among people, based on incomes, has increased during this disruption.
- This disruption has increased the use of social networks, some with embedded algorithms that have and could change people's thoughts and behaviors.

Within the aviation sector, this disruption has already affected both the demand and the supply sides much more significantly, because of its impact on economies and health, as well as the changes in people's social lives. And the impacts are being felt by all sectors of the aviation industry, airlines, airports, aircraft manufacturers, and providers of tourist facilities and services, for example. As such, moving forward after restarting the businesses, transformation within the airline industry needs to be not only fast, but also within a different mindset—incorporating different thinking, that leverages existing digital assets (brands, loyalty programs, airport slots, and equities in global airlines) as well as new digital assets (new data, smart analytics, new networks, new devices, new working arrangements within and outside the organization, and new simulation systems) to provide much more agility. The object is to develop new business models that provide solutions to people's mobility needs, for example. Think seriously about Uber's business model. It solved people's need for much more convenient taxi services. The transformational thinking was not to look at the existing taxi business and see how a new app would add value. The non-conventional thinking was how a new taxi business could be developed around a new mobile operating system; a new taxi business that makes people's lives easier. Some airlines also developed sophisticated mobile apps but Delta went even further and explored the use of biotechnology to provide personalized information at the micro level (hear Ed Bastian's keynote address at the Consumer Electronics Show in Las Vegas in October 2019). As such, airlines need to think about how new business models can be developed that:

- get the business restarted quickly,
- make the whole air travel process much easier for consumers,
- deliver the promises made more conveniently and more consistently throughout the journey, and

- provide airlines the agility to adapt to the fast-changing marketplace, now and, going forward, relating to more frequent disruptions and changing needs of new generations.

The answer may lie in finding new ways to:

- collaborate more effectively with partners in the entire travel ecosystem, including labor, communities, and policy makers, at the bilateral and multi-lateral level,
- identify real solutions needed to solve customers' problems by reinventing the business by leveraging innovation coming from both inside as well as outside,
- leverage, in the near term, digital assets to maximize the value from physical assets, and
- leverage a broad spectrum of new technology vehicles, ranging from vertical take-off and landing electric aircraft, in the mid-term, to hyperloop systems, in the long term, capable of transporting people at speeds over 700 miles per hour and covering distances approaching 1,000 miles.

For airlines to pivot their business models in a timely manner, this book suggests a two-pronged approach. The first part of the approach is to use scenario planning, an established technique used by businesses in the past (pioneered by such organizations as the Rand Corporation and the Shell Oil Company) to identify, develop, and implement strategies to adapt to the unprecedented changes in the marketplace. This technique can add much value if the scenarios can be established and deployed within a disciplined framework, for example, with scenarios developed around not only uncertainty in key external areas, but also internal capabilities of airlines and the resources available within the aviation ecosystem. Think about the fact that IATA, in its vision paper published in 2018, talked about the possibility of global-changing pandemics as one of the drivers of change. Only two years after the publication of this vision paper, a pandemic did catch the industry unprepared.[3] However, even an airline developing strategies to deal with an external uncertainty is not worth much if the strategies selected cannot be implemented due to some internal constraints, or the unwillingness of various members in the ecosystem to collaborate. One critical success factor, discussed in this book, is for an airline to combine a broad spectrum of its assets to solve customers' ongoing problems. Some business writers call this "combinatorial innovation."[4]

The second part of the approach is to work within a "back-to-the-future" planning framework. This calls for different ways to (1) think beyond the short-term concerns, and (2) develop a disciplined way to convert a future vision of the business into current strategic plans. In both parts, the focus should be (1) on placing customers in the center of the planning process, and (2) on the use of digital transformation methods to achieve physical transformation. Think about how airlines developed the computer reservation systems (CRS) decades ago to facilitate the booking process for passengers; they totally transformed the distribution function by enabling the storage and retrieval of information to conduct transactions related to air travel. The critical success factor was the leveraging of data networking. Next, think about how Amazon transformed the retailing business, making shopping easier for customers by leveraging the internet and a broad spectrum of suppliers. Finally, think about Uber that transformed the taxi business by leveraging mobile technology. The new thinking leveraged digital transformation—a mobile operating system, an app incorporated in a mobile device that capitalized on the network (riders, cars, drivers) to solve riders' problems, while enhancing the use of physical assets—private cars and willing drivers.

## Two scenarios

Two scenarios are offered: *continuous improvements*, based on conventional or linear thinking, and *elastic supply*, based on non-conventional or non-linear thinking. These two scenarios of the future landscape are based, in turn, on (1) six external areas of uncertainty in the marketplace, (2) six areas of internal capabilities, and (3) six areas of potential partnerships in the ecosystem. The object in scenario planning is not to try to predict the future or outcomes, but to highlight the potential influencing forces. The first scenario, continuous improvements, based on conventional or linear thinking, projects that the traffic level will bounce back to its level in 2019 and its growth will continue at its historical level (4–5 percent per year), based on numerous assumptions, relating, for example, to economies, health, geopolitical developments (by region and by country), and the business models of partners in the ecosystem. Under this scenario, although airlines keep operating, fundamentally, on the same core business model, they do continue to make improvements in the operational and the commercial areas, described in some detail in the book. The second scenario, elastic supply, is based on a different set of assumptions. In this scenario, even if the traffic was to return to, or even surpass its base level of 2019 after a number of years, its rate of growth may fluctuate and oscillate widely.

While no one can predict the level of traffic and/or its growth, going forward, managements will need to be prepared to deal with whatever the level and growth turn out to be year after year, or even month after month. Planning within the elastic supply framework could totally change not only the size, shape, and structure of the airline industry, but also the relationship of airlines with all partners within the travel ecosystem. The elastic scenario deals with two areas of analyses. The first area of analysis relates simply to an increase or decrease in the supply provided to match with the changes in the quantity of demand. The second area deals with how major changes are needed to plan and market capacity using both the existing transportation services and the potential new transportation services, for example, intermodal services, door-to-door services, and urban air mobility. The expected changes are described throughout this book.

The main message throughout the book has four parts. First, airlines need to offer real solutions to people's need for travel and their changing concerns. During the recovery, the concerns are related to health and safety. Going forward the emphasis might be on "conscious travel" that relates to such aspects as more concern for the change in the climate, smart mobility, and sustainable tourism. Second, airlines need to be better prepared for frequent and deeper disruptions that could be localized or globalized. Think about it. Just as the Coronavirus is turning out to be a large natural disaster, could, not so distant in the future, climate change be the next major disruption? Third, the general view is that governments, and the public, will introduce changes to minimize risks related to climate change. With respect to governments, they could introduce tighter regulations and/or implement high-burden tax systems. As for the public, there could be a significant reduction in the type of air travel that may be damaging the environment—the flight shaming movement. And let us not overlook the governments' roles in facilitating the introduction of new forms of transport services. The object should, however, be on changing priorities to focus on the positive side of change, and not to view change as only a threat. Fourth, there will be much value in working within the internal and external ecosystems. Keep in mind an African proverb: "If you want to go fast, go alone. If you want to go far, go together."

Changes in the external environment represent opportunities to solve problems while developing strong airlines at the same time. Both dimensions of opportunities call for the adoption of new visions and new purposes to change internal capabilities, created by managements with imagination as well as turbocharged innovation, and facilitated by enlightened government policies. While the current unprecedented disruption has already produced an enormous challenge for the global airline industry (to manage ambiguity and uncertainty), it has also produced enormous opportunities for those airlines, both incumbent and new, that are willing to acclimate themselves to much greater volatility in the marketplace by creating a data-driven culture. As is often said, "never waste a good crisis." While the opportunity has always been there, it is now time to do things differently so that airlines and partners—for example, airports—can make travel much more convenient and pleasant, not to mention solution-oriented, while making themselves much more agile, robust, and resilient. Even for the first scenario, there is a need for a greater focus on innovation, and a greater willingness to deploy new digital assets (data, analytics, and networks) to integrate and convert raw data into actionable insights and actionable strategies. For the second scenario, there has to be much more flexibility to increase the speed for making decisions in the context of a new framework. Tomas Pueyo is the author of the "Hammer and the Dance" framework in which he described the period of the lockdown to flatten the disease as "the hammer" and the subsequent actions to deal with it as "the dance."[5] In the context of this book, a hammer represents a change brought about by an external event, such as an outbreak of a new virus in a given area or a geopolitical disruption. The dance would represent various actions taken by consumers, governments, and businesses to react in the uncertain aftermath of the event to provide solutions for consumers.

## Chapter outlines

Chapter 2 presents some details on the two scenarios for managements to design and implement strategies to mitigate threats and to seize timely opportunities. The credibility of each scenario will depend on, of course, the validity of the underlying assumptions. This chapter also outlines a range of potential outcomes for each scenario, based on both conventional thinking, in the case of the incremental improvements scenario, as well as non-conventional thinking, in the case of the elastic supply scenario. Elements of both types of thinking are described, relating, for example, to the emerging consumer trends and the development of new forms of transportation services, such as aerial urban mobility and ultra-fast travel "on the ground" at airplane speeds made possible by the hyperloop transportation concept. Also discussed are developments relating to climate change, and the potential policies by governments, as well as responses by the aviation community.

Chapter 3 focuses on the analytical exploration of strategies, traditional or new, by, first, making the network, fleet, and schedule planning process much more integrated and dynamic and, second, by leveraging digital capabilities to reduce complexity and to achieve a flawless execution of strategies. For the first scenario, while some strategies discussed may appear to be traditional in nature, they do highlight the need for speed to address the rapidly changing structure of, and the competitive dynamics within, the airline industry. Examples include different ways to focus on integration around the financial function. For the second scenario, airline strategies could be radically different, to deal with greater variation in demand, to offer nonstop services in ultra-long-haul markets, to capitalize on the new regulatory policies, to make cargo a core product, and to integrate with emerging transportation systems. Both scenarios can make use of digital assets to get much more value out of the physical assets and by undertaking the analyses on a truly bottom-up basis, involving, for example, door-to-door services or on-demand services.

Chapter 4 provides a discussion on not just the type of strategies needed in commercial and financial functions to deal with both scenarios, but also the capabilities needed to analyze and execute such strategies, effectively. While some strategies discussed may not seem to be new, the focus is, first, on removing the barriers and constraints to the implementation of even the conventional strategies. Second, the focus is on strengthening the traditional core competencies by leveraging three new core competencies as well as digital marketing. For the first scenario, examples discussed include a realignment of revenue management systems, distribution systems, loyalty programs, and branding initiatives. For the second scenario, new ways need to be explored to think very differently about managing demand, for example, through the use of demand-driven-supply planning techniques, as opposed to the conventional supply-driven-demand planning techniques. The new planning environment calls for new ways to cooperate and compete more effectively within the physical and digital travel ecosystems, through the use of, for example, full-service platforms and apps that leverage such technologies as artificial intelligence. A critical success factor is the development of customer management capabilities that focus on customers' end-to-end journeys with the fulfillment of desired outcomes.

Chapter 5 provides some thoughts, for both scenarios, on the best practices for improving the decision-making processes during unprecedented times, relating to uncertainty outside the organization and the capabilities inside an airline's organization. Examples of points discussed include transforming business models around digital assets, managing operations in real time, and realigning organizations to leverage digital assets. The chapter includes discussions on new sources of data (for example, location and movement intelligence coming from mobile devices and the usage of credit cards), new technologies (such as artificial intelligence), new smart analytics (for developing customer intelligence and business intelligence for both passenger and cargo operations), new networks (social media, supply chains, and apps), the value of data exchanges, and smart interactive visualization techniques for technical and non-technical planners.

Chapter 6 provides some thoughts for leaderships, in aviation businesses and governments, for unlocking new sources of value as they examine different strategies to adapt to the two scenarios discussed in this book. While the need for innovation has been recognized for a long time, the change in priorities is now to get innovation implemented judicially to create, capture, and deliver value by removing constraints. In the near future, clearly the top priority in the minds of leaderships is to survive and get the businesses restarted. And to minimize risk, it would make sense to utilize conventional thinking and work within the framework of the continuous improvements scenario.

However, adaption to the second scenario calls for acceleration in the scale and scope of transformation requiring: (1) a noteworthy change in corporate culture—for the development of entrepreneurial mindsets and the creation of a culture of continuous innovation and collaboration; (2) a long-term investment in, and the use of, digital assets (data, analytics, and networks) to optimize the value of physical assets (fleet, airport facilities, operations systems control centers, and maintenance systems and inventories); (3) a breakdown of the traditional constraints to unlock new sources of value; (4) a review of some insights gained from the best business practices from outside the aviation industry; and (5) a new vision to solve customers' problems while making organizations much more agile and resilient. Keep in mind that whereas, in the past, all members of the travel chain were able to derive higher profit margins than airlines, going forward, this is not likely to be the case. Government policy makers could create a tipping point by changing their priorities to realign the regulatory frameworks so that, in return for resources provided to, for example, airlines and airports, both sectors of the industry continue to support the social and economic development of their countries.

As with previous books in this series, based on input received from practitioners, this book also has a number of forewords and a number of thought leadership pieces in Chapter 7. The diversity of forewords provides readers some global perspectives from a wider angle on the theme of the book. The thought leadership pieces, and their diversity, also provide international perspectives relating to the theme of the book, but at the narrower subject matter. Next, again based on feedback, this book contains a number of references to the best practices from different business sectors, best practices with potential applications in the airline industry. References to the best practices incorporate (1) the thoughts of some leading practitioners and business writers, and (2) the actual experience of a number of businesses, such as Amazon, FLiXBUS, Hyundai, IKEA, ING Group, Nike, Nokia, Patagonia, Porsche, Sephora, Tesla, Uber, Unilever, Western Union, and Zara. Finally, as in some previous books, this book raises numerous questions in numerous places. Some readers have found this feature to add value for them by making them sit back and think differently about answers to some questions raised throughout the book. The process is now more critical given that the pace of change has increased. Think about the ramification of this in the context of a quote from Vladimir Lenin, former head of the government of the Soviet Union, about the increase in the speed of change. "There are decades where nothing happens; and there are weeks where decades happen."

## Notes

1 Keith Hayward, "Creative Destruction 2.0: Covid-19 and the future of the civil aerospace industry," *Aerospace*, Royal Aeronautical Society, September 2020, pp. 14–19.

2 David M. Morens and Anthony S. Fauci, "Emerging Pandemic Diseases: How We Got to COVID-19," *Cell Leading Edge*, Cell 182, September 3, 2020, pp. 1077–92.

3 IATA and the School of International Futures, *Future of the Airline Industry 2035* (IATA, 2018).

4 Ian C. Woodward, V. "Paddy" Padmanabhan, Sameer Hasija, and Ram Charan, *The Phoenix Encounter Method: Lead Like Your Business Is On Fire* (NY: McGrawHill, 2021), ch. 12.

5 https://abc7news.com/hammer-and-the-dance-update-tomas-pueyo-coronavirus-article/6199923/

# 2    Managing conventional and non–conventional scenarios

Although scenario planning is not a new concept, it is worthwhile to revisit the best practices in this area to deal with the increasing levels of uncertainty in the external environment in the near future, the internal capabilities of airlines, and the capabilities of partners in the ecosystem to deal with uncertainties. A good recent example of scenario planning within the airline industry is provided in a report produced by IATA and the School of International Futures that summarizes almost 50 drivers of change, synthesized into multiple themes (such as geopolitics, the environment, values and communities, and business models) that, in turn, are synthesized into four contrasting scenarios. The four scenarios examined in the IATA report are: (1) new frontiers (turbulent world/connected and open); (2) sustainable future (calm world/connected and open); (3) resource wars (turbulent world/closed data); and (4) platforms (calm world/closed data).[1] These four scenarios provide, even prior to this disruption, a thought-provoking insight into possible shapes of the global airline industry in the future.

Within the context of this virus-led disruption, this chapter reviews briefly challenges, opportunities, and best practices in scenario planning. Although many airlines do develop scenarios, they do not necessarily engage in its use effectively to plan their businesses in the context of weaknesses and strengths of their internal capabilities as well as the weaknesses and strengths of partners in the ecosystem. This chapter offers two scenarios of the future landscape, based on six external areas of uncertainty, six areas of internal capabilities, and six types of partnerships in the ecosystem, shown in Figure 2.1. Let us start with some examples of questions relating to uncertainty in external areas.

- What could be the length and depth of the current recession that is already global and that has already impacted both the demand for, and the supply of, air services? According to the National Bureau of Economic Research, the US economy entered a recession officially in the first quarter of 2020. The last recession started during the last quarter of 2007, more than 12 years earlier. Uncertainty relating to the economy worldwide will bring about uncertainty in the level of passenger traffic, its growth, and its mix.

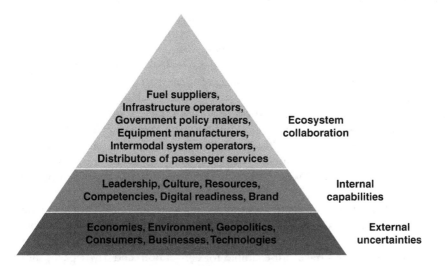

*Figure 2.1* Areas of external uncertainties, internal capabilities, and ecosystem collaboration

- This virus-led disruption has already impacted people's health and the demand for air travel. Over 2.6 million people have died of COVID-19 worldwide through the first week of March 2021. Could there be a totally new virus or some variants related to the current Coronavirus of equal consequences?
- While governments have already provided different kinds and levels of financial support, going forward, will there be government intervention that would impact business decisions of airlines directly (relating to networks, fleet, and schedules, for example), and indirectly (through the realignment of supply chains, the protection of the environment, and the development of the economies, for example), based on different political and economic agendas of different governments? The realignment of the supply chains could, for example, reduce unpredictability and insecurity and create more resiliencies.
- Would the globalization movement slow down as a result of economic considerations, technological changes, and the rise of populism and protectionism?[2] On one side are the recent policies of countries such as the US and the UK. On the other side, on November 15, 2020, 15 countries in the Asia–Pacific region signed the largest trade agreement (the Regional Comprehensive Economic Partnership) to develop deeper cooperation within the group. This group represents about 30 percent of the world's population as well as about 30 percent of the world's economies.
- How will the organizational structure of easyJet, Ryanair, and Wizz Air, relating to ownership and control rules, change following the exit of the UK from the EU in January 2021?

- Going forward, how much more will the demand for air travel be impacted due to health reasons, in addition to the economic reasons, mentioned earlier? How much of the reduction in demand for air travel could be permanent? How will airlines engage with consumers during their shopping processes on the ground, and in the air? How much could consumer behavior change further in the areas of spending and saving patterns, not to mention patterns relating to the way travel is purchased and completed, as well as attributes, such as the frequency of travel, stage lengths, and trip durations? Would passengers accept yet new types of inspections at airports, inspection relating to health, and with screening at both ends of the trip, especially in intercontinental markets? When will consumers see true intermodal services? Would virtual reality finally reduce a small amount of travel?
- The behavior of most businesses has already begun to change to reduce costs and to develop resiliency. Could the speed of digitalization of business processes (to reduce costs) increase further, leading to a reduction in some types of business travel, for example, for conventions and day trips for short meetings? Could business travel be impacted further by government-implemented and health-related, on-again and off-again travel restrictions, especially in international markets, making airline planning extremely volatile? Or, could the size of the business travel pie, in fact, increase, even though some slices (sub-segments) of the business travel pie decrease?
- How fast will airlines and related businesses adopt new technologies (such as machine learning, internet of things, advanced platforms, biometrics, and interactive chatbots) to develop and implement totally new business models (1) developed around the customers, as in the case of Uber and Tesla, and (2) with optimizations based at the systems level, as opposed to at the silo level (scheduling, pricing, revenue management, and so forth)?

Two scenarios are offered: *continuous improvements*, based on conventional or linear thinking, and *elastic supply*, based on non-conventional or non-linear thinking. Some examples of conventional thinking are:

- to continue to offer itineraries within the context of airport codes, passenger name records, and flight numbers,
- to continue to plan within a supply-driven-demand framework (based on schedules constructed well in advance of flights) and conventional revenue-management practices (based on traditional buckets, more to filter demand than to generate demand),
- to continue to plan marketing strategies based on traditional customer segments (business, leisure, and visiting friends and relatives (VFR)),
- for full-service carriers to continue to compete with the low-cost carriers, based on offering some seats in the main cabin at low fares, and to leverage the attraction of their more desirable loyalty programs,

- to continue to distribute airline products and services through the traditional distribution channels,
- to continue to offer loyalty programs with benefits based on transactions, such as number of miles or segments flown, and or, money spent on travel, and
- to continue to focus on a narrower business purpose, such as profitable growth.

Some examples of non-conventional thinking are:

- to manage risk relating not only to costs (for example, by hedging on fuel), but also to revenues (for example, hedging on passenger yield),
- to plan with a demand-driven-supply framework, coupled with next-generation revenue-management practices, to generate revenue and to provide flexibility and agility, for example, by trading customer flexibility to provide almost a real-time scheduling capability for airlines,
- to optimize the business at a systems level, instead of at the functional level,
- to focus more on digital assets (data, analytics, and networks) and totally integrated strategies (business, employee, and technology) to get more out of physical assets (aircraft, airport facilities, operations systems control centers, and crews),
- to provide door-to-door services rather than airport-to-airport services, leveraging digital marketing, platforms, and new vehicle technologies,
- to market itineraries based on total travel needs of consumers, rather than airport codes, flight numbers, and passenger name records (PNRs),
- to develop loyalty programs based on the customer experience desired and delivered, rather than past transactions, based on miles or revenues,
- to identify and work with partners in the physical and the digital ecosystems,
- to establish in some ultra-high-density markets air transportation services that reflect the characteristics of mass transportation, and
- to develop broader business purposes other than just the maximization of profits.

These two scenarios of the future landscape are based, in turn, on (1) six external areas of uncertainty in the marketplace, (2) six areas of internal capabilities, and (3) six areas of potential partnerships in the ecosystem (see Figure 2.1). The six areas selected of external uncertainties are economies, environment, geopolitics, consumer behavior, business behavior, and technologies. The six areas representing the internal capabilities are the priorities of leaderships, corporate culture, resources (financial, technology, and talent, to extract value from next-generation technologies), traditional core competencies (marketing innovation, operational excellence, and execution of strategies), digital readiness, and the brand. And the six areas of potential collaboration in the ecosystem relate to manufacturers (airframes, engines, and components, for example), infrastructure (operators of airports, air navigation service providers, maintenance repair and overhaul organizations, and ground services, for example), fuel suppliers, other modes of transportation, distributors of passenger services (global distribution systems and online travel agents, for example), and government policy makers (relating to the regulatory systems, the aviation infrastructure, the environment, and tourism facilities and services, for example). Particularly important are the areas of internal capabilities that can act either as enablers of strategies or barriers to the development and implementation of strategies that include collaboration and harmony within the ecosystem. It is the internal capabilities, individually or in combination, that will influence the decisions of managers that, in turn, will affect the degree of transformation and innovation achieved to respond to either scenario. And the success of some airlines to adapt to new challenges will certainly have an impact on those who can, and those who cannot adapt in a timely manner.

This book also suggests that the scale and scope of transformation of physical operations are most likely to be achieved through the scale and scope of digital transformation. In this context, there are three new core competencies—data, analytics, and networks (not relating to routes)—that can help managements sharpen and strengthen the three traditional core competencies—marketing innovation, operational excellence, and strategy execution (see Figure 4.2 in Chapter 4).

While it is easy to pose questions relating to uncertainties in the external marketplace, the real challenge is to recognize the weaknesses and strengths in the internal capabilities of airlines to develop robust strategies to adapt to the external uncertainties. Figure 2.1 shows also different areas of internal capabilities that can either be enablers of robust strategies to deal with the external uncertainties, or they can be disablers, or barriers, depending on the answers to the types of questions listed below.

- How will leaderships at airlines change their priorities after working in the survival mode, by creating, for example, different purpose-driven airlines and developing the necessary robust strategies around a selected purpose? How can a new purpose be identified and translated into action? What would be some bigger pictures of the future and how can leaderships work with a "back-from-the-future" framework to lead their organizations?
- How committed has the airline been to improving the entire customer journey, relating, for example, to door-to-door travel (see Figure 4.4)? Is the commitment to customer experience likely to accelerate or slow down during this disruption, due to revenue and/or cost considerations? Has the airline aligned its three strategies (employee, business, and technology) to become digitally relevant and digitally ready? Does the culture exist to promote innovation inside the organization and within the ecosystem? What is the spirit within airline groups that run multiple airlines or airlines that, having merged, continue to operate as separate airlines?

- Have sufficient resources (funds and talent) been made available to acquire and implement digital technologies? Does the finance department continue to insist on seeing a definitive analysis of a specific return on investment for every technology proposal? In fact, is the airline digitally ready to transform its business?

- Does the airline excel in marketing, or operations, or in the execution of its strategy? How about changing the priority to make the execution of strategies the first core competency, even in the traditional list of core competencies? Does the airline believe that value can be generated through innovation and digital transformation? In some cases, does the leadership believe that it needs to focus on the scale and scope of transformation or the scale and scope of digital transformation to adapt to either or both of the scenarios offered in this chapter?

- Does the airline believe that a brand can develop a strong bond with customers? Does the airline believe that its branding initiatives can drive a higher price point? Does the airline believe that its brand can build a loyal customer base? Where does an airline brand stand relative not just to other airline brands, but also to providers of other services, such as hotels, banks, and entertainment businesses? Are traditional airline brands tied to traditional cost structures (say, in a low-cost airline) or can airlines develop their brands and dramatically improve their cost structures at the same time?

These areas of uncertainty and capabilities are obviously not independent. For example, geopolitics can produce economic challenges that will, in turn, impact both consumer and business behavior. Similarly, the willingness and the degree of collaboration within the ecosystem are dependent on priorities of the leadership. For example, is an airline willing to share data and value, in the ecosystem? Based on these six areas of uncertainty, two scenarios are suggested. Both scenarios will change the size, the shape, and the structure of the airline industry, with the extent of change depending on the scenario and the time period: short term, medium term, and long term. The extent of the change will also depend on the internal capabilities, relating to managements' ability to scale operations quickly and efficiently, depending on the resources available, and the corporate culture to implement changes. In addition, the size, shape, and operations of the industry, relating to either scenario, will also be affected by a second set of influencers, the value of, and collaboration with, partners in the ecosystem, also exemplified in Figure 2.1. There are also numerous other influencing factors, related indirectly to the factors listed in Figure 2.1. Examples include future technologies to limit noise, fuel consumption, emissions, environment-related taxes implemented by governments (for example, pollution rights), the production of alternative fuels to limit the dependence on conventional fuel, and the hedge strategies of airlines to stabilize the costs of fuel. Additional technologies included are, for example, the development of aerial urban mobility, and the exceptionally high-speed "ground" transportation using the hyperloop capsules concept.

## Scenario 1: Continuous improvements

The development of any scenario requires an outline of some underlying assumptions and the estimated time when the passenger traffic might return to its base level and growth, and, going forward, the role of linear or non-linear thinking to manage the scenario. The first scenario, *continuous improvements*, based on conventional or linear thinking, assumes that traffic level will bounce back to its level in 2019 and growth will continue at its historical level (4–5 percent per year), based on the following types of assumptions:

- Based on the experience from some past disruptions, demand restoration was, and will be during this disruption, V-shaped or U-shaped, but not L-shaped. There may be some changes in consumers' spending behavior and travel patterns, but consumers will return to the old normal. Keep in mind that some analysts of economies have described the recovery of the economy in 2020 to be K-shaped, given that some sectors of the economy recovered fairly quickly (such as technology and e-commerce) while others went negative (such as travel). In fact, even within the air transportation sector, the movement in cargo traffic went in the positive direction while the movement in passenger traffic went in the negative direction. Think also about the initial public offering (IPO) of Airbnb (on December 10, 2020) which valued its shares at $68 with the price closing at $144 by the end of the day. According to a report by *The New York Times* the next day, Airbnb was worth $100 billion, more than Expedia and Marriott combined.
- Work from remote locations did not produce any meaningful reduction in business travel in the past and will not do so in the future, despite the improvements in communication technologies.
- Business travel will return as people on business need to travel to have face-to-face interactions and to form relationships. There will always be a desire to meet the business associates in person as business is about people and relationships. The return of business travel will be facilitated by the developments of new digital-health documents (coupled with the development of the necessary cooperation and infrastructure, such as the verification of the authenticity of tests), and the development of quarantine-free flights in high-visibility markets.
- There will be no significant changes in the structure of the airline industry, relating, for example, to full-service airlines, low-cost airlines, hybrid airlines, and sixth-freedom operators. Hub-and-spoke systems will also continue to provide competitive advantages for full-service carriers.
- Going forward, travel will rebound, given the resiliency of travel and the traffic mix will not change to any great extent. Leisure traffic and VFR traffic will rebound well before business travel for numerous reasons, including the availability of lower fares. Leisure travelers will always be interested in visiting places that they have heard about and read about. This interest will increase if airlines reduce fares significantly, coupled with some unusual

incentives provided by some airports. Business travel will take a little longer to return not just because of personal concerns of business travelers, but also the concerns of businesses, relating partly to costs of travel and all sorts of liabilities for businesses. However, business travel will come back, especially the segment relating to "bleisure." In the long term, business travel could, in fact, increase due to an increase in the globalization movement, growth and interconnectedness of economies, and the introduction of new types of transportation services, such as on-demand mobility as a service.

- The disproportionate percentage of revenue, and profit, from the two front cabins will also be maintained after the recovery. And some carriers, such as British Airways, will continue to derive higher margins from their premium cabins.

- Conventional revenue management systems, processes, and strategies will continue to be viable with continuous improvements. In other words, airlines will continue to plan their marketing and operational strategies based on traditional customer segmentation, based, in turn, on customers who make their decisions primarily on price (the lower-yield budget travelers) and those who make their decisions based primarily on itineraries and loyalty programs (the higher-margin business travelers).

- Ancillary revenue generated from the four major traditional sources (baggage fees, reservation-change fees, charges for seat location, and revenue from the sale of loyalty miles to credit-card companies, for example) will continue to exist and, possibly, even grow going forward. It could be assumed, for example, that even with a change in the policy to eliminate reservation-change fees, blocking the middle seat, individually or in a group, could be a new source of ancillary revenue. Think about Lufthansa's new product, Sleeper's Row, that allows passengers to book in economy class a row of three or four seats next to each other to sleep on long-haul flights.

- The contemporary loyalty programs, with minor adjustments, will continue to be effective. In fact, based on recent developments the existing loyalty programs have proven to be major assets of the large airlines. For example, not only have major airlines derived a significant amount of revenue from partners, such as credit-card companies, but also used the value of their loyalty programs as collateral to obtain loans.

- The conventional strategy of full-service carriers to offer some seats in the main cabin at low fares will continue to be viable to compete with the existing and new low-cost carriers and the business model of low-cost carriers will remain the same. For example, they continue to operate a limited type of fleet with high-density configurations and with labor and airport agreements that provide high utilization of assets.

- The relationship with airports will continue along the historical lines, with some variation by region. On their part, large airports will continue to work with the same model—develop and maintain capacity, facilities, and infrastructure. The expectation will be that the historical growth rates will continue as will the conventional models of different groups of airlines—full-service carriers, low-cost carriers, and so forth. Smaller airports will continue to market their facilities and services to airlines based on the economic strength of their communities and the diversification of the economic activities. See the thought leadership piece by Brian D'Amico in Chapter 7.

- With the exception of some continuous improvements, it is assumed that airline products and services will continue to be distributed using, more or less, the traditional distribution mix. Traditional global distribution systems (GDSs) could develop new platforms in partnerships with high-technology businesses, such as Amazon and Google, to improve their distribution systems and processes.
- Intermodal transportation services will make more progress in Europe but relatively little in North America.
- The impact of the "flight shaming" movement was minimal in Europe, except in a few countries, such as Sweden. It will not have a significant impact worldwide. On a worldwide basis, governments will not advance their timing requirements to meet the carbon neutrality policies.

Based on conventional thinking, coupled with examples of the types of assumptions outlined above, one could estimate the time for the traffic volume, and its historic level of growth, to return to the old normal (2019 base). The time could be between 3 and 8 years, as shown by the three dotted lines in Figure 2.2. The variation in the time will depend on details in the assumptions, relating, for example, to economies, health, geopolitical developments (by region and by country), and the business models of partners in the ecosystem.

Consider, for example, the degree of government intervention, relating to business practices of airlines. Even though it would vary by region and by

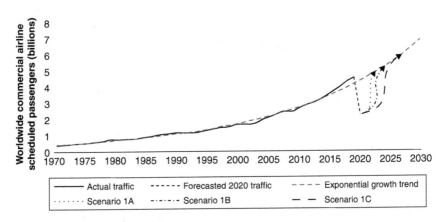

*Figure 2.2* Continuous improvements scenario based on conventional thinking

country, it could be limited, for example, in some cases to the makeup of the boards. In other cases, there could also be other conditions and constraints (relating to the financial support) that would impact some areas of the business, such as networks and fleets, the requirement to develop multimodal transportation, and the development of much more actionable strategies, on the part of airlines, for sustainability. In the case of economies, the recovery could be V-shaped, U-shaped, or, possibly even, W-shaped, but not L-shaped. If the recovery is V-shaped, for example, traffic could bounce back along the lines of the brand symbol of Nike, the "swoosh," and the recovery period could be only three years—shown by the first dotted line in Figure 2.2. In this case, the growth would start in domestic markets (led by such countries as Australia, Brazil, China, Japan, and the US), then it would move to intra-regional markets (led by the EU region and the ASEAN region), and, finally, it could move to long-haul intercontinental markets. Relating to the first dotted line sub-scenario, it is assumed that changes in the traffic mix are small, resulting from a slower return of the business sector, but the VFR and the leisure segments of the traffic, bounce back faster than the business sector. In fact, the VFR component may return at an even faster rate than the leisure segment. If the recovery of the economies is U-shaped, then traffic might take five years to bounce back—the second dotted line. And, if the recovery is W-shaped, and it is also accompanied by a number of other negative developments, then the level and growth of the traffic could take 8 years to get back to the normal curve—the third dotted line. Similarly, the recovery period will depend on the rate at which business travel returns. One example of the delay in the time for business travel to return would be related to the changes in the behavior of businesses, for example, through the creation of hybrid organizations, in which some work is conducted on-site and some at remote locations. The creation of hybrid organizations does lower the operating costs of businesses, based on the lower cost of the real estate, achieved by a reduction in the size of the office space. In another example, automation could also reduce labor costs, for example, from the introduction of driverless trucks.

The degree of structural changes in the size and shape of the industry, relating to the continuous improvements scenario, would be dependent upon the length of the recovery period exemplified in Figure 2.2. The variation in the recovery would depend not just on how economies recover in general, but in particular for some key countries and regions, such as China, India, the US, and the EU region. With respect to China and India, it is worth noting how their economies had been changing the complexion of these countries, with respect to the propensity of people to travel, just to pick one dimension, and the emergence of some industries and sectors, such as technologies and technology companies, in the case of China, to pick another dimension. And, while recovery of economies is one parameter for determining the time for traffic to bounce back, consumer consumption and consumer trends, for example, behavior, are two other parameters. It is also interesting to note that while the economies of most countries showed negative growth, in the case of

China, where the GDP had been growing at an average rate of about 12 percent per year (well above the world average), the decline in 2020 still kept the growth slightly on the positive side. On the other hand, the economy of India is expected to show a decline of almost 10 percent in 2020. Similarly, the economies throughout the world are likely to show very different levels of declines, for example, Canada, Germany, Japan, and the US posting a much lower level of decline than France, Italy, and the UK.

The continuous improvements scenario does not, however, imply that there is a specific point when traffic returns to the growth curve even though the arrows do reach the growth curve at specific points for illustrative purposes. Nor does it imply the existence of a specific point (or definition of success) to which an airline has to head. Rather, success will be achieved from a devotion to continuous improvements. Moreover, this scenario is neither negative, nor even pessimistic. It has been pointed out, for example, how after World War II, governments created new policies and established new organizations (such as the General Agreement on Tariffs and Trade and the International Monetary Fund) that fostered, promoted, and achieved broad-based growth in economies and businesses. Similarly, within the aviation industry, governments created new aviation policies and established new organizations to promote growth. Just three examples of new aviation organizations established were the International Civil Aviation Organization (ICAO), the International Air Transport Association (IATA), and the Société Internationale de Télécommunications Aéronautiques (SITA). Although the two situations, the spread of the Coronavirus and World War II, are not similar—for example, much of the infrastructure (such as airports) was destroyed during the War—there are some valid insights. As such, going forward, governments could realign their regulatory policies and enable the realignment of the functions of the global aviation organizations to not only get the industry back on track quickly, but also grow within a new framework that includes, for instance, sustainability considerations.

Under this scenario, although airlines and airports keep operating on, fundamentally, the same business model, they do continue to make improvements in the commercial and operational areas. Examples of continuous improvements in an airline's commercial area include changes in the design of websites to improve customer experience and dealing with the challenge relating to payments and, in turn, the relationship between airlines and the banks that process credit-card payments. Relating to the redesign of websites, the focus will be mobile devices as more and more searches (relating to airlines, OTAs, and metasearch engines) are made on mobile devices than desktops. Relating to payments, during the recovery period, the risk increased of an airline going out of business, before the completion of travel by passengers, holding confirmed reservations and having paid for the tickets. Banks processing payments wanted to hold the money until the flight was actually operated, a decision good for travelers, but not so good for airlines, which needed liquidity. As such, airlines developed incentives for travelers to use payment methods that provided cash to airlines directly, for example, through the use of virtual cards. Further examples of continuous improvements in the commercial area include (1) finding innovative ways to develop 360-degree views of customers to provide more personalized products and services, including through a higher level of collaboration and coordination with airports, for example; (2) stepping up the effort to implement the IATA-facilitated One Order and One ID initiatives; and (3) redesigning websites to improve customer experience.

Within operations, for example, management finds some ways to make up for the increase in aircraft turnaround times, the increase in time resulting from the changed ways of cleaning aircraft and boarding passengers. Similarly, some processes are changed to improve on-time performance and new arrangements are made with the cockpit and cabin crews to obtain higher levels of productivity. Also, within operations, airlines could increase the percentage of smaller airplanes in their fleet, given that unit operating costs of the advanced single-aisle aircraft are now comparable to the older, larger, wide-body aircraft. And, although the fleet-mix may change, airlines introduce the new generation of large wide-body aircraft, consisting of such aircraft types as the Airbus A350-900 and the A350-1000 as well as the Boeing 777-8 and the 777-9. Similarly, some processes and agreements are changed internally and within the ecosystem to improve aircraft and crew productivities.

Within the ecosystem, the current disruption did change the situation for airports, relating not just to the decrease in the traffic at airports, but also to revenues of airports (from aeronautical and non-aeronautical sources), as airports went from a situation of constrained capacity to one of overcapacity. Airports began to diversify their portfolios by marketing to new airlines and facilitating the development of cargo operations, as well as by becoming a little more open-minded. It is assumed, however, that after the traffic bounces back to the historical levels, particularly in the case of the first dotted arrow, larger airports worldwide continue to experience high growth rates and their infrastructure (runways, terminals, and roadways to and from the airport) would remain constrained. Under this scenario, most large airports would continue to manage the growth in traffic, using the conventional model of building additional infrastructure and then operating it, and then managing it. As with airlines, airports also continue to make improvements, such as through the deployment of biometrics and better plans developed from a better understanding of the needs of users, both suppliers of services (airlines, ground handlers, concessionaires, for example), as well as ultimate customers, the actual passengers. The most fundamental assumption, on the part of airports and airlines, is that travel does come back, as travel has become an integral part of most people's lives, even though this disruption may change the way people shop and the way they travel.

## Scenario 2: Elastic supply

To repeat, there are two aspects of the second scenario, elastic supply. They both involve the need to adapt to the changes in demand. One involves changes to the volume of travel and the second involves changes in the types of transportation services desired by consumers and provided by service providers, existing and new. The second scenario, elastic supply, is based on different assumptions, relating to key areas of uncertainty, listed in Figure 2.1, the need for different internal capabilities, and the need to collaborate and coordinate within the ecosystem to adapt effectively to the associated changes in the marketplace. For example, the economic recovery is assumed to be L-shaped or W-shaped, depending, in part, on government policies, relating, in turn, to the tax structure and interest rates to account for the extreme levels of debt taken over by governments. The impact could be severe on some governments that are not able to borrow large amounts of money, or at least, not at low interest rates. And, even if they were able to borrow a limited amount of money, in which sector of the business would they invest? Under this scenario, government intervention is substantial, relating not just to the economic and transportation policies, but also in the areas of policies toward globalization and multilateral initiatives (geopolitics). If the globalization movement was to slow down (as a result of changes in technologies and the movement of populism in some countries), the impact on travel and trade could be significant. On top of that, there could be a new disruption relating to health.

In all such cases, the level of traffic, its growth rate, and its mix will change dramatically. Consider the seriousness of two new areas of uncertainty overlapping—relating to health and geopolitical upheavals. The economic recovery is W-shaped and government policies dealing with the new health challenge are standard, but not coordinated. The result is that while all influencers are positive, traffic grows rapidly and then when influencers turn negative quickly, traffic declines just as rapidly, if not more so. The result is something similar to that displayed in Figure 2.3, requiring dramatically different strategies to adapt to changes in the marketplace.

Consequently, not only may traffic not return to its base of 2019 for a number of years, but its rate of growth may fluctuate widely, between high and low and between positive growth and negative growth. Figure 2.3 shows one

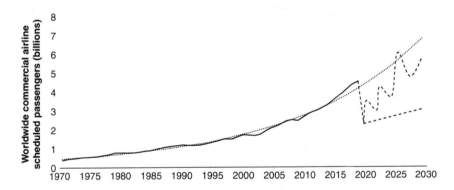

*Figure 2.3* Elastic supply scenario based on non-conventional thinking

dotted line growing at the old expected growth, based on the exponential curve (the higher dotted line), and one showing traffic growing at very low rate, such as 2 percent per year (the lower dotted line). The starting point is still from the lower base in 2020. The growth rate can then oscillate, meaning that the initial growth rate could be very high, say 10–15 percent, or even higher, and then instead of continuing to grow at that rate, it could actually decline, and then could start growing again, but at a different rate. The point is not that anyone can predict what the traffic level or growth will be, but that managements need to be prepared to deal with whatever they turn out to be, year after year. Moreover, fluctuations in growth do not need to be on a year-on-year basis. The demand might change on a week-by-week basis, depending on health-based lockdowns, politically induced travel restrictions by different countries, at least for the next 2–3 years, assuming the pandemic is not contained on a global basis and the political-economic disputes between major countries are not resolved. Airlines, therefore, need to plan for a broad array of capacity options in the medium term, with the capability to react on almost a daily basis. There are two important considerations to achieve such a level of flexibility. First, planning, both within commercial and operational functions, must start from ground zero with respect to the selection of fleet, the development of schedules, the realignment of cockpit and cabin-crew rules, and leasing arrangements. (See the thought leadership piece by Dietmar Kirchner in Chapter 7.) Second, key roles will be played by the chief commercial officer and the chief operations officer. However, it is the chief executive officer who will need not only to step in to ensure a balance between the operational considerations and the commercial considerations, but also to flip barriers to enablers. See the discussion in Chapter 6.

Under this scenario, there could be a significant reduction in business traffic for a long time—of the order of 20 percent. This reduction would lead to a much larger reduction in revenues and an even larger reduction in profits. Moreover, the reduction in business travel will affect many other areas, such as loyalty programs. The value of some loyalty programs could decrease if there is a significant reduction in frequent travelers, if some airlines become smaller, and if the viability of some airlines becomes questionable by financial institutions that have been investing in airlines, for example, credit-card companies. Relating to budget travel, the growth of the traffic generated by the emerging middle classes in some developing countries could slow down significantly for economic reasons and changes in social behaviors. Let us not forget that some developing countries not only have weak economies, but also relatively weak health care systems. Businesses reach a conclusion that working from remote locations can not only work, but it can be done within a distributive framework and it can provide flexibility for employees and productivity can be maintained through collaboration, without wasting time in physical meetings. If the global economy declines in 2020 by an average of 4.5 percent or more, there will be an enormous pressure on businesses to reduce their operating costs. At the beginning of October 2020, the International Monetary Fund was forecasting a decline of 4.4 percent in the global economy for the year 2020.[3] The focus on managing costs will then be on identifying and implementing structural changes to reduce costs, scale down operations, and find new ways to manage risk by finding new ways to work with labor, airports, aircraft manufacturers, aircraft lessors, and distributors. Airline network planners would need to explore new data sources and partnerships within different regions and they could get valuable information from both the airports as well as regional organizations. And the focus to reduce complexity will become a much higher priority, for both airlines and airports.

If this scenario were to play out, the change in the structure of the industry could introduce a somewhat new regulatory system, just as when the Chicago Convention, signed in 1944, created the International Civil Aviation Organization in 1945, even before the establishment of the United Nations.

- As mentioned above, there could be a strong interest by governments in the development of multimodal transportation systems that would go beyond the coordination initiatives at the edges, as might be the case in the first scenario that simply enables passengers to make smooth connections while changing modes of transportation, from a train to an airline, or from a bus to an airline, for instance. Now the interest would be in integrating totally different modes of transportation to provide door-to-door services seamlessly, based on locations of consumers in catchment areas and the socio-economic characteristics of these areas. Systems would be developed within a bottom-up framework and operated within a dynamic operational framework to manage intermodal trips. (See the thought leadership piece by Benedikt and Julian Mandel in Chapter 7.) Moreover, intermodality may not be restricted to the use of current vehicles. Also included could be a new generation of small electric airplanes and the likes of the hyperloop capsules, or autonomous vehicles in the ecosystem. And, let us not overlook the potential emergence of on-demand aerial ridesharing initiatives.
- If governments end up being required to provide huge amounts of ongoing financial support, there could be a significant number of mergers and acquisitions, a reevaluation of competition in key markets (relating, for example, to the operations of large sixth-freedom carriers), and a change in ownership and control rules to enable the development of multinational airlines.
- There could also be a need for a realignment of the business models of partners, for example, airports, that in some regions have simply built their business models on merely developing, operating, and managing the infra-structure to manage the ongoing growth, while assuming comparatively little risk. For example, airlines in the US could want to pay airports for only the services and facilities they use. On their part, airports in the US could insist that airlines release to the airports the unilateral control that they have had over terminals, and/or gates. At some airports, the hub-airlines and the airports have special arrangements to build facilities such as

terminals, including some decisions relating to concessionaires. This relationship may not exist going forward. At some large and congested hub-and-spoke airports, managements have assumed the continued existence of connecting traffic and the hub-airlines have assumed the value of their control of slots. These assumptions may no longer be valid and the higher profit margins generated by some partners, such as airports, may not exist, going forward.

- Governments could implement exceptionally stringent regulations to protect the environment (decarbonization) by forcing manufacturers to redesign new aircraft to use alternative power sources, and for airlines to find new ways to conduct their operations. Governments, especially in the EU region, could easily impose extremely high levels of taxes relating to the protection of the environment. Traffic could decline as a result of not only the higher price of tickets, but also the willingness of an increasing segment of the population to support the flight shaming movement. It is also possible that governments that impose high taxes on airlines may use the funds raised to subsidize other modes of transportation that are much more eco-friendly.

This scenario does not mean that traffic will not return to its original level or grow at the historical level. On the contrary, it could reach new heights in its level and in its growth. However, both the level and the rate of growth could just as easily decline by large amounts, and then bounce back rapidly, from year to year. The key capability needed would be to develop agile and smart strategies to manage the growth and fluctuations in demand. And, just as in the case of the first scenario, the second scenario is neither negative nor pessimistic. The air travel industry will continue to grow, even above the historical level of growth. The size, shape, and structure of the industry will, however, depend on how different sectors of the industry are managed and operated. And, how, for example, value is created, captured, and delivered through collaboration within the physical and the digital ecosystems, inside and outside of the organization.

Under this scenario, new disrupters could easily enter the airline business. Current generations of low-cost airlines entered the marketplace with a business model that basically started with point-to-point services at lower fares, using single-aisle aircraft. The fleet had high-density configurations and was used more hours per day. What if new types of low-cost airlines emerge that use even more efficient aircraft (such as smaller electric-powered aircraft) and operate to-and-from even smaller airports? What if they operate on an on-demand basis, or a ridesharing basis, just like Uber? Uber Air has reported its plan to start its urban on-demand aerial services in select cities in as early as 2023. Services could be provided with vertical take-off and landing electric-powered aircraft. These services would have a significant impact on not only hub-and-spoke systems, but also the airports selected for connecting services, not to mention the services provided to and from secondary airports. What if they decide to offer different pricing systems, such as subscriptions that would be acceptable to consumers and government policy makers as they would not be polluting the environment and will be keeping aviation green? What would be the response from not just the current generation of full-service airlines, but also the current generation of low-cost airlines? Keep in mind that the new breed of low-cost airlines does not need to have specific plans right from the start. Each airline could reinvent itself by pivoting its business model multiple times, based on a disciplined process of experimentation and learning, a concept that would not only be acceptable to financial investors, but also promoted by investors. Moreover, being agile, the next generation of new entrants could also take advantage of opportunities created from the slow and conventional responses of incumbent airlines, full-service and low-cost. New entrants will also be able to capitalize on the consolidation process among the incumbent carriers, the availability of lower-priced airplanes, the availability of qualified and experienced crews, and the scaling of their operations to cater to the level of demand that is depressed in some regions and rebounding in others.

Technologies were listed as one of the six areas of uncertainty in Figure 2.1. Here are just three examples involving vehicles, relating not to the quantity of capacity, but to the types of services provided.

Consider, first, the development of small electric aircraft. A lot of research is being conducted to replace small jet-powered regional aircraft with new technology electric aircraft. The research being conducted relates not just to the technical viability of the new propulsion systems, but also to the operational aspects, economic aspects, and passenger acceptance. Examples of operational consideration will be aircraft weight, speed and range, the infrastructure needed at airports (charging of batteries, for instance), and pilot training. Examples of economic aspects will be the initial investment costs and the daily operating costs. As for passenger acceptance, on the positive side acceptance will be facilitated by the knowledge that these will be non-polluting aircraft. However, questions may relate to the potential of higher fares. Once these concerns are resolved, the electric aircraft in regional service could be game changers.

Consider next the potential entry of capsules that can transport passengers at speeds similar to airplanes, with capsules traveling not on rails, but by levitating just above ground. Although the concept of such travel is not new, it was popularized and branded by Elon Musk, who then made it an open source concept in which other thinkers and problem solvers could participate to make the concept a reality. Hyperloop Transportation Technologies (HyperloopTT) is one of these organizations that has already made substantial progress in turning an innovative vision into reality by launching an innovative crowd-powered ecosystem.[4] A full-scale system has been developed in Toulouse, France and a commercial passenger version is scheduled to break ground in Abu Dhabi, United Arab Emirates. The concept is to connect cities, such as Pittsburg to Cleveland to Chicago in the US, and other cities worldwide. The capsule can also be used to transport people, in minutes, from large city centers to major airports where they can connect with other modes of transportation. The group, made up of a number of contributors, is studying the engineering, economic, and regulatory areas of viability of the concept that has the involvement of the private and the public sector. The plan is to go from design to delivery through a crowd-powered platform. Figure 2.4 shows an example of a passenger capsule that could travel at speeds approaching 760 miles per hour, carrying between 28 and 50 passengers. Figure 2.5 displays some information showing the incredibly high efficiency of this system, in terms of both speed and emissions. Not only will the carbon dioxide ($CO_2$) be absent, but the cost per ton mile will be much lower than the air mode, comparable to the levels achieved by the water and rail modes.

Finally, further out, consider the development of the hydrogen fuel-powered, zero-carbon aircraft. No doubt that such aircraft may not be available until around 2035, but their arrival would impact an airline's decisions on which and how many airplanes to acquire between now and then. Fleet planning is a very long-term exercise on the part of both aircraft manufacturers (airframe and engine) and airlines. Besides the environmental factors, airlines will be looking at the regulatory, economic, and operational aspects of such aircraft, such as payload-range and maintenance. Could such aircraft become available within the envisioned time frame—2035? It is reported that ZeroAvia flew its first flight of the hydrogen fuel-cell-powered Piper M (with six seats) in the UK on September 25, 2020. The development was reported as "one of the most historic flights in decades."[5]

One key critical success factor for the successful deployment of this technology would be the development of a partnership between the infrastructure providers (such as airports and cities) and the operators, such as the airlines, exemplified in Chapters 3 and 6. The concept is visionary and radical and does have risks. However, as elaborated in Chapter 6, it has the potential to become technically and commercially viable by the efforts of individuals who have "innovation capital," explained in Chapter 6.[6] The value of innovation available within the ecosystem cannot be underestimated. Think about the rise and fall of Nokia, a Finnish company that was a leader in the development of innovative mobile phones. Its mobile phones had embedded cameras, for example; however, its operating system had limited capabilities. Google and Apple, on the other hand, facilitated outsiders to develop apps to enhance the capabilities of their operating systems, the Android and the iOS systems, respectively. The innovations leveraged from the ecosystem represented one of the major problems faced by Nokia.

Under both scenarios, the structure of the industry is likely to change with the degree of change depending on the scenario. For example, there could be more mergers and acquisitions worldwide, if there is not enough traffic, or enough profitability, in the near term, to support all the carriers. This situation will call for a substantial reduction in networks. The surviving carriers would need to develop the capability to expand and contract their operations quickly to meet the changing needs of the marketplace, hence the name of the scenario—elastic supply. In the US, there could either be mergers among carriers within the second tier and the third tier, or among the three tiers, for

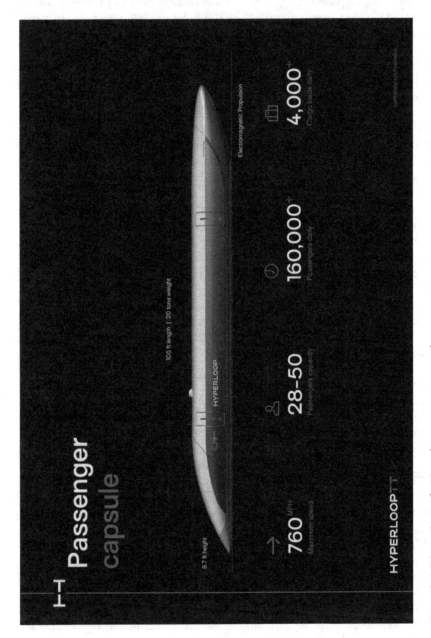

*Figure 2.4* Dimensions of a Hyperloop passenger capsule

Source: Printed with the permission of the HyperloopTT.

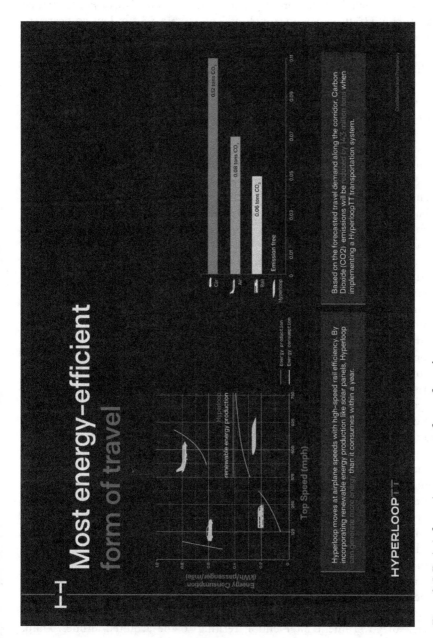

*Figure 2.5* Basic information on a new form of travel
Source: Printed with the permission of the HyperloopTT.

example, a carrier in the first tier acquires a carrier in the second tier. In Europe, there could be meaningful changes in airline groupings. Smaller carriers could become integrated in the larger groups. Think about Cathay Pacific which acquired both Cathay Dragon and Hong Kong Express. As for low-cost carriers, the positioning of the large carriers, easyJet, Ryanair, and Wizz Air, could change, for example, by one or more of the three acquiring a number of smaller carriers in the low-cost space. Think also about the possibility of Ryanair acquiring wide-body aircraft from one of the large manufacturers at really low prices. The carrier has reported in the past the viability of such a strategy across the Atlantic if the price of the aircraft was low enough. Finally, think about the possibility of one of the large low-cost carriers becoming part of the larger full-service carrier groups. Think about the diversity in the portfolios of large hotel chains. The Marriott Group has in its portfolio the classic luxury brands (such as the JW Marriott, the Ritz-Carlton, and the St Regis), the distinctive brands (such as W Hotels, the Sheraton Hotels, the Le Méridien, and Westin Hotels), its budget brands (such as Courtyard, Fairfield, and Four Points), and long stays (such as Residence Inn). And, just like hotels and technology businesses, airline groups could also make use of platforms. Imagine if platforms could be operated by airline alliance organizations?

Another area of structural change could be the development of multi-national airlines. Think about some airlines that have been financially weak and uncompetitive for years, even before this crisis. They have been dependent on government support for years—Aerolíneas Argentina, Alitalia, Air India, and South African Airways, just to name four. Now, some governments could see an opportunity for their national-flag carriers to be resurrected with changes in government policies to strengthen these airlines that could contribute a lot more to the economic development of their countries. One example would be for governments to change ownership and control rules to enable the development of multinational airlines that would not only generate capital for the weak government-owned airlines, but also provide the right strategic focus to strengthen the airlines to provide connectivity, and economic development of countries, including the development of tourism. In some ways, such initiatives would, in fact, reduce the complexity challenges faced by both governments and the airlines owned by governments. The movement toward the development of multinational airlines could change not only the location of hubs, and the make-up of hub-and-spoke systems, but also partnerships in alliances. In the development of multinational airlines, the operating costs of the acquired airlines will be decreased and their brand names will be raised to higher levels. The acquired airlines will also have access to higher levels of talent and technologies. The key would be to find the right partners, based on the location of the carriers, their strategic capabilities, their corporate culture, and the ongoing or lack of government intervention relating to the acquired airlines. Think about the potential restructuring opportunities within this context of relatively large airlines, such as Garuda Indonesia, Malaysia Airlines, Philippine Airlines, and Thai Airways.

This chapter has identified some key drivers of change and developed two scenarios based on possible outcomes. This disruption has already proven to be so different from any of the past disruptions experienced by the industry during the past 50 years. The result is that not only operations (the subject of the next chapter), but also the commercial plans and strategies (the subject of Chapter 4) need to be started from ground zero. The focus should be on the planning process, not on the plans. Keep in mind a quotation generally attributed to the former US President, Dwight Eisenhower. "Plans are nothing, planning is everything."

## Notes

1 IATA and the School of International Futures, *Future of the Airline Industry 2035* (IATA, 2018).
2 Steffan Waldron, "To Your Shore?" *Think: Act*, Issue No. 32, Roland Berger, October 2020, pp. 49–53.
3 www.usnews.com/news/best-countries/articles/2020-10-13/imf-projects-less-severe-global-economic-decline-for-2020-slower-growth-for-2021
4 Lynda M. Applegate, Terri L. Griffith, and Ann Majchrzak, "Hyperloop Transportation Technologies: Building Breakthrough Innovations in Crowd-Powered Ecosystems," *Harvard Business School Case Study*, No. 9-817-134, June 12, 2017.
5 Tim Robinson, "Airbus Spearheads Zero-Carbon Moonshot," *AEROSPACE*, Royal Aeronautical Society, November 2020, p. 40.
6 Jeff Dyer, Nathan Furr, and Curtis LeFrandt, *Innovation Capital: How to Compete and Win Like the World's Most Innovative Leaders* (Boston, MA: Harvard Business Review Press, 2019).

# 3 Rebuilding networks and operations from ground zero

During the initial phase of the recovery, most airlines were making short-term decisions to survive to meet their immediate needs for cash flow and liquidity without, in some cases, a comprehensive and a coherent long-term strategy, based on roadmaps for the commercial and operational functions. There were, however, a few airlines with a longer-term orientation that were asking some important questions regarding the fundamentally changing landscape in the coming years so as to rebuild operations within a back-to-the-future framework. These forward-looking airlines were also watching the strategies of other businesses outside the airline industry (such as Amazon, Nokia, Tesla, and Uber) to see how they were responding to the changing marketplace. Yet, planners, even within the forward-thinking airlines, were still working with conventional strategies for network, fleet, and schedule planning, based on conventional thinking, based, in turn, on conventional constraints, such as airport gates and slots, and labor contracts. However, new ways of planning are needed to address the two different scenarios, especially in the case of the second scenario—elastic supply to provide flexibility and agility. These new ways of planning need to be based on non-conventional thinking and, as such, would not only be hard to explore, but they would also be hard to implement in light of the ongoing constraints. On the positive side, however, resources now exist to enable planners to not only think differently, but also to explore dramatically different strategies as well as their execution with minimal risk. This chapter suggests that network, fleet, and schedule planners, as well as groups in operations systems control centers, consider the two scenarios, particularly the elastic supply scenario, and work backwards to frame their current tactics and strategies, and then develop the needed internal capabilities as well as the potential collaboration and coordination within the ecosystem.

If groups working on rebuilding operations from ground zero are to work with a back-to-the-future orientation, then what are examples of questions relating to the future landscape, say 5–10 years out? This is where the two scenarios come in to identify some longer-term options. A number of questions were raised in the previous chapter, relating to each scenario. The basic question is still not about when will markets grow and the conditions normalize, but rather what does "conditions normalize" mean? In addition to the questions already raised in Chapter 2, there are still a few more that concern specifically network, fleet, and schedule planners as well as planners of operations. For example:

- According to some experts, the world is becoming bipolar. What would be the impact on long-haul travel in the longer term, not just on the level of travel, but the potential ups and downs, relating to the demand? Next, while experts have pointed out that many viruses that originate in animals are transferred to humans, why has the speed of transfer increased? Is it because (1) the places where people live are changing due, for example, to the increase in urbanization, and (2) the changes in mobility of people? Assuming this to be the case, how would the location and mobility trends affect travel, going forward?[1]
- Will the decarbonization movement become global and imperative? Would governments, particularly those that have acquired equity in their airlines, push the sustainability aspects aggressively and force their airlines to adopt definitive strategies, and, at the same time, restrict the traffic rights of foreign airlines that do not comply to the same rules? Will CORSIA (Carbon Offsetting and Reduction Scheme for International Aviation) rules be adjusted to be in line with the Paris Climate Agreement or the UK's Net Zero Carbon obligations? At the same time, the reduction in travel during the pandemic seems to have raised the consciousness of the public for supporting the sustainability movement.
- Will some governments begin to implement protectionist and polarization polices and what would such policies mean for airline network and fleet planners? Would some governments, for example those with weaker airlines, try to reconstruct the regulatory structure to protect their carriers? Would some governments be interested in changing the ownership and control rules to enable the development of multinational airlines? Would some other governments, even with strong carriers, try to change the regulatory system to create more level playing fields, relating to competition, say, from large sixth-freedom carriers? To what degree would governments continue to support their airlines, given the airlines' contribution to the global trade, communications, and tourism sectors of economies, not to mention the social needs of the people? Would governments go so far as to change their regulatory policies to ensure the survival of their airlines? Could the policies of some governments change relating to the transportation of cabotage traffic?
- How much will the price of fuel increase from its level of $40/barrel in 2020? What is the viability of biofuels and synthetic fuels with respect to technology, ecology, and economics? If only small aircraft (say, with less than 50 seats) can be designed to operate with electric propulsion, how would the high cost of synthetic fuels impact the use of large wide-body aircraft, particularly those designed to fly ultra-long-haul routes? What if fuel costs become a much higher percentage of total direct operating costs?

- What is the expected year when major airframe manufacturers might bring out new aircraft, propelled by synthetic fuels? What would be the breadth of capacity-range options? What would be the impact on the residual values of aircraft delivered in the next 10 years?
- How will business models of the original equipment manufacturers (OEMs) and lessors change in light of potential cancellations and deferrals of the aircraft ordered, large numbers of permanently parked aircraft, and the push for more environment-compliance aircraft? Will OEMs start large leasing businesses to market their excess production? Would the Mitsubishi Aircraft Corporation (based in Japan) and COMAC (Commercial Aircraft Corporation of China) succeed in developing commercially viable aircraft, along with Embraer and Bombardier, at the sweet spot of trip-cost versus seat kilometer cost?
- Will end-to-end journeys, let alone door-to-door service and mobility-as-a-service concepts finally be developed and implemented? How much will conventional short-haul travel by air be replaced by surface (auto and train) and by the next generation of trains and by new forms of aircraft (small electric aircraft, for example)? Consider the planned improvements in the infrastructure and the collaboration and coordination among the rail service providers in the Blue Banana zone, a corridor of urbanization that stretches from Manchester in the UK to Milan in Italy, with a population of more than 100 million. How about Google's introduction of its Waymo One driverless ride-hailing services in early October 2020 in the greater Phoenix, Arizona area? How about when the hyperloop concept becomes technically and economically viable?
- Would traffic continue to grow at disproportionately high rates in Asia? Consider, for example, that the top ten global markets, in terms of seat capacity in the summer of 2019, were domestic and, all but one, located in the Asia-Pacific region—in Australia, China, India, Japan, South Korea, and Vietnam. The exception was the one located in Saudi Arabia—between Jeddah and Riyadh. Even the next ten high-capacity non-domestic markets were located in the Asia-Pacific region, such as Kuala Lumpur to Singapore and Hong Kong to Seoul. Keep in mind that according to some experts, the size of the middle class in Asia could be larger than the middle classes in the US and Europe combined, even though there will continue to be a difference in the levels of incomes in the middle classes of these regions.
- What would the structure of the airline industry look like on major inter-continental routes, such as the North Atlantic? Even prior to the current disruption, there was "consolidation" in this market, given that about two-thirds of the market was controlled by the three multinational groups that had antitrust immunized joint ventures. (See the thought leadership piece by Keith McMullan and James Halstead in Chapter 7.) Could there be changes in the makeup of the carriers in the three major groups within Europe? Could the Visegrád Group of four Eastern and Central European countries (the Czech Republic, Hungary, Poland, and Slovakia) work with

a single airline, such as LOT Polish? Not only would this group's population (about 60 million) be of a similar size to France, Italy, and the UK, but there are three significantly sized airports—Budapest, Prague, and Warsaw (Chopin).

- What is the future of alliances in general, and the antitrust immunity/joint ventures, in particular? Could all three Persian Gulf-based carriers join the three global alliances? Could alliances play a different role, for example, in the development and operation of full-service platforms, discussed in the next chapter?

- Could the original concept of virtual airlines materialize and, if yes, in what form, and by when? Will high-technology platform-based companies such as Google and Amazon play a role in helping airlines manage their capacities when there are large variations in demand? Will there be consolidation in the leasing sector and will some lessors develop into "white label," Aircraft, Crew, Maintenance, and Insurance (ACMI) operators to allow airlines to manage their capacity with more flexibility to adapt to the elastic supply scenario?

- Based on the two scenarios presented, should network and fleet planners reduce the size of their operations and, if yes, by how much, and how? If the spread of the virus continues and an effective vaccine takes a much longer time to become available worldwide, will some airlines simply leave the marketplace or reduce their size? How much will the structure of the global airline industry change as a result of both consolidation and fragmentation in different regions of the world—the EU, the Persian Gulf region, North America, and Asia, for example? How would the fragmentation and consolidation processes vary by region?

- Could a decrease in business travel be irreversible? Could a significant decrease in long-haul international travel, particularly within the high-yield segment, lead to a major challenge for large global network carriers with limited to no domestic market, for example, British Airways and Singapore Airlines, respectively? Think about the dependency of British Airways on the transatlantic market, not just with respect to the size of the market, but also its traffic (higher percentage of business travelers), and the disproportionately high level of premium-class fares. Could some of this impact be offset by an increase in the high-yield cargo traffic carried in the bellies?

- Would secondary airports be threatened or could they actually grow? Would threats and opportunities be created by network carriers that decide to focus on their hubs? Would opportunities come from the availability of new aircraft, such as the exceptionally long-range single-aisle aircraft, or the initiation of new services by new entrants, and the desire of some passengers to avoid large and overly congested connecting airports? Could Ryanair acquire wide-body aircraft at considerably low prices (old or new) and start transatlantic operations? What is the future of slots in the context of the two scenarios?

- Could some airports in the US, those experiencing severe financial challenges, decide to undertake the public-private partnerships (P3) initiatives, involving equity and debt? Such initiatives became more viable with the FAA Reauthorization Act of 2018.
- After the disruption caused by this pandemic, could the use of private airplanes increase? It is reported that this mode of transportation did increase during the initial phase of the recovery. While this mode of transportation is limited to high-net-worth individuals, could usage increase, based partly on the experience and acceptance gained during the pandemic, the potential loss of services, and/or frequency in thinner markets, and the emergence of on-demand platforms, developed around the concept of the Uber model? Could the Uber taxi model apply, both for the new, small, electric aircraft under development and the existing small aircraft that are privately owned and operated by individual people, or that are operated by a collection of charter carriers who might work with a platform to consolidate demand? Could the operators of small business jets feed international carriers at major hubs? Such a concept has been tried before but the operators did not have access to the digital assets and digital networks discussed in the next two chapters.
- How will travel patterns change if the growth in urbanization slows or even reverses, based on the concern that viruses are transferred from animals to humans and the likelihood of rapid spread is higher in urban areas?

If working with a back-to-the-future framework is reasonable, then answers to such questions as those listed above may provide some indications for the current plans for rebuilding networks and operations. For example, how much should an airline reduce its network, fleet, and schedules now and how, would depend on the expected answers to some of the aforementioned questions. Working backwards may help network planners (as well as revenue managers) to identify both short- and long-term strategies.

## Strategizing for the continuous improvement scenario

During the first phase of the recovery, the focus of airlines was on flying both freighters and passenger aircraft, to transport expatriates and to transport cargo, especially the shipments containing essential products. Often passenger transports carried only cargo shipments. In some cases, large aircraft, such as the Boeing 777s, transported cargo only in their bellies with no passengers on their main decks. In other cases, passenger aircraft carried cargo in their main cabins, with seats removed, or even with boxes placed on top of seats in the economy sections. Both cases required approvals from regulatory authorities (for transporting cargo in passenger cabins, for instance) and operational considerations (weight and balance, for instance). In the second phase of the recovery, the focus was on restarting operations by getting the grounded crews and aircraft flying again, while complying with the regulatory requirements.

As discussed in the next chapter, commercial groups in airlines focused more on stimulating traffic with lower fares and by engaging with consumers about the implementation of health-related practices, such as sanitizing the aircraft and keeping the middle seats vacant. Then, beginning in the middle of 2020, airlines started to think about the aircraft that they were planning to park permanently, an enormous challenge given the uncertainty relating to demand, going forward, and the logistics of training some crews that were moving from larger aircraft to smaller aircraft, the opposite of standard practices in the past.

Challenges and opportunities relating to some network, fleet, and scheduling strategies discussed in this chapter may appear to be similar to those faced by planners in the past. There is, however, a possibility of "constructive destruction" as discussed at the beginning of the first chapter that could change what economists refer to as the fundamental "structure, performance, and conduct" of the airline industry and related businesses in the aviation sectors. Consequently, there is a need to change strategies, for the following reasons, not so much to deal with threats, but to capitalize on opportunities.

- Competition is increasing, not only in speed, but also in depth and breadth. And, while some new entrants may not survive in the long term, they will create competitive challenges in the short term.
- While there are some serious threats, there are also some powerful opportunities that can be seized by changing business models to truly find ways to determine customers' problems and to offer solutions. Consequently, the need is now more critical than ever to get, even for the first scenario, change strategies implemented in a timely manner.
- The traditional internal and external constraints to the implementation of strategies can no longer be accepted. New ways must be found to work around these constraints while minimizing risks relating to the radically changing marketplace, for example, the development of intermodal transportation.
- The dynamics of the slot market could change, based partly on government policies, and partly on the competitive repositioning of major global hubs and their locations.

Even the most optimistic sub-scenario, in Figure 2.2, assumed that it could take up to 3 years for the traffic to return to the level achieved at the end of 2019 and to pick up the rate of growth at the historic level of between 4 and 5 percent. As such, most network, fleet, and schedule planners have begun to think about different ways to downsize their networks and fleet to adapt to this situation. Strategies differ by airline categories (for example, full-service carriers versus low-cost carriers versus hybrid carriers), by region (domestic or international), and by the type of business model. Take, for example, one low-cost carrier group, based in Europe. Within this group, take, for example, the growth plans of Wizz Air in Europe. Right in the middle of the Coronavirus disruption, when most airlines were reducing their operations by large amounts, Wizz Air, a well-capitalized and more liquid low-cost airline, reported its growth plans to the western, central, and eastern regions of Europe, as well as to and from the Persian Gulf region. These growth plans make sense, given:

- the well-capitalized position and higher liquidity of Wizz Air, demonstrated by the decision not to take government financial assistance,
- its well-suited fleet (young and relatively simple),
- its lower operating costs than easyJet, and possibly even Ryanair,
- the craving of some airports, under economic pressure, to offer a desirable working relationship,
- its existing relationship with Indigo Partners,
- its progress in adopting digital technologies, exemplified by the capability to enable customers to take care of their own bookings and the unveiling of its new service feature (called WIZZ RIDE) on a platform enabling passengers to access a taxi via the airline's existing mobile app,
- its innovative strategies, exemplified by its decision to start a "cabin-crew-to-captain," program that provides flight attendants an opportunity to train as pilots,[2] and
- its new relationship with the Abu Dhabi Development Holding Company.[3]

These growth plans began to be implemented despite the uncertainty relating to demand and despite the challenge of the growth plans of other low-cost carriers within its regions. For example, in the Middle East, the challenge came from flydubai and Air Arabia. In Europe, the competitive challenge came mostly from Ryanair. Ryanair (or other members of the Ryanair Group, such as Malta Air) and Wizz Air began to expand their operations in Europe, with new bases in Germany, not only at the Frankfurt and Munich Airports (high-cost and slot-constrained airports), but also at smaller airports, such as Dortmund, Düsseldorf, and Stuttgart. Both Ryanair and Wizz Air could grow at a fast rate given the contraction of both easyJet and Norwegian, particularly the latter. Could Norwegian become part of a large European incumbent airline, a full-service network airline or a large low-cost carrier?

Think about opportunities instead of threats. These competitive moves by Wizz Air and Ryanair began to change not only the dynamics within the low-cost carrier group, but also the competitive dynamics within the full-service carrier groups. In the case of increasing competition within the low-cost sector, Wizz Air's strategy is plausible in light of conventional thinking, namely, that low costs in the airline business provide a competitive advantage in a commodity business. As mentioned above, Wizz Air has lower costs than easyJet, and, as such, the strategy started to work right away. EasyJet, with its higher costs, began to develop strategies to penetrate the business sector. The expansion of Ryanair (and its group members, such as Malta Air and Laudamotion) as well as Wizz Air could easily take significant traffic away from Austrian Airlines (part of the Lufthansa Group), to and from its home base in Austria, despite the decision by the Austrian Government to put a fare floor, during the recovery period, to limit competition from low-cost carriers.

In the US, Southwest Airlines, based on its higher level of liquidity and the desire to maintain flexibility, reportedly declined to apply for a government loan. Instead, besides building up its supply to match the ongoing changes in demand, Southwest is also making some fundamental changes to its network to take advantage of new strategic opportunities. One example is the recent announcement by Southwest to start new services between Chicago's O'Hare Airport and Houston's Intercontinental Airport, both major hubs of United Airlines. Southwest already serves Chicago's nearby Midway Airport and Houston's nearby Hobby Airport. This appears to be a strategic move from another perspective, to claim some slots and gates at congested airports. The next question could be: Would Southwest consider opening up some international destinations from the two new major airports, especially from Houston's Intercontinental Airport, to transport passengers to and from its existing international destinations?

Let us move to a different part of the world, India, where some low-cost airlines began to think about starting to serve long-haul intercontinental markets, again. Take just three examples of carriers based in India—IndiGo, SpiceJet, and Vistara—that believe that they can succeed, given the bankruptcy of Jet Airways and the ongoing financial difficulties of Air India. Air India has been a weak carrier for years and the government has not been able to attract any buyers, given, in part, the exceptionally high level of debt that the airline carries. Air India also had high labor costs, not because of high wages, but because of a disproportionately high number of staff. IndiGo, India's largest low-cost carrier (transporting more than 50 percent of the domestic market), had discussed the possibility of serving, for example, one of the airports in London, either using its single-aisle fleet of Airbus A320s, with a stop in one of the cities in Eastern Europe (such as Baku, Azerbaijan, or Tbilisi, Georgia), or flying nonstop with the use of a wide-body aircraft. While the use of a wide-body might not have made sense prior to the current disruption, it might now, at least in the near term, with the availability of parked airplanes, available at low prices. Moreover, the price of fuel was also low in the middle of 2020. Vistara, a full-service Tata Sons–Singapore Airlines joint venture, had already acquired a Boeing 787-9 in March 2020 and had planned to fly nonstop between Delhi and London in 2020. Then, SpiceJet reportedly began to proceed with plans to serve the market between India and the UK. Besides serving domestic markets in India, SpiceJet also has experience in serving some international markets, for example, services to and from some cities located in Asia and in the Middle East. On top of the interest by these low-cost carriers to serve Europe, Jet Airways is also hoping to relaunch its services.

There is no question that potential opportunities are enormous, given the large size of the market between the two countries (estimated to be around 300 million passengers) and a proportionately large percentage of business travelers. However, while these three carriers look at new opportunities, they need to be mindful that not only is the market between India and Europe highly competitive, but there are also infrastructural constraints. Let us start with the challenge of competition. Extensive services are available from the operators of nonstop services, not to mention competition from the operators of connecting services, both from the carriers based in the Persian Gulf region, but also in Europe, such as LOT Polish. One only needs to look at the extensive networks offered by the three carriers based in the Persian Gulf area. Figure 3.1 shows the networks operated by these three carriers that connected, in summer 2019, 13 cities in India and a number of cities in the UK, France, and Germany, alone.

Leaving aside the strength of competition, based on capacity, there is also the challenge that the two low-cost carriers (IndiGo and SpiceJet) would need to provide business class configurations, at least for the sub-segment traveling for business purposes. Even if the low-cost carriers were to offer a two-cabin configuration, would the business-class service be competitive with the services offered by incumbent brands? What is likely to happen is that the new entrants could attract, at best, traffic from the premium-economy section of the incumbent brands, based in Europe and the Persian Gulf region. As for the

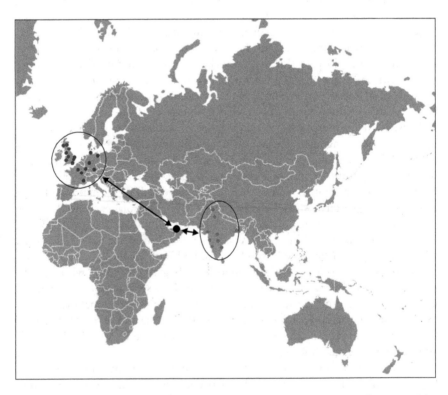

*Figure 3.1* Connecting services between 13 cities in India and cities in three countries in Europe served by the three Persian Gulf-based carriers (summer 2019)

infrastructural constraints, examples include the lack of slots at both Heathrow and Gatwick (at least prior to the current disruption) and the high costs of airport operations, more so at Heathrow than at Gatwick. However, even if these carriers do not succeed, they will change the competitive dynamics in the short term.

Consider, next, the emergence of totally new entrants and their potential to disrupt the marketplace. New entrants claim that they will offer less expensive but higher quality products and services as they would start the business with a clean slate—no debt, no financial losses, no legacy systems, and no legacy mindsets. And, some think that they can achieve quickly both scale and scope and a lower cost structure with the use of aircraft, grounded by large existing airlines, and the employment of furloughed, lower-cost, but experienced crew, that would be willing to work with less-constraining employment rules. The basic strategy would be similar to the low-cost and the ultra-low-cost carriers in the past when full-service carriers managed, eventually, to develop strategies to compete with them effectively. The key question now is what could be the new strategy of the new entrants, the so-called disruptive entrants? Would they be the conventional strategies of the past that worked for the new entrants, namely, leveraging lower costs to enter underserved and overpriced markets?

Given the greater uncertainty going forward, not only relating to the marketplace, but also the new business models of existing networks and existing low-cost carriers, what new, non-conventional strategies would the new entrants follow? If non-conventional strategies could be developed and executed intensely, then in some regions and in some markets, the "future" of air transportation could easily be in the hands of the totally new entrants, rather than the incumbents. Think about some totally new service models, such as extremely user-friendly shuttle services in high-density domestic markets in which high-speed surface transportation is not an option, for example, Gimpo–Cheju, Hanoi–Ho Chi Minh City, and Haneda–Okinawa. The shuttle service aspects would not just be related to a high level of frequency, but they would also include such features as no reservations, payment on board, subscription pricing, and Uber type of ground transportation at either or both ends of the trip. The disruptive thought process would be in the commoditization of mass transportation in which travelers have access to totally hassle-free transportation. In the top ten high-density domestic markets in Asia, an airline could begin to offer air services that resemble mass transportation that operate like utilities. As one former airline executive asked: Could the service provided be just as easy as hailing an Uber? This executive went on to say that mass transportation in these high-domestic markets should not require the use of any mental energy on the part of travelers for using a transportation mode. Another executive is reported to have said, "Don't Make Me Think" when I need to travel in these markets. Think about the application of the hyperloop capsules to provide transportation in high-density markets, based on a commodity-type service, "like turning on the light by a switch," or "like getting water by opening a tap." This is another example of elastic supply, but one that relates not only to the potential changes in the volume of demand, but also to the desire for and the availability of new forms of transportation.

A real route to success would be the combination of the previously mentioned reasons, coupled with the use of:

- digital assets (data, analytics, and networks),
- new sources of data (such as location and movement intelligence),
- new partnerships with secondary airports,
- new types of aircraft (such as single-aisle aircraft with a long range),
- new distributors (with access to demand, powerful platforms, and the capability to access data and mine data),
- micro-targeting capabilities, using the new digital assets, and, perhaps most important
- new thinking about disruptive products leveraging "innovation capital."

Critical success factors would be the use of digital assets and digital marketing strategies—the core competencies that did not exist when low-cost carriers entered the long-haul intercontinental markets. Think about the poor experience of some low-cost carriers that did not succeed because of their reliance on marketing their physical assets using conventional strategies. AirAsia X experimented with a nonstop service to London and Paris from Kuala Lumpur in 2012, with an Airbus A340-300. The services were not viable partly due to:

- the high unit operating costs of the aircraft (relating to the high cost of fuel in 2012),
- the lack of feeder traffic on the European side and, perhaps even more important,
- the lack of collaboration with partners in the dynamic digital ecosystem, and
- the use of conventional business models.

Norwegian also experimented in the London–Singapore market for about a year. These services also did not prove to be viable, due in part to the high ownership costs of a wide-body airplane and in part to the lack of cooperative arrangements with partners in the dynamic digital ecosystem. Other failures could also be studied, for example, the transatlantic services offered by Eos Airlines, MAXjet Airways, and Silverjet.

On the positive side, low-cost carriers do have the potential to succeed in long-haul intercontinental markets, or at least in long-haul markets, if they have some unique physical assets and if they can develop new digital assets to optimize the use of their physical assets and different mindsets. Consider the use of new long-range, single-aisle aircraft. Even the existing single-aisle aircraft can operate in much longer-haul markets. Figure 3.2 shows, for example, that the existing single-aisle aircraft have primarily been used in markets less than 1,500 miles. And, yet, some of these aircraft have the capability to fly almost 3,000 miles. The real challenge does not relate to the aircraft, but it relates to

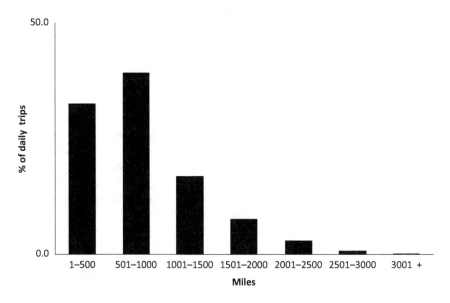

*Figure 3.2* Worldwide stage-length distribution of flights flown by Boeing 737 and Airbus A320, combined (summer 2019)

the existence of a mindset to "think out-of-the-box." AirAsia is a good example of a low-cost carrier that is not only realigning its network within the AirAsia Group, but also has developed a strategic platform to increase the e-commerce part of the business to diversify its revenue base. Consider, for example, the carrier's announcement of the introduction of its "ASEAN's super app," not only to improve customer experience with the use of a digital platform, but also a platform that could transform the airline from a low-fare airline to a "digital lifestyle company."[4] Air Asia is reported to have an ambition of having 50 percent of its revenues from non-flying activities by the end of 2024. The carrier is also planning to sell tickets of other airlines on its platform. The development of an e-commerce platform could add value as long as it does not add further complexity to its operations within the group structure or move the business away from its basic vision of low-cost, low-fare operations in South East Asia.

How about providing nonstop service in intercontinental markets, such as across the Atlantic? It is viable, if operated by carriers with the right combination of physical and digital assets, as well as a different way of thinking. Consider the decision of jetBlue to enter the transatlantic market. Consider, first, the strength of its assets, physical and digital:

- the right type of aircraft—an advanced version of the Airbus A321 series,
- an enormous number of slots at New York's Kennedy Airport, some of which could conceivably be traded for slots at London's Heathrow Airport,

- a strong presence in the New York region, including a large feeder network,
- a well-curated and desirable business class product (labeled as the "Mint" service),
- a well-recognized brand and loyalty program,
- a track record of having developed and implemented viable strategies, and
- a market in which the revenue per seat is relatively high and in which premium fares would most likely be coming down.

On top of these assets, jetBlue also has been developing its digital assets and has good experience in the use of digital marketing. Consequently, the carrier is in an excellent position to disrupt not only one of the most competitive, but also one of the most powerful markets in the world. By leveraging networks in the digital ecosystem, jetBlue could easily develop new marketing initiatives and new disruptive products, such as subscription pricing and intermodal door-to-door services, capitalizing on the use of new data (location and movement intelligence). Moreover, jetBlue is in an excellent position to practice micro-target marketing.

Do full-service carriers also have new opportunities in the emerging marketplace? Consider, for example, the Lufthansa Group, which has powerful physical and digital assets. Consider just two of its physical and tangible assets—a diverse fleet and five hubs that encompass a huge catchment area in Europe. Examples of valuable digital and intangible assets include a globally recognized brand name, a valuable loyalty program, and valuable slots at key airports. And, senior managers have a lot of experience in the use of analytics. Think about the last point—proven analytical capability. Lufthansa was one of the first airlines to have developed the capability to compute, with incredible accuracy, the lifetime value of customers in its loyalty program. It was also one of the first airlines to have developed an effective way to implement "continuous pricing" policies. The opportunity now is to further develop and leverage its three existing digital assets (brand, loyalty program, and slots), along with the new digital assets displayed in Figure 4.2 in Chapter 4, to maximize the value that can be derived from its physical assets—its diverse fleet and its hubs, displayed in Figure 3.3.

Consider, first, the diversity of the fleet. While fleet diversity does provide complexity, it also provides an opportunity to match demand with supply, a balance that will be required much more frequently, going forward. There are about a dozen types of aircraft operated by different members of the group. Even within a single type of aircraft, operated by one member, there are differences in seat configurations (in both wide-body and single-aisle aircraft) to meet some specific needs of specific markets, for example, heavy business traffic versus heavy leisure traffic. The fleet diversity provides network, fleet, and schedule planners the ability to change capacity in small increments to analyze route profitability by evaluating capacity, range, unit operating costs, demand (including the benefits of feeder services), and fares. There is no question that this level of diversity comes at a price: the costs associated with complexity. And the costs of complexity must take into consideration not only maintenance,

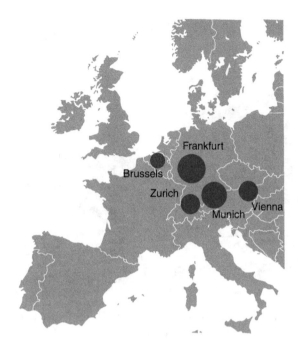

*Figure 3.3* Hub locations and relative sizes of the five hubs of the Lufthansa Group

spare parts, crew training, ground systems and services, but also certification, additional manuals, additional chief pilots, and additional engineers. However, the total costs of complexity generated from the use of fleet diversity can now be traded off with the true benefits of fleet diversity to generate more revenue by breaking down the silo systems in which fleet planners, revenue managers, sales divisions, and operational groups provide different inputs. See the discussions below.

Consider next, the second physical asset, the five closely spaced hubs (Brussels, Frankfurt, Munich, Zurich, and Vienna). In Figure 3.3, the circles represent approximately the relative size of each hub, based on the number of departures during a month in summer 2019. While the close proximity of the hubs does add some elements of complexity, there are also the benefits that come from the large and overlapping catchment areas of the five hubs, shown in Figure 3.4.

The presented airport catchment areas of the five hubs are a result of the route-specific catchment areas of the respective hubs, which compete with the services, offered at the airports located in the hinterland. Figure 3.4 shows the geographical dominance of hubs and reflects the shares of attracted regional air transport mobility. A diversified destination portfolio tailored to the local mobility needs of each hub location maximizes both local and transfer passenger traffic. At the same time, cannibalization effects in the overlapping areas are minimized. Fleet diversity supports this type of network fine-tuning.

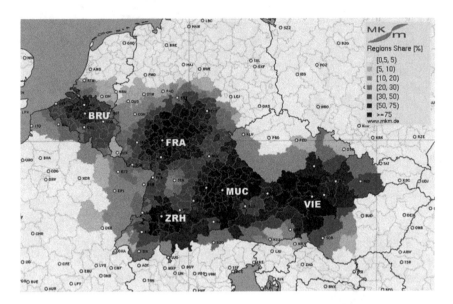

*Figure 3.4* Catchment areas for the five hub locations of the Lufthansa Group (2019)
Source: Printed with the permission of MKmetric GmbH.

Language barriers with the Czech Republic, which can be identified by the shape of the national borders, and geographical barriers, such as the Rhine, still have to be overcome. Local areas around Linz, Salzburg, and Innsbruck in Austria, as well as Düsseldorf in North Rhine-Westphalia and around Stuttgart in Baden-Württemberg are strategically assigned to the subsidiary Eurowings. Stuttgart is expected to be connected to Frankfurt in Hessen and Munich in Bavaria by new high-speed railways which are still under construction. And, let us not overlook the opening of the new airport (Berlin Brandenburg Airport (BER), which opened on October 31, 2020) that could provide some new opportunities for Lufthansa for long-haul nonstop services. There could be not only an opportunity to capitalize on the traffic potential from the new airport, but also an opportunity to slow down the expansion of Copenhagen Airport and the potential traffic that could be captured by the new Warsaw-Central Polish airport.

Lufthansa will thus be able to accelerate the expansion of its market position with minimal resources, by using intermodal services, customer loyalty through its loyalty program, and the fine-tuning of the entire network, flanked by its fleet diversity. In addition, slots occupied with grandfather rights can be used for network expansion. The size of the combined catchment area is phenomenal for developing new business models that offer comprehensive door-to-door travel, and/or urban air mobility, within the combined catchment area as well as connecting services to destinations, worldwide, in the next few years.

However, in the near future, think about the benefit of the combined catchment area to offset the disadvantage that Frankfurt and Munich have— lower levels of local origin-destination long-haul traffic compared with London's Heathrow and even, to a small extent, Paris's Charles de Gaulle. On the positive side, think also about the diversity in the traffic-mix among the five catchment areas. The Zurich hub, presumably, has a disproportionately higher level of premium traffic to justify the use of lower-capacity aircraft to offer higher frequency (not to mention the use of limited slots) to deliver and capture a higher value from travelers in its catchment area. According to a recent study by John Grant, using the data from OAG Traffic Analyser, the average revenue per seat from Switzerland, during the 2018/19 period, was $634, compared to $333 from Germany and $535 from Belgium.[5] And, Brussels Airport, while being squeezed between Amsterdam Airport and Charles de Gaulle Airport, represents an important block to reduce the geographic influence of KLM and Air France.

Nevertheless, to optimize the value of all physical and digital assets, and to perform the analysis at a systems level, the process must start from ground zero and take place within a bottom-up framework. A similar realignment of the network and fleet would provide even more benefits for the International Consolidated Airlines Group (IAG) that owns a portfolio of branded airlines that operate on an integrated platform. The parent company, IAG, decides how capital is allocated among the member airlines, based on a rigid rate of return on investment. This allocation of capital is most likely to change, given the expectation of a lower contribution from British Airways that had been generating a disproportionately higher level of profit margins from its transatlantic operations through the higher percentage of passengers traveling at premium fares: business class and first class.

In a similar manner, consider the opportunities created by the changing competitive dynamics within the US, relating, for example, to American Airlines, Delta Air Lines, and United Airlines, as they realign their networks, fleet, and schedules to adapt to the new marketplace. Figure 3.5 shows the locations and relative sizes of Delta's top ten hubs, estimated by the number of departures during a month in summer 2019. Although the realignment began prior to the current disruption, the speed of change has increased. The question might now be about the intensity of the realignment relating to the scenarios and the flexibility to shift the strategy, based on, for example, competitive moves in the marketplace. What if American was to decide to dismantle its hub-and-spoke system at Chicago's O'Hare Airport and focus instead on strengthening the other four hubs—Charlotte, Dallas, Miami, and Philadelphia? American's decision would totally change the decisions of network planners at United and Delta.

Delta had already reported its decision to expand its operations at Miami Airport, leveraging its newly formed joint venture with LATAM, challenging American's dominance at the airport, for the traffic to and from South America. To counter this, think about American's decision to develop a partnership

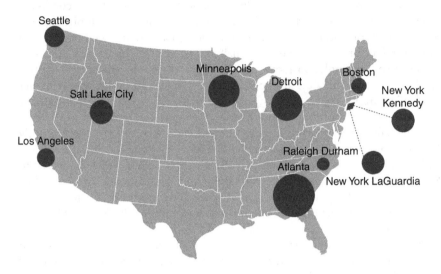

*Figure 3.5* Delta Air Lines hub locations and relative sizes by number of departures (summer 2019)

with Alaska Air to expand American's services from Seattle. Alaska Air had already been extended an invitation to join the oneworld alliance. In addition, American developed a partnership with jetBlue, based in the East Coast of the US, to codeshare flights from the New York region, as well as the Boston region (both hubs of Delta as displayed in Figure 3.5). Both moves by American are being designed, presumably, to (1) compete more aggressively with Delta, (2) increase access to leisure travelers, and (3) expand services in international markets, across the Atlantic and the Pacific. Examples of new international services envisioned by American are from Seattle to Bangalore and from New York, Kennedy to Athens and Tel Aviv. The challenge is that not only could the transatlantic market remain depressed for a number of years, but jetBlue could start competitive service with a single-aisle aircraft and a business-class product at a much lower fare.

The key message for network planners in both cases, Lufthansa and Delta, is to leverage both physical assets (hubs and aircraft) and digital assets (brands and loyalty programs) to change the business models to find new ways to serve customers—new ways to create value, capture value, and to deliver value. In the case of Delta, management has yet another major digital asset, equity in foreign airlines (Aeromexico, Air France, China Eastern, GOL, Korean Air, LATAM, Virgin Atlantic, Virgin Australia, and WestJet). The business can be reconfigured using the variety of hubs at major locations (on both coasts, for example) as well as an effective feeder system. The equity in Virgin Atlantic provides, for example, presence in the most important transatlantic market while an equity in Air France provides presence in the third largest transatlantic market (Germany being number two). And, it is the stitching together of digital assets that can help full-service airlines to seize new opportunities to reconfigure their businesses.

Another key to seizing new, powerful opportunities is, first, to start the network/fleet planning from ground zero and within a bottom-up framework and, second, to integrate the planning initiatives in real time (see Figure 3.6). Let us start with the objective of ground zero and bottom-up approach. Given the unprecedented level of uncertainty going forward, the far-thinking airlines are already beginning to look at the viability of their networks and their fleet. Large numbers of aircraft (with four engines or even those with two engines if they are old and have high capacity) are under consideration to be parked permanently. And, since in the past network/fleet planning tended to be performed with a top-down approach, the timing is now good to start with a bottom-up approach. In this approach, not only should the economic analysis of each route be performed individually, but the analysis should be conducted with numerous simulations relating to different economic, political, and competitive scenarios, but also with the use of different aircraft, existing and under design. Then the optimization can be examined on a network basis.

For a good description of the bottom-up approach, using simulation analysis, see the thought leadership pieces by Karl Echtermeyer and Benedikt Mandel in Chapter 7. In fact, according to Karl Echtermeyer, the bottom-up approach, including the use of simulation techniques, can be used by aircraft manufacturers, too. In the design of new aircraft, manufacturers have always worked closely with the lead airlines for a given aircraft design. However, the analyses have always been conducted in the context of their existing networks with minor changes, as expected from the announced plans of airlines or developments in the industry. However, going forward, there is much value in looking not only at a much greater number of airlines, compared to just a couple of "lead" airlines, but also at simulations of the scenarios of their potential networks. The scenarios can be examined for individual airlines, or airlines with equity relationships, or airlines within alliances, or multilateral airlines that could emerge. Manufacturers have taken such potential development into consideration in the past, but not at the level needed going forward. One only needs to see the very limited success of such aircraft models as the Airbus A340-500 and the Boeing 777-200LR.

As for an integrated approach, typically, optimizations at large airlines are achieved at the silo level—network planning, pricing, and revenue management, for example. Similarly, the operational groups optimize their initiatives in their own silos. Not only is there a need to optimize at the system level, but the system needs to include other functions, such as those shown in Figure 3.6; for example, sales and its sub-functions, such as corporate travel, distribution, and alliances. And, the central group in the integration process is the finance function that must provide rules to evaluate the results from its perspectives relating to fleet (and real estate), risk management (relating, in turn, to fuel and currencies, for example), and the traditional sub-functions in accounting. Just as the interest of marketing and sales might be to stimulate demand by improving

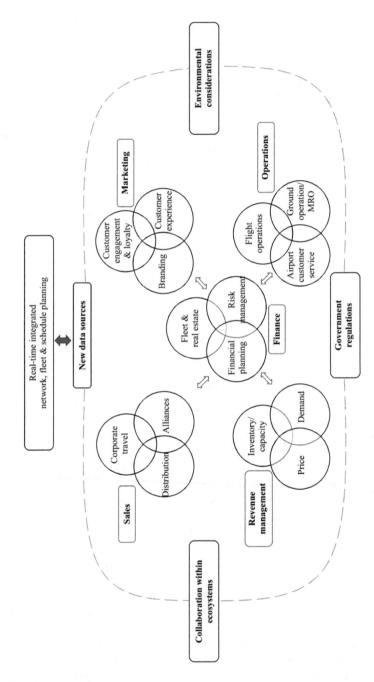

*Figure 3.6* Real-time integrated network, fleet, and schedule planning

customer experience, the interest of finance might be to de-risk the business. As John Lancaster points out in his thought leadership piece in Chapter 7, passenger revenues involve both market and systematic risk, risks that need to be acknowledged and managed. The answer lies in diversifying revenue sources beyond ticket sales, and by distributing the risk across the distribution chain. Digitalized systems are now available that can incorporate demand, network, fleet, schedules, revenue management, and sales, all linked by loops, to produce optimizations to be used for different competitive scenarios, and all within the perspectives of the finance group. Having different hubs (with different catchment areas and different traffic-mix) and different aircraft (with different unit operating costs, different capacity, and different seat configurations within the same aircraft type) can provide benefits that can outweigh the added cost complexity. Eric Leopold provides, in his thought leadership piece in Chapter 7, a discussion on the development of strategy based on three pillars: commercial, financial, and digital.

At the risk of repetition, let us consider the conventional process of the key decisions in three sub-functions. Network planners identify routes and schedule planners develop marketable schedules based on the characteristics of the market and competition. The revenue management group allocates the inventory in different buckets, based on fares and conditions. The operational group assigns the aircraft and crew, based on numerous operational considerations. The question is: Why is the "optimization" process undertaken in sequential steps? The answer seems to be that:

- the entire process is too complex,
- the developments in the marketplace are taking place at a fast rate,
- some global airlines have very large networks, a very diverse fleet, and a broad spectrum of constraints, such as slots, and
- the operation groups have to deal with numerous exceptions, relating to facilities (such as gates and slots), and crews, relating to unique requests (such as the desire to fly certain routes or even certain flights).

However, systems, processes, and data are now available that can be used to overcome the sub-optimized planning processes in the alignment of the fleet, the crews, and the hubs. Moreover, new technologies, such as artificial intelligence, are available to further improve the results. For example, major airlines have very experienced schedulers, pricing managers, and revenue managers. And, as mentioned, they perform their optimizations within their silos. One key aspect of artificial intelligence is to recognize patterns. Until recently, artificial intelligence was looked at as a black box that could conclude if an image was a car or a dog. But artificial intelligence has the ability to look at patterns within a data set, for example, the numbers relating to bookings and the numbers relating to yields, to provide incredible benefits. This technology can analyze not only patterns, but also whether there are any correlations among the patterns to determine the root cause of a problem. Suppose the forecast results of a market do not match actual results. This technology could identify the root cause, such as the loss of a large corporate client. In other words, patterns in one set of data and patterns in another set of data can be used to determine the existence of correlations. Finally, technology can also provide the capability to experiment and iterate, a critical success factor for internet startups. Is there an insight for airlines from the success of some internet startups?

Going forward, the key decision of airlines will relate not just to the amount and the type of reduction in the size of the network, but how this is accomplished. And the how part is not just for now, but it will be on an ongoing basis. Think about the ongoing question of cyclicality discussed for the second scenario. How will traffic patterns change and what would be the impact on network, fleet, and schedules? How about the reverse, the impact of changing network, fleet, and schedules on traffic patterns? With respect to the reduction in the size of the network, should the reduction be in the size of hub-and-spoke systems, or the number of nonstop markets served that do not touch the hubs, or simply in the realignment of hubs, such as by reducing the number of connecting banks? Then there is the question of frequency for business travelers. Even if business travel comes back to its previous base (as shown in Figure 2.2), at what yields would it come back?

For fleet planners, the tradeoff between trip-cost and seat-kilometer-cost has always been important, but its importance now needs to increase as airlines focus on mitigating their risk in the network-fleet-schedule planning process. Again, as discussed in the next section, and in the thought leadership piece by Dietmar Kirchner on this subject in Chapter 7, the mindset of network-fleet-schedule planners will need to change from supply-driven-demand to demand-driven-supply. This would be a challenge for conventional planners, as they would need to think in a non-linear manner. To start with, they would need to think about totally new ways of optimizing revenue instead of the sophisticated but, nevertheless, conventional bucket system. They need to think about maximization of revenue and not necessarily load factor. They would need to think beyond the low unit operating costs. As pointed out by a forward thinker at an airline, the Airbus A321XLR has similar unit operating costs to the Airbus A321, but provides extra range for the extra-long-haul routes. Similarly, the planner went on to say that the Airbus A220 might have a similar unit operating cost structure as the smaller Embraer 190 aircraft, but it has longer range, as an additional benefit. For an analysis of economies of scale relating to operating costs and yield, see the thought leadership piece by Karl Echtermeyer in Chapter 7. Besides the capacity-range considerations, the price of fuel will play a significant role. In the future, the price of fuel might be separated from the development of the crude oil price, as the purchase of "pollution rights" might add considerable cost.

Going forward, there would be an added twist. Whereas in the past, most schedule disruptions were on the part of the airline, in the future a disruption could be brought by passengers. Imagine if a group of passengers is not allowed to board an airplane due to a health-related situation. To say that the group can take the next flight might not be a reasonable option if the airline has reduced the frequency in the market by a large amount, due to insufficient demand.

Airlines obviously want to cut costs, particularly incremental costs that are usually in the range of 50 percent of the total costs (generally a little higher for low-cost carriers (LCCs)). Two major components of the fixed costs are related to labor and ownership of aircraft. The finance group (in Figure 3.6) might be interested in transforming some fixed costs to incremental costs and might be interested in different strategies—sale and lease back, for example. This might be the case with airlines, such as Lufthansa, that have a very large percentage of the aircraft in the fleet that are owned by the group. However, this is where the real-time integration of the decision-making process comes into play, as the prices of aircraft would depend on the condition of the market that is depressed during the recovery period. Technologies to integrate at the system level have been available for many years; the challenge has been for managers to use them due to the existence of exceptions that led mangers to use automation at some times and intuition at other times.

As illustrated in Figure 3.6, in addition to a new way of thinking on the part of network, fleet, and schedule planners, agility and reduction in costs can be derived from a realignment of contracts with labor, airports, aircraft manufacturers, and aircraft lessors. Therefore, from the perspectives of the finance group, relationships within the travel chain could be to explore win-win situations. Take the case of airports. The goal would be to reduce the constraints relating to the infrastructure and to achieve more operational flexibility while also enabling airports to achieve greater productivity and efficiency from the assets they own and operate. Take the case of aircraft manufacturers where the relationship would need to be realigned, relating to aircraft orders. Whereas network planners would consider mostly the capacity and frequency aspects, the finance group would want the capability to make decisions fast and to build resiliency.

Then there is the question of non-conventional thinking. Could the power-by-the-hour concept be applied to the whole aircraft, and not just the engines, to transfer risk within the value chain? Take the case of aircraft lessors. Would lessors work with shorter-term leases, for example, between 1 and 3 years, instead of between 3 and 7 years? Would planners work with the use of wet-lease aircraft? Would marketers and schedulers accept aircraft with standard cabin configurations? Think about the win-win situation. Lessors, which owned about 50 percent of the aircraft in the past, may experience an increase in their business with the end result of providing flexibility to the airlines leasing the aircraft and to the lessors themselves in terms of having standardized fleet that can be rotated much more easily within the industry. On the other hand, lessors may need to accept lower monthly rates if an airline decides to simply park the aircraft. The dynamics between the lessors and the lessees are expected to change significantly, partly based on the financial condition of airlines and partly based on some consolidation within the lessor sector. In the case of weaker airlines, there could now be much more interest in the sell-lease-back options. In Figure 3.6, while the finance group of a weak airline may wish to lease more aircraft, the lessor might need to have a higher-quality security package (for example, with respect to deposits and maintenance reserves) and higher credit qualities.

In the past, some airlines' finance groups have used some risk-management techniques to manage risk relating to such areas as fuel, interest rates, and foreign-currency rates. These areas would be examples of uncontrollable risk. There is, however, now interest in also managing the risk relating to the revenue side of the business, a more difficult challenge. Skytra, a recently formed subsidiary of Airbus, has developed an infrastructure for airlines to "hedge" their passenger yield. The technique involves the use of price indices that represent the average daily prices of air travel (by region) that can be used to develop Skytra index derivatives contracts and be traded on the "Skytra MTF."[6]

True integration in Figure 3.6 also requires different organizational structures and planning processes to reduce planning cycle times, both for the development of longer-term networks and the annual schedules. Systems used for the longer-term and annual scheduling planning processes should allow for both horizontal and vertical transparency and the deployment of the same "validated" sources of data. Decision-support technologies, discussed in Chapter 5, need to be used to make decisions in almost real time. Non-conventional data need to be collected and integrated with existing data to enhance the richness of the information. As such, the network, fleet, and schedule planning processes need to change radically,

- to optimize resources in real time, relating to the movement of customers, aircraft, employees, and subcontractors,
- to develop different ways to forecast demand without historical data,
- to utilize new types of data and analytics, and
- to incorporate consumers' emerging desires, for example, the need for door-to-door travel with a seamless and consistent experience.

Consider a relatively common situation involving network carriers and their mega hub-and-spoke systems at congested airports. It is true that mega hub-and-spoke systems provide flexibility for airlines and higher frequency and choices for passengers, but, going forward, some passengers may not want to go through congested airports, leading to the question of reducing some long-haul international flights that could lower, in turn, the viability of hub-and-spoke systems. Keep in mind that low-cost carriers are increasing their networks and frequencies in intra-European markets, creating challenges for full-service carriers to continue their long-haul operations to and from their hubs. Add on top of that the future of short-haul flights, not just from the pre-crisis "flight shaming" movement by consumers, but also by some governments' policies, such as in France where an interest has been expressed in placing limits on the use of aircraft for domestic flights, except in the case of international connections. And, let us not forget the policy of some governments to push the use of high-speed trains.

Going back to the silo systems in Figure 3.6, large airlines, typically, have had one group for planning fleet and another group for planning network and schedules. From a very simplistic perspective, a network and scheduling planning group develops schedules and hands over the results to a revenue management group that works with advance bookings and changes the contents of buckets and fares within buckets to maximize revenue. In the end, the execution provides optimizations at the local level, but not at the global level. It is true that the revenue management group can go back to the network and schedule planning group and suggest changes in the aircraft scheduled and/or frequencies, but changes made are infrequent, with reasons given by the network and schedule planners, as constraints relating to crews, maintenance, airport gates, slots, and so forth. Some airlines even have one or two representatives from revenue management and/or sales that work directly with the network and schedule planning groups when schedules are being developed. But the ultimate decisions are made by the schedule planning department. To summarize, again from a simplistic point of view, revenue management groups sell the capacity provided by the schedule planning groups through changes in prices to make up for capacity shortages or overcapacity. In some cases, this situation has had a double impact when the existing network and schedule planning systems also took information from the manipulated passenger flows (manipulated by revenue management and/or sales) for allocations of additional capacity. As such, in these cases, the sub-optimal decisions impacted the financial group, in Figure 3.6, twice, not to mention the potential impact on longer-term fleet plans.

## Strategizing for the elastic supply scenario

As mentioned above, a number of airlines have begun to look at the dynamically changing marketplace to convert threats into opportunities. Consider the following reasons, some individually and some in various combinations, that would enable network, fleet, and schedule planners to implement strategies to convert threats into opportunities:

- Working with "back-from-the-future" concepts provides a different framework and a different vision to develop viable strategies.
- In leading airlines, the internal situation is already becoming more conducive to think very differently. One example discussed in this book relates to the concept of demand-driven-supply and the use of "white-label" capacity to deal with the second scenario to handle the higher levels of variability in demand.
- There is now also a realistic opportunity to develop new products, such as intermodal door-to-door transportation for passengers. This opportunity is driven by the assumption that every passenger will be equipped with a

smartphone, enabling communications in real time and enabling the location of the passenger during the mobility mode.

- There is also an opportunity to expand some existing areas of the product line, for example cargo, including the possibility of redeploying the "combi" aircraft. The "combi" aircraft could make much more sense now that the separation of the cargo and passenger space can be changed efficiently during a turnaround. However, we must not overlook rules relating to safety, relating, in turn, to potential for inflight fires in an aircraft that carries passengers and cargo on its main deck.
- Given the economic pressure resulting from the impact of this unprecedented disruption, labor is more likely to change employment rules that provide higher levels of productivity and flexibility. Labor groups are also likely to accept the development of low-cost subsidiaries (operating with different airline operating certificates) to transport different segments of traffic, for example leisure travelers in general or on particular long-haul routes.
- There are opportunities not only for new agreements with partners in the supply system (airports, aircraft manufacturers, and aircraft lessors, for example), but also to develop new ways to collaborate and coordinate within the ecosystem. Governments are also key players in the ecosystem. It appears that United Airlines obtained a $5.2 billion government-backed loan from the US government, based on the airline's international routes as collateral.
- The next-generation network, fleet, and schedule planning systems are now available that enable "real-time" integration of different inputs from the internal groups and the external groups, if managers can get around to dealing with exceptions (see Figure 3.6).
- Digital assets are available to enable airlines to drive much higher values from the physical assets, as discussed in Chapters 4 and 5.
- The next generation of full-service platforms is already here that enables the delivery of end-to-end solutions with flexibility to make changes. See the discussion in the next chapter.
- As discussed in Chapter 5, new data is now available on location and movement intelligence, with the data coming from the location and movement of mobile devices.
- There are different amounts and types of pressure from governments to improve performance to reduce the financial resources required from governments. In some cases, airlines are required to return the capital provided, with interest and dividends.
- The industry is likely to go through an intensive process of consolidation, creating not just challenges, but also powerful opportunities. Consider, for example, the announcement in the middle of November 2020 regarding the takeover of Asiana Airlines by Korean Air. The combined operation could not only produce lower operating costs, but also make the combined group more competitive from a global perspective by making, for example, the hub at Incheon Airport stronger.

- Technology is now available to enable airline planners to make decisions in real time. Examples of such technologies include machine learning, the internet of things, and cloud computing. In addition, it is not just the availability of more data, but the costs of collecting, storing, and processing data have been decreasing rapidly.
- Single-aisle aircraft, capable of flying long-ranges, are now available.
- Less-efficient aircraft that are being parked could be used to establish divisions that could provide additional capacity to handle additional demand to deal with the elastic supply scenario.

Going forward, consider five examples of challenges relating to network-fleet planning:

- variable demand,
- ultra-long-haul routes,
- interline agreements,
- belly freight, and
- integration with different emerging transportation systems.

### Variable demand

First, the concept of demand-driven-supply has been discussed throughout this book. There is no question that such a planning concept would be a radical departure from the current network-schedule planning practices. However, this is exactly the planning process that is needed to adapt to the elastic supply scenario. Can it be done? Based on numerous examples, both within the industry and outside of this industry, the answer would be yes. First, think about how integrated carriers, such as FedEx and UPS, operate their services. They started their business models centered truly on the customer. They also developed their fleet plans and schedules to accommodate variable demand. Second, think about Allegiant Air which developed its business model, using inexpensive aircraft, to develop and market demand-driven-supply. The model was also developed around the marketing of hotel rooms and other tourist facilities and services. But now, with the use of advanced technologies, Allegiant's model can work within the demand-driven-supply framework in almost real time. Going outside the airline industry, go back to the taxi business again. Uber leveraged its digital networks to change the business model to connect drivers with riders in ways that are mutually beneficial and in which capacity is matched with demand in real time. Moreover, the use of digital networks enabled Uber to scale the business to meet the needs of both drivers and riders and used the surge pricing technique (discussed in the next chapter) to create a working example of demand-driven-supply. Next, think about Amazon which also developed a digital operating system to match the needs of suppliers and customers, a system that is efferent and effective in creating a demand-driven-supply, not to mention its effectiveness to achieve scale. Finally, consider how

Porsche manages to work in a demand-driven-supply framework by working with Valmet Automotive (based in Finland and formerly called Saab-Valmet), which offers flexible "on-demand" production capacity to Porsche, as discussed in Chapter 6. For more details on the demand-driven-supply, see the thought leadership piece by Dietmar Kirchner and Peter Glade in Chapter 7.

### Ultra-long-haul routes

Second, consider the challenges relating to ultra-long-haul flights. Table 3.1 shows the top ten ultra-long-haul routes operated in 2019 (all between 7,300 and 8,300 nautical miles) and operated with such aircraft as the Airbus A350 and the Boeing 787. Singapore Airlines was the first to start flying the ultra-long-haul route, nonstop, between Singapore and New York (Newark, New Jersey) in 2004 using the Airbus A340-500. Due to limitations of the range of the aircraft, capacity had to be restricted and the airline offered about 60 seats in business class and about 120 seats in executive-economy class. The flight was dropped in 2013 for economic reasons. Since then Singapore Airlines has not only restarted the service, but a number of other airlines started ultra-long-haul flights with at least a major hub on one side of the route.

Qantas was one of the first airlines to start an ultra-long-haul flight starting from a relatively small hub, Perth. It was successful because there were a sufficient number of passengers who preferred to fly point-to-point and avoid making connections at congested hubs, even prior to the current health-related concerns. Qantas even started competition between Airbus and Boeing to come up with a viable aircraft that could fly nonstop between Sydney and New York, as well as between Sydney and London. Although Qantas started the nonstop service between Perth and London Heathrow, it could make it a double daily with one flight starting in Sydney and the other starting in Melbourne, and both making a stop in Perth, before starting the long-haul intercontinental flight. If successful, two additional destinations could be started, one to Frankfurt and the second to Paris, as displayed in Figure 3.7. After the

*Table 3.1* Ultra-long-haul routes flown by airlines in 2019

| |
| --- |
| Newark–Singapore |
| Auckland–Doha |
| London–Perth |
| Auckland–Dubai |
| Los Angeles–Singapore |
| Houston–Sydney |
| Dallas–Sydney |
| Kennedy–Manila |
| San Francisco–Singapore |
| Atlanta–Johannesburg |

Source: Information reported by the OAG.

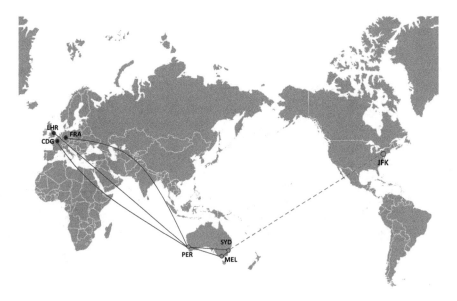

*Figure 3.7* Qantas actual and potential ultra-long-haul flights

recovery, it is possible that Qantas could start a nonstop flight between Sydney and New York-Kennedy, a flight that could even be made a double daily, with one flight starting in Perth and the second one starting in Melbourne. This schedule could easily become viable given that:

- Australia has a unique geographical location,
- many passengers desire to fly nonstop, even on flights taking 17–19 hours,
- hub-and-spoke carriers operating with hubs in Asia, for example, may not be able to obtain the necessary regulatory operating rights for nonstop flights,
- other European carriers, such as Lufthansa and Air France-KLM, may not consider nonstop services to be economically viable or even sufficiently strategic to operate on a non-economical basis,
- the available aircraft are sufficiently cost efficient, and
- value can be derived from the use of digital assets (data, analytics, and networks) discussed in Figures 4.1 and 4.2.

Similarly, Singapore Airlines, which is already flying three ultra-long-haul flights nonstop (Los Angeles, San Francisco, and Newark, New Jersey), could begin nonstop services to three additional cities in the US (Washington Dulles, Chicago O'Hare, and Houston Intercontinental), all three hubs of United Airlines, an alliance partner. The reasons are similar to those listed above for the viability of Qantas' potential flights (see Figure 3.8).

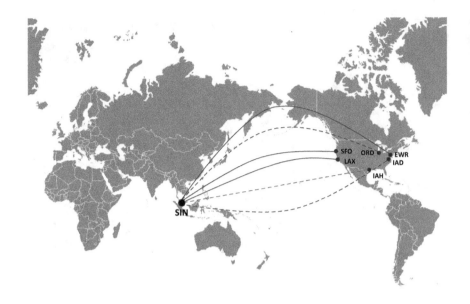

*Figure 3.8* Singapore Airlines actual and potential ultra-long-haul flights

### Interline agreements

Third, relating to the interline system, mentioned in the previous chapter, network and schedule planning may be facilitated significantly by the resurrection of the old IATA pricing and interline system, for at least three reasons.

- As mentioned in the next chapter, passengers may want the vouchers issued, for the flight not taken, to be redeemable on any airline.
- An airline may decide to make an offer that if a passenger is stranded at an intercontinental destination, due to unforeseen circumstances, the passenger will be transported back to the home base, even if it means transporting the passenger through an interline arrangement.
- An airline with only a small number of passengers booked on its own flight may decide, at the last minute, to book the passengers on another airline's flight and cancel its own flight.

The historical interline system, and the related pricing system, provided mutual benefits for all carriers.

The younger generation of network, fleet, and schedule planners may not know how the old IATA interline and pricing system functioned and how it provided benefits for both airlines as well as for passengers. A disruption at one airline did not necessarily strand passengers as they were accommodated on the flights of any and all carriers in the system, without any discussion on fares and conditions, the status of passengers, or the price of the tickets. Now, there can be questions even for the transportation of passengers on the flights of the carrier with the disruption, leaving aside the rules of strategic alliance partners, and competitors. A new version of the interline system can provide even more benefits, given the value coming from the use of advanced technologies and new data. The new interline system can even be accommodated in the full-service platform discussed in the next chapter. However, it will require a very different mindset not only for network, fleet, and schedule planners, but also for marketing and sales groups, not to mention managers in the antitrust divisions of governments. Think about it. Will the current crisis lead to different priorities of customers? Would a traveler be more interested in whether an airline has a 15-inch screen or a 17-inch screen, or getting to a destination as quickly as possible?

### *Belly freight*

Fourth, there is a real opportunity for cargo to become a core part of the business of passenger airlines. On a worldwide basis, revenue generated by cargo for passenger airlines represents a little more than 10 percent of the total revenue. The percentage has varied significantly by region, the lowest percentage is for the carriers based in the US and the highest percentage for carriers based in Asia. In the US, in some ways, carriers have viewed the revenue generated from the transportation of cargo as "ancillary" revenue, whereas some airlines based in Asia have treated cargo as a core part of the business. In more recent times, some carriers, based in the Middle East, have derived an even higher percentage of revenue from the operations of cargo. Take, for example, Qatar Airways that had a fleet of about 24 freighters out of a total of 235 aircraft in 2019. While the growth in freight has been minimal in the past few years, going forward, the situation is likely to change. Part of the reason could be the reduction of passenger flights for a number of years and part could be the need to transport the vaccine for Coronavirus. However, even with an increase in the demand for cargo services, can passenger airlines develop cargo as a core product of the business? It is possible if some historical barriers can be converted into enablers:

* The existence of "pallet pricing" (as well as minimum pricing) did reduce the operating costs of airlines, in particular, the handling costs at airports. However, these pricing policies enabled forwarders to enter the marketplace.
* Historically, cargo managers at passenger airlines did not take sufficient initiatives to understand the true needs of customers. Freight forwarders did, but groups managing the transportation of cargo in the bellies of passenger aircraft did not engage effectively with shippers. Subsequently, when some managers did think seriously of engaging directly with shippers, they were reluctant to do so to avoid the possibility of upsetting forwarders.

- Unlike in the passenger divisions, managers in charge of marketing belly freight did not develop 360-degree views of shippers and consignees, similar to what their counterparts did for passengers. Freight transportation has been seen as a commodity business. To counter this perception, the 360-degree views are important, not just for shippers, but also for consignees to identify their true problems and offer them meaningful solutions.
- Some cargo managers at passenger airlines did not develop viable strategies to go for the value of shipments as opposed to the volume of shipments. The cargo business is far more complex. Shipments have three dimensions and revenue management is far more complex compared to the passenger side of the business, because, for example, booking patterns are very different, relating, for instance, to advance purchase plans that tend to have short windows.
- Some cargo managers at passenger airlines were not able to find ways to compete effectively with integrators (transporters of express shipments and small packages) that understood the true needs of shippers and consignees of such shipments. Furthermore, a segment of these managers did not have a true appreciation of the key elements of logistics.

Going forward, some passenger airlines can make cargo a core product of the business by understanding the key elements of next-generation logistics that involves data handing, data transparency, smart apps, and smart dashboards. A key message is that it is not sufficient to offer just speed and security, but it is also necessary to provide transparency. If airlines are to carry more cargo in the bellies of their wide-body aircraft, then differentiation must come on the ground, at both ends of the trip. Moreover, belly freight may be less attractive to shippers of high-value goods if shipments go through hubs that would be no different than the services offered by integrated airlines. The real value is in transporting shipments in the bellies of direct flights. Consequently, the effort must go into:

- the digitalization of processes on the ground, starting with the elimination of paper airwaybills, and moving on to the development of smart dashboards, showing real-time location and progress of a shipment,
- collaboration with digital forwarders who have access to a lot of relevant data, including collaboration with fourth-party logistics,
- collaboration and coordination with airports to work with ground handling agents to not only reduce the costs of ground handling, but also improve the quality of services provided, as well as fast turnaround times,
- the management of claims activities, customs, safety, security, quality, interlines, promotions, pricing, revenue management, and the creation of unique selling propositions,
- the talent for marketing cargo, on the passenger side of the cargo business, to not only use electronic bookings, but also to use predictive and prescriptive analytics, in particular, in the area of revenue management, relating to cargo shipments and capacity.

There are clearly opportunities in the emerging marketplace, but there are also threats. First, let us consider, the opportunities. New wide-body aircraft, such as the 777-300 and the A350-900, have a lot of cargo capacity in their bellies. And, air cargo in the bellies can play an important role in the breakeven analysis if load factors drop, for example, by 15–20 percent. This potential revenue, from the cargo carried on passenger aircraft, is a real possibility if a passenger airline was to work with innovative forwarders who work with smart platforms that provide information, booking capabilities, and transparency. Some passenger airlines might even consider converting some of the parked planes into freighters—depending on the age of the airplane as well as the cost of conversion, not to mention the time required for the conversion. On the other hand, there are also threats. Just consider how Amazon could go after the shipment of high-value goods. The emerging marketplace may also present an opportunity for some airlines to consider operating the "combi" aircraft again, assuming that the safety issues, mentioned earlier, can be managed according to the regulations established by authorities.

### Integration

Fifth, consider the challenge facing network, fleet, and schedule planners of the emergence of new transportation systems: say, urban air mobility in the near term and high-speed hyperloop capsules in the somewhat distant future. The emergence of such new systems raises a number of questions. For example:

* Would network planners consider them as competitors or potential partners?
* If Uber started technically and economically viable systems, would a large hub-and-spoke carrier try to compete in short-haul markets, partner in these markets, or simply acquire the operator to become a division of the major carrier?

The key question is: Can an airline transform its business model to become a new transportation company that provides, for example, door-to-door transportation while taking care of its passengers' end-to-end journeys? This would be a radical transformation, but it can be done, based on the experience of other businesses. An airline can take a look at the experience of the ING Group that transformed itself three times: from an insurance company to a conventional bank, and then from a conventional bank to a digital bank, and, finally, from a digital bank to a technology platform company. What are the critical success factors? According to business researchers, Dyer, Furr, and LeFrandt, it takes a vision, the willingness to develop the necessary capabilities, and an internal and external communication strategy to "deliver both growth and traditional metrics."[7] Consider the rise, fall, and rise of Nokia. In the late 1990s and early 2000s, in the pre-smartphone era, Nokia dominated the mobile phone market, and, according to reports in the media, its revenue represented about 4 percent of

Finland's GDP. However, according to some analysts, Nokia's corporate culture was not innovating fast enough to compete with Apple's upcoming iPhone. The iPhone ended up offering a superior product, for example, a more user-friendly touch-screen capability and more user-desired apps, enabled by the iOS operating system that leveraged developments created in the dynamic ecosystem. For these and other reasons, Nokia failed and was acquired by Microsoft. Some of the former Nokia executives had a different vision and managed to acquire back the business from Microsoft and set up a new company, HMD Global Oy. Management then had the foresight to add to Nokia's well-recognized features (workmanship and simplicity) the use of the more flexible Android operating system that enabled timely software updates. Nokia was back in business.

## Notes

1  Fareed Zakaria, *Ten Lessons for a Post-Pandemic World* (New York: W. W. Norton, 2020), ch. 1 and ch. 9.
2  "Inspired Leadership," an interview with József Váradi, *Air Transport World*, October 2020, p. 11.
3  *Aviation Strategy*, May–June 2020, pp. 12–16.
4  www.futuretravelexperience.com/2020/10/how-airasia-is-pivoting-from-an-airline-to-a-unified-e-commerce-platform-powered-by-technology-and-data/
5  John Grant, "Transatlantic Turmoil Potential US$10 Billion Risk Looming," An OAG Report, September 29, 2020.
6  https://skytra.airbus.com
7  Jeff Dyer, Nathan Furr, and Curtis LeFrandt, *Innovation Capital: How to Compete and Win Like the World's Most Innovative Leaders* (Boston, MA: Harvard Business Review Press, 2019), pp. 210-16.

# 4  Plotting commercial strategies in a dynamic marketplace

Marketing and operations are right at the front line of airlines when it comes to restarting their businesses. In both areas of the business, airlines began to restart from ground zero, given that this unprecedented disruption changed the landscape so intensely. This chapter focuses on the commercial strategies and tactics while changes in operations are discussed in the next chapter. In marketing, it is not just that shopping and purchase behavior have changed, but also that the amount, the type, and the channels of communications and distribution have changed. Some basic questions facing airline marketers now are:

- How do I now reach and engage with my digitally savvy and more complex customers, existing and new, and online and offline?
- How do I implement new initiatives (for example, direct to consumer) by deploying comprehensive platforms and smart technologies?
- How do I now forecast passenger demand, given the on-again, off-again changes in government travel restrictions, consumer sentiments relating to travel, and the financial constraints for some customer segments?
- What kinds of products and services do different segments need now, and will need going forward, to make their lives easier in the new environment?
- How do I leverage the next generation of omni-channel retailing in the changed, and changing, marketplace?
- How do I realign my loyalty program and my brand by leveraging digital marketing?
- Given the increase in uncertainty, how can the internal marketing capabilities be scaled with agility?
- How can I make use of social media transparently and honestly to influence customers' choices?

While some of these questions are not necessarily new in the marketing departments of airlines, there is now a critical need to find new ways to develop viable strategies and tactics in commercial planning,

- given the inadequacy of historical data and planning models, and
- given the need for speed to identify viable strategies, their implementation, and their continuous alignment.

In light of these two constraints (irrelevancy of data and the need for speed), this chapter starts with a section on the value of:

- transitioning from managing physical assets to developing and managing digital assets,
- speeding up the use of next-generation platforms to introduce disruptive products and services (flexible schedules and reservation systems, as well as up-to-date health-related information systems, for example),
- refocusing on digital marketing and social media, and
- focusing on not just experience, but also trust, loyalty, and brand.

## Transitioning from physical assets to digital assets

Airlines have made high investments in their physical assets (aircraft and airport facilities, for example) and, as such, they spend a lot of time optimizing the return of these physical assets. Some airlines have also committed additional resources to develop some digital assets: for example, their brands and their loyalty programs. However, it is now possible to explore the development of additional digital assets that can be used to maximize the return from their physical assets and the existing digital assets. Figure 4.1 shows three major components of additional digital assets—data, analytics, and networks. It is the combination of these digital assets, coupled with the existing digital assets that can provide an airline with meaningful predictive and prescriptive insights

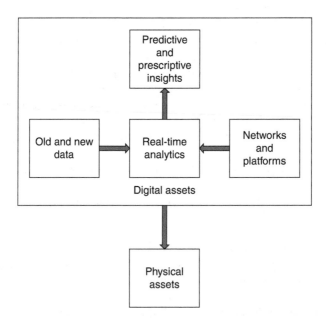

*Figure 4.1* Transitioning from managing physical assets to digital assets

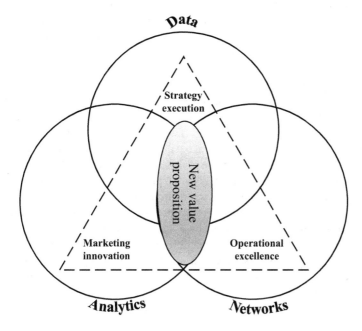

*Figure 4.2* New core competencies reinforcing traditional core competencies

that can help maximize the value of physical assets. The central part of digital assets, in Figure 4.1, is the box containing analytics that is fed by data from one side and networks (including platforms) from the other side, which enable the analytics (in the box) to build on any one or more of the three traditional core competencies—marketing innovation, operational excellence, and strategy execution, shown in Figure 4.2. The key insight from the best practices of some leading businesses is that the three traditional core competencies of a business can be reinforced by the three new competencies, especially professionals becoming known as "analytics translators," who have a working knowledge of analytics, but a deeper knowledge of the business and the company. See an article on "analytics translators" by McKinsey and Company.[1]

Leading airlines have clearly been using more and more data to help make more informed decisions relating to the use of their physical assets. However, the value of data (both traditional and new) can increase much more with the use of real-time analytics (relating to the business and customers), and then increase even more significantly with the use of networks, including platforms. While some historical data has become less valid, as highlighted in the previous chapter, there are new sources of data, such as the data coming from locations and movements of mobile devices and the usage of credit cards, discussed in the next chapter. Networks (not relating to airline routes) cover such areas as social networks, networks relating to supply chains, and apps. Take, for example, the value of social networks that can not only connect an enormous number of people, but also be used to persuade people, very cost effectively. Sinan Aral, in his book *The Hype Machine*, discusses this concept within the context of "personalized mass persuasion."[2] Aral also provides an excellent description of the phenomenon "hypersocialization," in which the behavior of people is influenced by their friends through the use of social media. Moreover, networks can relate to physical aspects or digital aspects. Physical networks relate to the physical aspects of an organization's structure while culture would be an important component of a digital network. One obvious question in this context is if an airline is willing to change its corporate culture (part of the digital network) to make the organization more agile (physical network). For example, is the airline willing to develop and work with a platform that collects data from the airline's website, different touchpoints in the end-to-end journey, different apps, airline's apps as well as apps used by customers for other travel-related services? Think about the app introduced by a startup company, called RYDES, that enables travelers to search and book different components of travel. The key message is that the travel behavior of customers is changing rapidly and airlines' strategies must go far beyond the strategies to reduce costs and realign their low-cost subsidiaries.

There is no question that strategy is developed by people and not by raw data or machines. However, strategy can now be explored more analytically, while taking into consideration many more variables, and it can be executed more judicially with the use of digital assets. So, while strategy is still being developed by people, it is being operationalized much more effectively with the use of data, analytics, and networks, both by physical networks and digital networks. And it is the physical networks (for example, an organizational structure) that can make digital networks (for example, corporate culture) either enablers or barriers. Furthermore, it is the networks in digital marketing, coupled by digital technologies and digital media, that can build customer management capabilities, discussed later in this chapter.

New ways of doing business in the commercial space, however, bring new challenges. The first challenge is the ability to forecast demand with limited amount of historical data. On the positive side, new sources of data (the location and movement of mobile devices, discussed in the previous chapter), can provide new intelligence for not only marketing groups within airlines (through digital marketing), but also for airline network planning groups, discussed in the previous chapter. The second challenge, with respect to retailing strategies, is that while the focus will still be on customer experience and personalization, the parameters connecting the two will be very different, relating, for example, to a greater emphasis on health (cabin layouts, social distancing, and masks, for instance) and care assurances, caused by unforeseen situations. The third challenge is that while customers may want new service features, such as the seats next to them to be empty, how much would they be willing to pay for such a requirement? The answer, according to one experienced airline executive, could be nothing, or almost nothing.

Let us start with the limitations of data, both the historical data on traffic and capacity, and the survey data on consumer sentiments. Traffic data collected by governments, for example, the US Department of Transportation, now is less timely. In the US, the 10 percent sample data on tickets sold by reporting carriers (DB1b) is, first, quarterly and, second, has a lag time of one quarter. Similarly, financial reports (Form 41) that contain balance sheets, cash flow, income statements, aircraft operating expenses, including crew and fuel, are also quarterly, also with a lag of one quarter. Finally, air carrier traffic and capacity reports (T-100), that report passenger miles flown, passenger enplanements, and load factors, are available on a monthly basis. While this data still adds value, the value has been less during the initial phase of the recovery. For example, the origin and destination passenger survey data for the first quarter of 2020 was not available until the end of the second quarter of 2020 and, even then, the data was for the whole of the first quarter of 2020, not by day, or even by week, or even by month.

Second, all kinds of surveys came out during the recovery period showing different sentiments of consumers relating to travel to help airlines get their operations restarted. However, a number of times the results of surveys presented in the media did not support the actual experience observed by airlines of consumer sentiment about travel, and the demand based on customer-intent, displayed in the surveys. While effectively designed and conducted surveys can and do provide valuable insights, care must be taken to think about the viability of the results being quoted. Think about the limitations of the information gathered by monitoring clicks relating to travel search or tourist websites— double clicks, different IPs used by the same person, and the divergent interests of travelers within a group.

- How was the sample designed and selected?
- What were the sample size, the selection process, and the terminology used?
- Was the sample selected within a probability framework?
- Was the survey conducted online or through interviews in the field? What were the demographic, the geographic, and the socio-economic characteristics of consumers sampled?
- Were they business or budget travelers?
- What was the frequency of their travel?
- How much do the consumers surveyed spend on travel?
- Finally, what is the audience of the survey results, the general public, hotels, airlines, or the network and schedule planning departments of airlines?

Often the results quoted in the media are taken too seriously by managers in the commercial and financial departments when making hard decisions. Serious information is needed about the validity of the survey results, along the line of the questions raised above. On the other hand, Google's input, discussed in the next chapter, seems to have added some value for airline marketing groups and airline network and schedule planners during the initial phases of the recovery.

However, even then, there are some fundamental questions, such as (1) what percentage of the people who show intent to book, will actually book, and (2) what percentage that do make a booking, will actually travel? It is also important to segment consumers by type and not just by demographics and socio-economic characteristics when considering buying behavior. *Euromonitor International's* annual Consumer Types Series provides particularly relevant insights into what consumers want and need, even within the same demographic group.[3] This report provides important insights about consumers' purchasing behavior based on such aspects as personal finances, influence from social media, feelings about the green movement, and the role of achieving balance in people's lifestyles.

Take the case of experience. Prior to the current disruption, most airlines around the world had been making substantial amounts of money for a number of years. As a result, some airlines made substantial investments to improve customer experience. The question, going forward, is if airlines will reduce their investments in products and services that would reduce customer experience. If the plans of far-thinking airlines are to introduce disruptive products and services, then these new products and services also need to be accompanied by greater flexibility and greater experience. Experience from other businesses shows that having just disruptive products may not be sufficient. Businesses introducing disruptive products in the marketplace must also focus on experience. How many resources should airlines allocate to the improvement of experience in adapting to each of the two scenarios, as well as the three sub-scenarios within the first scenario, discussed in Chapter 2?

Uncertainties in the marketplace are creating serious challenges, given the limitations of the historical data for forecasting future demand and its much greater volatility, going forward. During the initial recovery phase, passenger demand was not returning for three primary reasons: (1) lack of confidence in travel and consumers' unwillingness to travel, (2) restrictions on travel (especially in international markets due to policy measures), and (3) financial constraints resulting from the sharp downturn in economies worldwide (impacting, in some cases, the ability to travel). At the beginning of the recovery, the financial challenge related not only to people who lost their jobs, but also to those who feared that they might lose their jobs. As such, airlines began to look for new ways to forecast and manage demand as the historical data was less relevant and the development of new product features (insurance, health-related information, cancellation and re-accommodation conditions) required, in some cases, a realignment of distribution channels; for example, the mix of direct versus indirect channels. As a result, airlines and distributors, such as agents, began to explore new ways to regain customers' trust and to provide reassurance, in light of some failures of airlines and some travel agents.

Marketers might also consider the use of another aspect of networks—platforms. To adapt to the elastic supply scenarios, full-service platforms can meet the changing needs of customers through the use of hyper-personalization and micro-segmentation. Although platforms began to emerge prior to the current disruption, for airlines to manage their revenue, new platforms have emerged to derive deeper customer intelligence and business intelligence, and that work with a broad spectrum of partners, in real time. (See the discussion on this topic in a previous book in this series.[4]) Full-service platforms incorporate a broad spectrum of the capabilities needed: for example, the dimensions of multimodal travel, changes to reservations, payment systems that have different parameters than in the past, health-related information and documentation, and inflight entertainment. The inflight entertainment system, now part of the full-service platforms, can be made more comprehensive and extremely user friendly, provide wireless entertainment or entertainment through the seat-back system, integrate content, and handle the purchase of ancillary products and services, on board or on the ground, and can connect with an airline's passenger services system. Health-related information and documentation can, for example, provide information on the test requirements of various countries, locations where tests can be performed, verification of the authenticity of documents, and the location of the availability of vaccines. The use of such a full-service platform can help an airline obtain real information on the needs of its customers, actual and potential—actual who purchased a product or a service and potential, meaning, those who searched but did not buy. The key message is not just to better serve customers who did make a purchase, but also to identify who did not make a purchase, and why not. And, creating and delivering value to both groups will enhance the brand of an airline, discussed later in this chapter.

Full-service platforms, discussed above, can be made up of a number of platforms, each devoted to a specific function. Antoine de Kerviler, in his thought leadership piece in Chapter 7, provides examples of four specific platforms that should be considered by an airline—customer and loyalty, flights, aircraft, and people and finance—with the customer and loyalty platform being the most important. For a full description of these platforms, see his piece in Chapter 7. It is also interesting to note that the two aspects of collaboration, discussed throughout this book, collaboration within the organization and collaboration within the ecosystem, are also achievable with the use of platforms. There are two other important points made by Antoine de Kerviler in his paper. First, different aspects of collaboration must be centered on the needs of customers. Second, collaboration within the organization (among the four areas mentioned above) and within the dynamic ecosystem can be achieved through the use of apps that already exist. Sophisticated full-service platforms can now be established with more ease, given the availability of hosting services for developing software projects, for example, DevOps.

Full-service platforms can basically handle all aspects of retailing, including, for example, the sale of ancillary products and services, distribution and fulfillment, implementation of IATA's New Distribution Capability (NDC) and One Order (which will play a major role in replacing electronic ticketing), and the growth and optimization of revenue through the use of dynamic pricing and dynamic bundling. Dynamic bundling no longer needs to be restricted to rule-based decision systems, based, for example, on an "if-then" reasoning.

Now machine learning technology can be used to enable airlines to offer much more relevant personalized offers that include third-party products and services. Personalized dynamic bundling, created within the context of real time, is becoming a reality with the formation of platforms, based on artificial intelligence, such as those announced by Sabre and Google in late October 2020. Moreover, full-service platforms can also give travelers access to data and analytics to improve their travel experience.

A customer can get access to information, for example, that she will not make the flight, using a display of the road conditions on her way to the airport. Or, that she will not make the connecting flight, and then provide her with different options, using data (such as the next available flight with seats available, based on her status in the loyalty program). She can also be provided information on how to make a connection in a timely manner, given her real-time location, such as information on the location of the gate for the connecting flight and congestion in that part of the terminal, along her way to the gate. Customers can also be given access to analytics (including visualization techniques and capabilities) to enable them to take actions. They can troubleshoot problems and solve them, such as shop for rates and rebook flights. This capability of a full-service platform can not only help an airline monetize data, but also enable it to undertake data-driven marketing, an important part of digital marketing. This aspect would be an added feature of an airline's product line, leading to product differentiation (at a micro-segment level) in the digital world. If the amount and type of data and analytics made available to customers were to be based on customer profiles, then an airline could get more insights by tracking the usage of the data and analytics.

In addition to retailing, full-service (end-to-end capability-based) platforms can also integrate operational functions—flight operations (including crew management), ground operations, and maintenance repair and overhaul organizations (MROs). It is the comprehensive capability of an end-to-end platform that will enable an airline to scale up and down effectively, relating to time and scope. In short, a full-service platform can help an airline anticipate and respond effectively to the marketplace dynamics, relating to demand, in virtually real time, given that platforms will have the capability to compile data and use analytics, particularly prescriptive, to suggest innovative travel solutions.

There are, however, some basic questions regarding the development of such platforms:

- Who would develop such platforms?
- What data and analytics would add value for customers to improve their experience?
- Could analytics be deployed at scale?
- Could algorithms be deployed, especially for using unstructured data relating, for example, not just to text, but also to voice and images?
- Would an airline be able to track usage?

- What would be the value of such platforms to an airline relating to its loyalty and its brand?
- How can full-service platforms create, capture, and deliver value by offering personalized and dynamic bundles, based on information on the product/service features desired as well as the willingness to pay?
- Most important, would participants on the platform be willing to share data on customers?

While the personalization process was already on a fast track prior to the current disruption, the speed of innovation and the speed of its implementation will increase, not just to generate cash, but also to reduce costs and have extremely lean operations. As stated above, it was reported in October 2020 that Sabre and Google are developing a platform using artificial intelligence and the Google Cloud to improve personalization by being able to "sense, analyze, and predict customer behavior."[5]

Let us keep in mind that such platforms will be open-technology platforms, enabling any provider of travel-related products and services to make a connection and where consumers can connect with suppliers using any device, from any location, and at any time. Let us explore, for a moment, the first question as to who would develop full-service platforms. It would be hard to imagine an airline taking on such a task, given the resources required—funds, technology, and time. Keep in mind that airlines tend to be risk averse on the demand side. They do take risks on the supply side, hedging on fuel, for example. Global distribution systems could do it, as could major technology businesses, such as Alibaba, Google, and Salesforce. However, the ideal developers could be the three global strategic alliances. In the past, alliances helped their member airlines to promote their combined networks and worked on developing processes to develop seamless journeys. A recent initiative was the development of a comprehensive app to address the various needs of a customer. As a first mover, an alliance could develop a full-service, passenger service system (PSS)-agnostic platform that enables its members to make much more strategic decisions.

Let us start with multimodal connections. Some airlines have already started to work with railroads. Recently, Swiss International Air Lines introduced, for example, its new Airtrain service between Geneva's Cornavin central station and its Zurich Airport hub, in collaboration with the Swiss Federal Railways—up to ten daily services in each direction. Selected trains, operated by the Swiss Federal Railways between the Geneva railway station and the Zurich Airport, are assigned Swiss Air Lines flight numbers. This new Airtrain service is the third initiative after the rail services between Basel and Zurich Airport and between Lugano and Zurich Airport. Now, it is time to think seriously about intermodal door-to-door transportation. A customer looking to go from Toledo, Ohio in the US to Manchester in the UK should not simply be shown a list of short-haul regional flights at both ends to connect with the nonstop transatlantic flights from hubs (such as Chicago O'Hare and Detroit in the US and London Heathrow and London Gatwick in the UK, or Amsterdam in the Netherlands). The customer can also be given the choice of traveling in a limo (directly from the home) to the hub airport on the US side and in a limo from the hub airport in the UK to the exact final destination. Different types of limos can be provided for travelers on different budgets. For example, taxis, or even mini-buses, leaving from different locations in a town, can be provided for different segments of budget travelers. A full-service platform will also be able to handle changes in today's "food chain," such as distribution systems becoming tour and travel operators, and airline alliances running mega-search marketplaces. Most important, perhaps, think about the capability of a full-service platform, developed by an alliance, to enable its member airlines to share capacity within the elastic supply scenario, while enabling members to offer customized products and services, and offering them at scale.

Without the use of platforms, airlines based their decisions, to some extent, on the experience from past disruptions, such as September 11 in 2001 and the financial crisis in 2008—events after which travel bounced back to the historical base level and the historical growth trend. If one assumes that this disruption is different from the previous disruptions, going back to the 1970s, then the mid-term and the long-term strategies need to be proactive and experimental in nature. Under the second scenario, strategies need to be more visionary and, to some extent, more imaginative, to adapt to the changing dynamics of the landscape, as discussed in Chapter 6. Three key components of the strategy would be relevant levels of service, lower operating costs, and flexibility to change quickly. Such strategies can be developed and implemented with the development of digital assets, displayed in Figures 4.1 and 4.2, to manage the size, the quality, and growth in travel. However, priorities of the leadership (including the board of directors) may need to include different visions and purposes, while showing more imagination. Even for the first scenario, there needs to be a greater focus on innovation, and a greater willingness to deploy digital technologies to integrate and convert raw data into actionable insights and actionable strategies. Think about the time it took for airlines to introduce premium-economy-class cabins. Now there has to be more flexibility to enable an increase in the speed of making decisions in the context of the hammer and the dance framework, mentioned in Chapter 1.

The second scenario calls for a need for much more effective marketing planning through more informed and integrated decisions during this particularly uncertain period. There are two dimensions to marketing decisions being informed and integrated. First, the decisions being made must combine not only the perspective of all internal divisions (commercial, financial, and operational, as well as employees, for instance), but also external parties, customers, and partners in the travel chain (stockholders, government and community advocates, airports, hotels, and car-rental businesses, for example). Again, although this is not a new concept, now integration (with internal and external partners) is much more critical to deal with the expected constant turbulence.

Second, while decisions have always needed to be action-oriented, it is now possible to make this happen, through digital transformation, given the availability of insights derived from data, and not just intuition and past experience.

Airline managers could look at two examples of best practices to digitally transform the airline business. Elizabeth Altman and Frank Nagle provide one example of a best practice based on their research of one initiative of the United Nations Development Programme (UNDP) that created a global network of accelerator labs to develop its own ecosystems. They also show the application of such a technique by Syngenta, a large Swiss agribusiness, which used a global network of innovation labs to digitally transform agriculture.[6] While the concept of innovation labs is not new within the airline industry, the critical success factor is how to scale innovative ideas. Airlines could also obtain some insights on how to deal with new digital disrupters. In this area, Rita McGrath and Ryan McManus suggest a way to deal with digital disrupters through an approach called "discovery-driven digital transformation." The basis of this approach is for a company to identify a problem to solve, using the company's core strengths (knowledge of its customers and its operations, for example) and by using digital technologies within a discovery-driven framework.[7] Think about the idea for an airline to want to learn about the outcomes desired by customers and not the means offered to customers. Various customers need to achieve various outcomes, such as attend meetings, visit friends and relatives, and vacation at certain locations. Travel is just a means to achieve outcomes. How would airlines "discover" the outcomes desired? This is where digital technologies can play an important role if managements are willing to market "outcomes" rather than "itineraries."

The accelerated changes in the marketplace call for a need to develop new products and services, new distribution channels, new ways to sell new services, and new ways to brand to help customers achieve the outcomes that customers desire. On top of this, the new environment also calls for substantial reductions in operating costs and the development of new sources of revenue. Reduction in costs and identification of new streams of revenues mean creating different ways to work and collaborate with partners in the ecosystem (airlines, airports, aircraft manufacturers, hotels, and car-rental companies) while increasing flexibility in operating the airline business. The answer lies in:

- working on platforms to collaborate in the digital networks to not only reduce costs and enhance revenue, but also to manage risk, and
- reinforcing digital marketing strategies to acquire and retain new customers and grow revenue in non-traditional ways.

Let us not forget that airlines have always had two key advantages. They have a captive audience and they have data in their frequent flyer programs. Now they have a third advantage, namely, the interest by credit-card companies to collaborate to create "a real person behind a PNR," or "a real person in seat 23B."

## Developing customer management capabilities

The focus on customer centricity, or the use of digital technologies to improve customer experience, or the need to enhance brands, is hardly a new idea. However, the current pandemic has changed many dimensions relating to these areas, requiring a different way of thinking. Think about Sephora, which had been taking customer experience to new heights, and seems to have benefitted during the Coronavirus pandemic. Using artificial intelligence the business was able to match customers' skin tones to the company's available products. Next, Sephora was able to deploy virtual reality to enable customers, using an app, to sample different products in their homes rather than in physical stores. This process avoided the need for beauty assistants in stores to touch customers' faces and, at the same time, enforces the social distancing requirements. In the travel sector, the primary concern has been, and will continue to be in the foreseeable future, people's safety, health, and wellness. And, while consumers' desire for an improvement in the customer journey is also not new, the degree of emphasis on the aspects considered with the customer journey has changed. Let us start with customer centricity. Airlines have clearly been improving their products (itineraries, premium-economy seating, inflight services, and so forth) and customer experience. However, the core of the product has not changed. It is still scheduled services between airports. Some thought has been given to end-to-end journeys, but it has not become a reality, let alone frictionless end-to-end journeys. True customer centricity involves, as detailed by Simone van Neerven and Jirka Stradal, in Chapter 7, developing "continuous insight into the needs and emotions of your customers," and forming a purpose around these needs and emotions. They give one possible example of a purpose, "to bring meaningful experiences and connections everywhere, everyday." These aspects of customer centricity are important once airlines have gone through the recovery phase.

One important point relating to segmentation of consumers is the size of the Z generation and how leading businesses have already begun to change their strategies to meet the needs of this segment. One estimate of the size of this segment of the US population, born between 2000 and 2020, is about 86 million.[8] This segment of the population is sufficiently different to require different ways to connect and engage with them, from the perspectives of marketing and sales as well as employment. In some ways consumers in this group are trendsetters in their own right. They grew up along with digital technologies, are very well connected among themselves (locally and globally), have strong opinions about social issues, and have the power to influence businesses through the use of social media. They are incredibly effective users of such media channels as Snapchat and YouTube. Jason Dorsey and Denise Villa provide just one example of the influence of this generation on the brand of a company. Recently, Nike put out a controversial ad featuring a black-and-white photo of a "social justice activist Colin Kaepernick" with white text, "Believe in something. Even if it means sacrificing everything." The ad created such an outcry leading some people (presumably within the older generation) to "burning their sneakers and cutting the swoosh logo off their sock." Yet it is reported that Nike took a chance with this ad realizing the priority of the Z generation relating to social causes. The end result was a surge in the stock price of Nike.[9]

During the recovery phase, it is true that consumers' interest has been in such areas as contactless operations and nonstop services to avoid connections at busy airports, for instance. Similarly, while consumers have always been interested in consistency across channels, the focus now is in the digital channel as that is the primary channel of usage. Then there is the need for transparency with respect to pricing and conditions of service. While consumers have always been interested in being able to reach airlines through any digital channel and through any device, now the interest is also on speed and round-the-clock access. As such, human contact can be switched with robots, as long as communications with customers are interactive and user friendly. Consequently, digital transformation implies that technologies must be integrated and made available to the relevantly skilled staff at the right time, and with the right processes. This leads to the question about who should be given the responsibility to lead digital transformation within an airline organization. Chapter 6 discusses this challenge.

Consumers' demands are changing even more rapidly and are becoming more diversified. The challenge, however, is that while there are some concrete desires that consumers can state and relate to, others are hidden wants—features and products that consumers don't even know they want. This is an area where digital assets, in general, and digital marketing, in particular, can help in finding out customers' problems and then helping airlines to develop and offer solutions to those problems. One component of digital marketing is the development and use of customer management capabilities, displayed in Figure 4.3. For an airline, its website is one place to build relationships for passengers looking for solutions to their problems, not just a place to make reservations. As such, an airline needs the capability to show how an offer will make a customer's life better and achieve the outcome desired. There is no question that some airlines had attempted to find out the outcomes desired and offer the means to achieve the stated desires. Take, for example, a couple that states the desire to go skiing. In some cases customers are also able to reveal their budgets and airlines have offered packages, such as for this amount of money, you can go to these places and go skiing. However, with a total redesign of websites, with the use of digital technologies, digital networks, and analytics, it should be possible to find out, at scale, the outcomes desired and relevant offers to be made.

In Figure 4.3, one capability would be to determine what is the outcome that a customer is looking for and how can a customer provide the information on the outcome desired? The starting point is an image of the total customer journey, an example of which is displayed in Figure 4.4. Right there is an example of one improvement needed. How can a website offer the means for the customer to achieve the outcome? Why did the customer leave the site without booking? The key aspect of the design of the website is not just

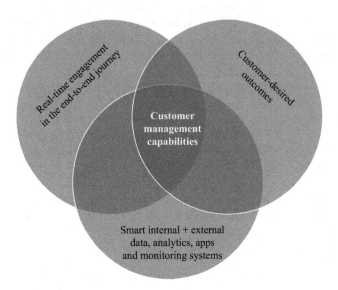

*Figure 4.3* Customer management capabilities

to improve functions and make navigation easier, but to be able to identify a consumer's problem and provide solutions to the problem. It is much more than showing schedules and prices and booking capabilities and payment capabilities. Right now, most consumers go to an airline's website to get their problems solved, not just to book a flight. The same is true with an OTA's website. Consumers say that they want experiences. What are the new drivers of customer experience? What are the systems to engage with customers and to monitor the degree of their satisfaction in real time and at each touchpoint, not through some general measurement of the Net Promoter Score at the end of a journey? Are there not only ways to measure a customer's satisfaction on the website, but also incentives to make a booking? How about providing some samples—a coupon for a seat selection or an upgrade or a free baggage service? What is the purpose of an email after a consumer leaves the website? Is it to provide confirmations for purchased itineraries, changes, or a sales campaign: for example, a promotion to sign up for a branded credit card? Or, is it to build relationships?

The need to have 360-degree views of customers has been an ongoing challenge for a long time. Airlines wanted to have 360-degree views of their customers to be able to provide rich and personalized content and to provide seamless and consistent experience. However, it has now become more critical during this health-related disruption. The challenge in the past has been related to not only data sitting in different silos, but also the inconsistency of the data residing in different silos. First, groups in different functions wanted to have specific types of data in specific formats to suit their own needs. Not only

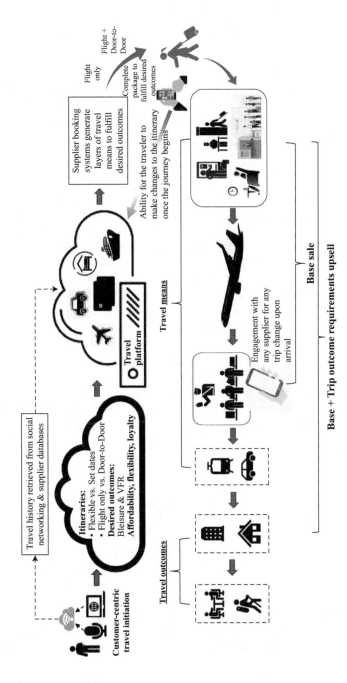

*Figure 4.4* Customer journeys starting with customer-desired outcomes

were each function's data needs different, but there was no design for the data to be shared. Then there were problems relating to data coming from external sources. Later there were challenges relating to the privacy of data (privacy regulations like the General Data Protection Regulation (GDPR)). Then there was the view that some customers prefer to control their own data regarding who gets what. There are also concerns related to the use of cookies. However, despite all these considerations, it is now possible to have 360-degree views of customers, using digital assets as represented in Figures 4.1 and 4.2 to develop the customer management capabilities displayed in Figure 4.3. Consider some new developments affecting the management of customers.

- Consumers now depend even more on online shopping and experience.
- Businesses need to focus on virtual operations.
- Security at airports has become more complex, as governments add health and hygiene regulations to the security regulations caused by the September 11, 2001 events. Going forward, governments could demand the introduction of globally accepted vaccination certificates along with passports.
- Pricing became a real challenge during the recovery as some leisure and VFR travelers were not coming back even at discount fares.
- Advance purchase aspects of pricing were not working during the recovery as consumers could cancel reservations without penalties.
- On the part of airlines, schedules were being changed at short notice to juggle flights to meet health-related changes.
- Demand was declining not only because of uncertainty, but also due to the cash considerations of some consumers.
- In the case of business travelers, not only were businesses concerned about the costs of travel, but passengers were also concerned over the risks of travel (travelers' well-being, sickness, safety, and so forth). There was also the concern relating to the unpredictability of the trip, created either by an airline (schedule changes or operational disruptions), or by the traveler (relating to health concerns at the origin or the destination).
- All three considerations (relating to costs, health and safety, and itinerary changes) were having a significant impact on the distribution channel selected. Could travelers, for example, address all three considerations satisfactorily when booking on an airline's website?
- Some consumers apparently are willing to use virtual reality to meet their travel needs. Consider this interesting statistic contained in the paper by Simone van Neerven and Jirka Stradal. Fourteen million people visited the Louvre in Paris in 2019. With the closure due to the lockdown, the museum offered a virtual tour of the site as an alternative to a physical visit. Within the first two months of the lockdown, about 12 million people visited the museum virtually.

In Figure 4.4, the starting point is for a consumer to be able to state clearly the outcome desired. The statement can be made orally, talking with a system such as Apple's Siri or Amazon's Alexa, or by typing a text on a keyboard or a mobile device. The information provided should be going to a travel platform, not just a website of an airline, a platform that already has detailed and secured information on the traveler, information such as product features desired and loyalty. It is the collection of service providers on the platform that can then come up with offers to help the consumer select the best option to achieve the outcome desired—participate in a business meeting, visit a friend or a relative, or (not just any vacation) a certain type of vacation, ski resort, beach, and so forth. The consumer should also be able to provide some information on the available budget and the degree of flexibility. In Figure 4.4, representing an outline of the customer journey, there should be a capability for constant interactive engagement, in real time, with the platform. The platform should be able to recognize all aspects of the trip and respond with options where needed. For example, the flight arrives at 6:30 a.m. but the hotel room is not available until 3:00 p.m. What would be the amount that the hotel would require to get a room ready by, say, 8:00 a.m., having investigated the rooms that would become vacant and could be prepared for occupancy by special staff to improve the experience of an individual traveler?

Even if airlines and distributors improve the experience relating to the booking process, there is still the question of end-to-end experience. For example, what happens after the booking has been made? Consider, for instance, the experience of consumers who had booked flights but then had to change, or cancel, or get refunds. The experience relating to these situations was relatively poor, given the inefficiency of the conventional processes. Would it have helped if airlines and distributors had provided customers with the capability to serve themselves? The developments relating to the implementation of the IATA NDC and One Order initiatives are clearly in the right direction, but they had not reached scale prior to the current disruption. It is ironic that while consumers are hyper-connected in other areas, when it comes to air travel, they do not have the self-service functionality. The key point in Figures 4.3 and 4.4 is to have the capability to stay engaged with consumers in their end-to-end journeys. If corporate travel takes a hit, as is predicted, then the fare gap between business travelers and budget travelers will decrease. This will increase even further the need for airlines to find new ways to penetrate the remaining segments of business travel by helping travelers achieve the outcomes they desire.

Let us go outside of the airline industry to look at the role of experience in addition to the introduction of disruptive products offered by such companies as Amazon and Netflix. Brian Halligan, the CEO of HubSpot, a customer experience software platform, makes three suggestions:

- give customers the experience that they did not know they wanted,
- make interactions frictionless, and
- personalize the relationship.[10]

Let us put these suggestions in the context of airlines. Consider the first point. How many airlines can claim that they can deliver the customer experience that customers did not know they wanted? Consider the second point. Have airlines reached a stage for making their interactions with customers frictionless? With respect to the pricing element of the product line, the focus is likely to be on dynamic pricing and that will require a much stronger interaction and integration between revenue management and network and schedule planning, as shown in Figure 3.6. This level of interaction and integration will require the development of market and customer intelligence, with a deeper use of data and analytics, as well as the use of artificial intelligence algorithms and mathematical simulations. The results presented will have to be evaluated in great detail related to the following types of questions. What were the independent and dependent variables used? Were the algorithms "over-trained"? The human element can and will still play an important role in the interpretation of the machine-generated options. With these considerations, the focus can now be more on total revenue and not market share, and the optimization of revenue to be based across a passenger's entire journey, and the passenger's willingness to pay for different components along the journey.

Customer experience can be improved using technologies as technologies can facilitate the understanding of customer behavior and expectations and then suggest appropriate actions that can be taken. It is a double win, an improvement in customer experience and a reduction in operating costs by leveraging, for example, self-help systems, processes, and channels. Data can be gathered in real time from numerous touchpoints in the end-to-end journeys and analytics can be used to derive actionable insights not only to create opportunities for upsell and cross-sell, but also to increase the conversion rate at relevant points. The key message is not just to develop a capability to connect data from different sources, but also to connect the data differently.

While some airlines have dabbled with the use of artificial intelligence (a subject discussed in Chapter 5) in their pricing policies in recent years, going forward, artificial intelligence can play a bigger role, given that the historical data on travel patterns and seasonality may not be as valid. Instead, it is digital marketing that can provide more useful information through posts on social platforms, non-travel related purchases made with credit cards, and, as already mentioned, Google searches, to predict consumers' travel plans, their spending patterns, potential destinations, and choices made relating to airlines and airports. Again, it is the use of data, analytics, and apps (shown in Figures 4.1, 4.2, and 4.3) that will enable managers to plan differently. However, as mentioned above, care must be exercised when relying on the data generated by monitoring clicks and vague intentions. As such, artificial intelligence, coupled with the use of unstructured data, can help managers in charge of pricing, to take dynamic pricing and target-marketing strategies to new heights in their short-term decisions. Valuable insights can also be gained in this area from the experience of the financial sector. Moreover, adapting to the elastic supply scenario, product planning will need to be on the basis of demand-driven-supply as opposed to supply-driven-demand. Some airlines that may think the demand-driven concept is too radical, may consider the fact that Allegiant Air has been practicing some elements of this concept for almost two decades.

## Changing perspectives for revenue management

In the commercial space, revenue management systems and processes are likely to go through a fundamental change. In the past, the primary levers of revenue management were schedules, fares, booking patterns and prices relating to the time of the booking (14 days, vs. 7 days, vs. 3 days, ahead of the flight, for example), customer segmentation (business, leisure, and VFR), and load factors (anticipated, based on booking vs. breakeven load factors). Going forward, information on all of these levers is likely to change. And, there could be new levers, relating to not only health-related concerns and regulations on the one side, but also to the degree of pent-up demand, on the other side. While some revenue managers had begun to use machine learning, prior to the disruption, to help manage demand, this new technology can in future play a bigger role to create sub-buckets within the traditional buckets to account for the constant changes in the data. New technology can help not only in the area of forecasting demand, but also in the optimization process. For example:

- Analysts need to forecast not just the number of customers willing to purchase travel, but the probability of selecting a specific itinerary and the preparedness to accept a specific fare.
- There needs to be a revenue strategy, for example, specific customers to be targeted at specific times while in specific channels.
- Artificial intelligence can incorporate "adaptive learning" in the revenue management process from the use of recent experience and new data to update forecasts on a continual basis.
- New sources of data can include information coming in from health-related agencies.

However, the value generated from the use of this technology will depend heavily on cross-functional integration, between flight schedulers, pricing managers, and now health agencies, as discussed in the previous chapter and displayed in Figure 3.6. Right now the goals of different groups are less than optimally integrated. Schedulers tend to coordinate aircraft and crews around government-instituted and labor-contract rules. Pricing managers tend to adjust fares to stimulate demand and to comply with the distancing rules in the cabin (the middle-seat challenge, for example) instead of dynamic pricing and dynamic bundling in the conventional framework. And, revenue managers do an extremely good job of maximizing the revenue from a given flight. Each sub-functional group optimizes the outcome within each of their silos. However, machine learning can enable optimization at the system level. Machine learning can detect and analyze patterns in each sub-optimization within each silo and then "see" the linkages among the patterns to suggest changes that will lead to optimizations at a systems level.

In some ways, the realignment of the revenue management systems is likely to be just as deep as it was when the revenue management process changed from using leg-based systems to using origin-and-destination-based systems. The next step improvement could be innovative pricing-based revenue management. The idea would now be twofold: not only to match supply and demand, but also to generate more demand. In the past, revenue management groups managed demand, given supply that had already been scheduled. And, revenue managers allocated the demand rather than generated demand. For example, managers filtered demand or they allocated demand. The systems did not really generate demand, except in some cases through an offer of some discounts within a bucket. Through digital marketing, an airline can now go to social networks and generate demand that comes via using social networks and pricing. Keep in mind that if the load factor is under 70 percent, there is really no need for using sophisticated revenue management techniques. However, the key goal is to manage supply and demand in real time. Think about Uber's surge pricing system. If it is raining and the demand for taxis is high, it is reasonable to expect the price quoted to be high too. However, the higher price also leads more drivers to provide more services. Consequently, the pricing system is dynamic and works to benefit both drivers and riders. And, it works in real time.

An innovative pricing-based revenue management system would be able to generate demand, while maintaining a transparent shopping experience. Under the current mode of operation, airlines wait for the demand to come to them, instead of going to where the demand is. How about revisiting some innovative uses of subscription pricing as in priceline.com (discussed below)? In the case of subscription-based pricing, Air Canada, did introduce in 2007, for example, its flight-pass system, for an unlimited amount of air travel for a month for a given price. Some airline executives may remember the online travel agency priceline.com, established in 2000, to help consumers find discount rates for air travel and hotels. The online travel agency was called by a unique name, "Name Your Own Price," through which a consumer could name her offer of a price for an airline ticket between two points. The agency provided the details of the itinerary after an airline accepted the offer. Both types of programs can now become much more viable within the context of digital marketing to adapt to the two scenarios discussed in Chapter 2.

If the current disruption, under the elastic supply scenario, has a long-term impact, how can a global airline accelerate its innovation initiatives? What would be the best practices to digitally transform the airline business? One strategy would be to reinforce digital marketing that leverages digital devices, digital technologies, digital platforms, and digital media. In a nutshell, the internet can be used to identify potential customers and provide them with access to relevant information through digital channels, such as emails, search engines, and social media, while ensuring the availability of a unified customer experience. The key difference in digital marketing is that connections with customers are made online and online channels are used to influence customers. And, since it is reported that more than half of internet activity takes place on mobile devices, the mobile channel needs to provide an exceptional experience. Can users navigate just as easily on an airline's mobile site as they can on an airline's site on the desktop? How about creating a single mobility app that will not only address the total mobility needs of customers (for example, information and booking capability for the use of different modes of transportation, as well as hotels), but also offer a capability to chat, not to mention the availability of loyalty benefits across businesses. Keep in mind that content, in the context of digital marketing, relates less to services, frequencies, prices, and itineraries, but relates more to the outcomes desired, including the experience that a consumer gets, while being on the website of an airline.

## Rethinking distribution systems and processes

The IATA NDC, which transformed airlines' abilities to merchandize their offers, continued to add value during the recovery period as airlines focused on generating sufficient cash flows to survive by providing different elements of the content. Initially, rich content during the recovery period related more to the health-related measures taken by airlines. In some cases, where sufficient information was not available from the agents working through the global distribution systems (GDSs), some airlines started to focus, even more, on increasing their direct sales. Prior to this disruption, the interest in direct sales was intended:

- to reduce the costs of distribution,
- to engage directly and more effectively with customers to offer (1) customized content, and (2) to learn more about the demand,
- to capture more revenue by providing rich content (from a traditional point of view), and
- to work around the limitations that a low-cost carrier may not be present in a GDS.

The new interest in direct sales, at least during the recovery phase, was based on the need to generate immediate cash. However, if airlines want to move into the direct channel more aggressively, they need to know if they have access to new data (such as location and movement and credit-card usage) and have the brand to make the direct distribution channel a success. Consequently, there is a need to have, not only a better understanding of travel search, but also a more in-depth analysis of channels and the channel-mix, not to mention the connection with the brand. As of the middle of 2020, airlines had only 10–20 percent of their bookings via the NDC, with the percentage varying by airline.

Going forward, it might be more valuable, adapting to both scenarios, to create a more harmonized relationship with indirect distributors for a number of reasons:

- to manage a large percentage of customers coming via indirect distributors, with the number varying between 50 and 75 percent, depending on the airline, and the likelihood of consolidation within the GDS and OTA sectors,
- to connect with suppliers of other travel-related services, such as hotels, cruise lines, and rental cars,
- to enable travel agents to compare schedules, prices, and availability across all suppliers,
- to develop innovative ways to market an airline's products and services,
- to enable consumers to make more transparent comparisons during the shopping process, as it has become quite a challenge with content becoming increasingly fragmented,
- to have a wider reach and access to higher-margin passenger reservations, and
- to address customer outcomes, not to mention the desire for more personalized and seamless experiences, displayed in Figure 4.3.

Only now, the personalized bundles may be based on different criteria, such as the ability to provide comprehensive vouchers for trips not taken—vouchers that can be used on non-alliance airline partners as well as hotels and car rental. Another major difference could be based on the unique needs of some corporate clients.

Selling direct to customers did help some airlines during the first phase of the recovery by engaging with customers at the point of sale to reduce customers' concerns for travel and to provide customers with different forms of reassurances. However, moving forward, the relationships will need to change between airlines and distributors as well as among distributors. The realignment is only partly related to commercial areas, such as GDS fees, including the additional distribution cost charges (for bookings made through GDSs), and incentives provided by the GDSs to agents. The bigger challenge relates to the trust between airlines and the GDSs, in terms of access to customer information as well as the personalization of the shopping experience, particularly with respect to the sale of ancillary products and services that can become much more dynamic. The GDSs upgraded their systems to enable airlines to display their full content (not just fares, itineraries, and seat availability), but also ancillaries—often the higher-margin products and services. The display of full content has already become critical, given that shoppers can now get detailed information from the use of metasearch engines. Moreover, the current practice of filing fares with a third party (for example, the Airline Tariff Publishing Company) will need to be reevaluated if airlines decide to move aggressively in the implementation of dynamic pricing strategies—the capability to create not just personalized fares, but also personalized bundles. A key requirement will be developing partnerships within the digital ecosystems to create, capture, and deliver value for partners and customers. Clearly, more products and services can be added through digital networks. Critical success factors relate, however, to a discussion on how value will be created and how it will be shared. The central points in this discussion are:

- having similar visions and goals,
- working with contemporary systems that enable airlines to display their differentiated content much more competitively,
- working through a platform that enables the use of "plug-and-play" capabilities, including apps,
- having different partners offer not only unique products and services, but also unique core capabilities,
- having the ability and the willingness to share data, and
- having a common view and understanding of the value generated by big data, smart analytics, and value-adding networks, as shown in Figures 4.1, 4.2, and 4.3.

Airlines have often commented about the legacy nature of PSSs holding them back from the deployment of next-generation retailing strategies. The GDSs did invest significant amounts in upgrading their legacy systems, and making them compatible, for example, with the NDC framework. However, a few new companies are now emerging that believe it is possible to simply bypass the existing PSSs (even the updated versions) and get the functions of the PSSs performed outside of the PSSs. While PSSs basically handled reservations, inventory, and booking classes, could these functions now be performed in other ways? For example, airlines in the US announced in September 2020 that they will not be charging change fees for travel within the US domestic markets. The implementation of this strategy was a challenge initially in the reservation systems. The incumbent GDSs clearly have the technical skills and the financial resources and they will be committing both to stay relevant. Could the next step be to develop the next generation of PSSs within an open-source framework that would provide a lot more agility for the commercial groups? Could they provide new platforms—the Enterprise Resource Planning (ERP) systems of the future for airlines?

The starting point would be the changing customer bases and their changing needs. Just as one example, payment systems have already begun to change rapidly. In the past credit cards were used which helped cash flows of airlines. During the recovery, credit-card companies and banks wanted to limit their risk in case a flight was cancelled, or more seriously, an airline declared bankruptcy. Could a new platform, developed by a GDS, not only handle new payment systems, but handle them with a trusted brand? Next, could flexibility be built into third-party distribution systems where an airline chooses the content to be displayed to an agent? The key benefit of the NDC was for airlines to have greater control of their content, their distribution networks, and their ability to implement surcharges on bookings. From this perspective, an airline chooses not only the degree of interaction with an agent, but also to have the capability to get a better handle on customer demand. A key insight, contained in John Lancaster's thought leadership piece in Chapter 7, is that the current structure of distribution of airline products creates a significant amount of uncertainty and risk that needs to be managed by restructuring the distribution model by creating an exchange that works with supply aggregators on one side and demand aggregators on the other side. The goal can now also be to reduce costs relating to passengers—costs of passenger acquisition, retention, and distribution.

While it is true that additional value could be added by the traditional GDSs, there is also a potential for deriving new value from new partners. Google, for instance, has developed a new program, called Demand Explorer, that can provide airlines with valuable information to help them develop schedules when they do not have relevant historical data. This information can be derived, to some extent, from the travel-related searches made by consumers, data coming from shopping on airlines' websites powered by Google, and from the use of Google's products, such as Google Flights and Google Ads.[11] However, care is needed in the interpretation of such data, given that the information relates to just search and not actual reservations, and the diversification of the information relates to users themselves and their locations. Information available from sources like advance bookings, as well as search and customer surveys, may not be of much help in forecasting demand, going forward. As such, forecasting route profitability has now become even more complex, given the inadequacy of the data on passenger demand, passenger yields, and aircraft economics, as to which aircraft would be used closer to the actual operations. Returning to distribution, even agents are being included in the partnerships in the distribution space. For example, during the recovery phase, strategic partnerships began to be developed with platforms such as Alibaba and Trip.com. And platform operators such as Trip.com and Expedia earmarked, during the initial phase of the recovery, large amounts of money to help travel partners not only develop and implement health and hygiene measures, but also with their cash flows. The real value for airlines, however, is in the detailed and up-to-date monitoring of policy measures (travel restrictions and health measures) around the world, framed into categories and harmonized values.

Take the case of travelers' capability to use the credit for travel on any airline, not just the airline holding the booking and the funds. Network and schedule planning groups might now want to consider the value of the older interline operations and pricing system for customers as well as for airlines and upgrade it to adapt to the new environment. The older generation of interline capabilities (prior to the development of strategic alliances) provided more options for customers and for airlines for travel in case of disruptions caused by passengers' own decisions or the decisions of airlines. Similarly, these capabilities provided more flexibility for airlines. An upgraded interline system can, once again, provide mutual benefits for passengers and for airlines. For example, not only can a passenger decide to use a ticket on any airline in the interline agreement, but also if an airline has only a few passengers booked on a particular flight, the airline can put the passengers on the flight of any interline partner, over and above the strategic alliance partners. Consequently, if interline itineraries can now add much more value for customers and airlines, should the old IATA interline system and processes be revived for the digital era—with parameters relating to standardization of interline prices, products, and connecting times? The key lies in the evaluation of the complexity added versus the benefits derived.

In the elastic supply scenario, new players could enter the distribution space to sell distressed inventory, just as they did after the events of September 11, 2001. Two examples of new distributors that entered the marketplace after the 2001 events include Booking.com and Expedia, both now major players in the distribution space. Going forward, Amazon and Google, which have already been active in the travel space, could become much more dominant, based on their core competencies, search in the case of Google and e-commerce in the case of Amazon. And let us not overlook the advantage Google would have from its lower customer acquisition costs. Both are already powerhouses on the digital front and could easily succeed in carving out a good piece of the distribution market, particularly in the distribution of intermodal trips. Think about just one minor difference between Amazon and an airline. A customer's credit card is not charged until Amazon ships the product. This has not been the same with airlines that charged the credit card the minute the reservation was made even when the actual flight was not taken for months. Google has reported that it will now display new information on the percentage of open hotels with availability and the percentage of flights operating at the city or country level. In addition, Google is also planning to provide consumers the ability to screen their accommodation searches to view properties and to see the information on their free cancellation policies. Google and Amazon's penetration of the distribution space will also be facilitated by the hyper-connectivity of consumers. Finally, there could be consolidation in the travel management company sector with the business model of the travel management companies changing, particularly in the area of corporate travel policies and duty of care.

## Redeveloping brand and loyalty

The fundamentally changed commercial aspects of the business require new ways of branding the business as well as the product line. Let us start with branding. Prior to this disruption airlines typically branded their businesses in the context of their networks and schedules (size and location of hubs as well as frequency, for example), their products (cabin configurations, inflight systems, airport lounges, and so on), their frequent flyer programs (awards and third-party partners, for example), and alliance partners (access to partners' networks, frequent flyer programs, and airport lounges, for instance). Now, after the disruption, some of these branding dimensions may need to be realigned, especially if new players enter the marketplace, such as "Uber Air" and "Amazon Travel." See the thought leadership piece by Moé Weisensee in Chapter 7.

Would a significant percentage of passengers be more interested in becoming more loyal to brands that provide more service in underserved markets or provide more point-to-point services to avoid connections in congested airports? How about Delta, the only US airline that has extended its decision to block the middle seat in the main cabin through the end of April 2021?

From a broader branding perspective, as mentioned in the previous book in this series, effective storytelling can play a critical role in transforming the airline business.[12] Kindra Hall explains so eloquently in her book how the storytelling process can help a business differentiate and capture customers through an incorporation of the "Value Story, Founder Story, Purpose Story, and Customer Story."[13] Donald Miller, the CEO of StoryBrand and the author of the book *Building a StoryBrand* (2017), suggests building a compelling story brand to connect with customers to promote brand familiarity. It is more important for customers to see meaningful benefits than the features relating to a company's products and services. The key, according to him, is to simplify the brand message that customers will listen to so that they understand the unique value offered by a brand that would make their lives easier. Think about a concept that Al Ries and Jack Trout developed about 40 years ago—a concept called "positioning." In their book, they explained how a company's brand needs to penetrate the consumers' mind and "fill a hole in the consumer's mind with the distinct attributes" of the company's product. The basic message was to become number one or two in the consumer's mind since that is all the consumer is likely to remember.[14]

Going forward, the existing brand messages and the existing loyalty programs may not provide competitive value. For example, in the introduction of new products and services, extra care will need to be taken not to "overpromise and underdeliver." Consumers are more empowered not only through the use of technology, but also from the success of the direct-to-consumer brands in the retailing sector. While it is true that consumers are now well-informed, they are also now overloaded with information and they are more impatient and more intolerant. It is also important to keep in mind that while consumers tend to be self-centered, many are influenced by social media. Finally, while consumers might say that they make rational decisions, many decisions end up being made on an emotional basis.

Lawrence Ingrassia provides numerous stories of how startups are transforming the branding space.[15] One only needs to look at the brand power of Amazon in the retailing sector. What if Amazon were now to succeed in the distribution of travel products and services? What if Amazon expanded its air cargo fleet and transported not only its own products but also met the needs of other shippers? Keep in mind three key factors.

- Amazon developed its web services system and associated services for its own use that began to be used by numerous other businesses.
- Amazon already has the infrastructure and the logistics to operate its own fleet of cargo planes. Now, Amazon can simply scale that component of its

business to transport not only its own packages, but also freight for other businesses.

- Consider the brand recognition of Amazon worldwide.

Can large global airlines get some insights on brands and branding from other unrelated businesses? To start with, see the thought leadership piece by Moé Weisensee who provides, in Chapter 7, some detailed insights from furniture business, IKEA, relating to such considerations as the buyers' budgets, experience in the store, transportation of the furniture from the store, and assembly of the furniture at home. Particularly insightful are the potential parallels for airlines. Next, consider Myriam Sidibe who provides sufficient evidence of the value of studying businesses involved in the global health care space. The key opportunity is for a marketing group to develop strategies to influence consumer behavior by connecting "a purpose to its business and increase its social impact."[16] The author provides an insightful example of the branding strategy developed by Unilever with a social mission to change behavior to enhance public health.

As for loyalty, frequent flyer programs have played a critical role since their development beginning in 1979. Although American Airlines is often given credit for introducing the first loyalty program in 1981, it was, in fact, Texas International Airlines that introduced it two years prior to that, in 1979, when this airline began to track the miles flown by passengers in the program. Since then loyalty programs have evolved so much that some financial analysts claim that the market value of some frequent flyer programs of some global airlines are higher than the market value of the airlines themselves. These analyses are based presumably not only on the earning power of the programs, but also on the value of the data contained on the members listed in the programs. The value of these programs has clearly been demonstrated in recent years by the ability of some airlines to sell their miles to financial institutions, such as credit-card companies, and some airlines to pledge their loyalty programs as securities to obtain loans. Consider the following information provided by United Airlines in its MileagePlus Investor Presentation, dated June 15, 2020. In 2019, the airline, with more than 100 million members, generated over $5 billion in cash flows from sales (representing more than 10 percent of the total revenue), and almost $2 billion in earnings before interest, taxes, depreciation, and amortization (EBITDA). These earnings represented for United about 25 percent of its total adjusted EBITDA.[17] Leading airlines began to see the real value of their loyalty programs long before the current disruption. As stated above, in some cases a question was raised about the loyalty program being of higher value than the airline itself. These kinds of considerations might have contributed to Air Canada's decision, having sold its loyalty program, Aeroplan, to buy it back after a number of years to reframe it, and then to make it a core component of its airline business, given the strategic value of a loyalty program. American Airlines reportedly used its loyalty program as collateral for a government loan under the Coronavirus Aid, Relief, and Economic Security (CARES) Act.

The key message is that while an airline's loyalty program can have significant value as a stand-alone division, the value generated by the loyalty program can be much higher if it is made an integral part of the airline business. Let us not overlook, for example, the role of loyalty when competing with potentially strong new entrants in the second scenario. The key to capitalizing on the loyalty program is to reinvent it by going beyond "miles and points." The strategy should be to tap into new sources of data, new partnerships, and new customer incentives, based on customers' changing behavior. Again, there is an increasing role for digital marketing in enhancing the loyalty programs. Examples of new data sources would be the data and software platforms of credit-card businesses and telecoms, social media feeds synthesized by third parties, and customers themselves through the direct sale distribution channel. Let us not overlook the point that while the new data, available from the location and movement of mobile devices, can be very helpful for network and schedule planners, it can also add much value for marketing planning groups for target-marketing initiatives, in real time. New value comes from not only real-time marketing on a personalized basis, but also from receiving almost real-time feedback. While these are sources of rich data, there are different conditions worldwide relating to the use of these sources.

As for changes in the loyalty programs for customers, new loyalty programs could be designed with new booking patterns for different segments and a new status-tier structure, for example, a fee-based status or a value-adding travel status, based across partners in the travel chain. A new form of subscription travel could also be developed and connected with a loyalty program. And if the percentage of consumers traveling for non-business purposes increases, then some aspects of the loyalty programs may need to be redesigned to appeal to this segment. There are some key questions to be answered. For example, what is the value of the loyalty program of a weak airline, given that it could go out of business? However, what if the weak airline is a member of a strategic alliance and the miles earned by customers can be redeemed on alliance partners, or the purchase of non-travel products and services? Answers would be of significant interest to the buyers of the loyalty programs within the financial investment community.

As for customers' changing behavior, think about consumers' concerns about making purchases during a recession, including having sufficient financial resources to make purchases. To deal with such concerns, airlines would need to think of new ways to engage with potential customers. Think about the approach used by the Hyundai Motor Company back in 2009 and repeated in 2020. In January 2009, during the recession brought about by the financial crisis, Hyundai introduced its Assurance Job Loss Protection program. It assured buyers of its cars that they could return their vehicles if they lost their jobs and they did not need to make any additional payments. This program provided peace of mind to a buyer of a Hyundai vehicle. Similarly, Hyundai relaunched this program in 2020 and offered to make up to six months of payments to new buyers in the event of job losses, as well as a 90-day deferral on new purchases.

This was a bold strategy in January 2009 and shows the company's commitment to its customers. This initiative transferred the financial risk from the customer to the company. Changing consumer behavior also has implications for the need to realign loyalty programs as well as the metrics to measure loyalty, metrics that go beyond the traditional Net Promoter Score. Coming out of this disruption, airlines will need to focus much more on customers' needs, with more focus on emotional needs than actual needs. Customers would need to see some concrete actions—exemplified by the Hyundai program—rather than generic statements of customer centricity.

Loyalty programs in the past have been based on the loyalty earned through transactions such as miles or segments flown or the amount of money spent on travel. Some thought had been given to the incorporation of other factors, such as customer experience and the lifetime value of a customer. However, lack of actionable data prevented any actions in this direction. Going forward, however, experience, personalization, and transparency (all three through effective engagement) are likely to become the drivers of customer loyalty. Take the case of engagement. It has to be not only proactive, but also to suit the desire of a customer. The choice of channel refers not just to major categories such as social networks versus online and offline sales, but also to sub-categories within a category. For example, is the preference of a customer to engage through a particular social media network, such as Facebook, Instagram, LinkedIn, TikTok, Twitter, WeChat, or Weibo? In any case, there is the desire to engage in real time, through mobile devices, and from any geo-location. Finally, consider another potential development relating to loyalty programs. What if, to protect the environment, governments decide to implement charges for not only the frequency of travel, but also the distance traveled? Consequently, whereas the previous frequent flyer programs have been incentivizing passengers to travel more, the additional costs imposed by governments could result in disincentives to join frequent flyer programs. As with other areas of the airline business, branding and loyalty programs need to be redesigned from ground zero. This is an opportunity. Keep in mind a quote by the former UK Prime Minister, Sir Winston Churchill, "A pessimist sees the difficulty in every opportunity; an optimist sees the opportunity in every difficulty."

## Notes

1 Nicolaus Henke, Jordan Levine, and Paul McInerney, "Analytics Translator: The New Must-Have Role," McKinsey & Company, February 2018.

2 Sinan Aral, *The Hype Machine* (New York: Currency, Random House, 2020).

3 Amrutha Shridhar, "Understanding the Path to Purchase: 2020 Consumer Types," *Euromonitor International*, June 2020.

4 Nawal K. Taneja, *Re-Platforming the Airline Business* (New York: Routledge, 2019).

5 Jill Menze, "Sabre, Google to Launch Tech Platform Driving Personalization in Travel," *PhocusWire*, October 23, 2020. www.phocuswire.com/sabre-google-to-launch-tech-platform-driving-personalization-in-travel

6　Elizabeth J. Altman and Frank Nagle, "Accelerating Innovation," *MIT Sloan Management Review*, Summer 2020, Vol. 61, No. 4, pp. 24–30.

7　Rita McGrath and Ryan McManus, "Discovery-Driven Digital Transformation: Learning Your Way to a New Business Model," *Harvard Business Review*, May–June 2020, pp. 124–33.

8　https://knoema.com/infographics/egyydzc/us-population-by-age-and-generation-in-2020.

9　Jason Dorsey and Denise Villa, *Zconomy: How Gen Z Will Change the Future of Business—and What to Do About It* (New York: Harper Business, 2020), pp. 93–94.

10　Brian Halligan, "The Experience Disrupters," *MIT Sloan Management Review*, Spring 2020, Vol. 61, No. 3, pp. 77–81.

11　Dennis Schaal, "Google is Providing Search Data to Air France, Lufthansa, Other Airlines Looking to Decide Which Routes to Restart," *Skift*, June 26, 2020.

12　Nawal K. Taneja, *Transforming Airlines: A Flight Plan for Navigating Structural Changes* (New York: Routledge, 2020), ch. 7.

13　Kindra Hall, *Stories that Stick: How Storytelling Can Captivate Customers, Influence Audiences, and Transform Your Business* (New York: HarperCollins, 2019).

14　Al Ries and Jack Trout, *Positioning: The Battle for Your Mind* (New York: Warner Books, 1981).

15　Lawrence Ingrassia, *Billion Dollar Brand Club: How Dollar Shave Club, Warby Parker, and other distributors are remaking what we buy* (New York: Henry Holt, 2020).

16　Myriam Sidibe, "Marketing Meets Mission: Learning from Brands that Have Taken on Global Health Challenges," *Harvard Business Review*, May–June 2020, p. 137.

17　United Airlines, "MileagePlus Investor Presentation," June 15, 2020. https://ir.united.com/static-files/1c0f0c79-23ca-4fd2-80c1-cf975348bab9

# 5 Moving toward an "informationalized" business

The emergence of either of the two scenarios (continuous improvements or elastic supply) will require a new paradigm for making decisions to adapt effectively to the changing marketplace. Some key dimensions of decisions, going forward, are:

- the need to start the planning processes from ground zero, given the lack of relevant data to forecast traffic, leading, in turn, to the need for planning with bottom-up approaches,
- the need to make decisions with greater speed, in light of the speed of change in the marketplace,
- the need to take greater risks with the use of data that is no longer robust,
- the need to plan with the use of decision-driven data as opposed to making data-driven decisions,
- the need to make decisions that are much more proactive rather than reactive,
- the need to monitor operations in real time, and then make appropriate decisions, and
- the recognition that the experience of recoveries from past disruptions is less relevant.

These dimensions of the decision-making process alone imply an urgent need for the development and use of digital assets, the realignment of organizations, and the movement toward the development of "informationalized" businesses to increase the scale and scope of digital transformation, not just physical transformation.

Even during normal times, decision making was challenging in the airline business, given the enormous complexity and huge investments in assets, such as aircraft and long-term contracts with labor. But the decision-making process has become more challenging during this time of increased uncertainty, not to mention a sequence of uncertainties. Even prior to the current disruption, data-driven decisions represented more of a hope than a reality within the airline industry, despite the fact some airlines do have access to data some of which may no longer be relevant. The limited use of data-based decisions, a relative statement, tended to be a cultural issue. Now, with the availability of digital assets—increasing amounts of new data, real-time analytics, advanced technologies (such as machine learning), greater use of networks, and insightful visualizations to conduct real-time analyses—it is possible to improve the decision-making process under much greater uncertainty. In addition, it is not just the availability of more data, but the costs of collecting, storing, and processing data have been decreasing rapidly.[1] As for real-time smart analytics, their use had also been limited. What is needed now more than ever, are changes in mindsets and organizational structures and cultures to work with meaningful data, real-time analytics, and data scientists who can translate business challenges into data-analytic-technology solutions to develop and implement viable strategies. Working with meaningful data means looking first at the questions that need to be answered and then collecting the relevant data to analyze (decision-driven data) as opposed to using the currently available data to make decisions (data-driven decisions).

Take, for example, the limited relevance of the experience from the past, such as the terrorist attacks in 2001 and the financial crisis in 2008. In fact, some of the past experiences could even be to guard against biases based on the experience from some past disruptions. Take, for example, the strategy to reduce prices, in some markets, to bring traffic back. If a person is afraid to fly for health reasons, a lower price is not likely to be of much value. Now, more than ever, an airline needs to analyze the behavior of consumers and businesses and the reasons for changes in their behavior so as to offer different segments different bundles to address their needs, while at the same time improving, as discussed in the previous chapter, changing dimensions of customer experience. For each customer, it is now necessary to examine travel behavior relating to logic and emotions. The object now is to reinvent the airline business by developing more flexibility and more agility:

- by evaluating innovative market-oriented ideas, by conducting disciplined experiments to make data-based decisions that are aligned with an airline's vision,
- by enabling managers to use relevant data and analytics to analyze the situations themselves rather than relying on data analysts and data scientists, given that they know the business context, and
- by collaborating and coordinating with partners in the ecosystem, particularly within the dynamic digital ecosystem.

Similarly, the need to conduct operations in real time and in an integrated framework is now more urgent. Such a planning framework will reduce costs and make planning groups in other functions much more productive and provide more flexibility.

## Transforming business models around digital assets

Airlines have clearly invested heavily in their physical assets (aircraft and airport facilities, for example) and a few digital assets (brands and their loyalty programs, for example) that can be leveraged to optimize the returns from the physical assets. However, as discussed in the previous chapter, it is now possible to explore the development of additional digital assets to drive additional value from the physical assets. Figure 4.1 displayed three major components of additional digital assets—data, analytics, and networks. It is the combination of these digital assets, coupled with the existing digital assets that can, in fact, help to transform the airline business, not just the maximization of the value that can be derived from the physical assets. Moreover, the key insight from the best practices of some leading businesses is that the three traditional core competencies of a business can be reinforced by the three new competencies (see Figure 4.2).

The impact of this disruption has been so intensive that the business now needs to be restarted from ground zero, given the unprecedented nature of changes and the future uncertainty. In some ways, it is like starting with a blank sheet. The question, as raised by Eric Leopold, in his thought leadership piece in Chapter 7, is: Should the rebuilding process be conducted using conventional norms, or new norms? The benefit of using conventional norms is that the process is relatively easy to implement. However, it does not provide the agility needed to handle new disruptions. While planning with new norms is much more difficult, it can provide flexibility and agility, going forward. And, it is in the context of new norms that airlines and related businesses (such as airports) can think about the use of digital assets to maximize the value of physical assets. Chapters 3 and 4 provided some examples of the development and use of such assets within the airline sector. Consider two others sectors, airports and aircraft manufacturers.

Take, for instance, the need for integrated planning between airlines and airports. Whereas, historically, the financial risk for large airports was fairly minimal, going forward, business models of airports will also be expected to change significantly. The realignment of their business model will involve more than forecasting the timing of the return of the demand. On their part, airports will need a more comprehensive understanding of the business models of all of their stakeholders—passenger airlines, cargo and express carriers, ground handlers, concessionaires, aircraft manufacturers, and government policy makers, for example. And, of course, they would need to have a thorough understanding of the behavior of passengers using their airports. This is where the need for integrated planning between airlines and airports comes into play, not to mention the role of digital marketing. There are major differences relating to the needs of passenger airlines that operate mostly origin-destination (O&D) flights versus those that conduct hub-and-spoke systems and between full-service airlines and low-cost carriers. There are also differences among airlines relating to their operational units (see Figure 5.1).

How much information do airports have on passengers in general, let alone passengers segmented by O&D versus those making connections, or frequency of travel? How much effort should airports devote in segmenting customers and using data analytics? At some airports, traffic forecasts were way off anyway,

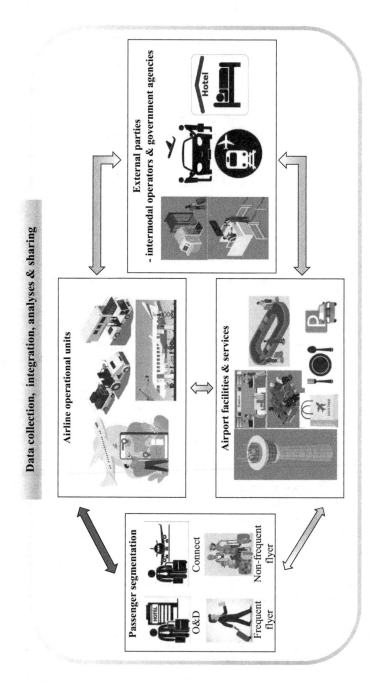

*Figure 5.1* Collaboration between airlines and airports to create, capture, and deliver value

as they did not see some long-term trends, such as the increasing market share of low-cost carriers in such countries as India. The thought leadership piece by Kapil Kaul and Binit Somaia in Chapter 7 points out, for example, that the domestic traffic in India shifted from being almost 100 percent on full-service airlines to more than 60 percent on low-cost carriers, six years later in 2010. Airports can now obtain a lot more information on passengers by using technology to engage with them. As the arrow in Figure 5.1 shows, the link between airlines and passengers is stronger than the link between airports and passengers. That requires an understanding of the role of technology from its role in functional areas to its role in strategic areas. How should this information be collected and shared between airlines and airports? How about coordinating the airports' loyalty program with those of airlines? Going forward, there could be a disagreement about the impact of government policies, relating to changes in bilateral agreements and open-skies policies. Finally, how about a common understanding between airlines and airports about the role of long-haul, single-aisle aircraft, about intermodal transportation systems, and about aerial on-demand services offered with the use of existing aircraft or new electric vehicles and by existing operators, or new operators?

Leading airports have already begun to rethink how they would build their operations from ground zero, by improving their own internal functional capabilities as well as the opportunities to collaborate much more effectively with their different stakeholders—passenger airlines, cargo operators, general aviation operators, ground handlers, concessionaires, and government agencies. The integration process displayed in Figure 5.1 goes much further than just the integration of technologies. It also relates to the large-scale expansion plans of some airports, not to mention the regulation of airport charges, and the related decisions on the use of the single-till approach or the dual-till approach. The conventional business model of airports has focused on managing growth by (1) simply keeping up with the development of the needed infrastructure—runways, terminals, gates and ramps, parking garages, roadways to and from the terminals, and spaces for car-rental businesses and hotels, and (2) complying with regulations, relating to the environment (noise, emissions, and so forth), and the usage of airspace. The risk has always been considered to be low, primarily due to the ongoing growth in passenger traffic, despite the temporary reductions due to disruptions. See the thought leadership piece by Kapil Kaul and Binit Somaia in Chapter 7.

Strategically located and capacity-constrained airports, such as London Heathrow, New York-Kennedy, Hong Kong, and Tokyo-Narita have also had significant pricing power with their primary customers, namely airlines, and, in turn, with related businesses, such as concessionaires. Traffic in some regions, for example, Asia, and some countries, for example, China and India, was growing at such high rates that the development of new airports could not keep up with increases in demand. Now restarting operations from ground zero could finally focus on not just door-to-door travel, but also the often-discussed "last-mile" dimension of travel. Airports can play an important role in this area by collaborating and coordinating with existing stakeholders, such as governments, but also new players.

The availability of new technologies can enable the development and implementation of timely strategies to develop demand and get the industry back to the old normal, if that is the goal. Some of these technologies were not available during some of the past disruptions, such as the terrorist attacks in 2001, or even the financial crisis in 2008. Now airlines not only have different products, but there are also different channels of distribution, social networks (Facebook, Twitter, etc.), online platforms, and so forth. Examples of new products include subscription pricing and travel all you want passes, as recently introduced by an airline in China during the initial phase of the recovery. Plus new marketing tactics can now be implemented, tactics that are proactive rather than reactive. Airlines and airports have better technologies to listen to customers and employees and to engage with both of them. Examples include live chats, conversational chatbots, self-service systems and processes (enabling customers to find their own solutions), as well as technologies to collect much more data on consumers (qualitative and quantitative data) and to analyze data to see changing patterns. Airlines now have the capability to customize products and provide integrated experiences at the same time. They also have the capability to develop lifetime value of customers and, as such, the ability to segment customers differently and to interact with them differently.

Finally, they have access to real-time data on the key segments of customers, for example, information in the frequent flyer programs, segmented by much more meaningful criteria. These resources should enable better management of operational disruptions, for example, through the transmission of critical information via mobile devices, coupled with the use of relevant insightful predictive and prescriptive analytics. The key to achieving agility is to have real-time access to relevant data and to convert it into actionable insights. Airlines do have a lot of information to implement personalization techniques from the data on customer profiles, and from marketing systems, such as loyalty programs. And they can now use machine-learning algorithms to update the information on customers to be targeted while making them more effective personalized offers.

Can the power of data and systems help revenue managers in situations when revenue might be down, by as much as 80 percent? The answer would have to be a yes and a no. Yes, if it was just due to fewer people traveling, but no if the behavior of travelers has changed too, such as booking and cancellation patterns that were incorporated in the systems. Consequently, if the degree of uncertainty in the behavior has changed then managers need access to real-time data. As such, managers need not only more reliable data but also new sources of data. Demand is changing by the hour, depending on changes in health-related restrictions. As such, one new source of data could be the local governments' decisions on restrictions. The advance purchase segment has become much smaller. There is also the challenge of balancing the lower levels of demand and the desire to charge higher fares to passengers that are still traveling, to compensate for the empty middle seats.

The data-driven decision discussion, presented above, is valid as long as the data used are relevant and the business models are valid. Going forward, what would be the business models and the criteria: cash flow for the immediate future, or longer-term profitability and market positioning? When passengers are making bookings, they are looking at not just the itineraries and the prices, but also the brand of an airline, with respect to health and safety measures, as well as policies, such as social distancing procedures in the aircraft. As such, direct channels may be preferred to get relevant and real-time information. On the other hand, airlines need to balance the value of direct bookings versus bookings coming from third parties to simply generate traffic, not to mention the possibility of capturing higher-margin traffic. Airlines now have access to models and systems to find, evaluate, experiment, and monitor different options. And, data and technology can make computations possible and inexpensive. The requirement now is to have data that is relevant.

## Data and information technologies

Although the concept of big data and its value has been discussed since the beginning of this century, its role and value have been changing. To start with, the volume of data has been increasing at an exponential rate. A few years back, someone coined the phrase, data being the "new oil" for airlines. If one assumes that the author of the term was thinking in terms of "crude oil," then crude oil needs to be processed and refined before it can become jet fuel for an airline. Similarly, "raw data" can only become useful once it has been processed. Think about just a medium-size airline transporting 20 million passengers. Now think about even such a medium-size airline obtaining data from a variety of mobile devices and the internet of things. But now it is possible to store and process data more cost effectively to make it usable. The need for cost effectiveness is essential, given the increasing volumes of data that are needed for the use of some technologies, such as machine learning (a subset of artificial intelligence). On the other side, the availability of large volumes of data and the capability to process large volumes of data at speed and at low cost means that in some cases, it is not necessary to use samples. Or, now it is possible to increase the size of samples to get better information on patterns and behavior. And, the ability to recognize patterns and exceptions now adds more value for decision makers in a broad spectrum of areas, from engagement with customers and employees to the prediction of aircraft component failures.

The value of machine learning and algorithms has increased in the current environment where historical data has become less relevant and current data more important. Think about the value of predictive analytics in whether a shopper will make a reservation given the uncertainty of the flight departure for lockdown conditions or given their health-related concerns. Think also about the use of prescriptive analytics. Should the flight be scheduled, given the uncertainty relating to government regulations? It is also the availability of big data and advanced technologies that enable the use of increasingly sophisticated platforms (for example, full-service and open-collaboration platforms discussed in the last chapter) for airlines to not only meet the total mobility needs of customers, but also provide seamless and consistent experiences throughout the entire journey.

One key feature of big data (over and above the size of the data base and the speed with which data is being generated and stored) is the type of data that is being collected. The data being collected is no longer limited to the transactional and structured data framework. We can now have data relating to the behavior of customers derived from, for example, their behavior on the website of an airline. Data can also be in an unstructured form. Data can, for example, be in the form of images and videos (posted in social platforms), or human voice, captured during a conversation with a customer-contact agent. Again, the value of collecting, storing, processing, and evaluating behavioral and unstructured data, from every interaction with customers, can be more valuable than ever during this virus-led disruption. Moreover, valuable data exists outside of an airline's organization that can add more value. Here are some examples of the data coming from outside of the airline industry:

- location and movement of mobile devices,
- searches made using the powerful engines of Google and metasearch organizations,
- postings on social platforms,
- consumers' spending behavior observed by the use of credit cards,
- information coming from conventional and new types of distributors (for example, social networks), and
- pertinent information coming from partners in the travel-related value chain—airports, hotels, and car-rental businesses.

Although some of this information is not new, its use has been limited in the past, given the insufficient consistency and integrity of the data, not so much for the data coming from internal sources, but for the data coming from external sources. Even more important, there are challenges relating not just to the consistency of the data (different formats, for example) and to the untimeliness of the data, but to its use, relating, for example, to visualization. However, state-of-the-art developments relating to data sources, data usage, and data display have progressed substantially. For example, until recently, airlines were still using the conventional visualization systems. Now advanced visualization techniques (based on artificial intelligence technology, for example) are available to not only show data in much more meaningful ways, but also relate to key performance indicators. Different decision makers can use different key performance indicators to use interactive visualization tools—interactive dashboards—to track, analyze, monitor, and visually display information to users within the operational, commercial, and financial areas. Interactive dashboards are now more useful, as they can not only handle more and different types of data, but also be hooked to systems with models so that they have the capability to predict, and not just monitor.

The real value of data, analytics, and networks is not just related to bringing more innovation within the operations and marketing spaces, but also in the execution of strategy. Given the complexity of the airline business and frequency as well as severity of disruptions, the speed in the decision-making process is now more essential. Think about how slow the progress has been with decisions in strategic alliances among the airlines, not to mention the partnerships with airports. And the key to developing relationships with partners, whether airports or distributors, is trust. And that means finding a way to include partners in the strategy-development phases at the right times and in the right places. It is trust that will enable the sharing of data in real time and the alignment of processes. Now, more than ever, there is a need for "outside-in" thinking to generate ideas and take a serious look at experimentation than the conventional approach of "tried-and-tested" beliefs. The focus is now on flexibility and resiliency, applying not just to the whole airline organization, but also to individual functions, such as commercial and operational.

In the airline industry, data has been growing at an exponential rate, with data being generated by airlines themselves and by partners in the travel chain (for example, airports), not to mention data generated by customers and employees. And, more data is now coming from many other sources, as described above—from social media posts, location and movement of mobile devices, and the internet of things. The challenge, therefore, is not the lack of sufficient data but its effective consumption—to obtain insights from the raw data and to take actions, through the use of real-time analytics, expanding networks, and insight-adding visualizations. Basically, there have been a number of semi-related barriers to the development of actionable insights from data. For example:

- Older generation data continues to sit in different silos in different functional units within an airline. Although some airlines are progressing in the breakdown of the silo system, they have a long way to go. In some cases, even within a given silo, data is not integrated. Some departments and individuals continue to have strong control over the data they have and the way that data is used. And, data is not available in different formats that can be used by different decision makers within the operational, financial, and commercial functions.
- Data has been coming from different channels and different devices used by customers and generated at different touchpoints. The challenge is to connect the data coming from different channels and place it in consistent formats.
- There is the challenge of not understanding the behavior of customers, not to mention that the behavior is changing. Some channels are relatively easy to monitor, such as the data coming from the passenger service systems

(PSSs) and airline websites. Some are more difficult, such as social media platforms.

- There is also the problem of a customer using different forms of identity to acquire different elements of the trip. The person is still the same person although the identities used are very different, for instance, a passport used at one place and a driver's license used at another place. There is also the challenge of one person using her desktop computer to make a reservation for someone else.

- Within the airline industry, the use of real-time analytics (for example, prescriptive analytics) has been limited for converting data into insightful information to make decisions. The use of advanced technologies, such as artificial intelligence (along with complex econometrics) and the internet of things, discussed below, is only at a beginning stage. Moreover, some users of data have been concerned about the limitations of the data, such as the integrity of the data, and the difficulty to separate noise from signals.

- Many airlines continue to work with legacy systems and legacy processes that cannot use new forms of data that are becoming available. Where airlines have taken some steps toward becoming data driven, the steps taken have been small. For example, a few airlines have brought on board data scientists in their IT departments, a decision that does not help much if airlines continue to work with legacy systems and legacy processes, and even worse, legacy thinking.

- There is still a need to reskill and upskill relevant employees at all levels to maximize the use of information in real time and to provide personalized services. Moreover, there is now a serious need to evaluate, employ, inspire, and retain the right talent—professionals that have both the technical knowledge and the management knowledge to handle business issues.

Airlines often claim that they are extremely rich with data. In some ways, they are as long as we are talking about old types of data. However, airlines tend to be relatively poor on information and insights, due to the inability to "informationalize" data, even if it is the old type of data. The value is in converting data (old and new) into insights. This would be the same for processing crude oil to convert into jet fuel. And, it is the insights from the data that lead to disciplined thinking that, in turn, leads to actions to develop and implement strategies that minimize risk. Even with access to abundant old data and the enlightening analytics available, there have been times when decisions were made based more on instinct rather than an analysis of data, relating to, say, patterns. On the positive side, data can now be converted into information that, with the help of, as mentioned above, online visualization techniques and innovative and interactive dashboards, can even be used by non-technical people to make effective decisions. In some cases, even the use of models has been simplified for non-technical managers to test scenarios relating to routes, markets, and competitors.

There are two key considerations for basing decisions on data. The first is to ask the right questions, to define clear key performance indicators, and second, to find the right data to answer questions, and to substantiate answers. Think about some key questions relating to customer experience (as discussed in the previous chapter), and the insights needed to answer such questions. Even worse is the situation when what is important is not being measured, for example, (1) the market value of loyalty programs, and (2) the value of proactive engagements with customers and employees. Recall the value of the statement, "what gets measured, gets managed." And it is data, coupled with real-time analytics and changes in processes that can help to accelerate the development and implementation of strategies during disruptions, not to mention the ability to conduct experiments. Consider, for a moment, the role of key performance indicators. Conventional indicators can lead to wrong decisions when markets are changing so rapidly. Thus, there should be a creative, multidisciplinary team that is permanently monitoring and questioning the indicators, data, models, algorithms, and processes.

Commercial departments can now have access to a broad spectrum of data, some coming from their finance, commercial, and operations departments at granular levels, for example, data on revenue accounting, consumer sentiments, and crew concerns. The important question, however, is how this data can be mined with the use of analytics for internal decisions and how it can be monetized, when used by partners. Moreover, qualitative data, coming from surveys, emails, and social media, can be just as important as quantitative data, if not more important. Moving forward, the two types of data combined can enable airlines to create new opportunities during this unprecedented time to predict trends and optimize current operations. However, both quantitative and qualitative data need to be cleaned, filtered, and put into contexts from the perspectives of different decision makers to add much value in commercial and operational functions.

Locational data can now be used by airlines, in addition to the conventional data from DB1b sources (data coming from the US Department of Transportation), to understand behavioral characteristics to identify purchasing decisions. In the airline industry, there is the concept of "latent demand," trips that are either being made by other modes of transportation or trips starting from different airports than the airports of preference. The decision could be due to lack of air service or lack of desirable service, such as nonstop flights. If service from a nearby airport is not purchased, it could be due to the quality of the service, or if it is purchased, it could be due to a lower fare. As such, one example of latent demand would be when a passenger flies in and out of one airport, say San Francisco, when there is a much more convenient airport nearby say, San Jose. Or, a person uses surface transportation because airline service either does not exist, or the price is too high, or some combination.

Location data, being captured from smartphones, can help airline marketers identify consumer behavioral characteristics important to the purchase of air travel. This data can come from a variety of sources, such as towers, and apps on devices, such as weather apps and apps that are used to show location of stores, for example. Users have the option to allow the use of the location of their devices, by opting-in and allowing the data to be shared. Consider, first, the case that requires a better understanding of the underlying behavioral characteristics of existing demand for air travel. Location data can identify where people live or start from, which airport they fly from, and which airport they fly to, and finally, their ultimate destination after landing at an airport. In particular, location data can identify the true point of origin and destination (not just the airports for enplanement and deplanement) to help airline route planners and pricing groups. In some cases, larger airports, in densely populated areas, attract more passengers because of the availability of higher frequency, for example, San Francisco vs. San Jose, or Toronto vs. Buffalo, or Cologne vs. Frankfurt.

To a passenger, the frequency advantage might be of higher value than the extra time needed to get to the airport, including the hassles of traveling through congested airports. Travel through less convenient and congested airports could also be explained by memberships in airline loyalty programs. It is the locational data that can help identify the exact geographical starting point and the ground travel time for passengers using the larger airports (with higher frequency of service), to see if passengers could be diverted to smaller airports from a ground time perspective. Location data can also identify long drive times, in general, as well as the long drive times accepted by groups, say a family of four. Moreover, location data can be used to determine whether the starting point is a home or a hotel, based, for example, on how long the mobile device was at that location, say, 8 hours. If the location has changed by 500 kilometers in, say, 4 hours, it is probably a trip. The mode of transportation can also be identified, based on the speed of movement of the device.

Moreover, location data can be overlaid on other data, such as the census data, and the airline origin and destination data. And the location data can also enrich the loyalty programs. Consider also the fact that visualization techniques can be used not just to look at large quantities of data, but also to discover trends. As such, location data can be useful for both schedulers and for marketers. Schedulers can see, for example, not only the exact point of origin and the exact point of destination, but they can also determine if the flight taken was nonstop or made a connection. Airlines can "see" passengers who are making connections and suggest that they could have taken a nonstop flight. Marketers can also see the exact location of a traveler at an airport to undertake direct marketing in real time. From the privacy perspective, the location data shows just the location of the device, and does not provide information about the user, such as name, age, and gender.

Let us consider the role of emerging technologies. Although emerging technologies have been available in the business world for some time, their use in the airline sector has been limited. Take artificial intelligence and the internet of things, just as two examples. With artificial intelligence and its various divisions (machine learning, deep learning, and neural networks), the concept is for machines (computers) to learn from data and to make inferences. In extremely basic terms, machine learning deals with computer algorithms through which machines can learn from data and then "train" themselves through experience. Deep learning and neural networks are more advanced applications of machine learning and they are beginning to learn from different representations of data, such as text, images, and sound. In the airline industry, the increasing volume of data, the newness of data, and the relevancy of the data can be particularly helpful to deploy different divisions of artificial intelligence to improve decision-making processes.

For a large airline, artificial intelligence can add much value in the commercial space (in the areas of pricing, personalized services, and conversational shopping, for example), in the financial space (retention of customers—corporate accounts and travel management companies, for example), and in the operations space (flight, crew, maintenance planning, and the day of operations, for example). To get the full benefit of artificial intelligence, however, requires the transformation of many business processes, as diverse as passenger reservations and aircraft dispatching. Moreover, occasionally, an individual technology may not be deployable by itself and may require a combination of technologies, sometimes referred to as "technology stacks." Sophisticated web and mobile applications require, for example, the use of technology stacks—software products, programming languages, and so forth, within the framework of both the front-end and the back-end functions and processes. This raises a significant question about new technologies. Can a business case be made for the deployment of a specific technology, say artificial intelligence, or the internet of things, let alone a technology stack, in the conventional framework of an airline's ROI and scalability? The answer is yes, if the focus is on achieving outcomes, not on the use of emerging technologies to improve some aspect of a function.

Leaving aside the financial considerations of a technology or a technology stack, the real challenge relates to the mindsets of users. Are decision makers in airlines willing, for example, to accept the recommendations generated by an artificial intelligence system? Are they willing to provide meaningful feedback? Major challenges continue to exist in the conventional planning departments of airlines, such as revenue management and pricing, as well as the dispatching of aircraft. The acceptance of the recommendations made by an artificial intelligence system is particularly difficult for people working in the operations systems control centers in the management of disruptions. This situation is unfortunate in that these systems can make recommendations, having taken into consideration orders of magnitude more variables than possible by humans and the results produced can be game changing. The areas impacted can be as diverse as operations (predictive maintenance and inventory management, for example) on one side and commercial (pricing and customer experiences, for example) on the other side.

Take a second example of technology, the internet of things, which can have an increasing number of applications within the aviation sector, airlines and airports, for example. Internet of things can add even more value when combined with other technologies, such as artificial intelligence, biometrics, and robotics. The airline industry works with numerous sectors within the aviation sector where each sector has its own processes, systems, and technologies. Take, for example, airports. They continue to work with their own sensors, beacons, and biometric systems. There needs to be a common vision for the use of advanced technologies, such as the internet of things. The point is that airlines and airports need to collaborate at a deeper level to create, capture, and deliver value (see Figure 5.1). The important point in this collaboration is not just the collection, analyses, and integration of data, but the willingness to explore new data sources and to share data. Consider, not only the strategic value of the biometric data for improving the degree of personalization of services provided to individual travelers, but also the issue of privacy that needs to be protected, in the use of biometrics that deals with facial recognition. The real power of sensors now is not only in collecting and monitoring information in real time, but also in transmitting the information using wireless technologies, particularly the newer generation of cellular networks, such as 5G. Some of these technologies described can also be combined to provide new capabilities, such as hyper-connectivity, resulting from the combination of the internet of things, cloud computing, and 5G.

Vast amounts of data being collected in real time, from different sources, can now be analyzed and mined using cloud-based technologies to produce insights, again, in real time. As such, the use of sensors can take some areas, as diverse as operations and customer experience, to new heights. Again, it is the combination of technologies (beacons, sensors, and biometrics, for example) that is now more critical than ever to improve operations (for example, on-time performance) and customer experience, in terms of airport processing. Then, within the aircraft, inflight connectivity is increasing as is the connectedness of electronic devices. These technologies can now take care of, not only passenger security, but also health-related aspects, for travelers, airlines, and government agencies.

## Managing operations in real time

Consider the value of data-based decisions in the operations space. Decisions in the operations space need to be made in real time, but the constraints relate generally to data. Figure 5.2 displays four dimensions of data that can constrain the decision-making process in real time—data access, data management, data sharing, and data monitoring. Data management, in turn, relates to data consolidation, data retrieval (that needs to be instant), data analytics (broadening the use of both predictive and prescriptive analytics), and the use of visualization techniques. Consider the operations within operations systems control centers. Typically, these centers are responsible for four functions. Flight dispatching provides critical and detailed information to pilots to navigate from an airport of origin to an airport of destination: such information as payload on board, fuel needed, flight altitudes, flight speeds, and so forth. The second function, flight following, is involved through the entire trip, from take-off to landing. The

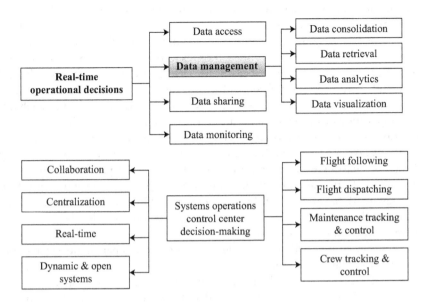

*Figure 5.2* Managing operations in real time

third function is the tracking and control of maintenance. The fourth function is related to the tracking and control of the crew.

Controllers in the center make decisions by monitoring data, by coordinating operations, and by controlling operations. They need to make decisions in real time while ensuring the safety of passengers, crews, and aircraft. And, decisions must reflect not only safety-related compliance (for crew and aircraft) but also operating cost considerations. In order to achieve both goals (safety and costs), controllers need to make decisions that are:

- collaborative—involving consideration of all stakeholders (including aircraft manufacturers and not only airports, but also groups within airports—ground handlers, for example),
- centralized, using one set of data that is shared,
- made in real time with respect to control, and
- made within a dynamic and an open system.

On the costs side, think not only about the costs of maintenance, but also about the costs of compliance, and the added costs of complexity, not to mention the added costs of using legacy systems and legacy infrastructure. The value of relevant data and analytics is not only to enable the management of operations in real time, but also to simplify operations. Think also about the aircraft that have been stored, some in the "active group" and some in the "prolonged group." These two groups have been stored in different locations based on such considerations as weather conditions, available staff, and the availability of the relevant maintenance facilities.

It is digital assets that can provide enormous value for controllers in the systems operations control centers. For example, data can be consolidated and placed in the cloud so that it can be accessed by any sub-function in real time and shared among different sub-functions. The sorted, consolidated, and integrated data can then be used smartly with the use of real-time analytics and applications to produce relevant and actionable insights, using new visualization techniques to monitor trends and to take actions proactively. These decisions take into account, for example, during irregular operations, not only the traditional three considerations (aircraft, crews, and passengers), but now also the satisfaction and experience of passengers (plus baggage and connection management), based on the values of passengers. Moreover, optimizations take into consideration not only savings in operational costs, but also the value of an increase in on-time performance.

Consider some challenges facing the operations department—challenges relating, for example, to unplanned maintenance and the relatively poor on-time performance. The challenge and opportunity lie in the ability to obtain even more data and to manage data, old and new, more effectively to produce data-driven and actionable insights. And managing data much more effectively will provide an opportunity not only to implement dynamic pricing in the commercial department, but also dynamic scheduling in the operations department. Think about it. Airline schedulers thought that they had a real problem when they had to change their schedules due to the grounding of the Boeing 737 MAX aircraft in spring 2019 and the uncertainty as to when the aircraft might return to the skies. That challenge was relatively minor compared to the current challenge when schedules are changing by the week; in some cases, by the day. The challenge of managing aircraft delays and improving on-time performance can be resolved by managing the "day of operations" function much more efficiently. According to Captain Michael Baiada, variance "is the root cause of most airline delay/congestion we see in our airspace and in our airports." His extensive research shows that airlines must drive variation "out of their entire curb to curb production process, especially in the arrival flow."[2]

The focus on network, fleet, schedule planning and pricing, going forward, as discussed in Chapter 3, will be on agility, at the tactical level and the strategic level, as well as at the operations and customer levels. This virus-led disruption is shedding important light on the need for ultra-fast decisions. In the previous disruptions, airlines could move aircraft and capacity around their networks fairly quickly. During this disruption, everything can and did come to a standstill. Nothing was moving for months during the recovery period. And, there could easily be other disruptions that are just as powerful as the Coronavirus-related disruption. A new disruption could come in the short term and be related to the Coronavirus in the form of new waves. It could come in the longer term and be related to dramatic changes in the climate (discussed in

Chapter 2), or geopolitical events, or cybersecurity, or totally new forms of transportation (such as urban air mobility, door-to-door services, hyperloop capsules, and so forth), or some combination.

## New forms of organizational alignment

Airlines run complex businesses. All functional groups face a common challenge, resolving conflicts between different objectives. While data, analytics, and technologies can help to resolve conflicts, the challenge is to know what the company's objective is—on-time performance or customer experience, for example. This is easier said than done. How does a controller, in a systems operations control center, measure customer experience? Is it the experience of customers that are on the ground, or those on an airplane? How are the tradeoffs to be evaluated? How can performance be measured in any case? Whose performance, an aircraft, or its crew, or both? Is it even possible to do both, maximize on-time performance and customer experience? Relevant data and real-time analytics can now help optimize decisions with full consideration to all aspects, aircraft, crew, ground operations, maintenance, airport services and facilities, and, of course, passengers. Keep in mind the complexity of the problem. It is not just that the passenger experience must be considered, but that customers are looking for experience that is now different, even though they still want it to be seamless and consistent (see Figure 4.3 in the previous chapter). However, what does that mean to controllers in operations, whose priority is always, first, on safety, and then on the operational aspects, aircraft and their crews? Yes, customers are considered, but lower on the priority list, and even then, in broad terms, such as the number of passengers affected and, with some information on their connections, but with very little information on their needs or their value to airlines. The challenge is threefold.

• There are too many variables and too little time to make a decision.
• Many systems being used are legacy systems and they are not even integrated.
• The processes are also legacy to deal with the dynamic situations that are now much more complex.

As a result, decisions made by controllers, working with limited resources (in terms of data, systems, and processes) lead to optimizations based on the short term, rather than a longer-term optimization. In any case, decisions tend to reflect the local situations rather than the broader operational aspects of an airline. For example, a decision can relate to the immediate responsibility of a particular group, a particular aircraft or fleet, a particular connecting bank, or a particular airport. What happens at this hub matters only to a particular group of controllers. What the impact is on the next hub is of less concern to this group. Moreover, the sum of optimizations of numerous local decisions may not necessarily provide an optimization at the global level.

With the use of large data bases (old and new), real-time analytics, and emerging technologies discussed above, it is now possible to automate many decisions within an operations department. In the past, controllers struggled with their decisions as there are too many related areas—flight ops, ground ops, and maintenance, for example. Then there are sub-areas within a given area. Take the area of crews, for example. There are considerations relating to crew assignment, crew rostering, and crew training, just to name three. Even when controllers were helped by automated decisions within one area, say crews, they faced difficulties in integrating all functions within operations, let alone with the commercial groups and sub-groups within the operations and the commercial groups, too. Now, situations have become even more complex and more dynamic. On the positive side, however, decisions can now be automated with the emergence of new technologies, such as artificial intelligence. However, while artificial intelligence is a powerful technology, learning systems, consistency, stability, robustness, and the interpretational capabilities also have a role to play. As such, human input is still required in the case of a major operational disruption. However, relevant data and analytics can now facilitate the decision-making process by people through a realignment of the organization. For example, technology can now help to break, to some extent, the data silos and some analytics can be applied at the enterprise level, rather than at a functional level. Next, data can not only be updated in real time, but also accessed by all, and with greater transparency. As for legacy systems, the real challenge continues to be the existence of legacy and linear-thinking ways of working within the control centers, and the strong leaning toward risk-aversion and toward experimentation.

Of all the departments within an airline, the decision-making process within operations needs to be not only more data-based and based on relevant data, but also integrated within all sub-groups within operations and within the sub-groups within the commercial and financial functions. And it is this level of integration that is now possible with the use of large amounts of new data (coming from new sources), real-time analytics, and new technologies, such as artificial intelligence. The data-based aspect does, however, require that the data be comprehensive and represent a single source of truth. It is the integration aspect of the decision-making process that will automatically take into consideration all objectives, some of which are likely to be conflicting. Sophisticated algorithms can now take into consideration multiple aspects of the decision and convert data into insights and insights into actions. It is the quick analyses of all options that can help identify the ideal option. Again, the idea is not to replace a human, but to support a human in selecting the right option, based on all the variables, and the creative input of cross-functional considerations.

Let us suppose that on a particular day four aircraft are down out of a fleet of 100 at the major hub. Which flights are to be cancelled and which ones are to be delayed? Which aircraft are to be exchanged and which crews are to be exchanged? These decisions are not new. Only, now complexity has increased, partly because of the uncertainty of customers keeping their reservations (due to health concerns), and partly due to the uncertainty of competitors' schedules. There is also now more uncertainty about the crews and about their health. Past data is not of much relevance. Whereas before, people in operations did pay some attention to economic considerations, such as the number of passengers impacted and, in some cases, the value of the passengers impacted, decisions are now more complex and the situations much more dynamic, requiring organizational realignments. The economic impact is greater, given the tight financial condition of airlines and the added challenge and opportunity of transferring passengers on interline flights, not just the flights of alliance partners. On the positive side, controllers now also have access to predictive analytics that can predict the availability of crews and their connections, aircraft and their gates, and catering trucks and their gates. The key difference that data and analytics make is to provide operational controllers more comprehensive information and in real time to assess different options.

In addition, prescriptive analytics can come up with recommendations that a human can accept or reject, based on unique situations and unique priorities. Even more important, these advanced systems, using large data bases, real-time analytics, and technologies, such as artificial intelligence, can help controllers know the impact of a change in the entire network of the airline, not just at a particular location, something that is next to impossible to accomplish with human intervention only. The idea is to optimize the decision-making process, leveraging the power of the data, the analytics, the technologies, as well the capability of controllers. There are four key considerations relating to the optimization: economics (revenue and cost implications), operational performance (on-time performance, and utilization of aircraft, crew, gates, and so forth), customer experience, and employee experience.

Take the first consideration—economics. In some cases within airlines, the issue is not the role of technology, but its justification on an economic basis. Take the case of the increasing interest in developing touchless and frictionless travel. This concept is not new. In the recent past, airlines could easily have used new technologies, such as blockchain, the internet of things, and biometrics to develop touchless and frictionless travel. However, the progress made was limited, given the difficulty to justify such initiatives on the conventional basis of the return on investment, data privacy considerations, and the considerations of sharing data. Now, the justification is related not only to customer experience, but also to the goal of getting the business started. The concept is much more feasible now from the viewpoint of the available technology and the capability to work on full-service platforms that encompass areas, ranging from the self-service bag drop offs, to biometric screening (including the new health-related checks), to consumers bringing their own devices on the aircraft. Contactless operations will not only be desired by customers, but they will also reduce airlines' operating costs and improve customer experience. This concept will go far beyond the current crisis. Think about the value the medical sector has achieved from tele-health. Going forward many office visits will be replaced by conference calls. There is no turning back of the tele-health system within the medical space.

Take the second consideration, relating to operations, say, maintenance. Technology can now take predictive maintenance to even higher levels. For example, multiple sensors are monitoring data on a particular engine on a particular aircraft, while artificial intelligence can be used to analyze data coming from sensors on all other aircraft, to show patterns and exceptions, for example, to improve the predictive capability of component failures. Similarly, sensors located in the entire aircraft can connect data and combine the data coming from other aircraft in the fleet. Sensors providing data from an entire aircraft, as well as the entire fleet, increase the volume and richness of data and increase the value of using artificial intelligence and cloud computing. Moreover, it is now becoming clear that artificial intelligence can help not only in the area of predictive maintenance, but also in the management of broader aspects of the management of maintenance costs, relating to inventory of parts (needed and available) and the availability of aircraft, before and after the maintenance work is completed.

The key message is that the decision-making process can be improved with the use of data through the use of algorithms—particularly helpful in three areas, commercial, financial, and operations. Decisions based on rules, instincts, and intuition can now be upgraded. In practice, however, there is still a conflict as to who is making the decision, the system or the human. The important point is not that human intervention is not needed, but it is the data coming from the human intervention that trains the artificial intelligent systems. After all, a human can always override an algorithm-based recommendation, even though the machine-made recommendation is likely to have taken into consideration many more variables and much more data. Consequently, the human can look at the situation differently. It is not that the human has been replaced by a machine, but that the human now has the time to monitor and analyze other developments to mitigate threats and seize opportunities.

Take the third consideration, relating to customers. How is the information on delays presented to passengers, for instance? It would have different impact depending on how it is presented. Is a 2-hour delay presented at one time, at the beginning, or in increments of 30 minutes? It is one thing to say that operational staff should consider customers, but does the frontline operational staff even have the full information on the delay and on the customers? Again, this is not a new challenge. Only now powerful data-based systems are available to support controllers in real time through which optimizations can be made not only having considered all aspects (operations-related such as aircraft, crews, maintenance, slots, and customers), but also with optimizations made at system levels.

Take the fourth consideration, relating to employees. In the case of the crew, considerations relate not just to hard facts, such as crew legality, but also some dimensions of employee engagement that can impact costs and employee satisfaction—the "hidden costs and values." Data-based systems can now add even more value, given the availability of new types of data, coming from existing and new sources.

All four considerations—economics, operations, customers, and employees—involve the use of metrics. However, operational performance is not easy to define and measure, although some elements, such as on-time performance, are. What about other considerations, such as the performance at a system level, as opposed to at a local level? Is it on-time performance of a particular aircraft, or of the connecting bank? How do we account for the fact that in some markets block times have been artificially inflated? Going forward, block times will be impacted by the adaptation of health-related measures and reduction in the number of operations. Then there are differences, such as the value of an on-time departure from a hub, or an on-time departure from an outstation with an aircraft flying to another outstation. Even with respect to passengers, are we talking about connecting passengers, or all passengers? Are we considering frequent travelers (who may travel once every week) or infrequent travelers (who may travel once every two years)? Some flights are identified as critical flights, by market or the time of the day, such as the first flight in the morning so as not to end up with creeping delays. What about the passengers on a flight that is considered to be less critical from a controller's perspective? How much should the last flight of the day be delayed to ensure that all connecting passengers are accommodated to avoid hotel costs? How much consideration should be given to the baggage of the connecting passengers? Again, none of these considerations are new, but now data-based systems can facilitate the decision-making process of controllers in timely and cost-efficient manners with much more comprehensive information on aircraft, crew, and passengers.

The need to make decisions with speed and data exists in all departments of an airline and across all airlines working with different business models. Think about the challenge that the ultra-low-cost airlines faced during the recovery phase in the consideration of blocking the middle seats. One primary reason for having lower operating costs was based on high-density configuration of the single-aisle fleet; for example, 180 seats in a standard Airbus A320, instead of 150 seats. Think about some carriers that decided not to block the middle seat when other competitors did. Think about the decision to focus on the direct channel for distribution to save distribution costs and to have earlier access to cash coming from reservations, as discussed in the previous chapter. What about the tradeoff with greater access to higher-margin traffic provided by the travel management companies using GDSs? How about the tradeoffs that fleet planners must make in their decisions about fleet replacement based on economic considerations, operational considerations (such as slots and night curfews at airports), and the environmental considerations, as discussed in Chapter 3? These are just a few examples of a broad spectrum of new decisions arising during this virus-led disruption. Going forward, it is the digital transformation of the airline business, being enabled not only by the convergence and the intersection of new technologies, but also by the willingness of managements to do things differently, that would facilitate the speed of the decision-making process. This disruption has already begun to encourage some managements to think differently. Here are just three examples.

First, airlines are clearly turning to the use of data, analytics, and new technologies, as discussed in this chapter, to improve the decision-making processes by detecting vital trends more proactively and to respond to challenges and opportunities effectively. There are, however, a couple of concerns about the use of analytics. For example, historical data is of less value. Next, it is incredibly difficult to predict consumer behavior and competitors' behavior while the marketplace continues to change rapidly and fundamentally. Consequently, the decision-making process is now requiring a strategic blend of analytics and business intuition. This requirement calls for the use of what McKinsey analysts are calling "analytics translators."[3] As mentioned in the previous chapter, these professionals have a working knowledge of the value of analytics but a much higher level of understanding of the business and the organization to help data scientists to identify business problems and their potential solutions.

Second, a new way of thinking differently involves the use of data exchanges. Since large data bases are required for operating online platforms and services, training algorithms, and for scaling various initiatives, should airline managements consider working with data exchanges to share data? These entities, developed generally by foundations, or private companies, or cooperatives, "generate value by structuring, aggregating, and anonymizing" data. The data is provided voluntarily by different sources and it can be accessed by third parties.[4] Not only is the data provided voluntarily, within the framework of privacy, but it can also be protected to some extent by the use of blockchain technology. Think about the value of such data exchanges in two different contexts—one dealing with health-related challenges and one related to the development of customer travel value scores (somewhat similar to the consumer credit scores used by different organizations). Travel value scores could provide much value for both suppliers of travel services (such as airlines, hotels, and car-rental companies) and consumers.

The third way of thinking differently is to develop and implement disciplined and systematic approaches to experimentation, used often in the technology sector. Experimentation can add much value for airlines to explore and, possibly, influence consumer behavior in various aspects of their marketing practices. Think about the need to know more about price elasticity of demand right now, as to whether to reduce prices or increase prices. What if the premium-fare traffic goes down in key intercontinental markets, such as across the North Atlantic, and prices of economy-class tickets may need to be increased? The key questions relate, of course, to when and how to experiment. The approach is data-based with the data coming from customers and it can be particularly valuable during this time of unprecedented uncertainty. Again, since historical data is not relevant, the decision-making process can be improved significantly with the use of carefully designed experiments. Think about Uber's decision to experiment with the diversification of its customer base and its revenue base by developing a new division, called Uber Eats. Uber Eats has been capitalizing on the lockdown situation by delivering food directly to customers' locations. Luca and Bazerman provide an insightful example of value that Booking.com has been receiving from the use of experiments to test new features before their introduction to customers.[5] It is incredible to hear of the number of experiments that some companies are conducting now with the availability of more relevant data and analytics as well as the greater use of the disciplined experimentation process. Keep in mind a saying by Stephen Hawking, "The greatest enemy of knowledge is not ignorance; it is the illusion of knowledge."

## Notes

1 Thomas M. Siebel, *Digital Transformation: Survive and Thrive in an Era of Mass Extinction* (New York: RosettaBooks, 2019), ch. 3–5.

2 Michael Baiada, "Airline Delays/Congestion Need Not Happen," in the book by Nawal K. Taneja, *Transforming Airlines: A Flight Plan for Navigating Structural Changes* (New York: Routledge, 2020), pp. 143–44.

3 Nicolaus Henke, Jordan Levine, and Paul McInerney, "Analytics Translator: The New Must-Have Role," McKinsey & Company, February 2018.

4 José Parra-Moyano, Karl Schmedders, and Alex Pentland, "What Managers Need to Know About Data Exchanges", *MIT Sloan Management Review*, Summer 2020, Vol. 61, No. 4, pp. 39–44.

5 Michael Luca and Max H. Bazerman, "Want to Make Better Decisions? Start Experimenting," *MIT Sloan Management Review*, Summer 2020, Vol. 61, No. 4, pp. 67–73.

# 6 Unlocking new sources of value

The breadth, depth, and speed of the Coronavirus disruption caught airlines totally unprepared, causing most CEOs to shift their priorities to first just survive and then to get their operations restarted using conventional strategies. They obviously knew that at some point in the future they would need to recalibrate their entire businesses to adapt to the radically changed marketplace. However, priorities to change, from operating the business with conventional processes, systems, and thinking, to reinventing their organizations' robustness and resiliency to mitigate future threats and to seize powerful opportunities, would need to wait. They recognized that at some point they will stand back to look at the bigger picture, not just to transform their businesses with respect to scale and scope using conventional methods, but to use the scale and scope of digital transformation, to adapt to the changing dynamics of the marketplace. At that time, the decision would also be made, not just how to win the game, but to decide which game to play. Simone van Neerven and Jirka Stradal go even further and say that the idea is not just to win in a "finite" game that has a beginning and an end. Rather, it should be to keep playing in "infinite" games in which, "players come and go, the rules are changeable, and there is no defined endpoint."

Chapter 2 offered two scenarios to help leaderships reconsider the timing of their priorities relating to the scale and speed of transformation of their business models:

- to better anticipate future disruptions, such as those relating to changes in the climate, geopolitics, and cybersecurity, individually or in some combination,
- to explore broadening the business to reduce the risk and capitalize on new opportunities,
- to make longer-term investments in better information systems and in the talent to use these systems, not only to monitor warning signals of change, but also to identify both threats and opportunities,
- to develop relevant strategies by leveraging digital assets (discussed in the previous chapter) to optimize the use of physical assets in real time and at the system level, and
- to collaborate within the ecosystem to create, capture, and deliver value.

There are basically four challenges in realigning business models. The first challenge is the willingness to take the bold step to even think about a radically different approach, such as the one to broaden the business. Think about it. The basic product of the airline industry is still scheduled services between airport pairs. Think about the insights from the oil and gas sector summarized by Frédéric Ducros in his thought leadership piece in the next chapter. This sector faces as many uncertainties, complexities, and risks as airlines, if not more. Yet CEOs in this business sector have managed their risk by broadening their businesses and integrated effectively within the value chain. Even staying within the same narrowly defined business, matching supply and demand in almost real time would involve radical changes in almost every function within an airline—network, fleet, and schedule planning, pricing and revenue management, loyalty, and operations systems control centers, just to name a few. The second challenge is to find new ways to reduce operating costs substantially, particularly the costs that are fixed. The third challenge is to decide on the timing and the approach of the transition from the conventional planning process to the non-conventional planning process.

The fourth challenge is to create a culture that stimulates and promotes innovation. As discussed in the previous book in this series, in some ways, culture is more important than even strategy since the implementation of strategy is highly dependent on the existence of a favorable culture.[1] To support the importance of culture, Satya Nadella, the CEO of Microsoft, wrote in his book, *Hot Refresh*, "the C in CEO is for curator of culture."[2] He then went on to say that he gained additional insights from Steve Ballmer (his predecessor CEO of Microsoft) about the theory of three Cs to build and sustain innovation. In a target, the first C (in the outer ring of the three concentric rings) represents concepts. The second C represents capabilities. The "bull's eye" in the third ring is the culture. Satya Nadella described his plan to change Microsoft's culture from a "know it all" to a "learn it all." As such, one question asked could be: How much effort is being devoted to creating a culture of innovation?

One could go further and ask a more specific question: Is there cultural resistance, meaning ideas that do not conform to the norm are rejected right away? Business researchers have pointed out that while many businesses recognize the need for innovation, in many cases there is neither a comprehensive plan nor an urgency to get it implemented. In many cases the reason tends to be the comfort level of staying with conventional planning systems and there is resistance to change. Now, for the airline industry, not only is there a need for change, but there is also an opportunity. One only needs to look at the problems faced by consumers. The problems and the solutions need to be looked at from different angles and through different lenses. It is true that some airlines have established teams with smart members, have held workshops and town-hall meetings, have held hackathons with clean slates, and conducted simulation exercises. However, the success achieved has been at a relatively low level given the lack of clarity of the value propositions and the lack of willingness to break the conventional rules. Jeremy Gutsche describes seven specific traps that keep businesses "fixated on the path" that they are already on and how to overcome these traps.[3] Gutsche's seven traps discussed are: the subtlety of opportunity, neurological shortcuts, the ease of inaction, optionality, the traps of success, linear thinking, and discomfort vs. breakthrough. One of these traps, linear thinking, has already been discussed throughout this book within the context of airline planning.

## Adapting to the two scenarios by removing constraints

In the first scenario—continuous improvements—passenger traffic level and its growth rate could return to the historical trend line, shown in Figure 1.1. The only uncertainty relates to the length of time needed to return to the old normal. Based on the assumptions made in Chapter 2 and based on conventional and linear thinking, as well as the deployment of business-as-usual practices, the time for the traffic to bounce back could vary from 3 to 8 years, shown by three different dotted lines in Figure 2.2. Executive teams at major airlines have always taken the time to develop long-term visions, some as far out as 10 years. After all, in some cases, fleet-planning exercises have required a 10-year horizon for ordering aircraft that might not be delivered for 3–5 years and then they are expected to be in use for a period of up to 25 years. However, these visions have normally been based on one view of the future, a growth along a straight line or, even more optimistic, growth along an exponential curve. Multiple possible futures have rarely been considered. In fact, even when more than one scenario is considered, the number is extremely limited.

Simone van Neerven and Jirka Stradal point out, in their thought leadership piece in Chapter 7, that organizations face many struggles because their leaders plan with a "finite mindset in an infinite game." As such, if the first scenario plays out, particularly the first subset of scenario number one, then planning with one or two types of futures and conventional processes could still work. Under this scenario, core processes are not likely to be transformed after the initial recovery period, although continuous improvements will take place, in both operational and commercial areas. Adapting to this scenario does call for a revalidation of some assumptions, based on, to a limited extent, the experience of recovery from the past disruptions, as well as the experience to date from this disruption. Consider just one example, the success of selling some high-margin ancillary products and services. Some executives did consider some warning signs, as many customers did not like the new fees that were implemented, fees to which most airlines became addicted. However, as one airline executive put it, "we looked at these fees as 'free' revenue." Consequently, there was pressure to continue the process. Even if the recovery takes longer, as shown by the other arrows in Figure 2.2, conventional thinking could still be deployed to manage the business with continuous improvements.

It is, however, within the second scenario (elastic supply, based on non-linear or tangential thinking), that the traffic level and its growth may or may not reach the historical level. Moreover, the traffic level and its growth could fluctuate significantly from year to year, depending on the nature of the future envisioned. For this scenario, there will be a need to explore more innovative ways to transform the business and to transform it at an even faster rate. As such, there will be a need to:

- look at an even bigger picture of, not one, but multiple futures through multiple lenses,
- achieve innovative transformation not only at an even faster rate, but without adding complexity,
- step back from the image of the historical trend line and the historical compounded growth of between 4 and 5 percent,
- rethink many assumptions, for example, the relationship between the growth in traffic and GDPs, and price elasticity of demand when prices go down, as well as when prices go up, and
- think how to integrate with the new forms of transportation under development.

According to Frédéric Ducros (in his thought leadership piece in the next chapter), there may, in fact, be some insights for airline CEOs in learning about the principles relating to "Shu, Ha, Ri," a term used to describe the progression of learning within the Japanese martial arts. The "Shu" part would represent following the rule, the "Ha" part would represent breaking the rule, and the "Ri" part would represent being the rule. Within this context, new ways will relate to not just how executives think or use new technologies, but the intersection of the two, to develop new business capabilities to respond to the changing marketplace much more effectively. The key, as discussed before, is to achieve scale and scope of the use of physical aspects of the business (fleets, airport facilities, and so forth), by leveraging the scale and scope of an airline's digital assets (brand, loyalty programs, and airport slots). And that involves developing new core competencies (data, analytics, and networks). Figure 4.2 in Chapter 4 showed the three traditional core competencies and a set of three potential core competencies. The idea to establish new data hubs was already discussed in Chapter 3 of the book, *21st Century Airlines*, in this series.[4]

While no one has a crystal ball for forecasting the future, using these new core competencies, starting with data hubs, management teams can stand back and look at the influential forces as well as their convergence and intersection (alongside the multiple outcomes) to make the forces of change work for the organization by converting threats into opportunities. While innovation is driven by customer needs (actual and latent) and business needs (not just efficiency and productivity, but agility and flexibility), leveraging new core competencies, with state-of-the-art simulation models, will help airlines grow without adding complexity and without increasing costs. Growth can, in fact, be achieved while reducing prices and improving customer service and experience. One only needs to look at the experience of Amazon as to how the company expanded its product line, while improving customer experience, not to mention reducing prices at the same time. In the case of Amazon, all three aspects took place without adding complexity.

Coming out of the recovery, forward-thinking airlines already began to focus on their true vulnerabilities and the agile transformations needed to survive and thrive in the overly uncertain, and increasingly complex, marketplace. As suggested in Chapter 1, this disruption is not like the disruptions experienced in the past five decades. According to some airline analysts, this disruption is so unique that just as government intervention was necessary in the aviation sector after World War II, it may be the case again to preserve social and economic development as well as the preservation of connectivity, trade, and communications. The degree of government intervention will, of course, vary by government, as it did after World War II, and include some areas, such as bilateral agreements and ownership and control rules. If government intervention takes place at the post World War II level, then this disruption would have created a true tipping point, calling for non-conventional and lateral thinking, and non-conventional processes to develop operational and commercial strategies, discussed in Chapters 3 and 4.

Some boards and leaderships at airlines have already begun to stand back and look at the horizon to see the value to be created, captured, and delivered. With this in mind, while most airlines were preoccupied with ultra-short-term decisions to mitigate threats during the recovery, using conventional wisdom, a few were looking at potential longer-term opportunities. Developing plans for dealing with the second scenario—elastic supply—requires not only stepping back and looking at multiple pictures of the future, but also adopting an even more holistic and innovative mindset to creatively embrace uncertainty and to see tantalizing possibilities using digital capabilities. Under this scenario, conventional thinking, conventional planning approaches, and traditional planning systems and processes may no longer be sufficient due to the:

- inappropriateness of the past data to make meaningful decisions,
- expected changes in the structure of the airline industry and regulatory policies,
- changing behavior of consumers and businesses,
- volatility in the demand created by localized and globalized disruptions, and
- potential emergence of new forms of transportation, ranging from air taxis operating in urban areas to hyperloop capsules.

As such, a few airline leaders are looking at key areas of uncertainty (relating to geopolitics, for example) and the internal capabilities required to adapt to such a marketplace. They are reevaluating their airlines' visions and purposes, traditional core competencies, and traditional strategies to remain relevant and capture sustainable growth.

While the need for transformation and innovation has been recognized for a long time, the change in priority is now to remove constraints to see if there are any new value propositions. Relating to both scenarios, both the scale and scope of transformation would need to change to remove constraints. Such a change in priorities would vary by airline—full-service carriers versus low-cost carriers, for example. Moreover, the scale, scope, and speed of transformation relate to not just internal functions (financial, commercial, and operations), but also outside of the organization, to collaboration among partners within the travel value chain. In the first scenario, transformation to remove constraints relates mostly to productivity, operations, and products, while relying on the existing business model. The second scenario, on the other hand, calls for transformation of the entire business model that is constrained by numerous factors such as a supply-driven planning framework, annual planning cycles, long-term labor contracts, lack of sufficient infrastructure, and, in some cases, government intervention in routine business decisions. Specifically, this scenario calls for investments in strategic digital information—data, smart analytics, and networks—and the establishment of small teams that look at the global marketplace from a very broad and long-term perspective.

As already mentioned, large airlines have a group of fleet planners that do have a longer-term perspective, typically 5–10 years. However, drivers of change considered by these groups still relate to conventional airline business models—looking at economic and traffic growth (by region), share of capacity and traffic by carrier group (full-service, low-cost, and ultra-low cost), by region, by hub developments (size and location), by airplane technology (capacity, unit costs, range), by airplane retirement plans, by infrastructure (airport and ATC capacities, by region), and by environmental regulations. These considerations can still work for the first scenario, or at least for the first sub-scenario of the first scenario. For example, within the conventional framework, one could still look at the long-term forecasts of GDPs and assume that the historical relationship between GDP and traffic growth would continue to exist at the historical levels. However, even for the first scenario, going forward, additional considerations might be required. For example, even if aircraft manufacturers start designing airplanes that are propelled with synthetic fuels, these airplanes might not be in service for another 10–15 years. This development raises three questions.

- What would be the operating cost structure of these aircraft? In other words, would fuel costs represent 30 percent, 50 percent, or 70 percent of the operating costs?
- What would be the residual value of aircraft that will be acquired in the next 10 years?
- Would airports be able to have the necessary facilities located at or near airports to produce the synthetic fuel needed?

Even more considerations might be required for the second scenario—the potential threats and opportunities relating to multimodal transportation, geopolitical upheavals, and totally new entrants working with full-service and open-collaboration platforms, supported by technology companies, such as Alibaba, Amazon, Google, Salesforce, and Tencent. Even the considerations of GDPs may need to be focused much more at the disaggregate level, for example, by country. In the past, country analysis had generally been examined from three standard perspectives—populations, GDPs, and geography. Going forward, country-by-country analysis needs to be deeper. See the reference, in the next section, to Ruchir Sharma, to the success of nations based on different perspectives.

The second scenario calls, specifically, for digital transformation to deal with the possibility of the emergence of one or more "black swans," individually, or in a group. Although the concept of digital transformation is not new in the airline industry, it carries different interpretations at different airlines. At one end of the spectrum are some airlines that view digital transformation to mean just making some investments, not only in technology, but technology specifically for their IT departments. Further along the spectrum are some airlines that look at digital transformation as a way to not only improve products, but also improve customer experience (by removing internal and external constraints), that may add more value than the products. Even further along the spectrum are a few airlines that see digital transformation as a totally new way of doing things, at the core level, and a means to reinvent the business to create new value systems to develop relevant differentiation, built on complete customer centricity. One example of digital transformation at this level would be the development of door-to-door services. Digital transformation can add value even for some existing initiatives within the context of the first scenario. For example, digitalization can now be undertaken to provide contactless experience at airports and in aircraft cabins. The process had already begun, enabling, for instance, passengers visiting websites to see virtually how they would be accommodated in their seats. However, for the second scenario—elastic supply—digital transformation will also provide agility and resiliency to deal with the appearance of one or more black swans. To foster agility, however, requires much more than the use of advanced technologies in ad hoc functional areas. There is also a need to change processes, think differently, and collaborate within the dynamic ecosystem to remove constraints. Think about the need to break down silo systems that preclude integration within an airline as well as among alliance partners (Figure 3.6). Think about the inability or the lack of willingness to share data with airports (Figure 5.1).

Let us look briefly at why progress in digital transformation has been relatively slow within the airline industry to remove constraints and to unlock the sources of new value propositions. It is true that some airlines did appoint Chief Digital Officers within their C-suites. However, the progress made for creating new value systems through the digital transformation of the whole airline business, not just within ad hoc functions, has been virtually non-existent. Here are a few reasons:

- Chief Digital Officers, especially those recruited from outside of the airline industry, became surrounded by conventional thinkers within the C-suites. There was confusion and misinterpretations within the C-suites on the concept of digital transformation and the responsibilities of different executives within the C-suites.
- Chief Digital Officers had limited authority and limited budgets. Financial departments did not generally see business cases developed along the conventional ROI metrics and Chief Financial Officers were not willing to either take the necessary risk, or use a disciplined experimentation approach. Sometimes, wrong key performance indicators were used to measure the contribution of digital transformation, even at functional levels.
- Airlines continue to work with legacy systems and continue to have data that resides in different functions (as discussed in the previous chapter). Some organizations are not willing to acquire and deploy platforms that can work around the limitations of siloed data and legacy systems due, in part, to the desire of heads of different functions that deploy their siloed data, to improve decision-making processes in their own functions. Lack of integration exists not only among different departments, such as commercial and operations, but also within each, such as between marketing, sales, revenue management, customer service, and loyalty within the commercial function.
- Digital transformation focused on a few limited areas, such as personalization, inflight shopping, customer-contact centers, management of disruptions, and predictive maintenance. However, it has not been pursued for the entire organization, let alone for integration within the travel value chain in light of the potential risks. One barrier to the success of digital transformation is the unavailability of sufficient resources for reskilling, upskilling, and reincentivizing the workforce, at all levels, to use new technologies coupled with new thinking. This aspect is unfortunate, given that some new technologies can, in fact, be used to reskill and upskill employees.

It is worth noting that challenges in the transformation of the airline business relate not to the lack of deeper understanding of technologies and their roles, but to the:

- existence of major structural constraints in the airline business,
- actual and the perceived complexity of the airline business, and
- ambiguity of the vision, relating to the business model.

Let us start with structural constraints. They relate to insufficient infrastructure (airport facilities—gates and slots, for example), government regulations (that vary worldwide), agreements with labor (relating not just to wages, but also to work rules), and legacy technology systems and processes, just to name four. As for vision, relating to the business model, one could ask: Is the vision to develop an efficient transportation system to transport people between airports, safely and at reasonable prices—the current vision? Or, is it broader, to redefine the boundaries of the business, for example, to provide efficient door-to-door mobility service? Or, is it even broader, for an airline based in a developing country, to provide connectivity for people, connectivity that promotes the social development and the economic development of the developing country? Even if one assumes that the vision is to remain constrained to the supply of scheduled services, can it be broadened to provide the means for travelers to achieve their desired outcomes, as discussed in Chapter 4, with reference to Figure 4.4.

Consider the context of all three points (constraints, complexity, and vision) relating to the entry of FedEx into the marketplace decades ago. The founders knew the complexity of the business and the conventional constraints. However, it was the clarity of the vision of FedEx that changed the structure of the air-cargo industry and its competitive behavior. The crucial finding related to the need of shippers and consignees for door-to-door services that were convenient and that provided peace of mind, related to the promise of delivery. Cost of the service was not a consideration at the time. Management could "see" new sources of value propositions by eliminating constraints to help shippers and consignees achieve their outcomes. Similarly, in the case of Uber, the vision was not to develop an app for the existing taxi business, but to design a taxi business around a digital network system. Again, customer centricity preceded the cost aspects that turned out to be lower, in some cases, anyway. Similar considerations apply to the planning activities at airports. The point is not that large airports have not considered these aspects before, but that there now is a need to change priorities.

Consider, for a moment, an airline's vision of door-to-door transportation as opposed to airport-to-airport service. It will require non-linear thinking relating to planning. Such a vision would require the use of a dynamic framework that is truly customer-oriented, as opposed to a static framework, involving suppliers, operators of trains and buses, for example. To start with, it will involve the development of an integrated and dynamic multimodal system. How would an airline team up with relevant partners? Who will be the relevant partners? In Europe, would they be bus operators or operators of trains, or both? In the case of operators of buses, would they be conventional bus operators, or new entrants, such as FLiXBUS that does not own buses or hire its own drivers—along the lines of Uber? If the multimodal framework is flexible and dynamic, it can even accommodate operators of new forms of transportation that will be coming in the near future, such as the on-demand Uber flying taxis. In addition to some questions raised above, what would be the basic product? How would prices be developed? How would services be marketed and distributed? Such a vision requires the use of a next-generation platform, highlighted in Chapter 4, a platform that can incorporate new suppliers, new data, new analytics, and new networks. A thought leadership piece by Antoine de Kerviler in the next chapter offers some valuable insights on the concept of such platforms.

Consider, next, a vision on the economic development of, and connectivity within, a developing region—a vision of a government-owned airline in a developing region. If an airline has been financially supported by its government for years, and has made losses year after year, it may be possible for a global-brand airline to work with the government to develop a multinational airline through a change in the ownership and control rules, as discussed in Chapter 2. Again, such a vision requires the use of a next-generation platform, highlighted in Chapter 4 and the thought leadership piece by Antoine de Kerviler. These platforms can enable a multinational airline to work with multiple partners, for example, different governmental agencies to ensure the economic and social development of a country and the availability of the necessary infrastructure, such as airport capacities and services. While governments would have the right to appoint directors to serve on the boards of multinational airlines, and as such could control business decisions, governments could also let the multinational airlines run the businesses, as they would have invested the money, and provided the talent to run the multinational airlines. In the past, development of multinational airlines did not materialize due to the unwillingness of governments and the complexity of implementation. Even the use of cross-border equities has only had limited success. However, going forward, governments may be more willing to discuss such initiatives, in light of the mutual benefits. As mentioned in Chapter 2, think about the value of multinational airlines in such countries as Argentina, India, Italy, and South Africa. One critical success factor would be the development and demonstration of mutual value.

Negotiations would clearly be more complex now in the development of multinational airlines, given the existence of (1) multifaceted interwoven interrelationships with governments, (2) different laws and different cultures of different countries, (3) varying degrees of influence of unionized workforces, and (4) the political aspects of public opinion. As such, the formation of multinational airlines, to progress from competition to collaboration well beyond partnership in alliances, would require much more complex due diligence (over and above the financial terms) as well as creative, but adaptive and constructive thinking, to meet the strategic goals of key stakeholders. And addressing much more delicate and sensitive issues would require the widening of the aperture and the inclusion of some different parts of the calculus. Examples include the potential imbalance in power and the different visions, the timing and transition of the agreement, the challenges and opportunities relating to the preservation of the brands, and the challenges relating to the preservation of national pride and egos. However, the ultimate value of multinational airlines for all partners cannot be overlooked as long as short-term interests are not sought at the expense of long-term interests.

Finally, think about the second scenario and some ways to mitigate threats and to seize potential opportunities. If, going forward, demand were to fluctuate widely, as envisioned in Figure 2.3, there could be, at least, four relatively unconventional options for a large global airline. The first option could be not to discard, at extremely low prices, all the airplanes parked during the recovery period, but to keep a select few in the fleet as spare aircraft to adapt to the elastic supply scenario. Special arrangements could be made with furloughed crew to operate aircraft on an "as needed" basis during the period when demand is high. It is true that fleet utilization would be low, given that the aircraft would only be used based on the existence of demand. This is not a new idea. Allegiant Air's business plan was based on such a concept when it started operations back in 1998. A second option could be to partner with an airline that would provide white label capacity during the period of high demand. Undoubtedly, this option would create some challenges that would need to be resolved—challenges relating to contracts with the labor unions and the brand, for instance. Within the airline industry, Atlas Air is already an example of an airline that offers ACMI services on a contract basis—Aircraft, Crew, Maintenance, and Insurance. Not only Atlas, but also Sun Country Airlines—an ultra-low-cost, US-based carrier—provides cargo services for Amazon. Going outside the airline industry and into the automotive sector, Valmet Automotive (based in Finland and formerly called Saab-Valmet) offers flexible "on-demand" production capacity to high-end car manufacturers, such as Mercedes-Benz and Porsche.[5] A third option could be the use of an effective revenue hedging system, an example of which is provided by Skytra, a subsidiary of Airbus.[6]

The fourth option would be to diversify the revenue base from a much broader perspective than the management of passenger revenues. This is not a new idea. Think about it. United tried to diversify its revenue base in the early 1980s when it acquired Westin Hotels and the Hertz Corporation and created a holding company, known as Allegis. The concept was viable, given the synergy among the three travel-related businesses—an airline, a hotel group, and a car-rental company. However, the strategy failed from the implementation considerations, including the lack of an effective resolution to the intervention of a labor union and the inability to secure the necessary financing. In February 2021, United took another initiative by announcing an investment in Archer to buy 200 electric air taxis. The strategy will enable the airline to diversify its revenue base, while improving customer service and decarbonizing air travel at the same time.

Similarly, the HNA Group, based in China, tried to diversify its revenue base a decade ago by investing in airlines, airports, hotels, and numerous other related business sectors. The diversification strategy, while conceptually viable, did not play out even prior to the emergence of the COVID-related disruption. One problem appears to have been the expansion, which was too rapid and too ambitious. The second problem appears to have been the breadth, the depth, and the complexity of the portfolio—not only numerous business sectors, but also too many organizations within a business sector. Take, for example, the airline group, which had about 20 airlines (with complex ownership structures) based in China as well as other regions of the world. Nevertheless, there is now an opportunity to restructure the HNA Group given the likelihood of consolidation, realignment of the business models of aircraft lessors and original equipment manufacturers (OEMs), and the growth of the civil aviation industry in China. The key opportunity is to look at different ways of operating airlines while reducing complexity.

There have always been resistances and constraints to the development and implementation of new ideas in the airline industry. However, it was the removal of resistances and constraints that eventually created new sources of value. Consider three historical examples.

- A first example relates to the numerous arguments presented against the proposed initiative of a US major airline to start regional services. The initial concept was to expand hub-and-spoke systems in the US by outsourcing feeder services to regional carriers. Here are examples of just three concerns expressed. The first concern was about the negative impact on the brand of the major carrier for putting its names on the aircraft flown by small independent and unknown airlines. The second concern was about travelers' potential reluctance to fly on turboprop aircraft, such as the de Havilland Canada DHC-6 Twin Otter and the Convair 580, that were in operations at the time. The third concern was about the reaction of labor to the use of lower-paid crew to operate these aircraft. Yet, airlines that decided to work around these constraints and introduced feeder services created new sources of value for developing hub-and-spoke systems through the use of code-sharing agreements. Regional carriers not only used the computer reservation systems of major carriers, but they also used their brands. Major carriers saved on costs and passengers accepted the services as these services enabled smaller cities to be connected to other smaller cities via connecting hubs.
- A second example of the removal of a constraint that created new value was the reduction of fees to travel agents. Airlines were concerned about the competitive reaction of agents from having their revenue reduced. Agents were also concerned about having to find new ways to charge customers for the distribution of travel. Yet, both sides managed to find solutions and new value was created for airlines through a reduction in distribution costs.
- A third example relates to the start of ticketless travel. This proposal raised a lot of questions, such as travelers' concern for not having a paper ticket in their hands to feel secure, the difficulty of passengers not being able to check baggage at airport curbsides without paper tickets, and concerns of some airlines that costs would increase in maintaining two systems, paper tickets and electronic tickets. Yet, the introduction of ticketless travel unlocked all kinds of value by reducing costs for airlines by eliminating paper tickets, and provided additional value for business passengers traveling to numerous cities within a same trip, and their need to change plans at the last minute.

Once airlines managed to get around the constraints to implement new initiatives, all kinds of new sources of value emerged.

And, if one thinks some of these ideas were radical and visionary, then think now about the visionary hyperloop concept, discussed in Chapter 2 and displayed in Figures 2.4 and 2.5. As mentioned in Chapter 2, leaderships with "innovation capital" can make such ideas a reality. According to business researchers, innovation capital consists of a number of components, such as "human capital, social capital, reputation capital, and impression capital."[7] And, it is the ability of leaders not only to show a track record of thinking creatively and "outside-the-box," but also to be able to leverage social connections and take actions that create attention. And the leadership at HyperloopTT has created (1) a vibrant crowd-powered organization with thinkers and problem solvers, and (2) an opportunity for potential collaboration and coordination within the ecosystem, to make the concept a reality—an eco-friendly and cost-effective concept with incredible benefits, not just for travelers, but also communities and nations. Think about it. What if, in addition to being eco-friendly and cost effective, this mode of transportation was also seamless and hassle-free, enabled by digitalization and simplification?

## Leveraging insights from best business practices

In realigning their business models, airline leaders might see some value by looking at some insights from the best practices identified by business researchers as well as from the experience of some actual businesses, such as Amazon, FLiXBUS, Patagonia, and Tesla. Here are some examples.

Let us start with how one can think about inflection or turning points. Rita McGrath provides insightful guidelines on how to spot inflection points and their implications.[8] She provides, for example, a list of eight practices that provide some clues to the emergence of potential disruptions. Although some points covered may seem obvious, they are important, nevertheless. For example, some senior executives get so involved with internal discussions and debates that they overlook the fact that the "corner office" is not getting real value from the information coming from the "street corner." This recommendation is followed by an equally powerful recommendation to "get out of the building" and see what is happening in the marketplace from customers' perspectives. Her message is to be alert in monitoring weak signals whether they relate to customers, or employees, or competitors. Consider a weak signal in the airline industry relating to a need for an urban on-demand aerial ridesharing network. Consider another weak signal that if governments are now injecting so much money into their airlines, private or government-owned, could policies be implemented by some governments to control the expansion of some sixth-freedom airlines? Third, how about the potential increase in ticket prices due to high levels of taxes imposed by governments relating to the protection of the environment and sustainability? While the industry has good experience about the price elasticity of demand when fares come down, should airlines be studying the impact of fares going up, not just due to the imposition of taxes, but specifically taxes imposed to protect the environment?

Let us consider visions and missions. David Rubenstein provides numerous examples of wisdom that he distilled based on his conversations with dozens of CEOs, founders, and game changers. Just as one example, according to Phil Knight, the Cofounder and Chairman Emeritus of Nike, "We're a marketing company, and the product is our most important marketing tool."[9] How can an airline become a great marketing company, like Nike, and use its services as a marketing tool? How could the marketing tool be used to help consumers achieve their outcomes that would then make them great marketing companies? And, according to Indra Nooyi, former Chair and CEO of PepsiCo, great ideas for improving products come from customers and "a nugget of an idea can actually translate to a big success in the company."[10] Kate Raworth, in her book *Doughnut Economics*, lists seven ways to think like a 21st-century economist. Although her book lists seven points in the context of economics, her thoughts presented are also applicable for businesses and business leaders.[11] Take, for example, her point number one (change the goal) and point number two (see the big picture).

Going forward, what can or should be the goal of a business leader in the aviation sector? Should it be to maximize shareholder value, or balance the value for all other stakeholders, such as employees, customers, suppliers, governments, communities, and society, just to name six? While such a goal is not necessarily new, it would mean working much more closely in partnerships with different stakeholders. Now that governments are investing heavily in aviation businesses, not just airlines, but also airports and aircraft manufacturers, the need to work more closely within the travel value chain is even more important. In some regions, conventional wisdom appears to be that commercial airlines developing a partnership with a government would be anathema to the C-suite. This does not need to be the case, if one looks at the value Singapore Airlines and China Airlines have gained over the years from their partnerships with their governments. Think also about the partnership being developed between the government in Korea, Incheon Airport, and the Hyundai Motor Company to accelerate the development of urban air mobility.

Going forward, sustainability will now be an even hotter topic to be addressed, meaning that the structure and operations of the aviation industry will have to change dramatically, again. Some business analysts break sustainability into two components, with one component relating to social aspects (such as supporting local communities and reducing energy impacts), and the second relating to the protection of the environment.[12] As such, managements need to think more seriously about the possibility, currently a weak signal, of governments implementing schemes relating to pollution rights that could be even more constraining than airport slots, and just as complex, if not more. How about the implementation of government-imposed regulations relating to both airport slots and pollution rights? Consequently, airlines will need to identify higher purposes—for example, supporting the protection of the environment, as well as supporting local and regional communities. The point is that airlines need to think about the environment in broader terms than just compliance. Sustainability aspects need to be part of the strategy, not just a compliance requirement to deal with the next inflection point. How about making cybersecurity a competitive advantage rather than an operational obligation and a cost?[13] Imagine if sustainability and cybersecurity were to become not only two central capabilities, but a strategy to develop a competitive advantage, and two primary components of the brand.

Think about Patagonia, a US company designing outdoor clothing and gear that is truly passionate about its purpose, its customers, and its employees. The brand has developed a laser-like focus not only on product quality, but also on the environment and sustainability by pursuing a resilient culture. Specifically, Patagonia has taken a weighty stand for protecting the environment and preserving the land through its employee strategies, its customer strategies, and its political endorsements. An example of its employee strategy is to motivate its employees to collaborate to understand and promote the company's vision and its goals and objectives—the creation of high-quality products while supporting communities and protecting the environment. Another example is an initiative to make its supply chain carbon-neutral by 2025. An example of its customer strategy is its attempt to promote customer involvement in environmental efforts, particularly the younger people who recognize both the purpose of the brand as well as the reality of the climate crisis. As for examples of political endorsement, Patagonia put its weight, for example, behind two Democratic candidates because of their efforts to protect natural resources—public lands and waters.

While the value of agility is clearly recognized, to adapt to both scenarios within the different aviation sectors, the question continues to be about what agility is and how to achieve it. Tilman and Jacoby clearly describe the term as: "The organizational capacity to effectively detect, assess and respond to environmental changes in ways that are purposeful, decisive and grounded in the will to win."[14] They provide a clear list of six main levers of agility and how to plan for agility, relating, for example, to the "detect, assess, and respond," process. Many examples are provided, including some, based on the experience of one of the authors (Retired General Charles Jacoby, US Army). A particularly illuminating example given is one relating to the digital transformation of a 165-year-old business, Western Union, which had a globally recognized brand and operations in more than 200 countries to facilitate the transfer of money across borders. However, the development of e-commerce and digital financial services created a real threat to the survival of this iconic business. Starting with a comprehensive understanding of the needs of its loyal customer base and its core strength, risk management, Western Union leveraged emerging technologies and the necessary organizational changes to reinvent itself. Think about how some older-generation airlines can reinvent themselves by identifying a loyal customer base, then focusing on the stated and unstated needs of this customer base, and then realigning the physical and digital assets to identify new sources of mutual value, value for customers and value for airlines.

The key to agility, according to Rigby, Elk, and Berez, is to find "the right balance between standardizing operations and pursuing (sometimes risky) innovations."[15] Let us say that an airline establishes a team to explore initiatives to achieve agility—the agility team. The challenge, according to these business researchers, is that the executives on the agility team have to play multiple roles, ranging from running their business units to developing and running the agile company system. Second, there is also a challenge relating to the relevancy of the talent. Are airlines attracting talent from businesses representing best practices? Investment banks have a lot of experience, for example, in avoiding the commitment of large resources to fixed assets, as airlines do to fleet, maintenance facilities, and long-term labor contracts. Should the finance department have some experienced investment bankers in key roles? How about hiring technologists from the likes of Google or dynamic pricing specialists from the likes of Amazon, or managers responsible for personalization from the likes of Netflix, or capacity planners from the likes of Porsche, or virtual operation specialists from the likes of FLiXBUS?

Agility, speed, and employee empowerment could also be achieved through the implementation of a "helix" organizational structure. Even though complexity has been increasing in the airline business, organizational structures have remained, more or less, the same. In a helix-based model (researched by McKinsey & Company) the conventional management responsibilities can be divided into two parallel lines or tracks. One line focuses on the development of employees, processes and capabilities of how functions can be performed, while the second one focuses on creating value through the actual daily work within the functions to meet business objectives. Both lines are linked. The helix organizational structure reduces the number of management layers, breaks down the traditional silos, and reduces the time to market.

Next, consider the insights identified by the following business writers.

* Based on the results of his extensive surveys, a business researcher, Amit Mukherjee, is proposing that the availability, and the potential use, of digital technologies call for business leaders to focus more on "creativity, collaboration, and inclusivity."[16] Think about the third dimension, inclusivity, that he relates to the willingness to recognize and address biases.
* Relating to technologies, according to Thomas Siebel, it is not just the four key technologies (elastic cloud computing, big data, artificial intelligence, and the internet of things), but their confluence that will change how business is conducted in the future.[17] Think about the role of artificial intelligence in bringing a step-change improvement in airline operations. And, according to Mukherjee, since digital technologies have already been transforming organizations and work, the changing priority of leaders must now be to transform more rapidly to adapt to the new marketplace and foster agility.
* Going beyond the need for speed, according to some researchers, for example, Arthur Yeung and Dave Ulrich, entire organizations need to be

reinvented to deliver greater value.[18] An example in the airline industry would be related to the development of door-to-door services.

- In their book, *Competing in the Age of AI*, Marco Iansiti and Karim Lakhani suggest four areas of competencies relating to data, analytics, networks, and learning.[19] Networks, in this context, do not relate to airline networks but relate, instead, to networks in social platforms, networks in supply chains, and apps. The four competencies can help airlines to manage passenger traffic levels and traffic growth that could range from high positive numbers to high negative numbers, and with wide oscillations in between.

- As for analyses of economies, Ruchir Sharma suggests numerous rules for successful nations relating to the growth of their economies. According to him, in addition to populations and geographic locations, the new rules also include politics, inequality, state power, investment, inflation, currency, debt, and hype.[20] He looks at the success of nations from a perspective of an astute, attentive, but pragmatic investor. He discusses, at length, for example, a measure of debt as a good predictor of economic crisis. This discussion is particularly relevant during this disruption when countries are taking on enormous amounts of debt to support a myriad of for-profit, not-for-profit, and public organizations. The "10 rules of successful nations," provided by Ruchir Sharma could provide significant insights for long-term network planners.

- Bertini and Koenigsberg suggest that companies should compete on "customer outcomes." Since customers buy products and services to achieve specific outcomes, tangible and/or intangible, then businesses can use technologies to track the delivery outcomes desired by customers and develop some relevant revenue models. They suggest three different revenue models: (1) access (with payments based on time frames), (2) consumption (payments based on use), and (3) performance (payments based on outcomes achieved).[21] Airlines have experimented with some versions of the first two revenue models when they introduced the subscription model and then when they unbundled the products. However, with the availability of new technologies, it may be possible not only to revisit the first two models, but also to explore the value of the third revenue model.

- Johnson and Suskewicz suggest, based on best practices in the business world, to "lead from the future." The concept is not only to have a long-term inspiring and actionable vision, but also to think systematically from the "future back to the present."[22] Emphasis is on the development of long-term horizons and systematic ways to convert challenges into opportunities, as well as visions into strategic plans.

- Woodward, Padmanabhan, Hasija, and Charan have coined the phrase "combinatorial innovation" to transform a business. They provide IKEA as an example of a company that had already disrupted in the furniture space. It "co-opted consumers to become co-producers—driving to the stores and picking and assembling in return for affordable design." This co-production provided lower prices for consumers. In recent times, as reported by these business researchers, IKEA co-opted with two new companies, one (TaskRabbit) that offers to work with consumers to help them assemble furniture—consumers who may not be interested in assembling the furniture by themselves. The second business (Reform) helps consumers to create designer spaces (say kitchens) at a much lower cost than traditional designers.[23]

The insights provided by these business writers can add much value for airlines as they think about changing their business models to respond to the two scenarios. Airline managements can consider the value, for example, to:

- think from the "future back to the present" for developing new forms of transformation and new delivery systems to meet the stated and unstated needs of consumers,
- develop and analyze multiple futures relating to, economies, politics, lifestyles, and new players providing, for example, door-to-door services by the likes of Uber, or local taxi consolidators, or FLiXBUS, or some combination,
- develop new ideas through the creation of innovation teams that provide real diversity, not by demography, age, gender, or functional experience, but diversity in the thought process (see the thought leadership piece by Simone van Neerven and Jirka Stradal that discusses the term cognitive diversity),
- develop and analyze the use of new technologies, such as artificial intelligence, to take both operations and commercial aspects to new heights through the use of pattern recognitions and exceptions (see the thought leadership piece by Peeter Kivestu in the next chapter), and
- create new value enabling consumers to become co-producers (as exemplified by IKEA).

For many for-profit businesses, including airlines, the standard interest has been in the impact on their business in terms of quarterly earnings and earning calls, even prior to the current disruption. In some cases, a focus on short-term plans has not only led to different management incentives, but it has also produced some challenges for the longer term. In contrast, think about some businesses that have always been focused on the long term. Think about two businesses, Amazon and Tesla, whose leaderships seem to always have focused on the long-term mission of their businesses rather than on short-term profits. One only needs to look at Amazon's decision to develop its Amazon Web Services (AWS) program for internal operations and its fleet of freighters to transport the shipments of its own products. The AWS is now used by many businesses and the fleet of freighters (used by Prime Air), which has already expanded in number (more than 80 by the summer of 2020) and diversity (Boeing 767s and 737s), could expand much more. Amazon could also use its growing fleet to transport cargo of other businesses, including airlines! What if Amazon decided to pick up, at low prices, some of the aircraft being parked by existing large airlines and convert them into freighters? Selection would obviously be based on the type of aircraft and the cost of conversion. Now that Amazon has gained sufficient experience in operating successfully a fleet of aircraft, what if the company decides to operate passenger aircraft? Brian Dumaine summarizes the key to the success of Amazon, "customer obsession, extreme innovation, and long-term thinking, all driven by artificial intelligence."[24] From a different perspective, think about Tesla which has had a longer-term focus relating to a "clean eco-friendly value proposition" (as opposed to short-term profits) and a digital technology orientation "built into its DNA."[25] Tesla is, for example, a "light-house" business not just within the auto sector, but for many other business sectors, because:

- it "does not abide by the customary rules of the car industry,"
- it practices very different "hiring practices," and
- it is obsessed with "speed" through a "flatter hierarchy."[26]

How can new entrants succeed in an industry? With research based outside of the airline industry, Rory McDonald and Kathleen Eisenhardt provide an interesting idea for developing effective strategies of new entrants, using an intriguing concept called "parallel play." Based on insights from child psychologists, the idea is to learn how young children (3 and 4 years old) "typically behave in a distinct fashion in a social setting."[27] How would a new entrant in the airline industry benefit from such insights? One answer would be through a greater use of well-organized and disciplined experiments. Based on studies of best practices of top-performing companies, some researchers are already concluding that better strategies can be developed through the experimentation process. Stefan Thomke, for example, elaborates on how experimentation can help in the design of products and customer experience.[28] If a new entrant has a radical idea that involves significant risk and uncertainty, then according to some experts the use of "impression amplifiers" can support the successful implementation of radical concepts. These amplifiers, such as "comparing, materializing, and storytelling," have proven to be more helpful than using the standard presentation of "data analysis, financial forecasting, and strategic planning."[29] These experts illustrate, for example, the use of the amplifier, comparing, "We're the Airbnb of the X industry." Another example, within the travel industry could be "We're the Uber of the X industry."

To compete more effectively with the stronger new airline entrants, older-generation airlines may need to rely more on the experimentation technique to test different ways of implementing old concepts, such as subscription pricing, the low-price guarantees, and the use of white label capacity. Another insight for airlines would be based on the research of Marco Bertini and Oded Koenigsberg, who suggest, as mentioned above, that businesses should sell "ends" (outcomes) instead of "means" (products and service).[30] These business writers ask some simple, but piercing, questions, such as: Are people buying groceries or nutrition? Finally, even if disruptive products were to help purchasers achieve the desired outcomes, the delivery and consumption of products must also be accompanied with good customer experience, along the lines of Amazon and Netflix.

Finally, consider an applicable insight from Zara (a division of Inditex). Zara innovated its business model designed to enable fast response to fashion trends and garment designs to ensure that its store shelves were always stocked, not only with the trendiest clothes, but also to match the changes in demand. Although Zara was not the first fast-fashion retailer in the fashion industry, it was perhaps the first one to respond to changes in market demand in, practically speaking, real time by transforming radically all of its core processes. Prior to the innovation of its core processes, Zara took about a year to create (design), manufacture, distribute, and sell its products—garments. After innovation of the business process the cycle, from product design to product sale, was reduced to less than a month.

There were three critical success factors. The first one was the ability to detect consumers' trends with speed and accuracy. In addition to receiving detailed feedback from employees in stores, analysts were sent to the actual marketplace (and in social media) to observe trends on what customers want now, forecast trends on what customers would want later, and work very closely with designers based within the company to provide flexibility to make changes. The second critical success factor was the integration of the information among all the teams—trend observers, designers, manufacturers, distributors, and sales. The third critical success factor was the reliance on production in Spain and nearby countries for most of the products, providing considerable flexibility in changing orders, in light of the close location of suppliers, relative to far-flung places in Asia. The shortened planning cycle, from a year to a month, increased the frequency of change of merchandise in stores, reduced the uncertainty in demand, delighted customers in all age groups, and increased margins on products. It is interesting to note that in studying the history of Zara's changes to its processes, while the company was not the first one to reduce cycle time to eliminate discounts for the end-of-the-season merchandise, its strategies were truly proactive to create "supply-based-on-demand."

The 2020s will be a decisive decade for airlines, a decade in which a few airlines will leave the marketplace and a few will remain in the marketplace, but they may become simply uncompetitive and/or irrelevant. On the other hand, the airlines that manage to survive, by not just adapting to uncertainty, but outsmarting it, will stay relevant, and thrive by converting constraints into opportunities and uncovering totally new value propositions. Leaderships at forward-thinking airlines have already begun to transform their businesses through the use of new technologies, the use of more pertinent data, the attraction of appropriate talent, the use of non-linear thinking, and the willingness to collaborate within the internal and external value chains. Priority now needs to be on the urgency of a sweeping transformation, built around customers and employees to develop a capability to become agile at scale to adapt to tumultuous times. Some airlines had already begun, even prior to this disruption, to reprioritize the third dimension of the older set of core competencies—excellence in the execution of strategies through the use of data as well as inclusion and diversity—the other two being excellence in operations and excellence in marketing innovation (see Figure 4.2). The focus can now be on leveraging digital assets to "future-proof" airline organizations.

There is a lot more value that can be created, captured, and delivered through participation within the travel value chain and by working not only on next-generation platforms to power suppliers of travel services and customers, but also in strategic partnerships, based not only on data, analytics, and networks, but also on trust. In times of unprecedented crisis, such as this one, the natural inclination is to avoid risks and use legacy systems, legacy processes, and conventional thinking. However, a few cutting-edge airlines are already getting out of their comfort zones and changing corporate cultures to develop capabilities that are enablers rather than disablers. They are beginning to change culture to manage uncertainty and ambiguity relating to situations that are complicated vs. those that are complex. Uncertainty, associated with change and its pace, concerns what cannot be determined clearly or accurately. Ambiguity, relating to the existence of multiple choices in making decisions, concerns situations that may have multiple meanings; that is, they may be understood in multiple ways. In a similar context, as elaborated by Margaret Heffernan, complicated environments are linear and predictable, while complex environments are non-linear in which "small effects may produce disproportionate impacts."[31] As such, leaderships of these cutting-edge airlines need to go further by reimagining the future and taking risks to convert threats into powerful and tantalizing opportunities. This disruption is an opportunity for serious renovation of airline business models within the "outside-in and bottom-up" framework to change the way people travel. Keep in mind a forecast of the changed global demographics and the changed global economies by 2030, as perceived by an original thinker, Mauro Guillén: "more grandparents than grandchildren; middle class in Asia and sub-Saharan Africa greater than in the US and Europe, combined; global economy driven by the non-Western consumer; and more global wealth owned by women than men."[32] To plan for such a changed marketplace would require a very different form of thinking—a three-dimensional thinking. Rosabeth Moss Kanter, in her book *Thinking Outside the Building*, provides some insightful success stories of leaders from the business, government, and community sectors who managed to bring about change and innovation.[33]

## Notes

1   Nawal K. Taneja, *Transforming Airlines: A Flight Plan for Navigating Structural Changes* (New York: Routledge, 2020), p. 41.

2   Satya Nadella, *Hot Refresh* (New York: HarperCollins, 2017).

3   Jeremy Gutsche, *Creating the Future: Tactics for Disruptive Thinking* (New York: Fast Company Press, 2020), pp. 7–114.

4  Nawal K. Taneja, *21st Century Airlines: Connecting the Dots* (New York: Routledge, 2018), ch. 3, pp. 39–41.

5  https://en.wikipedia.org/wiki/Valmet_Automotive

6  https://skytra.airbus.com/

7  Jeff Dyer, Nathan Furr, and Curtis LeFrandt, *Innovation Capital: How to Compete and Win Like the World's Most Innovative Leaders* (Boston, MA: Harvard Business Review Press, 2019), p. 5.

8  Rita McGrath, *Seeing Around Corners: How to Spot Inflection Points in Business Before They Happen* (Boston, MA: Houghton Mifflin Harcourt, 2019).

9  David M. Rubenstein, *How to Lead: Wisdom from the World's Greatest CEOs, Founders, and Game Changers* (New York: Simon & Schuster, 2020), p. 87.

10  David M. Rubenstein, *How to Lead: Wisdom from the World's Greatest CEOs, Founders, and Game Changers* (New York: Simon & Schuster, 2020), p. 184.

11  Kate Raworth, *Doughnut Economics: 7 Ways to Think Like a 21st Century Economist* (White River Junction, VT: Chelsea Green Publishing, 2017).

12  Lisa Holmes, "2020 Industry Insights," *Euromonitor International*, July 2020.

13  Manuel Hepfer and Thomas C. Powell, "Make Cybersecurity a Strategic Asset," *MIT Sloan Management Review*, Fall 2020, Vol. 62, No. 1, pp. 40–45.

14  Leo M. Tilman and Charles Jacoby (Retired General), *Agility: How to Navigate the Unknown and Seize Opportunity in a World of Disruption* (Arlington, VA: Missionday Publishers Group West, 2019), p. 7.

15  Darrell Rigby, Sarah Elk, and Steve Berez, "The Agile C-Suite: A New Approach to Leadership for the Team at the Top," *Harvard Business Review*, May–June 2020, pp. 64–73.

16  Amit S. Mukherjee, *Leading in the Digital World: How to Foster Creativity, Collaboration, and Inclusivity* (Cambridge, MA: MIT Press, 2020).

17  Thomas M. Siebel, *Digital Transformation: Survive and Thrive in an Era of Mass Extinction* (New York: RosettaBooks, 2019).

18  Arthur Yeung and Dave Ulrich, *Reinventing the Organization: How Companies Can Deliver Radically Greater Value in Fast-Changing Markets* (Boston, MA: Harvard Business Review Press, 2019).

19  Marco Iansiti and Karim R. Lakhani, *Competing in the Age of AI: Strategy and Leadership When Algorithms and Networks Run the World* (Boston, MA: Harvard Business Review Press, 2020).

20  Ruchir Sharma, *The 10 Rules of Successful Nations* (New York: W.W. Norton & Company, 2020).

21  Marco Bertini and Oded Koenigsberg, *The Ends Game: How Smart Companies Stop Selling Products and Start Delivering Value* (Cambridge, MA: The MIT Press, 2020).

22  Mark W. Johnson and Josh Suskewicz, *Lead from the Future: How to Turn Visionary Thinking into Breakthrough Growth* (Boston, MA: Harvard Business Review Press, 2020).

23  Ian C. Woodward, V. "Paddy" Padmanabhan, Sameer Hasija, and Ram Charan, *The Phoenix Encounter Method: Lead Like Your Business Is On Fire* (New York: McGraw Hill, 2021), pp. 220–22.

24  Brian Dumaine, *Bezonomics: How Amazon Is Changing Our Lives and What the World's Best Companies Are Learning from It* (New York: Scribner, 2020).

25  www.garyfox.co/tesla-business-model/

26  https://mondaynote.com/how-the-tesla-way-keeps-it-ahead-of-the-pack-358db5d52add

27  Rory McDonald and Kathleen Eisenhardt, "The New-Market Conundrum," *Harvard Business Review*, May–June 2020, pp. 75–83.

28  Stefan H.Thomke, *Experimentation Works:The Surprising Power of Business Experiments* (Boston, MA: Harvard Business Review Press, 2020).

29  Jeff Dyer, Nathan Furr, and Mike Hendron, "Overcoming the Innovator's Paradox," *MIT Sloan Management Review*, Fall 2020,Vol. 62, No. 1, pp. 70–77.

30  Marco Bertini and Oded Koenigsberg, *The Ends Game: How Smart Companies Stop Selling Products and Start Delivering Value* (Cambridge, MA:The MIT Press, 2020).

31  Margaret Heffernan, *Uncharted: How to Navigate the Future* (New York:Avid Reader Press, 2020), pp. xii–xiii.

32  Mauro F. Guillén, *2030: How Today's Biggest Trends Will Collide and Reshape the Future of Everything* (New York: St. Martin's Press, 2020).

33  Rosabeth Moss Kanter, *Thinking Outside the Building* (NewYork:PublicAffairs,2020).

# 7 Thought leadership pieces

Chapter 7 provides a number of thought leadership pieces that provide international perspectives relating to the theme of the book. These pieces are written by a very diverse group of practitioners with extensive experience, both in the aviation domain as well as in other business sectors. The contents of some of the thought leadership pieces suggest that managers are now free to consider new ways to respond to opportunities to restart businesses with fewer commercial and operational constraints. Moreover, there is now an opportunity to consider integrated planning and optimization at a system level. And, while historical data will have less relevance, new types of data are becoming available to plan for new volatility in the level and growth of the demand for air travel.

## Redefining air service development in a post-COVID world

*Brian D'Amico*
Air Service Program Manager, San Diego International Airport

In April 2020, passenger traffic at US airports declined by 97 percent nation-wide. By September, more than 120 airports around the world had lost all commercial service[1] and over 20 airlines had declared bankruptcy or ceased operations. COVID hotspots continued to rotate around the globe. After gains in bending the curve were made in the northern hemisphere over the summer a second wave took shape in the fall. Airport professionals are tasked to provide some level of certainty in an industry and crisis where there is little to be found. Despite this, there are a number of insights the current upheaval provides on how to craft strategies to regain lost passenger traffic, capture new demand, and better prepare for the next major disruptions on the horizon.

COVID-19 helped underpin the essential need to have a diversified air service portfolio. Just as a city dependent on one single industry is vulnerable to severe economic downturns when that industry struggles, so too are airports exposed to greater volatility if one carrier or type of service represents the overwhelming majority of the airport's operations. Much like in investing, where it is advisable to mitigate risk and exposure by diversifying assets, so too can airports better insulate themselves from future industry disruptions by having a diversified carrier and destination mix.

San Diego is an example of a market well-positioned to weather disruptions due to the diverse economy and mix of travel that the San Diego International Airport has long supported. With nonstop service to more than 70 destinations from 17 different airlines, the airport had built a diversified air service portfolio in the years prior to the pandemic. Home of the world's largest concentration of military assets, an innovation hub in biotechnology and telecommunications, and a top ten US tourist destination, San Diego also has a diversified economic base to draw from as the airport rebuilds passenger traffic. These three key sectors are uniquely positioned to thrive during and beyond the present crisis. Up to one-third of all COVID-19 testing kits produced in the country for example are made in San Diego.[2]

Airport officials must understand the strengths and weaknesses of their own markets and service portfolios when charting a path to recovery and planning for future growth. Most industry experts currently believe that it may take at least until 2024 for total passenger volumes to climb back to 2019 levels, but the recovery across different travel segments and individual markets will not be even. Domestic leisure travel started to come back in June 2020, but business and international travel for the most part did not. Airlines pivoted their schedules to favor leisure travel in response. When looking at which US markets with at least 100,000 departing seats between June 1 and August 31,

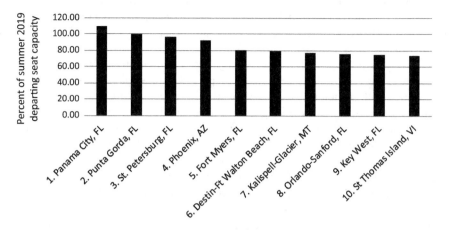

*Figure 7.1* Top ten US markets retaining summer 2019 seat capacity in summer 2020
Source: Cirium Schedules.

2020 best retained seat capacity compared to last summer, seven of the top ten best performing markets were in Florida (see Figure 7.1).

Business travel continues to be impacted by canceled conferences and trade shows, government restrictions at the local, state, federal, and global levels, budget cuts, employee aversion to travel, and increased organizational utilization of video conferencing. While government travel restrictions and travel aversion can be expected to go away with time, the long-term impact of increased reliance on and preference for conducting business virtually on business air travel is yet unknown. It is safe to say that at least for the short to medium term, the demography of air travel has shifted heavily towards leisure. The implications for this in markets that experience seasonality can be extreme if airports and destinations do not take a proactive approach in repositioning themselves in the marketplace.

None of this is to say airports should stop caring about business travel. The San Diego International Airport has stayed closely engaged with the business community and regional partners through webinars, travel surveys, and direct outreach to better understand how the crisis is impacting business travel decisions and future outlooks. Despite increased use of video conferencing, the overwhelming majority of survey respondents said they expect business travel to be "the same" to only "a little less" when their organization is ready to resume travel more regularly again. Some major employers even reported that broader adoption of telecommuting will actually stimulate an increase in travel for more company meetings and retreats to bring people together.

Restoring international traffic has proven more challenging, especially for markets similar in size to San Diego. Prior to the pandemic, San Diego had nonstop service to nine international destinations in Asia, North America, and

Europe with two new routes to Canada originally slated to begin in the summer 2020 season. In March 2020, President Trump issued presidential proclamations restricting travel from residents of the Schengen Area of Europe, the United Kingdom, Ireland, China, and Iran, and the Department of Homeland Security ultimately limited entry for flights from these countries to 15 designated US gateways. San Diego, along with other major US airline hubs such as Charlotte, Denver, and Philadelphia, were not on that list. After an internal review and months of lobbying and working with industry trade partners to better understand these procedures, the Trump Administration announced the gateway restriction would be removed in mid-September. While this opens the door from the US side for the return of transatlantic nonstop service to cities like San Diego, there is more industry work to be done to control the spread of the virus, restore consumer confidence in air travel, and unravel the web of additional government travel restrictions that remain. From the customer's perspective, the myriad of different safety procedures, protocols, testing requirements, mandatory quarantines, and outright travel prohibitions that vary from state to state and country to country is the biggest impediment to having the confidence to book their next airline ticket. Aviation industry professionals must continue working together to standardize safety measures, streamline travel restrictions and requirements, and hone messaging on everything being done to make air travel safe, reliable, and expedient.

### Four coming disruptions that will change air service development

The COVID-19 pandemic is unlike any disruption to air travel anyone alive has ever seen. But what are some of the next great industry disruptions lying in wait? Below are some thoughts on what's going to impact air service beyond the short term.

#### Climate change

Climate change is a serious threat to airports. There is extensive research around the subject of sea level rise, heightened tropical storm activity and severity, and the implications of both of these for airports around the world. Many airports were built near bodies of water thanks to the extensive low-lying and flat surface area such locations often provide to accommodate long runways. According to new data released by the World Resources Institute (WRI) earlier this year, more than 80 airports around the world could be underwater by the end of this century.[3] Even before then, as sea levels rise and storms intensify, the threat storm surges pose to airports will only increase. This is not a future hypothetical. It's already happening. In 2012, Hurricane Sandy infamously flooded all three major airports in New York City, shuttering LaGuardia Airport for three days. In 2015, Typhoon Goni flooded the runways at Shanghai Hongqiao International Airport and, in 2018, Cochin International Airport in India was rendered nonoperational for two weeks due to historic floods there.[4]

Sustainability in air service requires sustainability in airport operations, and this can only be achieved if airports take the necessary steps to mitigate the local effects of climate change on their facility. In the not-too-distant future this may very well become a calculation of airline network planners: with all else being equal, do I fly my $150 million aircraft into a market that has flooded three times in the last year or do I fly it into a competing market that has successfully fortified itself against such calamities and service disruptions?

While there has been well-documented research on the looming impact sea level rise will have on airports in coastal regions around the world, arguably not enough attention has been given to rising air temperatures which could impact a far larger number of markets. As the earth warms, the hotter air becomes less dense, making it more difficult for engines to create thrust and wings to create lift, thus impeding an aircraft's ability to take off efficiently. In the United States, Phoenix Sky Harbor International Airport for example has on more than one occasion infamously grounded flights due to extreme heat.

In the case of the Boeing 787-800 Dreamliner, with a payload of 436,000 pounds at sea level during a standard design day (or 59 degrees F) and typical engines, roughly 6,700 feet of runway is needed for take-off assuming no impedance by any other variables (such as headwind, slope or clearance obstacles). Assuming all these other variables remain equal, when the thermometer hits 120 degrees Fahrenheit that same airplane needs approximately 10,600 feet of runway. That's a 58 percent increase.[5]

Airports at higher elevations experience an even more profound impact from rising temperature, as illustrated in Figure 7.2. Using the same criteria as the previous example but at 2,000 feet elevation, the necessary runway required goes from roughly 7,700 feet at a temperature of 59 degrees F to approximately 15,000 feet at a temperature of 120 degrees F (see Figure 7.2).

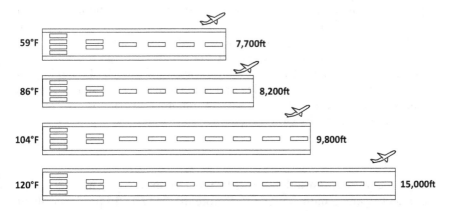

*Figure 7.2* Approximate corresponding required take-off runway length for a B787-800 weighing 436,000 lbs at 2,000 ft elevation with rising temperatures (typical engines), all else being equal

That's a staggering 95 percent increase in required runway length, or almost *double*.[6]

Some aircraft may still be physically capable of taking off from airfields experiencing extreme heat using higher thrust engines, but this is both less efficient and more costly to airlines' bottom line and the question then becomes what the impact on climate change would be if suddenly thousands of more operations per day around the world started doing *that*.

Absent major infrastructure investment, technological advancements or other meteorological developments, smaller airfields in hotter climates may eventually be rendered unserviceable. Global schedules will see more flights at midnight and fewer flights at midday. Hub banks will need to shift, and that may leave some markets out all together from the network as their geographic location may not be suited to the new required hub banking times.

Of course, all of these dire predictions about rising temperatures and sea levels assume we do not make further advancements in aircraft performance technology or do more as a civilization to address climate change. The worst-case scenario does not have to be inevitable. And several US airports from San Francisco to New York have initiated plans to spend hundreds of millions of dollars to buy more time by better fortifying their infrastructure.[7]

Meaningfully preparing for climate change at airports means engaging in community-wide mitigation efforts in addition to sustainably fortifying and operating the airfield. In southern California, the San Diego International Airport (SAN) has long been a champion of this. The airport has partnered for example with the Scripps Institute of Oceanography's Center for Climate Change Impacts & Adaptation, one of the world's leading research centers, to deploy a network of wave-current pressure sensors in San Diego Bay. These sensors enhance understanding of water levels and regional flooding potential. In 2013 the airport constructed the world's first Leadership in Energy and Environmental Design (LEED) Platinum-certified airport terminal and the airport's next project for a new administration building is being used to pilot the US Green Building Council's new RELi rating system, which focuses on socially and environmentally resilient design and construction.

While the worst is not inevitable, it does underscore the relevance and importance of climate change to air service professionals. Preserving an airport's reach, operational reliability and attractiveness to air carriers requires a concentrated effort to address these issues and properly plan for their mitigation, from the local to the global level.

### Flight shaming

One of the greatest disruptions to strike the aviation industry in recent years was quickly gaining momentum right before the COVID-19 pandemic: flight shaming as one component of the environmental movement most recently energized by the young Swedish activist Greta Thunberg. Aviation has long been the target of climate change activists' ire for its contribution to carbon emissions well before Ms. Thunberg arrived on the global stage. In response aircraft manufacturers, airlines, and airports have taken significant steps toward lowering their carbon footprint through initiatives like designing more fuel-efficient aircraft, offering carbon offsetting programs to passengers, and implementing zero-waste targets. Still, under mounting public pressure the carbon footprint generated by air travel was increasingly coming under closer scrutiny in 2019, particularly in Europe. And it was having a dramatic industry impact. Domestic air travel fell by 9 percent in Sweden compared to the year prior, with flight shaming cited as a primary contributor to the decline.[8] The movement was spreading across the pond too. Some airports in the United States began sounding the alarm as major corporations started announcing travel restriction initiatives aimed at reducing their business flying and overall emissions contribution. The need for more robust industry action to address climate change and message successes in mitigating aviation's contribution was a hot topic right up until the COVID-19 crisis struck. It may have taken a backseat for now, but it will return. And airports and air service professionals would be wise to use this time to advance environmental initiatives aimed at sustainability, operational efficiency, and carbon neutrality. Educating the public and instilling confidence in their choice for air travel will be a routine part of the air service professional's job in the near future and the measures taken today will help determine how easy that job will be.

*Modal shifts: From competition to integration*

Some environmentally conscientious passengers will not stop traveling all together, but will opt instead for modes with smaller carbon footprints, primarily rail and bus. Several European governments, like Germany, have signaled policy moves to encourage and accelerate this behavior. This modal shift, already developing in Europe, can at first appear to be an existential threat to the legacy hub-and-spoke business model which relies heavily on domestic short-haul flying to feed long-haul international services. If the short-hauls become unprofitable due to a large enough modal shift to rail, this puts the entire network in jeopardy. That is, if the modes remain isolated.

While Europe was a hotspot for flight shaming and promotion of rail over air travel where possible leading up to the present crisis, Europe has also long been an exemplar of successful modal integration between rail and aviation. From Amsterdam to Paris, passengers have for years become accustomed to beginning their journey on one mode and ending it with another in a seamless, integrated trip thanks to the connections offered between these major international airports and the vast European high-speed rail network. There has been little experience of this so far in the United States, with United's codeshare relationship with Amtrak in the northeast a unique but relatively small exception. But as high-speed rail projects develop in this country over the coming decades in California, Florida, Texas, and the northeast, and demand once again puts constraints on existing aviation infrastructure, the potential for future integration between these two modes increases and becomes mutually beneficial. Developing air service strategies and future airport infrastructure with a mind for greater multimodal integration, including rail and high-occupancy vehicle (HOV) lane dedicated intercity express buses, will be an increasingly important part of the progressive airport's future.

### Arrival of on-demand aerial ridesharing

According to its website, Uber Air plans to begin operating an urban on-demand aerial ridesharing network in select cities in 2023. With vertical take-off and landing electric aircraft, the service will dramatically improve door-to-door travel times inside metropolitan areas with congested surface transportation. Car ridesharing services have already had a dramatic impact on airports through decreased parking revenues and evolving surface infrastructure needs over the last decade, and the arrival of Uber Air will once again fundamentally change how many passengers begin and end their air travel journey over the next decade. Perhaps the airport parking garages that were emptied by Uber's ground services will be repurposed to accommodate Uber Air's services.

From an air service perspective, the arrival of aerial ridesharing opens up a number of possibilities for a destination's attractiveness to air carriers. What does that do to the demand for secondary airports in ski resort towns that used to be a three-hour, hazardous journey by car via the closest major hub airport but could be easily accessed via a 20-minute Uber Air trip from the much closer regional facility? How much more demand for a market will there be if suddenly that national monument, professional sports arena, amusement park or beach are brought much closer into range by avoiding crowded highways altogether? Passengers value time and convenience. They want to spend less time getting to their destination and more time enjoying it. Cities with a robust and efficient aerial ridesharing network will be at a competitive advantage to attract commerce, bleisure, and tourists in the future and airports will be well-served to ensure adequate infrastructure, regulatory policies, and protocols are in place to accommodate this next disruption sooner rather than later.

### Six step approach to air service development in the post-COVID world

COVID-19 and the industry-altering events that will follow may introduce unprecedented disruption and uncertainty into the aviation world, but there are a number of steps airport professionals can take to best position their market moving forward.

#### 1. Re-examine market segment diversification, strengths, and opportunities

The top air service priorities of the last 5 years may no longer apply or may simply have to take a back burner. The front few slides of your air service pitch to air carriers highlighting the economic strengths and market assets of your community may need to be reshuffled and reprioritized (i.e. instead of beginning with cruises and conventions, maybe talk about the growing opportunities for outdoor adventurism in your market).

In February 2020, San Diego's top air service priority at the time focused on expanding the list of nonstop trans-oceanic destinations and there was good progress in advancing that goal. Today, international connectivity remains a priority but refocused largely on restoring the links that were temporarily lost and working to better understand and remove the restrictions that make international travel presently prohibitive. Like before, developing trans-oceanic service is a multi-faceted effort that typically spans several years. While markets like San Diego hope to restore all service as soon as possible, there has been an industry shift toward developing new domestic leisure capacity, and the timeline for new international projects perhaps needs to be pushed back a couple of years.

*Perhaps.* The aviation industry is going through one of the biggest shake-ups in history right now. Fleets are consolidating, business plans are evolving, network strategies are changing. Network planners are scrambling to find anywhere they can fly a plane that breaks even, and they are more open minded than ever to consider outside the box opportunities. Do they put that double daily back into Los Angeles, as all of their competitors from that region of the world do the same in a period of suppressed demand and dwindled hubflow, or do they consider diversifying their southern California gateways by adding a few frequencies without competition a few hours south in San Diego instead?

Continued advancements in aircraft technologies (such as the Airbus A321XLR) will open new market opportunities particularly for mid-sized cities where present-day aircraft range and economics make service unviable. Shifting passenger preferences toward more eco-friendly travel will put higher premiums on nonstop point-to-point services. Successful multimodal integration can enable new short-haul services and non-aeronautical revenue opportunities for airports both large and small, as more intercity surface transportation networks are integrated with the airport terminal complex.

Diversify your targets. Capitalize on your market strengths that play during and after the crisis. Seize opportunities that uniquely fit the moment.

## 2. Fortify regional partnerships

Never before has having a close working relationship with your economic development corporation, tourism authority, hotel/motel association, convention and visitors bureau, and broader business community been more important. In times of budget cuts and the need to do more with less, turning to and relying on each other to share information and resources, identify market trends, and collaborate to address community needs is critical to getting your community back up and running as quickly as possible. It's also an essential component of air service development. These regional partners know and understand your community and the flying public in ways the airport never can. They have their fingers on the pulse of what's happening on the ground while you're working to connect as many dots as possible in the air.

Last year's O&D (origin and destination) passenger demand figures are not the most important data points in determining where an airline should fly during a pandemic. Airline network planners are looking for new data points to help guide their short- to medium-term decision making. Some of those data points might come from your regional partners who may know more than you about current hotel booking curves, attraction developments, and new business moves in your market.

### 3. Be nimble, flexible, and open-minded

The crisis is constantly evolving. Hotspots have rotated from country to country and from state to state. Airline schedules are still subject to change four weeks out. No one knows exactly what next month, let alone next year, will ultimately pan out to be. In this environment, airports need to be nimble and adaptable in their air service approach. The world has moved to be able to collect, communicate, and share information entirely virtually. Airports have had to put aside how they understood things before COVID, and take a fresh stock of everything as it is now and may be in the future. And while we do the best we can to identify and commit to a sustainable path forward, we have to be ready and willing to pivot with the next disruption that comes our way. If getting passenger numbers back up—any passengers—is the main priority, that may mean shifting efforts and air service priorities from pursuing a handful of seasonal flights to "sexier" international destinations to restoring increased frequencies to hubs or year-round service to new domestic cities. It may mean devoting more resources to connecting airports with additional short-haul, surface transportation services in order to feed new air service routes. If we are to not just survive but do better than the average in the present moment, we have to be willing to let go of everything we thought we knew yesterday, if it no longer applies today.

### 4. Maintain relationships with air carriers

Having close, personal working relationships with airline network planners has always been critical to staying informed on airline business strategy shifts and future network plans. Staying connected used to be facilitated by attending a half dozen or so industry networking events and in-person meetings that would typically occur throughout the year. Now, the whole relationship has become a virtual one. Maintaining those relationships is a key requirement to stay on top of the latest airline schedule changes and airline responses to the present crisis situation. It helps to know about cuts or additions before the schedules are published so you can adequately prepare your team ahead of inevitable media and public inquiries. For the foreseeable future, virtual communication will be the primary vehicle to stay in touch and let airlines know about what is happening in your market, from attraction re-openings, to new business ventures to success in controlling the spread of COVID-19. Developing a closer partnership between airlines and airports has never been more vital to ensure the survival of the aviation industry as we know it beyond the present moment and the turbulence that lies ahead. Together, airports and airlines can not only chart a course to navigate travel restrictions and new health and safety protocols, but also identify untapped markets and new revenue potential.

## 5. Become a multi-faceted expert

The job of the air service professional has evolved during this crisis. The role has become a critical data clearinghouse for strategic organizational decision-making, a key stakeholder liaison, and a community power builder. The air service professional works more closely than ever with airport operations, planning, and finance to optimize the airport enterprise for both today and tomorrow in light of evolving market conditions. In many respects, air service professionals did all this to some degree before. Today, by becoming a little more conversant in areas where multiple departments and agencies overlap, they can play a key role in better aligning them and that bodes very well for successfully navigating the disruptions of the future. This puts the air service development professional at the crossroads of strategic multidisciplinary integration critical to the airport's survival. It requires becoming a subject matter expert not just in one wheelhouse, but comfortable conversing in others and identifying early on market conditions that could impact any of them. This is important in solidifying the air service professional's contribution to the airport operation beyond simply maintaining and securing new flights, but in helping facilitate critical decision making that impacts the airport's day-to-day operation and long-term planning.

## 6. Anticipate the next industry disruptions

COVID-19 is not the first and will not be the last industry-altering disruption to impact aviation. It is unique in many ways as discussed throughout this book, but so too will be the disruptions that follow. We cannot expect a future simply based on what we know from the past. But we can use lessons learned from the past to better prepare ourselves for what may come next. While some discussion was given on the previous pages to four particular disruptions on the horizon, there will be others. Anyone tasked with managing and improving passenger air service in their community can apply the two forecast scenarios discussed throughout this book with respect to future passenger traffic levels and begin identifying, planning for, and positioning their market to best weather the next disruptions that will inevitably come. Disruptions may not always be preventable. But they can be mitigated, adapted to, and overcome. The best way to survive the next major disruption is to anticipate it ahead of time.

## In summary

If COVID-19 has taught us anything, it is that business will not go on as usual. While air service professionals continue to navigate the current industry disruption, we must begin anticipating the next one. Diversification, flexibility, foresight, collaboration, and adaptation are the underpinnings of a successful air service strategy and approach, and the tools to weather the coming industry disruptions of tomorrow.

## Notes

1  Cirium Schedules Analysis, airports with regularly scheduled passenger service that ceased after March 2020.
2  Sasha Foo, "San Diego Company Makes Up One-Third of All COVID-19 Kits in US," *Kusi News*, August 6, 2020.
3  Noah Maghsadi and Tina Huang, "Runways Underwater: Maps Show Where Rising Seas Threaten 80 Airports Around the World," World Resources Institute, February 5, 2020.
4  Hiroko Tabuchi, "Many Major Airports Are Near Sea Level: A Disaster in Japan Shows What Can Go Wrong," *The New York Times*, September 7, 2018.
5  Based on charts from "787 Airplane Characteristics for Airport Planning," Document Number D6-5833,3 Revision M, Boeing Commercial Airplanes (March 2018), 3-5 through 3-8.
6  Ibid.
7  See Chris McGinnis, "SFO To Spend More Than $1 Billion To Hold Back The Bay," SFGATE, October 15, 2019; and Alex Davies, "How Airports Are Protecting Themselves Against Rising Seas," *The Wired*, December 2, 2019.
8  BBC News, "Sweden Sees Rare Fall in Air Passengers, As Flight-Shaming Takes Off," January 10, 2020.

# What can oil and gas, the military, and complexity scientists teach us about weathering these turbulences?

*Frédéric Ducros*
Former Chief Transformation Officer, AirAsia, Former Head of Change Management, Cathay Pacific

These are trying times. Being at the helm of an airline has never been an easy task—massive size, 24-hour operation, big investments, high risks, high-maintenance assets, complex ecosystem, chaotic crises. And it has been getting harder over the years. Economies shift constantly between sudden accelerations you do not want to miss, and downturns you must weather. Every decade has its crisis. Markets collide unpredictably. Demand changes unexpectedly. Game-changing technologies come up faster than you can adopt them. Employees have more expectations and less loyalty. Signals are more numerous and harder to read. And with more factors to consider, more constraints to account for, there is no easy, definite answer. This is what Volatile, Uncertain, Chaotic, Ambiguous feels like. Transforming has become an ever-present necessity, and permanent focus. And then, COVID-19!

If flying an airline has never been an easy task, surely, flying an airline in such turbulent times will be a tough job for the next few years. Nonstop transformation was becoming the new norm. But now we need to transform while enduring chaotic situations. Those who do will not only outlive others, they will come out stronger.

Where to look for inspiring or insightful examples of practices and approaches to weather the storms?

In this brief paper, we will explore a few practices and approaches from oil and gas companies, venture capital firms, and the military. Airlines could gain by trying them. We will then summarize five ways of thinking about situations airlines are facing now, ways of thinking and acting you can impart to your team, and help your teams apply as you see fit (see notes 1, 3, 4, 5, 8, and 11).

## Oil and gas: Reinvention, integration and exploration

The oil and gas industry can be a great source of reflection and inspiration for airlines. There is much to learn from what they do well, the difficulties they face and major mistakes. Like air transport, the oil and gas industry is a diverse mix of small to gigantic government-owned or -linked companies and private businesses that share high risk, high use of technology and capital, long horizons of planning and operation, as well as overall long-term demand growth with sudden, dramatic falls. They have been significantly affected by the pandemic, although not as badly as airlines. For the long term, major players also surmise the end of oil demand relentless growth, while others note how much more difficult and costly it has become to find, setup and produce oil.

Historically, oil and gas businesses have split their activities among upstream, midstream, and downstream operations. These three businesses tackle distinct challenges with people who operate with vastly different mindsets and ways of working. Upstream focus on exploration, development, and production. Their teams search across land and sea for large, accessible reservoirs, then test the reservoirs and develop them before setting up massive operations to extract enormous quantities of raw material for years, often decades. Midstream focus on storing and transporting the extracted oil and gas through pipelines, ships, and trucks, to the refineries where they can be processed. These regulated activities are highly dependent on upstream but less risky. Downstream focus on operating refineries to convert raw materials into final products for industrial or individual use from jet fuel and heating oil, to asphalt, gasoline, and plastics. Many also run a large network of gas stations, owned or franchised.

As an executive in an airline, you may want to explore three topics the best oil and gas companies have done well:

### 1. Rethinking your company from being what it was to being much more

Over the last decades, some oil and gas companies have diversified as 'energy companies' that provide power to businesses and consumers, not just oil and gas companies that extract raw materials and sell their derivatives. Far from just a renaming, this shift is a necessity with the coming energy transition. This might come because of environmental policies, but it will much more likely happen due to the finite nature of oil and gas reserves. They expanded their portfolio of investments and offerings to renewable energy sources such as wind and solar, mostly, as well as emerging technologies such as nuclear fusion. They also expanded into energy storage and carbon sequestration down the value chain of their core activities.

Similarly, airlines have traditionally been defined by their fleet, crew, and destinations. As businesses, they carry around people and goods from A to B with airplanes. Yet, many airlines could reposition themselves to become more than an airline, and ultimately be more than an airline.

**Questions worth investigating**: Which could your organization become: a lifestyle company, providing exciting experiences online and offline as we started at AirAsia from 2018? A loyalty company, becoming the preferred wallet and homepage or even super app of your customers? A logistics company, providing end-to-end shipping and delivery solutions to the door? A travel company? An integrated transportation and mobility company? An engineering company? How would this shift impact the way you run the business? What new offerings would you need to provide? How could you leverage your current strengths and pivot your business to more stable and possibly more profitable activities?

## 2. Integrating the value chain

Many oil and gas companies are integrated companies. They have upstream operations for exploration and production, midstream operations for transportation and downstream operations for refining and distribution. And the integrated value chain makes them much more powerful and resilient businesses.

Similarly, airlines may explore integrated value chain options: digital lifestyle, digital business services, airports integration, last-mile transportation (public, semi-public or private). Of course, few airlines could now afford to acquire other businesses, but there are other routes: mergers, joint ventures, reverse acquisitions, among others. Many could prepare themselves to become a highly visible part of a larger, more solid, powerful group or public transport service.

**Questions worth investigating**: Which businesses or services could you integrate into your offerings? Which services could you offer to a larger group to complete the value chain upstream or downstream, closer to the end-user industrial customer or individual consumer? Which integrated value chain could you complete with an alternative, for instance adding air transportation to a land and sea provider?

## 3. Getting proficient with exploration and opportunities discovery

Oil and gas businesses understand that exploration is a different type of activity. It is not linear. It is not predictable the way most manufacturing or retail businesses are. It is ultimately a treasure hunt, an activity where your teams can be knowledgeable, use the latest insights and technology, follow good practices, do everything right, yet not get any positive result for a long time. So they handle these activities differently from the way they handle regular operations such as production or distribution, which can be reliable in normal times, and can by and large be managed and controlled.

Similarly, airlines may want to explore how they can grow these exploration and development teams that go out there, and search the land and sea to discover then develop new opportunities that the rest of the business would grow at scale—not just new destinations, new routes, new services through their customers' journey, new offerings and products in the cabins or in the airport lounges, but also entirely different services as described earlier.

**Questions worth investigating**: What could your teams learn from how oil and gas companies explore, test, and develop new oil fields before growing large scale operations? How could you embed these principles systematically to discover and estimate or develop the potential of new types of opportunities? Where else, beyond destinations and routes, could airlines apply these techniques? Who in your organization is methodical, bold and strong enough to take this responsibility? What can you do to become at the same time resilient and effective at exploration of new fields of opportunities?

### Military and insurgency, with team of teams, red teaming and Shu Ha Ri

Through history, wars have shown that little is ever set before the battle, through countless upsets. Military culture and strategy are seen on the battlefield, and analyzed in memoirs, a few of which have earned a place on the shelves of any leader today. Century after century, superpowers relying heavily on technological advantage and overwhelming numbers have suffered surprising defeats at the hands of much smaller and weaker enemies who used asymmetric warfare techniques.

> No battle plan ever survives contact with the enemy.
>
> (Helmuth von Moltke)

A battlefield, with thousands of individuals, vehicles, weapons, is the epitome of complexity, quickly falling into chaos. Outcomes can be estimated, but surprises are always in reach. C2 explains in *The International C2 Journal*:

> The word "control" is inappropriate … because it sends the wrong message. It implies that complex situations can be controlled … push the right levers; take this action or that; solve this problem. But this is a dangerous oversimplification. The best that one can do is to create a set of conditions that improves the probability that a desirable … outcome will occur… . Control is in fact an emergent property.[6]

To address this complexity, the military have been exploring a range of techniques and practices at the operational, tactical and at the individual level. And as an airline executive, you may find it useful to apply some of their findings to help your organization navigate these turbulences.

#### 1. Rethinking your organization for resilience and adaptability

**At the strategic level,** military commands have made it a priority to increase their forces' adaptability, responsiveness, and resilience, based on the premise that most conflicts will now involve asymmetric, quickly changing situations. To meet these objectives, military commands have focused their efforts on three main shifts:

- Giving authority and autonomy to the frontline, on the basis that officers and soldiers on the battlefield have a direct perception of what is happening in their section and are in the best position to make decisions.
- Investing in lateral connectivity across the force, helping units connect with other units they will interact with, to build a shared understanding, instead of operating in silos relying on top-down communications.
- Asking leaders to disseminate information and intentions instead of orders, so that teams can make decisions at all levels, to allow and support empowered execution on the frontline.

These principles evolve the organization. In the traditional command system, the connections and interactions that matter are within teams and between the teams and their managers, and the leader listens to facts and gives orders. In a command of teams, teams may operate autonomously but they report to a traditional, siloed structure. And in a team of teams, the connections that matter are as much within the teams as they are between the teams, and the leader shares intentions and facts with more local leaders who have their autonomy yet work in concert.

Similarly, airlines have immense experience with complexity, and even chaos. They also routinely hand over their responsibility for thousands of passengers to individuals with pre-flight briefings and post-flight review as a sole oversight mechanism. Air traffic control worldwide is also a complex system, which can quickly shift into chaotic situations when typhoons or volcanic eruptions affect large parts of the globe. From an operational standpoint, airlines and airports have responded incredibly well to these situations, thanks to crises cells, integrated operations centers, and the generally massively distributed system of responsibility where cockpit crews are in charge and air traffic control dispatches information. They are resilient to most weather conditions. But what about business operations and sales?

**Questions worth investigating**: How can you give the same decision power to the frontline that you grant to your cockpit crew and senior cabin crew? How can you increase lateral connectivity across the airline, with for instance marketing teams connecting with sales teams and product teams? How can you help them build a shared understanding, instead of operating in silos relying on top-down communications? How can you nudge leaders to disseminate information instead of orders, so that teams can make decisions at all levels?

*2. Discovering, recognizing, and addressing your organization's vulnerabilities in action*

**At the operational level**, military leaders have been exploring ways to test the effectiveness, adaptability and resilience of their forces. One of the techniques they use is red teaming. The aim of red teaming is to discover and exploit unknown vulnerabilities, to help the organization get out of its own complacency and hubris, and realize its weaknesses, so they can then be addressed. Red team members are highly encouraged to resort to unconventional methods, exploit the terrain and any opportunity they spot to their maximum advantage, ignore traditionally accepted rules, and generally "play dirty." This puts the blue team (the ones representing the main forces) in a position of weakness, by presenting risky, unexpected situations. Reaching these objectives requires an extreme level of vulnerability and acceptance from the command.

When it works, it provides heightened awareness and rich insights. It does not always work that way, though, because it is so humbling for commanders to see years of investments, planning, and training fail in days or hours, or minutes, that some are tempted to script the wargame to preserve appearances.

This is what happened in the case of Millennium Challenge 2002. This massive exercise is an example of a large wargame using red teaming that could have been better used. As it went, the Red Team led by retired Marine Corps General Van Riper won within 5 to 10 minutes of the start, sinking 19 US ships with lightly weaponized boats. But the organizers of the exercise had an expansive agenda, with the intention to test a number of new vehicles, weapons and techniques. As this stunningly quick defeat prevented them from showcasing the above, they canceled this victory on a technicality, and stacked the deck against the red team, changing the rules and preventing them from operating as they intended. A large report gives clues that the Pentagon may now see more use in letting wargames play out and debriefing to recognize weaknesses and address them.

As an airline executive, you know well that you cannot afford such complacency. Yet, many organizations have their weaknesses, and in these trying times, it may seem scary to people who inherited them to suddenly see their area under the limelight. Everybody wants to find weaknesses, but few are comfortable sharing weaknesses in their field of responsibility.

**Questions worth investigating**: How can you recognize both the people who created imperfect plans and the people who found holes in these plans, and invite them to keep iterating to make the plans better? How can you help your organization recognize and name hubris and complacency when it happens? How can you instill curiosity and resilience? How can you make it safe for people to name weaknesses, and "unsafe" for people to hide them?

*3. Creating more leaders across the organization, to get the best from the most engaged teams*

**At the tactical team level**, many commanders have embraced the complex nature of a crew and the importance of tackling human factors. For many warship commanders, for instance, letting go of traditional command and control means anything but letting go of their leadership; it means finding new ways to lead that create more leaders among the crew, and empower them to get better results, more resilience and adaptability. Captain D. Michael Abrashoff, former US Navy Captain of the USS *Brenfold*, explored the reasons why sailors were leaving the navy, which included: (1) not being treated with respect, (2) being prevented from having an impact, (3) not being listened to, and (4) not being rewarded with more responsibility. This is described in his book, *It's Your Ship!* He describes the key to being a successful skipper as being able to "see the ship through the eyes of the crew." Other key areas of focus for him as a leader include "trusting people, [because] they will usually prove you right," and being "a rising tide that lifts all the boats" by helping your people feel needed. David Marquet, former US Navy Captain of the USS *Santa Fe*, expands on the same in his book, *Turn the Ship Around*—with principles that helped him turn his submarine from the worst in the Navy to the best in a year.[10] These include more ways to turn interactions upside down to help people at the helm truly be at the helm:

- Engaging crew to declare their intentions with "I intend to...," "I plan on..." or "I will...," instead of asking for guidance or permission, and empowering them with acknowledgments "Take control" or "Very well."
- Promoting flowing and intentional conversations over traditional formal meetings. This includes allowing/inviting questioning, instead of making questions risky to ask.
- Replacing when possible the one-way delivery of briefings followed by directives and orders with two-way conversations where the commander specifies the goals (the why and the what), not the methods (not the how), hears the crew, and certifies (aka acknowledges) the plans that leaders from within the crew generated.
- Enriching orders with context and informal communication, which could give meaning to the request, and could help the crew understand if a request is now irrelevant, past-due or at least questionable given what they know.
- Learning, everywhere, all the time.

**Questions worth investigating**: As an executive, are you rewarding people to tell you that your plan is great? Are you punishing people who tell you your plan will not work?

*4. Rethinking your company from being an airline to being more than an airline*

Finally, since everyone realizes battles are won one fight at a time, it makes sense to expand on these practices **at the individual level**. We can connect to the above the path martial artists take to assimilate and master their art, and "become one with their weapon" the way an artist would become one with their instrument. This martial artist's journey of embodiment is often summarized as Shu Ha Ri (followed at times by the word *Kokoro*), a reference to Japanese martial arts concepts in Aikido and Shorinji Kenpo. It starts for them by teaching their body and mind to fit the form and the weapon, until it becomes appropriate to adjust their form and weapon to fit their needs.

The Aikido master Endō Seishirō explained this journey as such:

> It is known that, when we learn or train in something, we pass through the stages of shu, ha, and ri. These stages are explained as follows. In shu, we repeat the forms and discipline ourselves so that our bodies absorb the forms that our forebears created. We remain faithful to these forms with no deviation. Next, in the stage of ha, once we have disciplined ourselves to acquire the forms and movements, we make innovations. In this process the forms may be broken and discarded. Finally, in ri, we completely depart from the forms, open the door to creative technique, and arrive in a place

where we act in accordance with what our heart/mind desires, unhindered while not overstepping laws.

This journey does not apply solely to martial artists. It can apply to any highly trained warrior, be they pilots or commandos. And it applies to professionals:

1. Initially following scrupulously existing *katas*, methods or forms (**Shu**), the practitioner learns to execute and practice large blocks of knowledge, choreographies varying in length, from beginning to end.
2. As they grow in their practice, and start mastering certain forms with skill, they start engaging in short contests, where they get the opportunity to practice the *kata*, but also the necessity to break down the *kata* (**Ha**) in their core components, and arrange them to fit the needs of the situation, intuitively, spontaneously. Ha corresponding to actual fights, it is the place of much episodic learning, intense learning with very fast knowledge acquisition due to the intensity and high stakes. This is what soldiers do when they learn to dismantle and reassemble their guns under live fire at night in the field.
3. As they keep growing in their practice, they engage in more and more live contest and practice, which gets them not only to break the rules, but to transcend them and recompose them (**Ri**) into their own style, to leverage their natural strengths and unique preferences.
4. Finally, as years of fluid practice take over the initial training, they synthesize their practice into a small set of beliefs and practices (*Kokoro*) that capture the essence of the art, and encapsulate their learning—but would not make any sense to an apprentice that has not walked the path (see Figure 7.3a).

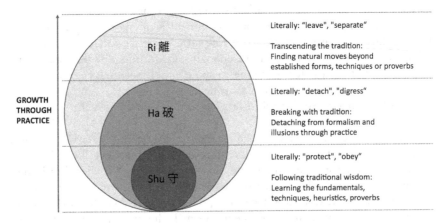

**GROWTH THROUGH PRACTICE**

Ri 離

Literally: "leave", "separate"

Transcending the tradition:
Finding natural moves beyond established forms, techniques or proverbs

Ha 破

Literally: "detach", "digress"

Breaking with tradition:
Detaching from formalism and illusions through practice

Shu 守

Literally: "protect", "obey"

Following traditional wisdom:
Learning the fundamentals, techniques, heuristics, proverbs

*Figure 7.3a* Shu Ha Ri: Continuous growth and breakthroughs through practice

For airlines, what this means is that talent—from an inclusive standpoint anyone who is willing to dedicate themselves to the business and has some skills—must grow, and that if growth has many paths, it surely is a personal journey towards excellence, which includes on-the-job practice of the learning in live conditions, mentored then coached deliberate practice, active recall, spaced repetition, episodic learning.

**Questions worth investigating**: How can you bring these practices into the many disciplines that make your business successful, aside from flight operations, where they are already at play? How can you benefit from their use?

### *Approaching our world with different lenses, and picking the right one to handle "the mess"*

> We cannot solve our problems with the same level of thinking that created them.
>
> (Albert Einstein)

Following management science practices beyond their applicability made airlines vulnerable to crises. Assuming that systems are deterministic and can be modeled, predicted, and controlled, management science led to models, timers, metrics, key performance indicators (KPIs), and drove incredible improvements in productivity and cost efficiency. But the very decisions that made them more productive and cost-efficient led to removing all the slack and flexibility that could help them be resilient and adaptive.

Since then, scientists have discovered and explained what some executives have felt all along: few situations and systems can be fully modeled, predicted, and controlled. It's not that simple. Most situations are instead open-ended and interconnected, complex, or chaotic; and their behaviors cannot be fully determined—for instance, knowing the employees in a team is not enough to determine what they will do. Complex systems often behave in non-linear ways—doing the same thing twice may yield different results. And new behaviors emerge unexpectedly—for instance, crowds may self-organize spontaneously (herd mentality).

All this impacts dramatically the work of executives. Teams, organizations, markets, and networks are what makes businesses and sectors. And they are organic, complex systems, not deterministic machines as schools had taught them. If companies are not mechanical systems as executives were taught, then they cannot be led the way executives were taught either. So, it is normal to see poor results when attempting to drive them as such.

This is where Cynefin can help airlines survive these turbulences and beat their competition (see notes 2 and 7).

**Cynefin** is a model that helps step back, make sense of situations, then apply an approach that fits the situation. Cynefin distinguishes five situations: clear, complicated, complex, chaotic, and confused (see Figure 7.3b).

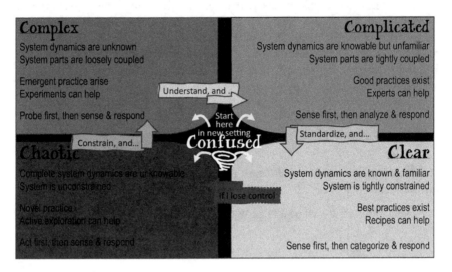

*Figure 7.3b* A simplified summary of the Cynefin model

To experience Cynefin firsthand, consider the following situations. When driving to work on a clear day, at their usual driving time, any executive would easily be able to handle a call in speaker mode, because they would drive in automatic mode, not having to think about the well-known path. If they were to drive to work at night, for an emergency, during a black out, what was simple before could become complicated. If for some reason the same happened the day you took on a new job with another airline, in a new city, this would quickly become a complex situation. And if there was a severe storm, the situation would leap into chaos. Different situations, different actions.

**Clear** (formerly 'simple') situations are *familiar*, with *obvious* links between cause and effect. They are hence *predictable*, and effective responses/solutions are well known. This allows for repeatable **best practices** and straightforward automation. This is what happens, for instance, in an airline contact center:

- An automated system allows to receive and "sense" the request/situation/need (dial 1 for…, 2 for…).
- It orients customers across categories of requests (routing to the right agent with the right authority).
- The contact center agent then applies well known **best practices** with check lists and standard operating procedures.
- As teams grow more familiar with the simple domain, they may **automate** many of the tasks.

Having a part of the business in the clear domain frees people's minds for more complicated or complex situations. Contact centers, employee-related procurement, and employee onboarding are some of the functions and processes that airlines can consider for the clear domain. At the same time, handling too many situations in a systematic way with the "clear" frame of mind is risky. It can quickly turn into a crisis/chaos if the context changes, and people miss these changes. For instance, odd requests due to unexpected chains of events cannot be tacked by the automated system, which is why people want to talk to an agent. When major storms strike, airlines must get out of this mode to help their passengers better.

**Questions worth investigating**: What parts of the business do you want to deliberately put in the simple domain? How clear and uniformly followed are your best practices? What do your team managers plan to do to keep things clear for everyone, and get the best repeatability? What activities in this simple domain do your team managers want to automate? What measures do you and your team managers want to take to ensure you all do not get blindsided if things change?

**Complicated** situations are *unfamiliar*, but ultimately *knowable*, because the relationships between the parts are *understandable*, although not obvious. For instance, a cause and its effect may be separated over time. The setup of the system makes its dynamics *predictable* by experts. In other words, the way the system works can be understood and controlled, just not by anyone, and not immediately. This lens assumes multiple plausible causes or contributions to any single event, and the default mode for working together is "collaboration": we agree on directions, do their part, then come back and check on each other.

Appropriate approaches involve sensing the situation through direct observation or data collection, analyzing the system and its behaviors because context makes situations unique, then applying **good practices** that experts could recommend and run. Another good approach is to **consult experts**. Experts thrive, and are useful, in this type of situation, as time and dedicated practice gave them precious knowledge that laypeople lack.

As you grow more familiar with a complicated system, you can formalize your understanding of what happens in it, and elaborate standard (albeit possibly complicated) ways to operate in it. You can then start interacting with it or its parts as if they belonged to the clear domain. This is what many methodologies are trying to do.

**Complex** situations are unknown. Appropriate approaches in the complex domain include asking a lot of people for their perspectives and recommendations, translating promising ones into safe experiments, running these experiments, and analyzing their outcomes, then amplifying or modulating what seems to work. This leads to **emergent practices** as you iterate and apply more or less of them as the system responds. Best practices are irrelevant in complex environments, given the sensitivity of the system to its context. Also, because the system is not fully understandable or predictable, there is no such thing as an expert there.

As you understand more of what happens in it, you can identify ways to tune or modulate the behavior of the system, and you can start interacting with it (or part of it) in the way you would handle a complicated system.

**Chaotic** situations are simply unknowable. It can be a crisis you fall into, or a voluntary exploration, very little information and meaning is available. An appropriate approach involves taking action first, because of the lack of available information or meaning, and adjusting as the system reacts. Another fitting approach is to constrain the system, to bring it from complex and unknowable to a complex system. Chaotic situations are dangerous because certain leaders will use these as excuses to shift to autocratic leadership.

We enter most situations with one of these lenses on. This default lens we approach situations with is usually the one we are the most familiar with, because of what we have done before, or what sounds true to us:

- Shane led large, repetitive operations and sees situations through a "clear" lens. He gives people simple instructions and make sure they follow the Standard Operating Procedures. He is considering automating the whole activity.
- Seamus led engineering or maintenance operations and reads situations with a "complicated" lens. He hires experts, makes sure all his people are well trained, know every page of the manual, and practice on aircraft parts until they can do repairs blindfolded. He then relies on them entirely for diagnostics and repairs.
- Samantha led highly collaborative operations (ticket sales, air traffic control) and sees the world through a "complex" lens.
- Sienna led the integrated operation centers during typhoons and before that war rooms during the first hours of global crises. She sees the world through a "chaotic" lens. She assumes she cannot understand everything, but she can act on parts that matter.

Did you notice that most management operate between the "clear" and "complicated" lenses?

Few of us ever remove our preferred lens and see the world through the other lenses available to us. **Misreading a situation can be extremely costly**.

Looking at the way work is done and decisions are taken, airlines' current level of thinking is assuming "complicated" situations. Complicated matters, such as aircraft maintenance, are handled with the "complicated" assumption. Complex situations, such as patterns and rostering or pricing are often brought back to "complicated" or "simple" (copy-paste) frames, although some effective operations embrace the reality of complexity and the necessity of experimentation and constant adjustments.

**Questions worth investigating**: What if, instead, you approached every new situation in an "open" state? What if you accepted, even invited the momentary **confusion**, with the first objective to understand what type of situation you face, what lens you need to use, and what mode of action you need to take? What if your first few thoughts, instincts, moments of attention were dedicated to one single goal: make sense of the situation you are in, so you can then use the appropriate lens and the appropriate approach?

### Summary and suggested courses of action

Many situations are complex or chaotic. These situations cannot be fully understood, predicted, and controlled. Approaching them as such makes situations worse.

Here are a few things airline executives can try, to lead their teams better in turbulent times:

### Mindset:

1. Recognize there are different types of situations and problems, and solving them takes different approaches.
2. Recognize their own biases, from a look back at their career history and personal preferences.
3. Remember how oil and gas manage different parts of their business differently, in particular exploration.
4. Remember how best-laid plans die with first enemy contact, and how planning is more useful than the plans.

### Practices:

5. Develop your ability to recognize situations and distinguish chaotic, complex, and complicated domains.
6. Practice naming the situations and expressing the appropriate approaches that would fit the situation.
7. Make it easier, as a leader, for your people to do the same with the situations they encounter.
8. Help your teams learn through training, but also practice live to make the techniques theirs.

## Notes

1. Dave Snowden and Mary E. Boone, "A Leader's Framework for Decision Making," *Harvard Business Review*, Vol. 85, No. 11, 2007, pp. 68-76, 149.
2. Dave Snowden, *Cynefin, A Sense of Time and Place: An Ecological Approach to Sense Making and Learning in Formal and Informal Communities*, 2011. www.researchgate.net/publication/264884267_Cynefin_A_Sense_of_Time_and_Place_an_Ecological_Approach_to_Sense_Making_and_Learning_in_Formal_and_Informal_Communities
3. Chris Fussell, *One Mission: How Leaders Build A Team Of Teams* (New York: MacMillan, 2017).
4. S.A. McChrystal, *Team of Teams: New Rules of Engagement for a Complex World* (New York: Portfolio/Penguin, 2015).

5. Stanley McChrystal, Jeff Eggers, and Jason Mangone, *Leaders: Myth and Reality* (New York: Portfolio/Penguin, 2018).

6. *International C2 Journal*, Vol. 1, No. 1. http://internationalc2institute.org/

7. Greg Brougham with Dave Snowden, *The Cynefin Mini-Book, InfoQ* (Morrisville, NC: lulu.com, 2015).

8. C.F. Kurtz and Dave Snowden, "The New Dynamics of Strategy: Sense-making in a Complex and Complicated World," *IBM Systems Journal*, Vol. 42, No. 3, 2003.

9. Captain D. Michael Abrashoff, *It's Your Ship: Management Techniques from the Best Damn Ship in the Navy* (New York: Hachette/GrandCentral Publishing, 2012).

10. L. David Marquet, *Turn the Ship Around! A True Story of Turning Followers into Leaders* (New York: Portfolio/Penguin, 2013).

11. McKinsey Global Institute, "Inside the Mind of a Venture Capitalist: An Interview with Steve Jurvetson." www.mckinsey.com/industries/technology-media-and-telecommunications/our-insights/inside-the-mind-of-a-venture-capitalist

## Profit optimized fleets, successfully designed airliners: The power of digitalized bottom-up planning

*Karl Echtermeyer*
Director Fleet Projects, Deutsche Lufthansa AG

### 1. Does size matter? Interaction of unit cost and yield

When manufacturers develop new aircraft types, they collect requirements from the airlines to derive the design and specifications for the new aircraft. This process is isolated from the airlines' fleet planning and is largely guided by a heuristic approach. This has led to the development of aircraft types that proved to be commercial failures and of which only a few have been sold, such as the Airbus A340-500 (29 units) or the Boeing 777-200LR (59 units).

Even the Airbus A380, equipped with about 500 seats, once euphorically welcomed by the airlines in their top-down planning, proved to be over-sized and a major loss-maker after only a few years. Over many years, Airbus had succeeded with a high marketing effort in convincing the airlines to buy the large A380, as it promised a significant unit cost advantage over the (smaller) Boeing 747-400 (see Figure 7.4). By exploiting economies of scale, the Airbus A380 achieves a unit cost advantage of around 15% over the Boeing 747-400. This unit cost advantage of the A380 is achieved through a volume growth of more than 40% additional seats versus the Boeing 747-400 (approx. 350 seats).

However, these (early) economic considerations failed to recognize that the postulated "profit advantage through the use of economies of scale (A380)" turned into a profit disadvantage on many routes.[1] The background to this is a demand forecast based on assumptions that resulted in too many relevant

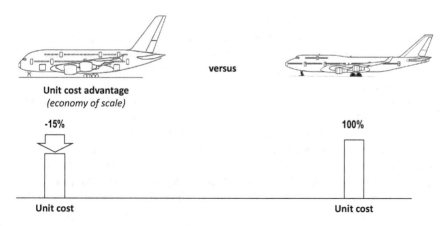

*Figure 7.4* Unit cost advantage of a large aircraft by using economies of scale

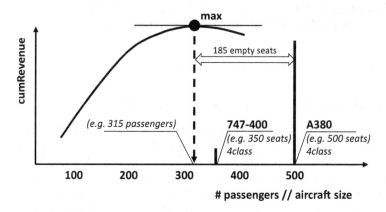

*Figure 7.5* The optimized cumulated revenue volume for a single flight: The answer of
the market as a result of demand and supply

operational areas for the A380 and a too high volume of passengers on these
routes. This lack of passenger demand could not be stimulated by a unit cost
advantage passed on to the customer. This is because revenue management
systems attempt to maximize the revenue potential for each individual flight, in
the best case selling scarce capacity at a maximum price (see Figure 7.5).

In this example (Figure 7.5), the maximum cumulative revenue that can be
generated is 315 passengers. The A380 is oversized with about 500 seats (185
empty seats), whereas the Boeing 747-400 with 315 passengers and about 350
seats achieves a seat load factor of 90%. But in the awkward situation of filling
an oversized capacity, seats are brought to market for little money, so that at
least a contribution margin can be earned. As a consequence, the cumulative
revenue potential drops, as Figure 7.5 illustrates. Incidentally other side effects,
such as the distortion of demand through price control on routes of the airline
network, must be pointed out, since their revenues, passenger volumes, and so
on are also included in a fleet optimization and thus influence the result. With
regard to fleet planning, the distorted data serve as a basis and implicitly lead to
suboptimal decisions regarding the fleet structure to be aimed at.

If one relates the respective maximum achievable cumulative revenue volume
to the available seats of an aircraft in service, the dramatic drop in yield of the
(larger) A380 versus a (smaller) Boeing 747-400 becomes obvious very quickly
(see Figure 7.6). The unit cost advantage of the Airbus A380 will not (always)
be exploited due to a lack of demand. The advantage of the larger A380 aircraft
(−15% unit cost), which can be achieved through economies of scale, (thus)
turns into a profitability disadvantage compared to the smaller aircraft (Boeing
747-400). This is because the average yield is calculated by dividing the maximum cumulative revenue of a flight (Figure 7.5) by the number of seats of the
respective aircraft (for the A380 approx. 500 seats).

Hence the profit potential of an individual flight is calculated from the maximum cumulative revenue minus the trip costs of an aircraft. It should be noted

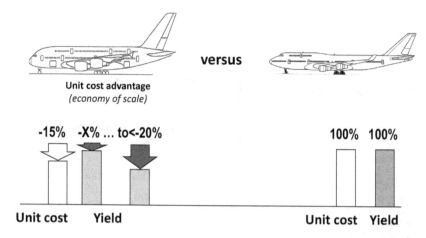

*Figure 7.6* Overcompensating of economies of scale due to size-related yield erosion

that, on the one hand, the flight (as a product) is like a perishable good, because after gate closing time the free capacities (unsold seats) only generate costs and, on the other hand, the product is subject to a rapidly changing supply market with high competitive intensity. Therefore, flights to the same destination but at different times (with the same aircraft type) can generate very different revenues. A generalization of the problem analysis using average values therefore leads to a completely different optimization result, since per se the elasticity of demand and the competitive situation is disregarded. As a consequence, the yield must be determined at a disaggregated flight level.

If this idea is extended to the entire flight network of an airline, the profit optimal fleet composition (fleet structure) of an airline can be found (see Figure 7.7). The optimal fleet composition (optimal fleet structure) is determined by maximizing the profit potential of the entire network. To determine this optimal fleet structure, the operation of the aircraft in the network is realistically simulated with the goal of maximizing the profit potential on the overall network level. Networks are varied (network scenarios), cumulative revenue values are differentiated for each target market, passenger numbers, trip costs by cost type are simulated by non-linear models, performance data (e.g. for take-off/landing per airport served) and payload range capabilities of the aircraft are taken into account. In addition, aircraft layouts are varied and operational constraints are taken into account. It should be noted that the market and network scenarios used here in the simulations also originate from non-linear "bottom-up" calculations. See the thought leadership piece by Dr. Benedikt Mandel in this chapter.

Figure 7.7 lists the above-mentioned parameters that are considered, varied and taken into account when simulating the scenarios. An optimization

**Simulate:** networks / markets / operation

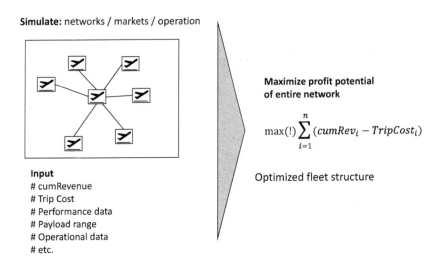

**Input**
# cumRevenue
# Trip Cost
# Performance data
# Payload range
# Operational data
# etc.

**Maximize profit potential of entire network**

$$\max(!) \sum_{i=1}^{n} (cumRev_i - TripCost_i)$$

Optimized fleet structure

*Figure 7.7* Bottom-up fleet planning: Optimization of fleet structure

calculation for a grown network shows the fleet structure that maximizes the total network profit potential of an airline and allows the adaptation of the existing fleet. Of course, this (optimized) fleet structure will gradually change over the years as mobility needs (markets), flight networks, competitor networks, airport infrastructures, new aircraft and engine technologies and political framework conditions are subject to constant development. From the context described above (unit cost advantage, demand-driven capacity and disaggregated earnings analysis as well as consideration of a constantly changing competitive situation), it can be concluded that there is enormous potential for optimization in the fleets of the world's airlines. And it can also be concluded that the world's airlines should be very interested in a planning process that helps them to structure their fleets as optimally as possible/develop an exit strategy in the current phase of the Coronavirus pandemic. This also includes airlines for whose network strategy (sixth freedom) the Airbus A380 seems to be optimal, but which in the pandemic crisis, with the accompanying dramatic drop in demand, leads to the problems mentioned above.

## 2. Reduce the high-risk of making commercial airliners: An innovative approach of working together

When a manufacturer develops a new aircraft, the design and specification are not only carried out by the aircraft manufacturer, but are carried out in several steps in close cooperation and coordination with potential and actual customers. Prior to the actual design and development phase, the manufacturer asks the customer for the desired technical, operational and economic characteristics of aircraft required in the market. This includes the airlines' network strategy, their

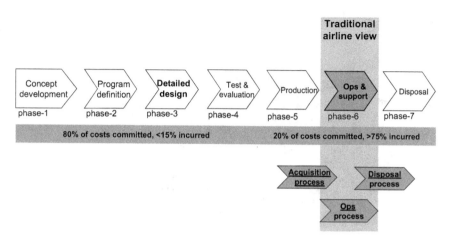

*Figure 7.8* The aircraft life cycle from clean paper design (phase-1) to disposal (phase-7)

market assessment and their assessment of competitors. In the next step, certain design parameters are determined as the basis for the design of a new aircraft model and a (cost) optimal design is developed in a synthesis process.

The course for the profitability of a new aircraft type is therefore set very early on. Figure 7.8 shows the temporal sequence of these relationships from clean paper design (phase 1) to disposal (phase 7). The highest leverage effect of a new design on the economic positioning in the business case of an airline can therefore be found in the first phases of the life cycle. From concept development (phase 1) to flight test (phase 4), the above-mentioned elementary decisions are made in the design of an aircraft and are irrevocably frozen. During this time window, a huge potential exists for influencing the design of the new aircraft and thus the later profit potential (costs/revenue) of the new aircraft in the respective networks of the operator airlines. This is because the design variables are fixed in this time window of the design process. This chance of a potential influence opens up in a positive sense for future buyers of this new aircraft. Also from the manufacturers' point of view, this phase of the design process sets the course for the future market success of a new aircraft.

From an airline's point of view, a change in the aforementioned design parameters can be translated into changed operating costs and changed revenue volume. Reduced or increased costs (due to an initially influenced design) result in a gigantic change in the cumulative cost and thus also in the cumulative revenue volume in the life cycle of an aircraft over a period of approximately 20 years. Therefore it is obvious to derive the effects of changed design parameters from the simulated operation of the aircraft in future markets/flight networks of airlines in a resilient way. These constraints (relevant design parameters) are assigned to stakeholders (airlines/manufacturers) (see Figure 7.9). The assignment of the design parameters to the stakeholders is based on the operational use of the aircraft in the airlines' networks. This is

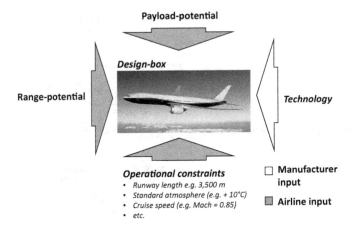

*Figure 7.9* Design-box: The relevance of stakeholders to the conceptual design of new aircraft

because a change in the design parameters (payload, range, thrust potential and operational constraints) will change the aircraft design. This will potentially change the operating costs as well as the revenue volumes (transportable payload) in the airline networks. The manufacturers' development focus is thus shifting to new technologies, such as new materials, new aerodynamics, new engine technologies, and so on.

Since the development of a new aircraft is associated with very high costs and manufacturers do not have detailed knowledge of the airline-specific requirements (operational aspects), manufacturers involve major airlines in the development process at the beginning of the "life cycle" of a new aircraft design. However it would be risky to optimize the effects of changed design parameters only for the operational use of a single airline that wants to have a high degree of influence on the design of an aircraft due to a large order. Therefore the use of innovative "bottom-up planning procedures" and a more efficient, improved format of working together/communication between airlines and manufacturers through the use of digital possibilities should be desired.

### 3. A redesign of working together: A prerequisite for successful aircraft design?

Although cooperation between airlines and manufacturers has a long tradition and although the manufacturers make an incredible time- and cost-intensive effort to involve the airlines, this process led to the design of many aircraft that were not in line with market requirements. The heuristic approach that has prevailed until now has not prevented aircraft developments, such as the A380, the A340-500, the 777-200LR and others from being classified as economic failures. Obviously, something needs to be changed to avoid developing aircraft that are completely written off by the airlines after 10 years of use. Since the development costs of new aircraft models are now in the double-digit billion range, manufacturers also have a strong interest in meeting the needs of the market. Thus the determination and definition of the design parameters is critical. An airplane could be configured in a way that is not in line with the market (design flop) and results in no buyers if the manufacturer and airlines interested in a new aircraft do not cooperate intensively at an early stage. In practice, therefore, the determination of the design parameters correlates with the ordering of aircraft, whereby a fixed and optional part is usually ordered. This thought process is thus an elementary part of the design process and should be carried out on the basis of differentiated scenario calculations taking into account the respective existing flight networks. This also includes a projection of future flight networks in the near and distant future, taking into account the airline-specific network strategy. This approach allows to determine potential aircraft quantities for today's and future markets.

However, changes of the aircraft in the focus of development create side effects, which are of positive/negative influence elsewhere; for example, in the networks of different airlines. Therefore, it is always necessary to investigate what effect the technical design parameters defined by the manufacturer have on the respective overall flight network in deviation from the design parameters defined by the airlines. The economic consequences resulting from the differences have to be quantified by the airlines for each of their strategic scenarios and evaluated in their risk. From the perspective of each individual airline, this results in a "different" correct dimensioning. This gains not only economic advantages by means of design parameters (aircraft design parameters) optimally aligned to their network structure, but also essential competitive advantages. This should be seen in particular against the background of a typical 20-year service life of an aircraft.

For the airline, "clumsy" design parameters can cause enormous costs (e.g. $100,000 additional costs per month mean $24 million over the total lifetime of an aircraft), while the competing airline saves costs (e.g. in the same order of magnitude). This results in a difference in production costs (in this example of $48 million for one aircraft, or $480 million, if ten aircraft are purchased). Correspondingly the profit margin is lower or higher, leading to the possibilities for re-investment, network expansion, and so on. This illustration of the correlation underlines the immense importance of these levers of influence.

All design parameters thus focus on the needs of an airline. There are considerable conflicts of interest here, which result from the different requirements of the individual airlines. Obviously, the airline tries to influence these design parameters and to convince the manufacturer of the optimal design parameters for their airline. This results in considerable advantages for the respective airline in terms of operating costs and competition in the market.

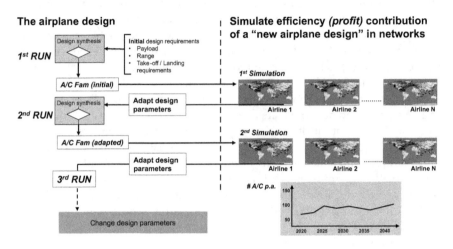

*Figure 7.10* The simulation of a new "paper aircraft" in airlines' networks: A bottom-up approach to define well-designed new aircraft

Clearly, competing airlines pursue different interests in the interpretation of the design parameters. This tug-of-war over the influence of these design parameters, which are so essential for an airline, stretches over many years, basically from the first initial discussions on a new design (Figure 7.8, Phase 1) to the design freeze of a new aircraft (Figure 7.8, Phase 4). The bases of this process, however, are evaluation approaches, which are mostly of heuristic nature and are based on simplifying or generalizing "top-down" calculations. Every airline as well as the manufacturer itself uses its own procedures, the compatibility of which is neither guaranteed nor allows for a consistent result. Thus, the consultation process is characterized by qualitative instead of factual quantitative arguments. This dilemma must be countered by a systematic procedural "bottom-up" solution and the cooperation between airlines and a manufacturer. See Figure 7.10 which shows the consolidated version.

Aircraft design starts with the first run and passes through design synthesis. A new aircraft design (e.g. as an aircraft family) is simulated in "bottom-up" planning procedures for different airlines in the context of their existing fleets in operational use and a sustainable profitability is analyzed in "bottom-up" fleet planning. The results of these "bottom-up" simulations (of the participating airlines) lead to the adaptation of the design parameters and to a second run of the design synthesis. The operational simulation in the networks of the airlines is repeated. This process has to be run through with many airlines (e.g. in digitally networked working groups of the respective manufacturer with working groups in alliances), so that the requirements of the future buyers of the aircraft can be generated consistently and taken into account in the design. This ensures that an adapted design will also lead to the desired optimal economic result for the respective airline. The results of the simulations show the economic risks or the economic advantages of a new design.

The new approach integrates both the design process and the simulation in networks. This process is illustrated by the patented "Method and System for Designing an Aircraft," which Echtermeyer/Coenen invented in 2013 while working for an airline and which has already been patented in several countries in 2019. The method allows the operational use of new aircraft in the context of fleet planning/fleet strategy. It enables the influence of a redesign in the life cycle of an airline on the profit potential, the competitive change(s) and furthermore to exert a significant influence on manufacturers and/or to sound out the interests of the respective airline. Instead of heuristic approaches, the procedure that provides consistent and reproducible detailed information is moving forward. It allows the risk area of the decision to be quantitatively assessed with regard to fleet mix and economic effects by means of a wide range of scenario formulations. The procedure is set up as a bottom-up process. It uses non-linear models based on the analyses of big data. If a manufacturer carries out simulation calculations for several interested airlines using the method described above, the similarities and differences can be identified between customer requirements, including their economic implications, at an early stage. On the one hand, the manufacturer can use these findings to optimize the design parameters and, on the other hand, the manufacturer receives economic information for price negotiations.

### 4. A bottom-up fleet planning/fleet structure optimization: Is it feasible?

In fleet planning, the task is to find the optimal number of suitable aircraft for a given network (quantity of flights) in order to maximize profits from operations. Since airlines usually have comprehensive, excellently quality-assured databases, these big data inventories form the basis of the model world described below. The modules are combined in a non-linear manner to form a fleet simulation model (see Figure 7.11). Bottom-up fleet planning uses "bottom-up" market and network simulations as the main input. Network classes are not formed in order to exclude possible error potentials in the optimization from the start. Consequently, there are no average values as input data. Instead, non-linear models generate the input data without exception. In other words, the "top-down" fleet planning is completely substituted by a "bottom-up" fleet planning.

For each time slice an optimal fleet composition (fleet structure) is determined by maximizing the network profit potential in each case. These fleet structure optimizations are successively developed over a timeline of, for example, 5 or 10 years. Existing sub-fleets (those aircraft that still have a considerable life) are integrated into the planning. This results in fleet plans that differ depending on the simulated market/simulated future network. Financial models are hard-coded into the system. These show key performance indicators (KPIs), such as financial requirements over time, cumulative revenue over time,

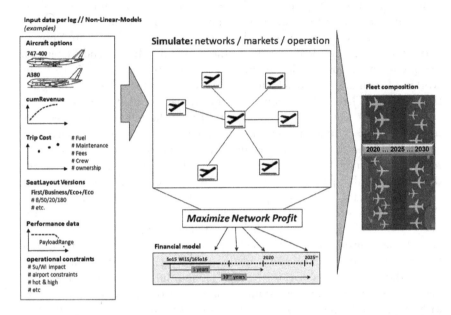

*Figure 7.11* Fleet structure optimization: A bottom-up planning approach, based on calibrated non-linear functions (big data usage)

among others. The KPIs are generated automatically. Simulations are based on a big data approach. A realistic operation of commercial aircraft in the network of an airline is simulated.

Here are some highlights of important modules:

- For each leg of a simulated flight network, revenue values are modeled as a function of aircraft size and market conditions.
- Non-linear cost models compute parameterized costs for fuel, various types of fees, crew cost, maintenance cost and ownership cost.
- For each aircraft type, version capability is provided with different seat configurations.
- Aircraft are characterized by different performance characteristics (e.g. payload range potential).
- The fleet simulation can be performed using different scenarios.
- A fleet financial model can evaluate the results of the scenario calculations from a financial point of view.
- The components of the overall simulation model interlock and function according to a "bottom-up" approach.

The bottom-up fleet simulation is extremely powerful. It uses non-linear models (which reflect technical and operational constraints as well as consumer

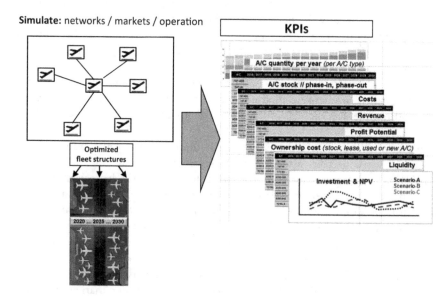

*Figure 7.12* Summarized overview of a profit potential optimized bottom-up fleet planning, based on bottom-up generated market and network scenario simulations (big data usage)

behavior) to compute optimized fleet structures, in the entire fleet planning (see Figure 7.12). The calculated fleet strategies/fleet structures (5–15 year plans) are based on bottom-up generated market and network scenario simulations. Fleet planning is a result of the optimization of entire network profit potentials. Multiple KPIs (economic numbers over time), like fleet plans, investments needed, revenues and costs, liquidity, capacity to phase in/to phase out aircrafts, among others, are determined. The system is scenario-capable and it can run sensitivity scenarios. As mentioned above, the results are based on integrated market and schedule forecasts (see the thought leadership piece by Dr. Benedikt Mandel in this chapter). Obviously, these flight networks and market forecasts, integrated into the simulation, play an essential role. The following section shows the importance of these topics.

### 5. Fleet planning and networks: How to simulate and integrate comprehensive topics

Fleet planning addresses three temporally differentiated problem areas. These are examined individually in the following:

- Current status (fleet structure optimization) in which the focus is on optimizing the existing fleet for the operated network. The goal is to structurally adapt the fleet to the grown network and thereby maximize the airline's profit. In this way the fleet is adapted to the competitive situation.

- Future status (fleet development) in which aircraft with the optimal characteristics for an airline's future network/flight plan are selected/ planned, taking into account the existing fleet.
- Aircraft design (design process) in which the development of an aircraft requires an immense capital expenditure over a period of 10 to 15 years and represents a high risk for the manufacturers.

Currently, methods are used which form representative route bundles with regard to an (uncertain) future network development, or which add representative routes to a given network. Growth is formed via the historical development trend for each network class. Basically, the use of representatives as flexible placeholders should reduce the risk of wrong decisions in fleet planning. In addition, the flights combined into network classes based on average values and aggregated values per network class seem to simplify the optimization problem and reduce the computing time.

This approach seems elegant at first glance, but it is inherently prone to elementary sources of error. This is because determining market development by projecting the past into the future ignores, for example, technical innovations, changes in air traffic rights, the behavior of competitors and socio-economic developments. Simplifying assumptions limit the use of some aircraft in subsequent optimization calculations, although they would have been highly economical. Furthermore, the use of aggregated values means that different destinations are treated equally, which is a fatally wrong assumption from a technical and economic point of view. Such errors cannot be subsequently extracted and corrected. Special requirements for the aircraft as well as profitability calculations are simplified, resulting in significant misjudgments in fleet requirements and achievable profits. Instead of an active strategy for shaping the future, taking into account innovations that have occurred or are expected, fleet planning then (only) reacts to historical developments and is of a passive nature.

This is countered by bottom-up fleet planning through high granularity, the use of sound mathematical methods with suitable optimization algorithms as well as resilient demand (market) and network simulations as input variables. This prevents errors in the operational and economic calculation, which cannot be quantified afterwards for an interpretation of top-down planning results.

In order to minimize the risk inherent in the conflict of objectives, a mathematically well-founded procedure must be used which reflects the real conditions of the airline as well as the economic variables (i.e. the influencing factors in total). A bottom-up procedure is better suited for this purpose than a generalized top-down approach or a heuristic mixed procedure. With the former, differentiated scenarios can be developed that comprehensively map the decision area, which only enables a decided risk assessment on the basis of which the ordering decision can be made. It should be emphasized that future flight network scenarios including passenger demand scenarios are of deterministic importance for fleet planning.

While in the case of fleet structure optimization the input variables are known, these must be determined for fleet development and aircraft design. Of deterministic importance is the future flight network of an airline including passenger demand. In addition to technical parameters, the competitive situation and the development of demand are decisive factors in this respect. The latter two in particular are subject to a high degree of uncertainty, but they are of fundamental importance, as they are the basic building blocks for determining corporate strategy in terms of market positioning through network development.

## 6. Evaluate and integrate new technologies

Obviously, technical advances are incorporated into the definition of the design parameters. However, the question is: In what way do they have implications for fleet planning? There is much discussion about technical innovations. Ambitious goals and demands on the part of politicians, manufacturers and social groupings/interest groups are being mentioned as a result of the Coronavirus crisis. These concern "summarized" zero emission aircraft, which are (also) operated with new (synthetic) fuels. The innovations are to be technically implemented, certified and brought to market within a short time. This also implies new developments in supply chains and the establishment of new work processes, which must be ensured worldwide. The economic situation of the buyers (i.e. the airlines) must also be taken into account. On the one hand, their liquidity for investments is limited for years to come due to the Coronavirus crisis, and on the other hand, the existing fleet cannot be written off overnight. The same applies to all companies in the air transport process chain.

From an aeronautical point of view, the Breguet equation provides an orientation for the feasibility of innovations in aircraft with gas turbine engines and the equation clarifies the interdependencies between the determining variables (see Figure 7.13). At a glance, the Breguet equation conveys the leverage of innovative technologies to improve the performance of an aircraft design. An improvement in overall performance translates into an increase in range. Performance improvements can be outlined in simplified terms with "new gas engine technologies" "redesigned aerodynamics" and "light weight structures." For example, it is interesting to understand the effect of technically induced counter-rotating forces on the overall performance of an aircraft, with the use of innovative technologies.

Since the improvement of the overall performance can be translated into an increase in range, this measure of range increase describes a potential for improvement; that is, to change the overall aircraft design. This is because every airline does not need aircraft with increased range and/or take-off potential in its flight network. If this is the case, the process runs "backwards," so to speak.

**Range equation of 'Breguet'**

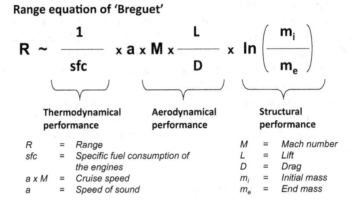

$$R \sim \frac{1}{sfc} \times a \times M \times \frac{L}{D} \times \ln\left(\frac{m_i}{m_e}\right)$$

| Thermodynamical performance | Aerodynamical performance | Structural performance |
|---|---|---|

| | | | | | |
|---|---|---|---|---|---|
| $R$ | = | Range | $M$ | = | Mach number |
| $sfc$ | = | Specific fuel consumption of | $L$ | = | Lift |
| | | the engines | $D$ | = | Drag |
| $a \times M$ | = | Cruise speed | $m_i$ | = | Initial mass |
| $a$ | = | Speed of sound | $m_e$ | = | End mass |

*Figure 7.13* The Breguet equation and its levers to quantify the impact of innovative technologies for commercial aircraft

One assumes a range/take-off potential that results from the requirements of operational use in the flight network. One questions which components of the aircraft are to be modified, how structural weight can be modified due to changed strength requirements, and so on. Thus, these improvement potentials can be used to reduce emissions and to reduce the overall cost position in operational use.

An important point remains the time dimension of the realization of new developments, which includes not only the airframe and engine, but also the challenges of a new type of fuel or the provision of energy with worldwide production and logistics. The development times of today's existing aircraft can vary between 15 and 25 years, without addressing the issue of a new fuel/energy source. In addition, within two decades there can also be considerable political, economic and social changes, which can have a positive or negative impact on the development of an aircraft. An in-depth comprehensive discussion of the technical feasibility of goals or demands within 15 years is beyond the scope of this contribution. However, from the point of view of the described procedure, all technical innovations can be transferred into a change of costs, a change of design parameters and a dilution of the residual values of existing fleets/aircraft currently in delivery, due to upcoming substitutions by new technologies, as far as these are part of fleet planning. In concrete terms, this is reflected in changes in costs (also ownership cost), revenues, range potential, payload potential, cruise speed and other operational parameters. These are comprehensively reflected in the present bottom-up process and also have an impact on the network design underlying the fleet planning. The latter must also take into account the socio-economic framework conditions.

### 7. Back to the future: The power and potential of digitalization

However, it can be stated that the bottom-up process presented creates the prerequisites for digitizing the entire process chain, starting with market forecasts, network generation, fleet planning/fleet strategy and the derivation of design parameters for the development of new aircraft. Thus, the many technologies can be evaluated very quickly and efficiently in the economic context of an airline's operational use. In retrospect, the negative economic consequences of many of the airlines' aircraft procurement activities could have been identified early on using this method.

To the same extent, the wrangling over design parameters for new aircraft in a conflict of objectives between the most diverse airlines can be evaluated. The particular interests of airlines to influence the design of new aircraft through gigantic initial orders can be observed (again and again), underpinning the necessity of the bottom-up procedure presented here. Due to the geographical location of their hub systems, the requirements of airlines from the Middle East naturally differ considerably from those of European airlines with their hub systems in the heart of Europe. The average daytime temperatures in the Middle East during the summer period are more than 30 degrees Celsius and in Europe (London, Paris and Frankfurt) these average temperatures are close to 20 degrees Celsius. This temperature difference illustrates the different interests to define design parameters of different airlines. This example illustrates that not only the economic dimension and future of an individual airline, but also its role in the environmental context can be quantified. Moreover, the scope can be much wider because the entire process chain of aviation stakeholders is taken into consideration. The economic effects for airlines, airframe manufacturers, engine manufacturers, suppliers, airports, and above all (also) the sustainable environmental consequences of air traffic as a whole can be quantified with the described bottom-up planning approach.

### Note

1  www.airbus.com/aircraft/passenger-aircraft/a380/benefits-to-airlines.html

## Reinventing airport business models in India

*Kapil Kaul*
CEO and Director, CAPAGlobal

*Binit Somaia*
Director, CAPAGlobal

Over the last 15 years there has been a remarkable transformation of the Indian airport sector. The two largest gateways in the country—Delhi and Mumbai—were privatized; greenfield airports were developed at Bangalore and Hyderabad as well as at a couple of smaller cities; and 37 airports were modernized by the state-owned Airports Authority of India.

Terminal development has been accompanied by notable improvements in airside infrastructure and processes, generating significant slot and parking capacity. Mumbai Airport is a prime example. In 2011 the airport could handle just over 30 runway movements per hour whereas today it has a declared capacity of 48 air transport movements (ATMs)/hour, and regularly handles 50 or more. Prior to COVID, Mumbai handled more daily movements than any other single runway airport in the world.

This transformation has supported tremendous growth. Indian airports handled 341 million passengers in FY2020, almost six times greater than in FY2005 (see Figure 7.14). The outcome has been a win–win proposition for all stakeholders. Airlines have been able to expand their operations and increase efficiency, while passengers have benefitted from a vastly improved experience.

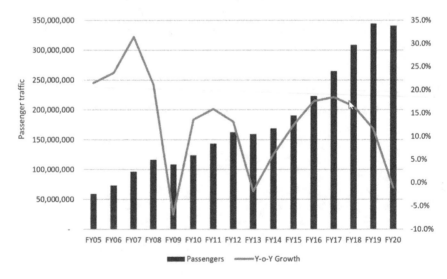

*Figure 7.14* Historical growth of passenger traffic at airports in India
Source: CAPAGlobal; Airports Authority of India.

Not only have the private airport operators achieved a significant upside in their valuations, but even the Airports Authority of India has earned close to US$7 billion in revenue share from the public–private partnership (PPP) concessions that have been awarded. Meanwhile, local and national economies have enjoyed a significant positive impact from the increase in business, trade and tourism flows.

Despite the significant investment in airport infrastructure, in the 5 years to FY2019 the surge in traffic significantly outstripped supply. Traffic forecasts had underestimated demand, and infrastructure which would otherwise have sufficed for 7–10 years was being utilized within 3–5 years.

Congestion was increasing within terminals, in the airspace above and even on the approach roads to airports. Some of the busier airports were constantly playing catch-up. In response to this emerging capacity crisis, decisions were taken to fast-track greenfield second airports in Delhi and Mumbai, while six non-metro airports were privatized.

Given strong traffic flows and with airports being thought of as relatively low-risk monopoly businesses, the mindset of operators was focused on managing growth and developing infrastructure. Strategic issues largely took a back seat.

COVID has delivered an unimaginable destruction of demand. CAPAGlobal estimates that Indian airports will handle just 90–115 million passengers in FY2021, a year-on-year decline of 66–74%. This would take traffic volumes back to FY2007.

Traffic—and by consequence, revenue—developed over the last 14 years has evaporated almost overnight. Airports alone are expected to lose US$1.5 billion in FY2021, out of total industry losses of US$6.06–6.5 billion (see Figure 7.15).

This has serious implications not only for airlines and airport operators, but also for on-airport concessionaires such as duty free, retail, food and beverage, and ground handlers. Access to funding for greenfield projects is also likely to be compromised. Financial challenges may precipitate ownership changes and consolidation.

The current crisis must force a rethink and reinvention of the airport business model over the next 5 years. From considering airports as close to risk-free, near-monopoly businesses, operating in an environment where growth can be taken for granted, operators will need to adopt a different set of skills and capabilities to re-build demand.

The focus will now need to be on understanding customers, partners and passengers, and using strategic thinking, technology and innovation to drive aero and non-aero revenue. Operators will need to ask themselves the following questions:

- What is working? How do we make it better?
- What is not working? What is an alternative approach?
- How do we not only aspire to global benchmarks but use this crisis to leapfrog to best practices?

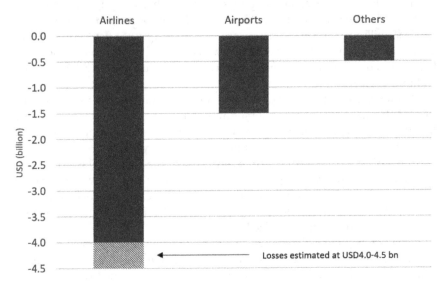

*Figure 7.15* Financial performance of the aviation sector in India
Source: CAPAGlobal estimates.

Only by stepping back from operational issues and making an effort to genuinely answer these questions will it be possible to reinvent airport business models to be applicable for the new environment in which we find ourselves. Reinvention will be required in multiple areas.

**Corporate governance**: There needs to be an understanding that good corporate governance is fundamental to transformation, not just for airports but for the aviation industry as a whole. If airports are to attract serious investors, they must relook at the capability of their boards and the experience of their independent directors. By bringing in experienced, professional directors, airport boards will be able to move beyond compliance to adding value.

**Institutional know-how**:Airports do not always have a good understanding of the business models and economics of all stakeholders, especially airlines. But without viable airlines the performance of the airport will be severely compromised.There is a need to reinvent the relationship with airlines, ground handlers, cargo and express companies, general aviation operators, and non-aero concessionaires, among others, to deliver a win–win proposition for recovery.

**Collaboration**: Having understood the priorities, challenges and drivers of other stakeholders, the next step is to institutionalize collaboration with them. This will be critical to restore demand post-COVID.

**Planning**: Our research shows that airports do not include airlines, passengers, ground handlers and concessionaires to the extent that would ideally be required. As a result, their requirements are not suitably incorporated.

Or critical trends—such as the impact of long-haul narrow-bodies on network planning and route development—may be missed. Given that the outlook for the next couple of years remains uncertain, the planning process will need to be flexible in response to shifts in the market if financial and operating performance is to be optimized.

**Forecasting**: Traffic forecasting has been repeatedly off the mark, more often than not under-estimating demand. This has a major impact on planning, costs and the passenger experience. Forecasting methodologies need to be reinvented to incorporate a continuous ground-up understanding of the key drivers of traffic, such as airline strategy, fleet plans, air access and bilateral policy. Airport operators have tended to be disconnected from these underlying market trends.

**Market structure**: India's domestic traffic shifted from being almost 100% full service in 2004, to more than 60% low-cost carrier (LCC) in 2010. But infrastructure development did not factor in this shift, despite the fact that this evolution was evident. There is a need to reinvent understanding of airline strategies and business models, to be able to foresee fundamental changes in the industry. The emerging issue which airport operators need to focus on is the impact of new aircraft technology on airline networks. For example, from Mumbai, the A321LR/XLR will open up the ability to operate to numerous destinations in Europe, Africa and Asia that were simply not possible with a current engine narrow-body (see Figure 7.16).

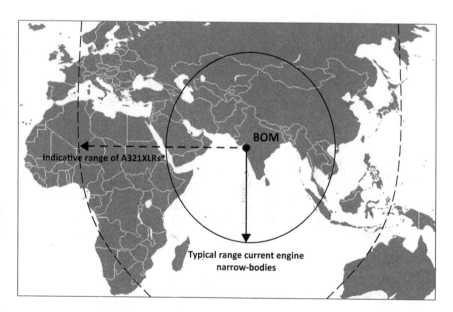

*Figure 7.16* Extended reach of long-haul narrow-body equipment
Source: CAPAGlobal; Great Circle Mapper.

**Route development**: Airports have historically pitched route opportunities to airlines based on historical traffic flows. But volume alone does not enable an airline to determine the viability of a potential route. And in the post-COVID era historical data is almost irrelevant. Airports will therefore need to reinvent their approach to route development.

A more holistic approach is required which also includes forward bookings, travel search trends, consumer surveys, travel trade research (some Indian airports now incorporate passenger and trade research but need to increase the sophistication of their analysis). But most critically, any pitch to an airline must consider route profitability based on airline and aircraft economics, especially as India is a low yield market. To increase aero and non-aero revenue, Indian airports will need to attract more nonstop, long-haul, wide-body services.

**Consumers**: Airports have very limited knowledge about the passengers that pass through them. Who are they, where are they going, why are they traveling through this airport, what are their travel preferences, what do they want to buy? The relationships and data are mostly held by airlines, travel intermediaries and concessionaires.

There is a need to reinvent the level of engagement between airports and passengers using technology so that their data can be used positively for planning, greater efficiency, an improved experience and increased revenue.

**Technology**: Technology can play a pivotal role in reshaping airport business models, but the boards and leadership of airport operators need to start seeing technology as a strategic lever rather than simply a functional one. The

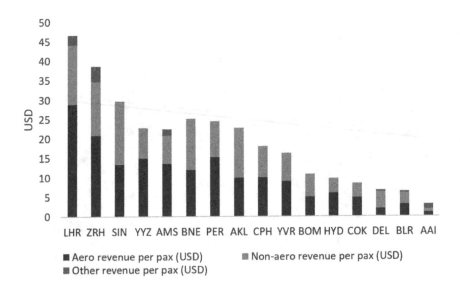

*Figure 7.17* Distribution of airport revenues at key global and Indian airports in FY2019

Source: CAPAGlobal research, company reports and filings.

organizational priority accorded to technology needs to be elevated. COVID has in fact accelerated this process by demonstrating the benefits that technology can deliver and by hastening consumer acceptance of it.

**Costs**: Some initiatives, such as the consolidation of operations into a single terminal, are already being implemented. However, savings need to be identified under all cost heads and, as noted, technology can be deployed to reduce both capex and opex.

**Revenue**: If airport operators evolve from simply being passive generators of revenue to becoming active, commercially driven organizations, the upside potential in revenue is immense, as demonstrated by reference to global benchmarks (see Figure 7.17).

There are numerous ways to drive non-aero revenue by investing in customer segmentation and data analytics, supported by initiatives such as a loyalty program, a digital and e-commerce platform, and collaboration with concessionaires and partners.

COVID is undoubtedly a crisis of unprecedented proportions. But as they say, a good crisis should never be wasted. This is a once-in-a-century opportunity for the industry to take a step back and to seriously examine, question and reinvent every aspect of their business model. This is the time to rewrite the accepted ways of doing things. Those that make the effort to do so may be able to compress transformation that might otherwise have taken a decade into a couple of years and emerge as far stronger and more viable organizations than before.

## Start with the customer

*Antoine de Kerviler*
Vice President, EMEA Field CTO Travel Transportation Hospitality,
Salesforce

We are going through an unprecedented sanitary crisis. It is impossible to use an existing model to predict when demand will reappear. Customers were forced to stay home, could not travel for months. Before the crisis, travellers accepted many inconveniences because they slowly but surely piled up over the years. Travellers have grown accustomed to them, but restarting and being confronted by them all at once is difficult: removing belt and shoes, scarf and jacket, putting your toiletries in a small plastic bag, nothing more than 100 ml, queuing three or four times, showing your passport and boarding pass at the end of each line to finally board a flight where you're crammed in a very small space for the next hours … and then at destination having to walk kilometres in an unfamiliar environment to queue and show your passport again, before waiting to get your luggage back … We're very far from the dream of flying…

Nothing has changed. Everybody expected or dreamt that the world would be different. Before dying from the thousand cuts, many are planning to travel less. They've organized themselves for that. They and their customers are now proficient in Zoom, Webex, Teams and Hangouts. They still plan to see each other face-to-face but for more social and friendly occasions. As a direct consequence, airlines are going to see fewer business travellers in their planes in the years to come.

During the same time, airlines have focused on staying alive and restarting their operations. They did not think too much about their customers and their post-crisis expectations.

The purpose of this article is to explain how airlines can restart, become more efficient through the use of platforms and value chain collaboration. Reconstructing the air travel value chain is not the sole responsibility of airlines, all other participants—airports, distribution, aircraft manufacturers—are invited to play.

We'll see how airlines can collaborate with all stakeholders to improve the value chain and make it more resilient for all participants. Next, we'll look at how airlines could make their customers' experience unforgettable and easy to attract and retain.

### Collaboration starts within the enterprise

Although collaboration is obviously a need for every company and very often mentioned, collaboration tools in most companies, not just airlines, are often very poor. Just to clarify: email is not a collaboration tool; direct messaging is not a collaboration tool. We need tools where the communication is not human-to-human with documents attached, but tools where the topic is at the centre and humans see all communications. With workforce spread around the world and rarely coming into an office,[1] collaboration is even more critical for airlines. To serve customers, airlines need new ways to collaborate around a customer's service request: everyone is sharing and commenting on the same information to promptly resolve the customer's query. Systems should be organized to facilitate this collaboration, linking any record to questions and answers posted by colleagues working together to respond to the customer. The team members solving the customer's request can also be assisted by artificial intelligence bots fetching and sorting information from other systems.

Beyond better serving our customers and being more efficient, it removes employee frustration as it makes it easier to ask for help from a colleague to solve the customer issue. Companies can establish service levels for customer service and each employee can measure their contribution to service level attainment. It's essential for employee motivation as it shows the company is really taking customer service seriously.

Both for keeping employees and improving customer service, airlines need to implement tools enabling everyone to collaborate to solve customer issues faster. Rather than asking the customer to connect to several employees, one employee is connected to the customer and she is collaborating with other employees to solve the customer's issue.

### *Value chain collaboration*

Figure 7.18 is inspired from "The Aviation Value Chain: Economic Returns and Policy Issues"[2] but instead of considering the passenger as a downstream participant, I suggest considering that the passenger initiates the value chain. All other participants are there to serve the passenger need, including the airline. Chronologically, airlines need to prepare before the passenger arrives, but without the passenger there's no value in the chain.

Airlines need to take a leading role in constructing a **customer centric value chain collaboration**. Often, airline customers are taken care of by a subcontractor. Yet the customer sees the service as being provided by the airline. How many times have we heard that an airline has lost someone's luggage? Yet, it's very rare that the airline would have anything to do with losing a piece of luggage. By opening a collaboration platform and making its use mandatory, the airline would have a much better view on the provision of the service to the customer. They would also have ways to measure performance transparently and nearly instantaneously. Data privacy rules are not obstacles as the temporary sharing of data for the provision of a service is generally authorized.

There are many examples of cross value chain collaboration. As a first example, an airline creates a case management application to manage customers' issues. Contractors and suppliers would have to respond to customers' cases in this platform. Airlines could impose service level agreements on their suppliers to respond within a given time to ensure they are, in turn, able to respond to the customer within a certain time.

As a second example, take a customer arriving on an early flight and requesting access to their room earlier than the usual check-in time. Efficient collaboration between the airline, the hotel, the cleaning company and other third parties enables a positive response to the customer. The customer agrees to pay an additional fee for the extra use of the room. The additional revenue should be split among all parties to ensure that the collaboration model benefits each party.

Let's look at another break in the value chain, when the passenger boards the aircraft: airlines used to know the passengers with their passenger name record reference; on board the passenger becomes a seat assignment: 6E or 21D. How can the aircraft and those working on board have knowledge of the customer? How can that information pass through? Airlines have distributed tablets to their cabin crews to compensate by making some information about customers available. Integrating the aircraft in the customer-centric value chain has always been difficult. Aircraft manufacturers are talking to flight operations departments about fuel saving and maintenance costs, and customer comfort; but rarely about end-to-end customer experience and very rarely using open systems where the airline would not have to use the aircraft manufacturer's software package.

There are other examples less visible to the passenger. Airlines are attempting to pay airports only for the services used, transferring the revenue uncertainty to the airport. As airlines operate a reduced service, activities are scattered thinly in large and mostly empty airports. A temporary moratorium or a rapid renegotiation of contracts leading to a more intelligent use of space should lead to cost savings for airports which can be partially passed on to airlines. Joint efforts should equally benefit all parties to motivate all to find new collaboration opportunities.

Identifying friction areas and improvements in the customer journey is easy, and bringing together the various parties able to improve the experience can bring rapid benefits to the customer.

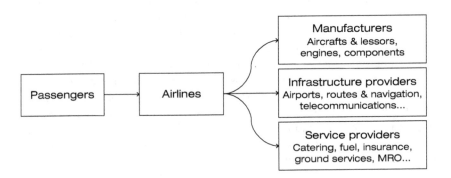

*Figure 7.18* The customer-centric value chain

*Facilitating collaboration*

The previous paragraphs illustrate a few examples of collaboration, visible and invisible to customers. There are many areas to improve collaboration. Airlines have long recognized the need to collaborate but rarely invested in the platforms to facilitate the collaboration. Using technology platforms and public APIs[3] to facilitate collaboration is a relatively easy response to the problem.

Airlines' information technology is becoming more and more complex, but the complexity has been subcontracted in many instances (passenger service system (PSS), revenue management, revenue accounting) and therefore is invisible. The complexity and its costs are rarely put in perspective with the value perceived by the customer. Simplification is a must. Airlines should run on four distinct platforms interconnected through APIs. In each platform, systems should be connected together through APIs as well, in a similar model to those imposed by Amazon in its API Mandate published in 2002.[4]

As an additional benefit, connecting systems through APIs allows additional services to be built rapidly. During the crisis, airlines using APIs would have been able to repurpose their passenger aircrafts to cargo capacity in their systems. It should take less time to do in the systems than it takes to physically remove the seats and protect the cabin.

Figure 7.19 represents a simpler yet very similar view to the one presented in Chapter 3, Figure 3.6: real-time integrated network, fleet and schedule planning with the customer platform "sales and marketing" presented on top, and revenue management and operations at the bottom. Figure 3.6 presents some of the interactions between various components as well as the pivotal role for financing assets and risk management.

| Public API | Private API | Partner API |
|---|---|---|
| Selectively expose services, content or data used by the company; user can be identified and data can be monetized | Make data, systems, workflows accessible to other departments: enable decoupling and integration with well documented API and clear mandate to use | Open systems beyond the organization to facilitate collaboration with little strain on internal resources |

| Customer & loyalty | Flight | Aircraft | People & finance |
|---|---|---|---|
| Customer service & experience, brand, trust, confidence, relationships, sales and distribution, notifications... | Reservations, scheduling, documentation, operations and disruption management, crews... | Utilization & scheduling, airworthiness, fleet management, MRO, pilots & training, stations | Financial planning, financing assets, revenue accounting, procurement, risk management and other compliance systems |

*Figure 7.19* Four inter-connected platforms to run an airline

### The most important platform: Customer and loyalty

Everything related to the customer is available in one platform including sales and distribution but also notifications and customer experience. Initially the customer is unknown and the airline will offer a standardized experience. Each time the customer gives additional data to enrich their profiles, the airline will adapt the experience and personalize more. Through each experience with the customer, the airline is accumulating more data driving better insights on the customer's expectations. The new data allows the airline to improve the experience, and to continually gather more data.

Once the customer is happy, they will also be happy to trust the airline with their data, giving a lot more data than the airline was able to capture. With that data, the airline will be able to build a personalized experience for *this* customer. Accessible through APIs, the customer data can easily be enriched with other data coming from other experiences, can be available for other systems, and can also be anonymized and shared as explained in examples below.

Almost anyone in the company should be able to access relevant metrics and measure their performance and their impact on the customer experience. It's possible to include data from many data sources and evaluate the impact of irregular operations on customer satisfaction. Employees are now using data to improve their performance and their customers' experience.

The personalized, delightfully easy experience leads to loyalty and customer advocacy. Without giving discounts and loyalty points, a company can convert their customers into advocates. Check out Apple or Amazon: when was the last time they gave 10 or 12% discounts on their flagship products? Ten percent is one free flight every ten. They have found other ways of making sure we're loyal advocates of their brands. Instead, airlines have made us unhappy customers because it has become very difficult to impossible to fly with air miles to the destination we're interested in (i.e. not the one we usually travel to).

The need for more connected customer experiences is omnipresent as businesses come to realize there's an opportunity in looking at what's happening in the wider world of their customers. The airline customer is not comparing their experience with another airline experience. They're comparing with Uber, Amazon, Zara... They're comparing with the imaginary experience combining the best of all worlds.

Once we have loyal customers advocating for our brand, we can think of the "flights" platform and then about "aircrafts" which are needed to deliver the flights. Looking at platforms in this order puts the customer at the forefront, and enables the airline to build a demand-driven system.

### CIOs must integrate with intent

Airline chief information officers (CIOs) spend most of their time making sure the lights are on. In normal times, they spend 80% of their budget on keeping the lights on, another 20% on governance, leaving nothing for innovation. It should really be the opposite.

CIOs should integrate with intent. Re-platforming the airline should be done with determination to decouple systems and to simplify. Integration is not an after-thought. It needs to be done with intent and determination as there should be no shortcuts, no special permissions to build something accessing the data directly or recoupling systems.

Besides, the value of integration should really be made clear to the business, so they're willing to pay for it. None of the agile methodologies includes a hidden budgeting area to finance developments that the business does not need to know about. In fact, if one assumes that the CIO, chief finance officer (CFO), CEO and all other CxOs are as smart and well educated as each other, one should also assume that all the CxOs will understand the value of integration, once properly explained. It's part of the CIO's role to explain what she wants to invest in, and get approval for it.

Airline IT should be in the cloud. Apart from a handful of apps like building access or video surveillance, 100% of apps must be in the cloud. Legacy, and even 15 year-young companies, are dealing with "technological spaghetti" made up of brittle legacy systems, unruly technology stacks, and shiny new applications that don't fit into the larger whole. All these applications should communicate with each other through private APIs. Applications can then evolve independently from each other, and APIs can be reused many times and exposed to external stakeholders. Integrated applications can provide data in a seamless manner that can be used by anyone in the company to get insights about customers and drive the best experience.

### Reduce costs and create collaboration opportunities

By exposing a public and a partner API, an airline can give their stakeholders access to some of its own data and services. Other than NDC,[5] a quick search on the internet provides interesting results: most airlines do not offer APIs; a few provide some APIs about their baggage policy or flight status. In many instances, we've seen pages where the last update dates back more than 4 years ago. Many airlines seem to have left this field to their PSS[6] provider or to startups who are trying to access and monetize the data.

Here are two basic examples, which, simple as they are, still do not exist. First, airlines, competing with each other and also often competing with airports for the customer, are not ready to expose simple APIs to the public.

Airlines and airports could expose a simple and secure public API with airport movement data—no named passengers for privacy compliance, just passenger counts with gender and nationality—offered for a nominal fee to all stakeholders: ground handlers could size their teams according to the number of turnarounds and passengers, duty free stores could get ready to adapt their displays and increase sales, police forces could adapt their staffing and so on. If airlines are "forced" to expose their data through such an API: what's in it for them? A much-improved service for their customers: immigration, duty free stores, coffee shops, for example. The first airline to offer this API will benefit from the first-mover advantage as they're setting the standard which will be followed by others.

The second example is an API to inform coffee shops that an airline is about to release hundreds of passengers into the airport with vouchers for coffee and a doughnut. To help them get ready and to facilitate the transactions—make it contactless—airlines could communicate with coffee shops. It would not be economically viable to collaborate individually with each coffee shop in each airport. But giving access to content through an API, or through a web page would facilitate the coffee shop's life. In addition, it can be made easy for the coffee shop to be paid back by airlines in exchange for data from the coffee shop. Once again, a simple API to improve the customer's life and improve the economics of the value chain. It could even tell the airline what customers are actually ordering, whether they are paying more for something else ... actionable data that the airlines could use during the next disruption.

With its AnyPoint Platform MuleSoft enables airlines and airports to build an API exchange where anyone can connect and consume data and services. Make data available and easy to consume: application developers will consume data to power their applications. These application developers will establish their own business models to monetize the reformatted and repurposed data.

In London, 600 applications are powered by the open data provided for free by Transport for London;[7] they're used by 42% of Londoners. According to Deloitte,[8] the cost of providing the data is estimated at £1 million p.a. and the cost avoidance is estimated at more than three times that amount.

Using the AnyPoint Platform and reusing APIs, airlines can create a specific experience API to give public stakeholders access to a limited version of their internal APIs, thereby reducing their cost of providing the data.

### Once in a lifetime opportunity

Airlines have a once in a lifetime opportunity to make the customer's experience delightfully easy, notwithstanding the collaboration improvements. And it's essential to work to improve the employees' experience. Otherwise, it will impossible for employees to make the customers' experience easier sustainably.

Systems must reflect reality or the disconnects—between the submerged and the emerged part of the iceberg—eventually become unmanageable. Ticketing and fares are good examples. Online check-in is the new normal. In the same way that no one ever says digital photography anymore, no one says online check-in anymore. Despite the system's complexity, airlines have done a great deal to improve the customer's experience. To reach the next level of improvement they need to simplify the back-ends.

Although the paper representation of an airline ticket does not exist any-more, tickets still exist in systems: e-tickets are just a representation of tickets which do exist in systems. It's the same ticket as 25 years ago when the move to the e-ticket started.[9] Airlines are not ticketless, they're paperless. The complexity inherited from the red-ink paper coupons is still present in the systems leading to complexity in real life. One cannot buy a ticket with more than four segments; it will be two tickets in conjunction. Think of the complexity of refunding only part of the overall itinerary and issuing a new ticket.

Take another example with fares. Fares must be simpler. Business and personal will be more and more mixed. If I am commuting to work, it's a business trip: not for my company as I am the one paying. But because, there's no Saturday night (the Sunday rule), it looks like a business trip so legacy airlines offer me a business fare. A quick search on the internet shows that a return flight over a weekend is at least 50% cheaper than mid-week.

According to Google flights, the cheapest fare for London to New York is €223 via Paris; on the same date, the cheapest flight from Paris to New York is €394. If I wanted to travel from Paris to New York, I should buy a ticket from London. After all, if I buy a concert ticket, I am allowed to come only for the main attraction. It's so critical for airlines that some did not hesitate to take their customers to court: now defunct Northwest Airlines took their passengers to court because they were not using coupons in the right order. Imagine a fast-food company telling you to eat the burger before the salad because you ordered a Happy Meal…

Yet, legacy airlines need to protect their revenue and their hub-and-spoke model. There can be many reasons why the price should be cheaper in London on that date. Workarounds do exist but they are nearly impossible to imple-ment with the existing system: issuing *one* ticket and *one* boarding pass with *one* barcode clearly showing London as the departure city: it's better than taking passengers to court.

Tickets and coupons are a thing of the past, which is probably why low-cost airlines are doing without both. There are only bookings and boarding passes. Get rid of tickets and coupons, get rid of the four-coupon limitation. Allow dozens of legs for one order, and allow a customer to book three return trips if they want to. Make it as simple as possible for the customer. But there are conditions, as when buying three pens with a quantity discount, I cannot return one and keep the discount.

Unfortunately, it's not that simple. But PSS providers, global distribution systems (GDSs), travel agents and airlines are all in the same boat and it's in their interest to simplify now and reinvent travel to make it really simple for the cus-tomer at the initiation of the value chain. Think of the amount of money and time sunk into managing that complexity, think of the slowness and the rigidity, at times when companies are supposed to be agile and reactive. Legacy airlines have accepted this complexity as a curse; yet, there is a way out.

### Opening new opportunities

Getting out of that complexity allows airlines to concentrate on new services for customers. For instance, if my travels bring me through Nice, I would be happy for the airline to allow me to stop in Nice for a day to visit some friends. The airline should offer me that stop for a small extra cost justified by extra luggage handling. The airline could also offer me additional services in Nice: transfer, storing my luggage, which I'd be happy to use. The airline could expose an API for taxis and other service providers to offer their services. Service providers are made available on the airline website and get some additional revenue while the airline takes a commission for offering the API. Most important, the customer's experience is better than lugging a large suitcase around and looking for taxis.

The airline has made the API available on their website for service providers to consume. No need to implement an EMD[10] for the additional service, only one more line in the order form. The customer is provided with a bar code; once the bar code is used, the service provider is paid minus commission. Provisioning the API and signing the contract is all automated and creates little to no additional work for the airline. Therefore, low commission levels are acceptable to the airline and the small revenue generates a profit.

### Building the customer and loyalty platform

At Salesforce, we're helping our customers build customer platforms to get closer to their customers. The airline can remember all the things their customer did and all the offers the customer has seen. When the customer comes back, regardless of the channel, she is recognized. Airline employees are "augmented" with artificial intelligence to remove menial tasks and have full visibility on all the customer's interactions on all channels. The airline can provide a better service than the customer expects. The experience is so delightful that the customer comes back every time.

Once the platform is built and APIs are available, what is most remarkable is the acceleration and the relaxation. In my previous professional experience, we've delivered in a few weeks a delay and repay system that paid for itself in weeks, increasing the net promoter score by 6 points. All connected to data analytics so we could analyse what our customers were doing and simulate different levels of compensation. We built in a few hours—decision made at noon, live at 18:00—a system to allow our customers to tell us what they wanted to do when their trains are cancelled. Contrary to what we thought, only 40% wanted to travel on the next available train. That allowed us to make sure to process their cases first while we automated the refund cases for around 20% of customers. We learned a lot from our analytics. We were able to tell our finance department precisely our exposure to delay and repay penalties.

There was never any excuse for delaying serving customers and improving systems for the customers. Today, airlines have an opportunity to modernize and radically simplify their systems. Airline and subcontractor employees must work together, must be provided the tools to collaborate, to enable a stellar experience for the customer. Information or business technology should be at their service to make this very difficult exercise much easier.

The customer initiates the value chain. Paraphrasing legendary Harvard Business School marketing professor Theodore Levitt[11] "people don't want to fly, people want to go to a remote location." With the recent crisis, customers have started questioning the need to actually go to another location. Depending on what one wants to do in the remote location, it might be possible to do it using technology like video-conferencing. Obviously, this is not the same thing as meeting in person, but there are so many benefits—time, ease, cost, for example—that video-conferencing has become a true competitor to air travel. Now airlines have to restore some of the dream of flying to bring their customers back to airplanes.

## Notes

1 Flight and cabin crew never come to the airline head office, unless it's located in the airport. They come to the office to prepare the flights a few hours before the flight, i.e. not always during office hours.

2 Michael W. Tretheway and Kate Markhvida, "The Aviation Value Chain: Economic Returns and Policy Issues," *Journal of Air Transport Management*, 2014, vol. 41, issue C, pp. 3–16.

3 An API is an application programming interface: a way to programmatically interact with a computer system. An API is a language to communicate with a system comprising vocabulary and grammar: how to name a piece of data and how to formulate a question or understand a response.

4 There's no official version of the Amazon mandate. It was an email from Jeff Bezos sent sometime in 2002, something along the lines:

- All teams will henceforth expose their data and functionality through service interfaces.
- Teams must communicate with each other through these interfaces.
- There will be no other form of interprocess communication allowed.
- It doesn't matter what technology they use.
- All service interfaces, without exception, must be designed from the ground up to be externalizable. The team must plan and design to be able to expose the interface to developers in the outside world. No exceptions.
- Anyone who doesn't do this will be fired.

5 NDC: New Distribution Capability from IATA. A set of XML messages to standardize the way air products are retailed to corporations, leisure and business travellers.

6 PSS: Passenger service systems providing services including inventory, reservations and ticketing for airlines. Providers include Amadeus, Radixx, Sabre, SITA and Travel Technology Interactive. In addition, a PSS can be extended with revenue management, departure control, revenue accounting, B2C and B2B distribution, among others.

7  The Transport for London example is not related to the MuleSoft Anypoint Platform. The author is not making any assumption related to the technology used by TfL to power its APIs.

8  See "Assessing the Value of TfL's Open Data and Digital Partnerships" http://content.tfl.gov.uk/deloitte-report-tfl-open-data.pdf

9  United Airlines was the first airline to issue electronic tickets, back in 1994. The industry was 20% on e-ticket in 2004 and 100% in 2008. As of June 1, 2008, agencies could no longer issue paper tickets to be processed by their local billing and settlement plan (BSP).

10  EMD: electronic miscellaneous document used by air travel providers to sell non-air services.

11  In 1969 Theodore Levitt published *The Marketing Mode: Pathways to Corporate Growth*, and he attributed the saying "Last year 1 million quarter-inch drills were sold," to Leo McGivena who added, "not because people wanted quarter-inch drills but because they wanted quarter-inch holes." Theodore Levitt, *The Marketing Mode: Pathways to Corporate Growth* (New York: McGraw-Hill Book Company, 1969), Chapter 1: "The Augmented-Product Concept", p. 1.

# Demand–based scheduling

*Dietmar Kirchner*
Senior Policy Advisor

*Peter Glade*
Chief Commercial Officer, SunExpress

The Coronavirus pandemic is about to completely change many parameters for the airline industry. Some can be considered as a threat; some are new and can be dealt with, some offer opportunities for forward-looking airlines to develop a new and better business model. This article elaborates on an operating model that has been successful in the express cargo business and that could be adopted in a modified way to the passenger business.

The dramatic decline of passenger demand, especially in international traffic, has led to bankruptcies and dire financial situations for almost all airlines. Planes were retired or put into storage. Flight crews, mechanics, operations and office staff became redundant in vast numbers due to the downsizing of capacity; governments and investors had to save airlines with large loans or capital injections. On the other hand, airplane capacity, airport slots, and experienced staff have become available at very favorable terms, both in cost and flexibility, which will eventually invite startups to enter the market at very competitive rates and with very flexible production systems.

Demand not only dramatically dropped, it also became erratic due to ever-changing travel rules and risk perceptions of the customers. Conventional forecasting systems, based on historical data, became useless, and will be so for a long period, as the projected recovery of demand will also provide a shifting database. Unconventional forecasting systems like research on Google keywords or analytics of smartphone mobility also can only give a snapshot of present behavior, which will be overridden by actual rules and concerns at the time of the projected travel date. Today, airlines are experiencing that even bookings will not automatically lead to passenger numbers, as people often have to adapt their travel plans at short notice.

During the pandemic, we experienced a "fast forward" of the introduction of digital consumer processes built around the usage of the smartphone. Smartphones were used for shopping and navigation, served as tickets and access management tools, provided streamed audio and video content and news feed, integrated biometric tools for banking and other functions, just to name a few.

As the pandemic may disappear during 2021 and 2022, the next challenge for the airline industry will be the task of "decarbonization" which is required to meet the targets of the Paris Climate Agreement. Airlines will have to become familiar with a transition to carbon-neutral mobility, which, according to today's scientists, can only be provided by the introduction of "synfuels" made of $CO_2$, water and ("green") electric energy. These fuels are expected to cost about twice as much as the average fossil fuel cost over the last years. Thus, airlines will have to burn substantially less fuel per passenger.

### Principles of a "demand-based capacity" system

Today's airline operating model starts with a given fleet, built around medium- and long-term market expectations. Scheduling tries to maximize its utilization by developing the "optimal" schedule. This schedule is published for the next 11 months in a "supply cloud" and then "pushed" to the market by a distribution system, using very sophisticated tools to influence demand. A published schedule is considered as fixed cost for the period of its validity, the marginal cost of a passenger is considered very low containing only a fraction of the landing charges, catering cost, passenger insurance and payload related fuel. Therefore, airlines very often offer rates that are only slightly higher than these marginal cost numbers. Today airlines carry many passengers at rates that are not sustainable as they do not cover the cost of a flight and have to be cross-subsidized by much higher fares in the front of the cabin.

A demand-based system starts with the travel commitments of passengers, stored in a "demand cloud." The data in this cloud describe the travel intention in a door-to-door format with a description of the intended travel "window," urgency level, comfort requirements and other trip relevant data.

According to those data, the airline (or airline system) develops a basic operational schedule that will be adopted as the data in the "demand cloud" evolve and will be finalized on the day before departure.

As incremental demand triggers incremental capacity the marginal cost of a passenger now becomes much higher, containing all the cost of an extra flight section (fuel, all landing, ATC, and overflight charges, variable maintenance, variable crew cost, etc.). "Non-sustainable demand" fares will mostly disappear.

Two built-in flexibilities allow the system to match demand and supply. Demand is defined from door-to-door, giving the airlines some flexibility to select start and final airport, as in many cases "doors" are in the greater vicinity of more than one "three-letter-code." In addition, passengers submit their travel "window" and other potential flexibilities (e.g. accepted travel time), as flexibilities "earn" better fares. On the other hand, airlines can adopt their capacity and routings according to the demand, once they are able to design such a flexible production system.

### The passenger's view

As in express cargo, in a demand-based travel system there is no need for a reservation system. Passengers submit their travel intent with the airline or airline system of their choice, describe their flexibilities, comfort demand and so on, and, in return, receive a "commitment of transport" against payment of the fare. The rate incentivizes flexibilities with regard to length of "time window" and acceptance of a longer length of trip, allowing for one- and multi-stop itineraries.

On the day before departure, the airline communicates the time of pickup at the departure address and the arrival time at the final destination address. In case of short-term disruptions (weather, technical, etc.), the passenger is rebooked automatically and then notified of an updated arrival time.

### The airline's view

Like with today's low-cost carriers, the operational bases are distributed throughout the network: Airports supporting four and more airplanes will become bases, where crews are residing and airplanes have their overnight home base stops. The airline develops a "skeleton" network around theses bases. This **baseline capacity** is operated by its most efficient aircraft with a high annual utilization. Flight rotations are simple ("Ping-Pong" flying from home base of sub-fleet and crew), overnight stays of planes and crews at out stations are avoided to save on crew cost and allow overnight maintenance at the base station. In addition, airlines can deploy extra capacity easier from the base station.

For seasonal demand peaks the airline plans for **seasonal supplement capacity**, operated by mostly written-off airplanes using crews with seasonal contracts.

**Further backup capacity** can be contracted from "White Label Carriers" specializing in short-term capacity supply. Carriers like that already exist in the cargo area (Atlas Air, Kalitta Air) or in the passenger charter business (Avion Express, Hi Fly) and are used as short- and medium-term capacity extension, for example to cover longer downtimes in the customer's fleet. The present crisis is an ideal "breeding ground" for many more of these airlines.

**Interline agreements** with most third-party airlines finally help to allocate the demand that exceeds their own capacity or would require extra flights with very poor load factors. Also, these agreements allow the airline to offer a really global network.

**The actual planning process** starts with allocating the commitments already stored in the "demand cloud" sequentially, starting with the passengers with least flexibility. An AI-powered computer system optimizes the operation to accommodate 98% of the demands at minimum operating cost. The remaining 2% are either distributed to other airlines via interline agreements or will receive the equivalent of today's Denied Boarding Compensation and will then be transported outside their requested "time window."

Dependent on the requested comfort levels the system then plans the ground transportation to and from the airport. Passengers may choose between limousine, taxi type, or group van services. For longer distances, trains and later maybe electrical drones may be selected.

Airlines and airports have to make sure that the intermodal processes at airports will be much smoother than today. "Transit lounges" for road or drone service with direct shuttle connection to the airplanes can save a lot of walking time and distances at major hubs. In addition, separating passenger and baggage flows might help to ease processes at airports.

## The airport's view

Today's perception is that travelers start and end their trip at airports. Taxis, rental cars, parking lots, friends and family, and, to a small proportion, public transportation serve as links to and from the origin or destination. Intermodality is performed on one or more lanes in front of the terminal building. Passengers are urged to arrive hours before the departure of their airplane and are expected to spend money in shops and restaurants. After arrival it might take another hour or two until passengers have passed through immigration, picked up their baggage, and finally picked up their rental car.

Airports operating as intermodal hubs try to limit connecting time as much as possible. Therefore transport to the airport will be turned to bus and rail lines which frequently operate from "satellite terminals" at the main residential and business areas. At those places passengers switch from "last mile transportation" (cars, taxis, etc.), drop their bags, and undergo security checks. Therefore they can be fed right into the "air side" of the terminal.

Bags should be stored in specialized baggage containers to allow for fast loading and unloading at the airplane.

Immigration procedures normally consist of submitting required data and an "analog biometric check" by an immigration officer. Also in a few cases some more questions are asked for clarification. Those processes could easily run on digital platforms with the additional advantage that rejected passengers would not have to travel to their intended destination in vain. Once immigration procedures are handled digitally, airport processes will become much faster and easier.

Consequently airports will have to adopt to new sources of revenue, as shopping, restaurants, parking lots, rental car outlets, and other concession services will only be required at a much smaller scale. Instead, airports will have to invest in facilities and processes to support fast intermodal transits for in- and outbound passengers.

## Some road blocks (as of today)

**Airlines have to operate in order to protect airport slots**: During the pandemic, all airports have suffered severe reductions in traffic; for the "time after" a recession with a slow recovery is expected. So airport slots might not be sparse for the foreseeable future.

**Airplanes have to be used at maximum utilization**: Many airlines today have parked or stored half of their fleet. Keeping those airplanes in a "usable" mode would add little cost, but provide a lot of capacity that could be deployed at short notice. Thus scheduling becomes much more flexible. Also, airplane manufacturers and leasing companies will offer "power-by-the-hour" leases to bring their capacity to the market with some upside potential.

**Airlines need reservation systems to control demand**: All cargo express carriers operate without any reservation systems, as they can "store" demand ("overnight" vs. "next day"), integrate ground transportation for better gateway distribution, and have access to stand-by airplane capacity at short notice. These built-in flexibilities allow them to operate with constant fares year-round (no seasonal surcharges). Shipment numbers are allocated to flights when the daily ops plan is available, not like in today's passenger services, long before the day of travel. Still, penalties for delayed delivery are more rigid than in the passenger business.

**Crews want their schedules well in advance**: In the future, for a typical crew flying in and out of their home base (maybe two, four, or six sectors a day) it should be sufficient to know at what time they have to be at the airport (morning shift, noon shift, afternoon shift). For long-distance crews, there will be a mixture of fixed schedules and times of stand-by periods as is the case during the current crisis, yet with a higher proportion of stand-by days.

### Advantages for airlines

Airlines will achieve much higher load factors and, at the same time, will avoid selling seats at today's "fill-up fares," as capacity will follow sustainable demand only. Thus airlines will have much higher revenue per flight, needed to compensate higher fuel cost and pay back the debt incurred during the crisis.

Airlines will become much more flexible to deal with short-term changes in demand and thus avoid both lack of capacity as well as over-capacity.

Those airlines managing "demand clouds" will develop a much closer relationship with their loyal customers, as they will be able to always offer a mobility solution, and, with the right interline agreements, even far beyond their present physical network. Scale and scope of those "virtual networks" as well as convenience of access and processes will become the key performance indicators (see Table 7.1).

### Migration strategy

In order to avoid a "hard cutover," airlines should test passenger response, internal processes, and IT functionality on one city pair with high daily demand (minimum eight roundtrips per day) and a typical distance of 60 to 120 minutes' flight time. At least one of the two airports should be a major hub of the airline. Planes and crews should be based at both ends with 2–3 planes, including crews in stand-by mode. An agreement with a ground transportation provider (e.g. Uber, Lyft, or any other local operator) could take care of the local ground

*Table 7.1* Comparison of supply-based demand and demand-based supply

| Function | Supply-based demand (today) | Demand-based supply (future) |
|---|---|---|
| Sales | "Distribution" of given inventory | Marketing of "travel solution commitments" |
| Fare types | Endless booking classes plus individual "personalizations" | Fixed fares with "flexibility bonus discounts" |
| Minimum fare based on: | Marginal cost per passenger plus small margin | Marginal cost per flight (@ 80% load factor) |
| Product sold (scope) | Air transport between "3-letter-codes" | Door-to-door mobility solution |
| Network offered (scale) | Own services plus codeshare plus alliance partners | Worldwide capacity via interline agreements |
| Typical sales transaction (convenience) | Screen-based multi-step dialogue (generation "mail-order retailing") | Voice message, analyzed by AI, produces "travel solution commitment" (generation "Alexa") |
| Loyalty program based on: | Miles/turnover with customer | Subscription of app-based service agreement |
| Fleet composition | Trend towards large planes | Trend towards smaller planes |
| Fleet variation | Multiple "specialized" types | Few standard types |
| Bases of operation | Few large bases | Multiple small bases |
| Lease types | Long term, monthly rates | Short term, "power-by-the-hour" |
| Typical routings | Multiple stops, overnights at "out stations" | Every second landing and overnights at home base |
| Scheduling | 12 months in advance, little short-term adoptions | "Baseline schedule" plus daily variations according to demand, developed by AI system |
| Peak capacity | Deployed year round | Deployed only during peak demand |
| Interior layout of airplanes | High individualization of airline | "Commercial-off-the-shelf" |
| Deployment of third-party capacity under own airline code | Only in cases of codeshare or as "regional express partner" | "White label airlines" as flexible capacity enhancers |
| Labor contract types for direct staff | Single standard contract | Mixture of standard, seasonal, stand-by contracts, depending on demand seasonality |
| Self-perceived role of airport | "Shopping mall with gate access" | "Intermodal traffic hub" with minimum connecting times for air–air and air-ground flows |

connections. Whenever possible and accepted by the passenger, there should be an option for combining itineraries (like UberXL) to save cost.

Once the first trial city pair is established the airline can add more, using the already existing gateways and their infrastructure.

Demand-based scheduling is a systematically new product approach combining customer-centric mobility solutions with a huge efficiency gain potential for passenger airlines. The needed technology is here, both at the supplier and at the customer side. It has worked with the cargo express carriers for decades. Hopefully, airlines, airports, and authorities will give it serious consideration.

## Business digital twins: Architectures of the future

*Peeter Kivestu*
Founder & Principal, Oplytix

*Andrew Fu and Ryan Williamson*
Co-Founders, Transity

### Overview

Stan Davis[1] once said, "if you want to understand new business you're going to have to understand new technology." When a new generation of technologies brings about a step change in business, transformation occurs.

One such emerging technology is the digital twin. Digital twins are examples of digital assets that will become the cornerstone of business strategy and competitive success. This piece discusses two emerging themes and the importance of digital twins for business.

### Introduction

When new aircraft engineering led to faster, jet-powered aircraft, the US Air Force needed a new approach to make full use of the greater speed, acceleration, maneuverability and other dimensions of fighter aircraft. The resulting concept called the OODA Loop is still taught today.

OODA stands for observe, orient, decide, act. The OODA Loop teaches that executing these four steps faster than opponents in an aerial dogfight will have the result of appearing to possess superior capability, to disorient and ultimately to defeat the opposition.

Airlines today should heed lessons from OODA. Executing this loop will be critical for winning the battle for revenues and for operational effectiveness alike. The technologies needed to do this will create step changes in advantage because airlines that use them will have the ability to execute at the system level, not just at the individual department or function level.

When I asked John Dasburg, CEO Northwest Airlines about why he invested in technology even while Northwest faced its darkest financial hours, he said "airlines are a B2C business; as such they need to renew their customer base each and every day; we invested in technology because there are some things technology can do that can be done in no other way."

John was talking about creating digital assets. Digital assets help airlines to "observe" and to "orient" around customer trends faster and more effectively than the competition. We will show how Observation and Orientation through digital twins provides detailed, high fidelity actionable insights for the "decide" and "act" parts of the OODA Loop.

## Digital assets blend three key ingredients

Earlier in this book Nawal describes a framework for creating digital assets. Digital assets do not replace traditional business focus (any more than OODA replaced the principles of flying) but rather are capabilities required in addition to traditional competencies, in order to execute better than the competition.

The airline frequent flyer program is an early example of a digital asset. Its success was heavily dependent on data management. Actually it would be accurate to say airlines created a new form of data (even though the transactions already existed) that ultimately became known as the frequent flyer mile.

I had a front row seat at American Airlines as they grabbed immediate first-mover advantage by automating the capture of customer transactions. By reducing data latency, they increased the value to the customer as well as reduced the burden on the end consumer. By creating digital assets to capture the underutilized detail data in airline booking and ticketing transactions, a digital asset immediately changed the dynamic between airlines and their target customers.

The frequent flyer program was just one of American's digital asset innovations in that era. The point is that the CEO was intimately involved in the strategies, aligned with the message "there are some things technology can do that can be done in no other way." Digital assets are an executive topic because they require a systematic approach to extract value:

- relentless data collection and governance, particularly in capturing detail,
- network development, of *both* internal and external digital sources and players,
- hunger for analytics embedded in the organization, a "what's the next question" culture.

American recognized the urgency to develop a digital asset strategy early. American's success was made possible by executive drive to always ask the next question, and for their supporting executive actions—for organizational staffing that valued analytics, and for data technology from companies such as Teradata that fueled their best-in-class digital networks.

By exposing the business value from exploring the data, they created a whole new way of understanding customers. It's not that the data was never there before—the data was never amenable to analysis before. By creating a digital asset, American created an open-ended opportunity to identify unanticipated topics, unanticipated relationships, where every question leads to the next question.

Today's data and tools are vastly superior, but key principles of the strategy remain the same. American used analytic discipline to realize real understanding and ultimately ability to forecast customer behavior from having such a comprehensive digital asset. Today's data, with all of its detail, makes it much easier to capture behavioral trends and patterns, from which predictive and prescriptive models naturally emerge.

By increasing the amount of detail available in the tools, by reducing the need for assumptions, and by continually expanding the ability to extract value, the tools of AI and machine learning, are reaching further into corporate processes to create new means for competitiveness.

### "Observe"

To renew its customer base each and every day, an airline will need keener observation skills. In the digital world, where it is so easy to reach customers, for you, but also for your competitors, airlines need a practical way to identify, target and gain customers they have never served before. The challenge is similar to creating a frequent-flier program, but at a scale many times larger. Airlines will need better observation platforms. A digital twin of the customer marketplace is such an asset, and its effectiveness will depend many times more on analytic skills than frequent flyer programs to date.

#### Reaching customers you have never served before

In a market where customers are being targeted aggressively, it is necessary to be both better aligned with prospects and more targeted in reaching them. With a digital twin of your target audience it becomes possible to micro-segment customers in a way that knows what can be known about the customer and better leverages every customer acquisition resource available. Such a digital asset contains a combination of real-time data together with history, brought together from a wide network of sources. It weaves a fine-grained understanding of customer preferences, especially from data outside the organization, including behavioral data and important location and other context data.

Using the behavior and context data we can build models to predict transactions. All the data can be used to help influence or change the transaction, whether it is a ticket transaction or any other kind of transaction.

A great example of the blending of a wide variety of different detailed data types, resulting in a continuously updated predictive model were the approaches used by the Obama campaign in 2012 to target micro segments for the purposes of campaign spending to influence voters. By using detailed information available within the organization, and selectively mining external information to fill the gaps, they were able to create a targeting strategy that was extraordinarily effective in stretching the available marketing resources.

#### Location intelligence: Where do people live, work and go in between?

Airlines today have a wide variety of data on the ground truth of their customer and prospect preferences. One example is location intelligence data—where people live, work and go in-between. Location intelligence data provides the physical context of their behavior and this can be used to understand their purchase transactions, regardless of whether physical or digital.

Location intelligence data will likely become an important ingredient in building a digital twin for customers. The data is collected from digital devices that accompany our day-to-day activities, whether smartphones or vehicle-based devices. Because these devices accompany human activity so frequently, the digital fingerprint they collect is extraordinarily detailed.

With numerous data collection techniques, data from different providers is complementary to each other, not duplicative. GPS data from cell phones is useful for understanding movement of people around large urban areas. The same data from connected vehicles can be good for understanding trips across road networks. Sources such as Bluetooth and Wi-Fi help understand people movement in smaller, well-defined environments such as airports, retail locations, stadiums, and event venues.

One such provider is Predicio. Sourcing GPS data from mobile apps, it offers a statistically significant sampling of all smartphone devices from countries all over the world, with over a dozen attributes useful for analyzing location interactions to mobility patterns and more. Later on we show how Predicio data can help airlines know the "ground truth" of where customers and prospects start and end their air travel trips.

Two aspects of this data make it particularly valuable. Knowing customer movements is helpful for transportation companies that need to understand end-to-end journeys for planning purposes. But equally important is the use of this location intelligence data as anonymous but targetable device information that can be used by marketers to reach customers with specific behaviors. What specific behaviors might we want to understand? We'll look at three of them and why they are of interest to airline marketers below.

The first objective is to **understand/size the market opportunity**. Location intelligence data is geospatial/temporal in nature, with physical coordinates and timestamps. For example, where did the customer start their journey before taking an air trip? Travel choices are affected by the entire end-to-end trip needs, and that may include ground travel options, choices of airport, and more. Figure 7.20 helps us understand the market potential in terms of trip origins.

There is a lot of direct information in the location intelligence data, for example visited locations and dwell times at each, which can be particularly valuable when integrated with other public information (e.g. demographic economic) or internal data a company may have on its customers (e.g. trip patterns and preferences). When integrated, the questions marketers can answer are:

- What is our market share by neighborhood? How are we doing with people of these preferences?
- Where do people work? How does that affect their travel choices and interests?
- How could we reach people as they travel to and from home and work?

*Figure 7.20* Knowing the customer based on trip origins of air travelers in the domestic United States

The second objective is to **improve trip planning and the trip experience**. Location intelligence helps us know more about the full customer journey, from their original ground location to their ultimate ground destination, with a journey in between. This helps to first understand and then to explore ways of improving the trip experience.

By knowing customers' ground travel needs and interests, airlines could use this knowledge to develop new route options, explore opening new cities based on interesting or attractive ground destinations and/or better understand demand stimulation opportunities. Through selective use of location intelligence we can help customers with travel plans, suggest ideas well ahead of time on options and alternative locations to be visited.

In understanding how people get to where they go, we learn about the following:

- Did people use the closest airport? How can knowledge about the choice of airport be used in marketing?
- Did the customer make a long road trip together with an air trip? Does this help us understand a "time versus air travel cost" elasticity choice?
- The end-to-end journey, to better understand the impact of total travel time on modal choice, their journey experience, for example speed and reliability, and identify latent demand for air travel.

Because of the complexity of human behavior some of the best ways to gain an initial understanding of opportunities is to paint a visual picture. Figure 7.21 shows a visual analysis of customer "use of closest airport." Our diagram shows ground journeys that connected to an air journey from an airport, and in the picture you can see both length of the ground journeys as well as selections of airports, not necessarily the closest. As the concept of mobility as a service expands in reach (with electric airplanes, air taxi service, etc.) it is likely to become increasingly important to have the capability to visualize the patterns of customer choice.

The third objective is to improve **competitive and collaborative marketing**. In a marketing environment already saturated with messages, it is imperative to micro segment customers we want to reach in order to stretch available marketing resources. We need to know who are/where are the people of most interest to us, and ask further questions:

- Where do these customers visit? How can we collaborate with establishments who have access to prospects desirable to us?
- How can we find establishments frequented by our competitors' customers?
- How could we approach potential travelers with propositions such as, "people who do this also are likely to be interested in this."

One particularly relevant example of targeting customers at your competitors' locations was brought to us by Continental Airlines. Years before digital options

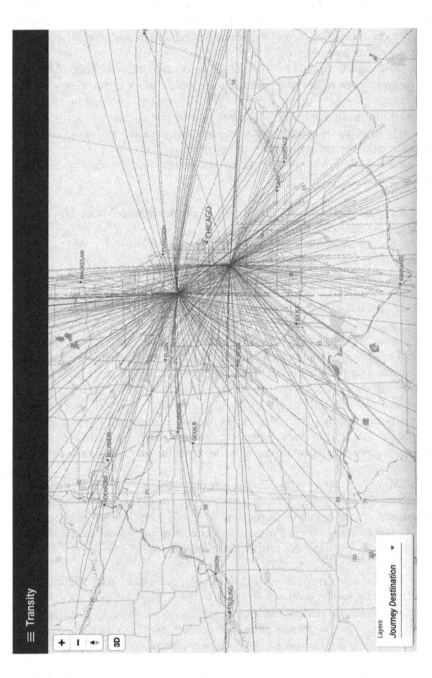

*Figure 7.21* Developing clearer understanding of closest airport to trip origins of travelers from Chicago to selected destinations
Source: Data provided by Predicio; visualization by Transity.

were available, they found a way to approach competitors' customers directly within an airport. It was one way of mining prospects whose travel needs were clearly identifiable. Over the decades they significantly updated those techniques as new data sources became available and digital techniques enabled scaling this approach. With location intelligence, many retailers are already exploiting this approach, and airlines are likely to maintain their tradition of using data to their advantage here.

### *"Orient"*

Improving orientation means operating at a system or even enterprise level. It means getting out of functional silos, and eliminating time wasted on finding sub-optimal solutions. It opens up the aperture on the consumption of data, which until today is often ad hoc analysis (perhaps just spreadsheets). This necessarily limits the amount of detail, causes every analysis to start mostly with data relevant to their own silo, and more often than not starts afresh without building on lessons learned from previous periods. Constant rework and confusing conversations originate from different interpretations of the same data.

The alternative is to orient around the true needs of the business, to use tools that aim for understanding at the process level, across the enterprise. Data is analyzed once (instead of many times in many places in many different ways) and analysis is reused effectively to further the business versus confusing discussions to sort out functional differences.

The increasing availability of AI-based solutions reflects such an enterprise approach. They have an output known as "explainable AI"—insight on system level patterns that decision-makers can use. We'll provide specific examples of where this is working already. But before we do so, to fully understand the potential power of this approach, let's look first at a topic familiar to everyone in the airline business—the problem of balancing demand and supply.

This problem today is solved in three silos. Network planning identifies feasible routes and schedules. Pricing decides what is acceptable from a marketplace position. Revenue management sub-divides the available prices and seats in a way that optimizes revenue. Why do we "optimize" in three steps, why not all at once? Because of modeling complexity of flight schedules and fast-moving developments, continuous competitive response is required all at once.

But even this complex problem is beginning to yield to the power of new technologies. It is partly because aviation has matured to the point where in some places, market conditions are right for doing all three simultaneously. Although there may be others as well, I believe what Kambr is doing may be an excellent example of where technology will lead us in this topic in the future.

Until we get to the point where technology can manage these most complex of processes, it can be instructive to see what can be done on smaller, but equally powerful airline process challenges. The following sections will describe two examples that are operationally available and implemented today. They address significant business issues, are practical applications of AI that produce explainable results and provide a roadmap for managing business in new ways.

The examples illustrate three key principles that bring impact on organizations:

- They use the power of AI to apply analytics at an enterprise level; instead of optimizing in silos, they aim to help decision-makers to "orient" across the overall process; one common opportunity in large corporations is the white space between organizations.
- They use AI differently from "black box" (often neural net) approaches we hear about so often; our examples are "explainable AI," which augments (not replaces) human capabilities, by providing process level insights (digested from vast quantities of detail) that managers need for decision-making.
- The technology unlocks a step change, not incremental benefits; with a process level view, multiple owners of a business process can start their discussions from a single version of truth, which frees up time for innovation instead of endless discussions on reconciling analyses done within silos.

Of the three characteristics above, perhaps the third may be most compelling. A single version of analytic truth enables organizations to collaborate ("orient" to the opportunities and the threats around them) with a new language focused on innovation. It is a powerful energizing force. Both our examples use technology to transcend organizational silos.

### Mitek Analytics

Our first example introduces AI to help manage one of the most complex tradeoffs in all of airline business—balancing aircraft availability with spare parts inventory and costs of maintenance. It's a very large space and management of rotable component maintenance is just one challenge faced by every operator of commercial aircraft.

There are literally hundreds of components on aircraft, and on any given fleet type, dozens or so may provide a recurring set of maintenance headaches that affect aircraft availability, maintenance workload, inventory needs and operating costs. Addressing the problem is challenging because:

- the overall process requires management of distinct sub-processes such as aircraft availability (line maintenance), spare parts availability (inventory management), and spare parts repair (repair shop or vendor management),
- the number of variables is huge, with literally hundreds of components per aircraft, multiple fleets, sub-fleets and component variations; keeping track of and making the connection between a fault reported, a part removal, and subsequent actions is not simple,
- it's a closed loop system where what happens on the flight line directly affects repair shops and other processes; however, the linkages are far from

clearly observable because of line maintenance workarounds, delays related to logistics, shop workload management, shops not always being able to confirm faults, among other things.

Much attention has recently been given to predictive maintenance—just one aspect of rotables management. Routines to identify a maintenance problem before it occurs are important, but that is not at all the essence of what we are addressing. While being able to detect a fault before it occurs can have huge operational value, this is not where the majority of cost occurs. The challenge with rotables maintenance is that the bulk of maintenance costs occur after part removal and across complex processes shared by multiple owners.

Because rotables are a very large cost item, a variety of groups within technical operations are affected by rotables maintenance and corrective actions. These actions are as diverse as engineering investigations, purchasing decisions, inventory management, overhaul and repair decisions and more. Each process owner participates in analysis, but each is done in silos. The net result is that any cost management is done in silos. Working in silos fails to optimize actions at the system level and, worse, perpetuates the cycle of partial solutions that never directly address the root cause. Consequently the analytic effort is dissipated.

The new analytical techniques of AI are about to change that. With the capacity of AI to absorb detail and understand performance across an entire process, much of maintenance and logistics data that is available today, but is never used, can be put to work to optimize the system.

Mitek Analytics uses AI to extract a treasure trove of value buried in this data. They started by working with the maintenance and overhaul operation at the US Air Force. Initial customer objective was to understand the workload in the form of units to be repaired and the problems with keeping aircraft available. Several years later, mature Mitek AI applications are operationally used by the US Air Force and are piloted by several commercial aviation players.

The explainable AI yields a single version of truth generally unavailable in maintenance analytics today. The result is powerful because it provides a process-level understanding of the results. More importantly it provides what is required to correct it, whether buying more parts, repairing them faster, eliminating logistics delays and more.

Engineers, maintenance managers and logisticians can start proactively with insights vs. usual practice of reactive response to symptoms in their silos. Best practices today for these kinds of opportunities are simulation capabilities, where users create and compare scenarios with multiple assumptions. AI offers a new approach and one with considerably less user workload. The AI approach continually updates itself, using all available data and requires no assumptions.

This AI development was driven by end users at US Air Force and they estimate $200 million in savings. But this is just the beginning. A byproduct of this process-level view is that side benefits will continue to multiply. Taking a process-level view builds an analytic foundation from which to evaluate other important solutions. Now this foundation is in position to help leverage predictive maintenance for improving aircraft availability.

While predictive maintenance ideally removes a part just before it fails, it is still an analysis and not an actual failure. And that means we need assurance with a metric to validate that parts are indeed being removed at the right time and not in fact way too early. A removal that is "way too early" is a false positive. As predictive maintenance algorithms proliferate, and become mainstream, there is a very real need to measure false positives with the same degree of rigor as any other metric that drives costs in maintenance.

The AI tools developed by Mitek do exactly that. It helps understand the impact on the overall removal rate and the costs of predictive maintenance—is it working as intended? In this way, digital assets create strategic value—when properly governed and extended across the enterprise, their value grows over time as the data coverage and user network expands.

### Outlier.ai

Our second example uses AI for enterprise-level identification of "outliers," exceptions brought to the attention of specific audiences while there is still time to react. It uses AI to accomplish enterprise-level analysis of data in details that humans simply cannot do and to identify those stories in which managers may be most interested.

Every enterprise that grows beyond a certain size has a challenge with regard to performance measurement. The enterprise has a strategy with associated goals, performance metrics and dashboards. However, once it gets beyond a certain size, some of the details that matter most to a business are not readily visible among the mass of signals and data.

Automated business analysis recognizes that every established company faces volatility and change. These changes can represent either opportunity or danger, and the earlier a company discovers these, the more time there is to act.

What automated business analysis does is to separate the signal from the noise, using AI to separate what is changing unexpectedly from what is stable and seasonal, before the problem has gotten too big or the opportunity has been grabbed by others.

Automated business analysis (ABA) has three key features.

First, it automatically flags any activity **outside of historical norms**. It finds places where data and relationships divert from historical trends and finds the best story on what is causing it. While the machine does not know the different data types it's looking at, the AI approach does drill down to identify any detail attributes and discern the ones that are most correlated with the exception. The net result is a superfast identification of any deviation the business might be interested in with an explanation understandable by the business. This is explainable AI.

Figure 7.22 shows how an e-commerce retailer uses Outlier "stories" to understand changes in customer engagement. Outlier automatically details a

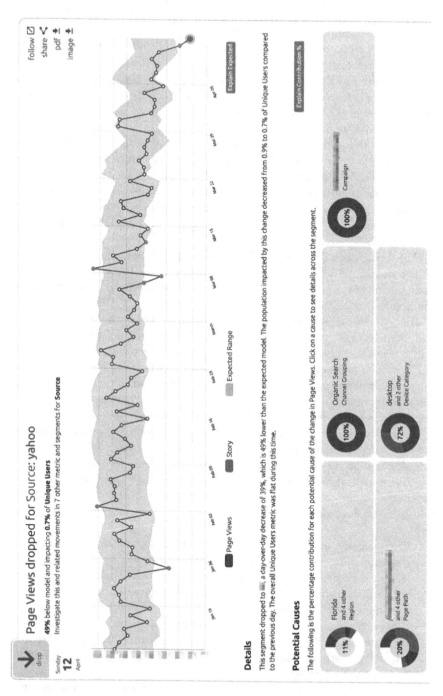

*Figure 7.22* Outlier provides a periodic feed of stories, interpreting outliers in business activity

trendline it sees (shaded areas of the graph), the exception identified (points outside shaded areas) and five analyses of contributing factors from its drilldown (in the pie charts) that flag the key contributing variables and contribution of each.

Second, ABA is a standard, scalable way to tap into any of the company's data, wherever it resides. It is designed to look at any of the data in your organization. It is not bound by the need to know the relationships between these data and can look at any level of detail. The AI approach scales across attributes, so it can see data used in your business dashboards as readily as a new data source that just appeared yesterday.

ABA is the ultimate fast implementation of business intelligence. It complements existing efforts by being able to get to root causes at a level of detail not readily apparent to business analysts, and it always makes use of any new data that is available to it. But more importantly, because the AI approach does not require any particular data alignment, it can readily add in any new data sources whenever they appear, whether from new internal or new external data sources.

Third, ABA is an analysis tool that works on timelines most relevant for your business. ABA probes your business data on a daily, weekly or monthly basis, whatever is most relevant, with an early heads-up on any exceptions the business may need to know about.

ABA works by looking at trend line exceptions within the time series data, and therefore does not need to look at any sensitive data in individual business transactions, such as details of any particular passenger name record (PNR), any particular flight operation, or any vendor transaction. Rather, by looking at the aggregations of this data, and using AI to understand any relevant history, it can identify on a daily, weekly or monthly basis the places where your business activity is diverging from historical norms.

Because of its reach across corporate data, when it identifies a story of interest, it prioritizes these stories for each business audience, so the deviations it finds could be very different for revenue management, from marketing, from sales. With such a broad capability of data examination, the possible applications of automated business analysis at airlines are quite broad and we will highlight just four of them below:

- Passenger sales and revenue management: in sales channels to detect loss of a specific customer segment (e.g. within corporate sales), channel leakage (e.g. in a particular online or travel agency), in regional sales (e.g. issues with seat availability bottlenecks) or in marketing promotional items (e.g. response on social media).
- Customer segment management: discern nuances by type of customer attribute that could represent targetable (e.g. customer churn in a particular micro segment) and valuable opportunities (e.g. new customer acquisition by particular micro segment).
- Ancillary and partner revenue generation: an early heads-up on acceptance levels/revenue impacts of customer behavior (e.g. product adoption),

emerging preferences (e.g. loyalty program partner offers), loyalty program behaviors (e.g. earning, burning or transfer effects), activity on codeshare alliance partners (e.g. desirable or undesirable trends or cannibalization).
• Flight or web experience disruption: identify "out of the norm" trends having either positive or negative impacts on the customer experience, customer experience challenges (e.g. interrupted trips, or broken online experiences).

Automated business analysis has been implemented in virtually every kind of industry, to catch exceptions from people behavior such as fraud to technical behavior such as web services inconsistencies. Within big pharmaceutical companies it has been used to identify end customer (e.g. patient) topics and channel changes (e.g. by doctors and pharmacies) as well as internal supply chain issues. It has been used in the travel industry to correlate marketing campaign activity with booking trends, and by retailers to identify early interest in products, enabling them to tailor availability to achieve greater market share.

ABA is not a replacement for the data initiatives of digitally savvy marketing firms, nor of the enterprise data management efforts of companies with data science and business intelligence investments. Automated business analysis is a fast-paced, business-oriented complement to the suite of tools that the most sophisticated businesses have for managing and creating digital assets.

### Digital twins advance competitiveness, by observing more

In a world of increasingly available data, especially from external resources that are rich in details and valuable to businesses, the opportunity for improving observation through digital assets is real. Digital assets gain their power through a combination of data, analytics and network. Of these, the networking is central. If there's any doubt about the power of networks and hubs, just look at the spread of social networks and the power that they have.

While airline physical hubs will always be important, complementing them with digital hubs[2] will create value that surpasses the value of physical hubs in a significant way. Just look at what the frequent flyer program achieved. Networks bring about hubs that strengthen it and attract more participants, and networks have a resiliency created from the multiplicity of connections they enable. Whenever implementing new technologies, the network effect cannot be ignored and building digital twins will no doubt exploit networks of data sources over time.

### Digital twins advance competitiveness, by orienting faster

With increasing amounts of observable data will come the challenge of being able to stay oriented. There are two challenges that a business faces in this, which are essentially about pattern recognition in both customer and operational activities.

First, as our systems become increasingly complex, driven by real time requirements and global in scale, the price we pay for analyzing patterns in silos and then (if ever) reconciling these, becomes too great. While organizational silos may be inevitable in large organizations, AI tools now help us overcome the silos in terms of the patterns we look for. AI will help organizations become more collaborative by giving us a new data language that transcends individual organizations.

Second, AI will extend human argumentation by working with our visual senses. Visually, we can ingest so many more dimensions at one time than we can numerically to respond to increasingly sophisticated pattern recognition. For airlines, as the patterns of travel places and operations are across increasingly complex networks, it seems that visual analytics built in actual digital process twins will rise in importance as we seek to orient around meeting customer needs and finding operational opportunities in the search for better business.

## Notes

1  Stan Davis, Professor at Harvard Business School and author of *Future Perfect* and many other books on the future of business.
2  Peeter Kivestu, "The Under-Appreciated Importance of Hubs as Disruptors," in Nawal Taneja, *Airline Industry: Poised for Disruptive Innovation*, Chapter 10, p. 201 (Abingdon and New York: Routledge, 2017).

# Evolving the next distribution model: Its impact on analytics and data requirements

*John Lancaster*
Founder and Chief Scientist, Lancaster Analytics

With each crisis, ticket sales disappear, and airlines fight to survive. With massive infrastructure investment and notoriously low margins, market shocks take a toll on the airline enterprise's viability. As a whole, the airline industry has returned a net profit of $0 over the last 50 years. Such performance does not inspire investor confidence in airlines "staying the same."

Yet, banks and credit card companies have placed their bets on airlines again, investing in airlines with large loyalty programs. Bankers and financiers do not gamble. They are betting that airlines can transform their business strategy. Otherwise, that investment will disappear.

Is the "pain of change" now less than the "pain of staying the same"?

Airlines have to show they can deliver sustained profitability, which justifies the long-term investment in their physical and digital networks. With 75–80% of operational revenues tied to ticket sales, demand fluctuations catastrophically impact profitability. This risk exposure is not limited to crises. Fare volatility and shifting demand patterns erode return on assets deployed.

In the parlance of risk management, passenger revenues experience market and systematic risk. Until these risks are acknowledged and managed, profitability will exhibit high volatility levels, making airlines a risky investment. As the executive leadership realize, attracting capital investment depends on finding ways to:

- stabilize cash flow from passenger revenue stream,
- diversify revenue sources beyond ticket sales, and
- distribute risk across the distribution chain.

This thought leadership piece proposes (1) the current structure of global distribution creates much of the uncertainty, (2) the model needs to be restructured to provide risk mitigation mechanisms, and (3) the analytic framework and data requirements must change to support decision-making in a new paradigm.

## Sources of risk in airline distribution

The airline's global distribution system (GDS) consists of three essential components: suppliers (airlines), a storefront (GDS and associated enablers like the Airline Tariff Publishing Company (ATPCO), OAG, BSP, and others), and consumers (agencies, OTA representing passengers). This model mimics the functional organization of the 1960s airline reservations center, in which airline representatives take reservations at set fares over the phone, then record them

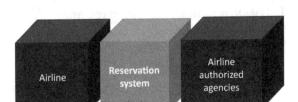

*Figure 7.23* Airline distribution model circa 1970

in an inventory management system controlling a fixed supply of seats. The move to e-commerce directly translated this business process into a network of computers and green screen terminals.

In the prevailing business realities of the 1960s and 1970s, airlines faced little uncertainty with this distribution model. Fares were regulated and travel agents represented their authorizing airline. Airlines owned their reservation system or were hosted by a partnering airline. Airlines owned the entire distribution chain. They could respond to the market by shifting capacity or using a promotional price, not easily discoverable by a competitor. The distribution model produced stable and reliable revenue (see Figure 7.23).

Over time, travel agents shed allegiance to a single airline and represented multiple airlines. Legal regulations stripped airlines of reservation system ownership. With independence, airlines' distribution partners formed separate missions, and pursued goals not aligned with airlines. Passengers formed relationships with travel agencies, who would guide their purchasing decisions. The use of percentage commissions encouraged agents to upsell passengers. When commissions were cut in the 1990s, agencies had no incentive to upsell passengers.

Reservation systems became storefronts for displaying the products and prices for many airlines. Airlines only saw passengers through the lens of a passenger name record (PNR) so their ability to learn about and influence passengers was restricted to what they sold in the GDS storefront. Airlines lost control of distribution. Unable to directly talk with passengers, their knowledge about market conditions and future demand volumes was restricted. Furthermore, airlines only controlled what inventory they placed in the storefront and how that inventory was priced.

Meanwhile, deregulation transformed the nature of competition in the industry. New entrants offered lower fares, and established airlines engaged in fares wars. Price competition became intense. Online travel agencies, such as Orbitz, Expedia, Travelocity, and Priceline, consolidated a position in the distribution model. Their model permitted passengers to browse and compare airline fares, increasing transparency. The airline landscape became considerably more volatile. But the storefront distribution model did not change.

Airlines still had to provide fixed products and prices to the GDS. Without ownership of the demand chain, airlines were forced to respond with supply-centric solutions. Revenue management, leveraging price elasticity between segments, was developed to align prices based on inventory availability. Decision-making centered on balancing a known supply with an unknown demand, optimizing scheduled supply and differential pricing of available inventory. The analytic framework, supporting scheduling and revenue management, optimized revenue received from a fixed supply. The linear optimization and stochastic heuristics relied on predicting where, when, and what demand will materialize from available inventory histories. A forecasting system dependent on history will introduce risk due to inherent inaccuracies in modeling past patterns and assuming tomorrow looks the same as yesterday.

As airlines grew their networks and origin and destination (O/D) demand forecasting became necessary, the risk of misaligning fixed inventory and dynamic prices increased. Forecasting the size of O/D demand threads over millions of O/D had little chance of detecting a pattern. The analytic framework has not significantly altered over the last two decades, so the risk profile has not altered (see Figure 7.24).

Risk mitigation efforts in the storefront proceed along three ideas:

- reducing forecast error,
- creating greater flexibility in pricing fixed inventory (e.g. continuous pricing[1]), and
- extending what can be offered in the storefront with, for example, New Distribution Capacity (NDC) and Next Generation Storefront (NGS).

Both of these solutions seek to build more flexible ways of using the storefront by extending its functionality. The new solutions are not designed for mitigating the revenue-side risk. Doing this requires constructing a risk management analytic layer in the model, which in turn needs a data architecture not expressed in the distribution model. Therefore, the way forward entails reimaging the roles, functions, and interfaces required to build a risk-resistant distribution model.

*Figure 7.24* Airline distribution model circa 2000

Two architectural paths appear fruitful to examine:

- conversion of the storefront into an exchange,
- extension of the storefront into a digital marketing platform.

Both paths lead to transformative change in the distribution model but with quite different compositions of roles and functionality. Consequently, the questions asked and answered diverge from those driving decisions today and from each other. Thus, the two transformation paths require innovations in analytics and data.

### The exchange path

Conceptually, an exchange supports a distribution model which is composed of five roles illustrated in Figure 7.25. In this model, the central exchange interface between the demand chain and the supply chain functions to facilitate a negotiation between sellers and buyers. The negotiation sets volume and price in each transaction, unlike the storefront where a small volume of requests are accepted or rejected on price alone. The two-dimensional nature of a transaction adds flexibility to the offering of a single product (see Figure 7.25).

The model accommodates five roles. Suppliers and consumers want to be very efficient in interacting with the market. They fulfill essential roles; without them there is no market, but focus on building efficiencies and flexibility in either production or consumption. Aggregators exist to act on behalf of suppliers or consumers in the exchange. For this they receive remuneration as a commission or fee. In this role they regulate the influx of supply and demand in the market to balance the two. But this is a low margin role. Since aggregators bridge the supply and demand, they develop a deep understanding of the amount and dynamics of supply and demand in the market. This knowledge can be used to undertake an opportunistic speculation. The greater part of their profit comes from speculative activities. These speculative actions distribute risk which absorbs shocks in the system, thus protecting suppliers and consumers.

A useful example of a successful exchange model can be observed in the maritime industry's Baltic Exchange which facilitated the tramp cargo trade. Ship brokers represented aggregated supply and shipping agents aggregated

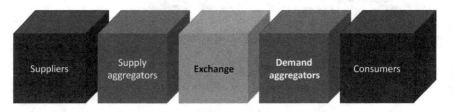

*Figure 7.25* Exchange-based distribution model

*Figure 7.26* Tramp shipping's distribution chain

demand. Negotiations determined how many vessels would be chartered, setting the supply carriage shipping agents have to offer (see Figure 7.26).

In turn, ship owners learn from the brokers how to size their operating fleets for sparse supply drives charter rates up and excess supply lowered charter rates. Shipping agents used charter rates to set prices quoted to shippers. Normal economic dynamics then balanced supply and demand. When market shocks occurred, brokers holding charter agreements modulate financial impact on owners. This model thrived successfully for centuries in various shipping exchanges present in the Hanseatic League and later the Baltic Exchange. Though much smaller in the age of containerized ocean shipping, the tramp trade still exists because of its ability to adapt to structural changes in the industry.

This suggests modification of the airline distribution architecture would be able to regulate market risks resulting from fare competition and systematic risks due to market disruptions. Using forwards (contracts between a supplier and consumer agreeing to future sale at an agreed price) and derivative products (granting the right but not obligation to buy or sell at an agreed price) would create greater risk sharing potential. This has been done in agricultural and manufacturing industries with significant uncertainty in future supply and prices.

The airline distribution model lacks two roles faced in exchange models, the exchange and supply aggregators. Exchanges differ from storefronts in how the terms of a transaction are made. Storefronts sell a fixed amount of supply at a fixed price. The buyer accepts or rejects the offer. In an exchange, the buyer and seller negotiate on quantity and price. The need for an exchange has been anticipated by Airbus's Skytra market, which announced it was building a forwards and derivative market for the industry. Within the exchange there are many roles for market intermediaries (e.g. GDS, ATPCO and BSP), one can assume, ranging from clearing and settlement, market makers, storage of volume and price offers, reporting of trading activities and other essential roles in exchanges.

The supply aggregator looks and behaves like a "virtual airline," a concept which has floated around in the airline industry for years. A purely commercial entity, owning no physical assets, it has great flexibility in its ability to enter and exit markets, shift inventory and engage in volume and price discovery.

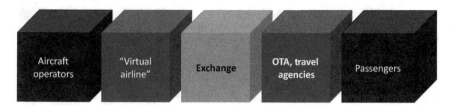

*Figure 7.27* Airline exchange model

The "virtual airline" assumes the functionality of a ship broker in the Baltic Exchange, creating and marketing capacity from a set of airlines. This role will appear organically to provide market intelligence and risk-sharing with airlines separated from the demand chain (see Figure 7.27).

This would open up the possibility of splitting a scheduled airline model into a network operating enterprise, free to sell capacity to several "virtual airlines," and a "virtual airline" enterprise, free to purchase capacity from multiple operators. This arrangement decouples the need to simultaneously maximize revenue while minimizing the risk of poor asset allocation.

The "virtual airline" is not new in the airline industry. The traditional Japanese airline distribution model builds a private, temporary exchange between Japanese airlines and tour agencies. Once a year, tour operators and travel agencies negotiate to secure seat allotments, which it then sells and manages independent of the airline. Nor is it far-fetched to see how an Amazon could become a "virtual airline." Imagine through a series of negotiations, the ten largest airlines agree to sell 10% to have access to booking inventory to an online retailer to survive 2021. With a large base of customers, no network costs, a more efficient marketing model and the ability to offer a customer a different carrier, they could readily out-compete airlines on price and selection. In this scenario, the online retailer would become both a demand and supply aggregator, capable of serving its own. Without the transparency afforded by an exchange, each airline would be thrown into a prisoner's dilemma, leaving the online retailer with an enviable negotiating position.

The possibility of such a scenario adds weight to arguments for the exchange model and generating an airline-friendly "virtual airline."

Many of the components needed to realize this distribution model exist today. The seat block mechanism can be repurposed to provide a "white label" product sellable in the exchange. As previously mentioned, exchange functions have logic analogs in ATPCO, Airlines Reporting Corporation (ARC) and BSP, and GDS.

In this scenario, financial engineering, derivative pricing, and risk management become the dominate analytic framework of "virtual airlines." Revenue management can be replicated by a real option strategy, called a swing option.[2]

Demand and pricing are discovered in the market rather than forecasted. Decision-making evolves into portfolio management. Analytics supports portfolio management with simulation, value-at-risk estimation and statistical analysis aimed at identifying correlations that signal market changes. Data requirements consumed in these analytics include market data, financial news, economic forecasts, and travel-related social media feeds.

### The digital marketing path

An alternate choice can be realized in fulfilling the vision of the NDC and the NGS. The logical end state is digital marketing. The path forward to digital marketing entails a change of identity from an airline selling online to a digital retailer selling air travel.

While several digital retailers are trying to enter the travel distribution space, airlines enjoy several advantages. They understand the intricacies of selling travel. Second, airlines can readily form "travel ecologies" capable of delivering a total travel experience. But most importantly, airlines already have a following of loyal travelers, their loyalty programs.

With a pre-existing following, airlines do not need to climb the first two rungs of the digital marketing ladder, **A**cquiring and **A**ctivating. They can leap-frog forward to the **R**etain and **R**efer phases. From these, **R**evenue will flow, completing the growth hacking AARRR strategy.

The vision of being a digital retailer expresses itself in a retailing platform, offering travelers a one-stop-shop for shaping their experience. The travel retailing platform enables a traveler to obtain travel-related information, shape their individual travel experience, shop for components of their desired experience, basket the components, then pay for it all in one place, their mobile phone.

If an airline formed a travel ecology to populate a travel retail platform, the resulting business model would resemble WeChat or Alibaba. In 2017, Alibaba conducted negotiations with a major ocean shipping concern to do this in ocean shipping. Alibaba or WeChat will face few barriers to entry when they decide to do this in the airline industry.

A simple key underlies the digital retailing; using digital technology to reach individuals, allow them to build their own product, and influence purchasing decisions. The digital retailer does this for each customer during each shopping session. Doing this at scale creates an imperative for digital transformation and a new analytic framework. Dynamic products and dynamic pricing (DP2) emerge as enabling technologies, replacing pricing and revenue management.

Digital marketing relies on understanding an individual's satisfiers, dissatisfiers, delighters then building the desired content in the dynamical constructed product. To improve the probability of purchase, context and price are to conform with an individual's observed behavior patterns. Artificial intelligence tests then analyzes customer reactions to build a model of product selection and purchasing behavior. Analytics provides four enablers to this process:

* data collection processes from customer interactions,
* experimental design guiding A/B testing,
* algorithms for cleaning data and extracting actionable information,
* deploying AI that learns how to interact with and influence the user.

The dominant analytic framework draws on insights from behavioral science, behavioral economics, and statistical analysis rather than operations research. In this role, the analytic framework solves many small behavior modification problems throughout the follower base. At scale, algorithms and analytic models favor simplicity and rapid response.

Underlying everything is **data**, lots and lots of granular customer data.

As the platform interacts with the user and the mobile phone hosting the platform, the app collects data. From GPS functions of the phone, geospatial (location, event timing, and life span) extracts data. Purchase histories, collected from the embedded payment platform, support constructing total travel spend, share of wallet, preferred products and merchants, and most importantly lifetime value profiles. Purchase behavior, interests, and product preferences are discerned from session histories and browsing choices. Biases and motivators are discovered using A/B testing experiments embedded into the suggestion mechanism. Personal attribute data can be collected from monitoring travel-related social media interactions. The list of potential datum is limited only by the imagination of the data scientists and data architects.

To build an understanding of the power of this data and algorithms, consider how real-time location data can be used to assist in navigating an airport, finding a hotel, and alerting partnering restaurant and retail partners in the vicinity to enable sending advertising and incentives. Knowledge of itinerary, lodging arrangements, and location of meetings allows the app to guide selection of ground transportation alternatives. Purchasing profiles and lifetime value enhance understanding of user willingness-to-pay and lifetime to the travel ecology.

Realization of digital marketing demands a one-to-one relationship with each traveler. This relationship does not begin and end within a single transaction, like the current airline distribution does. It encompasses interactions designed to interact with and aid the potential traveler through the travel experience, which includes dreaming, planning, shopping, purchasing, traveling, being at the destination and following up. The distribution model seeks to extract value over the user's lifetime, creating a long-term revenue generation model.

The platform's architecture delivers the functionality of a travel guide. A travel guide elicits desired experiences then takes the traveler to places to purchase the experience, but the guide directs the traveler to business partners. This goes beyond the functionality of a storefront displaying goods and services.

The GDS storefront will be hard-pressed to compete with travel platforms delivering total travel experiences.

The path of digital marketing presents an alternate vision for creating an investment-worthy transformed airline model. Embedding the airline within an ecosystem capable of generating revenue across a spectrum of transportation modalities (airplanes, trains, busses, cars, ships, and boats), services at destinations and transit points (hotels, restaurants, and entertainment), and retailers, diversifies revenue generation over sources. Participants in the ecosystem may agree on share revenues. Possible additional revenue can be generated from pay-per-click advertising revenues. Additionally, the owners of the engagement, retail, and payment platforms can charge other members usage fees. All these stabilize and diversify the revenue streams.

The digital marketing transformation disruptively changes the distribution and airline model. It requires a new mindset and different technologies, analytic methods, and data being deployed currently. Moving directly to such a vision would incur undue risk. This distribution model has to be evolved in incremental steps.

One possible roadmap is illustrated in Figure 7.28. The roadmap proceeds along a series of increasingly efficient distribution models.

Moving to an exchange model using over-the-counter futures and options would be a relatively easy application of NDC. This would be a good first step. Deployment of a simple exchange allows airlines to offload marketing low-value inventory and permits them to focus on high-value loyalty program members. During this first step, an airline would also be building alliances with travel-related ventures to extend its network to closely related industries.

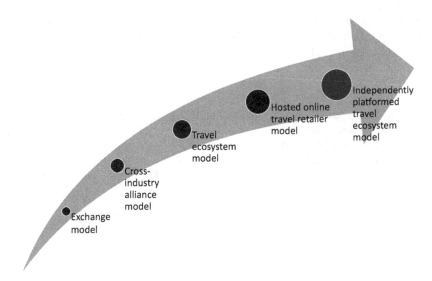

*Figure 7.28* Roadmap to a digitally platformed travel ecology

Developing and fully deploying the cross-industry packaging of air travel, hotel and rental car could be offered for loyalty program members by extending the NGS vision. This begins the formulation of travel ecologies and creates a hybrid model. As the travel ecology develops, travel packages could be sold to a "virtual airline" in the exchange. This creates a travel ecology model without a digital platform.

The travel ecology next moves to distributing travel products in a hosting online retail platform. During this evolutionary stage, the ecology constructs its own travel platform expressed in a WeChat- or Alibaba-like mobile super app. Now the airline has evolved itself into a travel retail platform selling air transportation as part of a fuller travel offering.

The coming evolution of the distribution model will be a major component in inventing a more resilient airline. There are many ways the industry may evolve its business model, as it seeks to build a more profitable and resilient revenue model. As we have shown in this paper, those choices impact the questions asked, the analytics providing answers, and the data required to provide those answers.

The airline model has changed a lot since hungry, unemployed military pilots and aircraft manufacturers joined forces 70 years ago to challenge the rail and ocean liner industries using speed and a relatively inexpensive, flexible network. The industry muddled its way through computerization, globalization, deregulation, and internet-ization. The industry will muddle through digitalization and COVID too. Airlines have accomplished a minor miracle in those 70 years, maturing a new technology and reaching scale. It took the maritime industry millennia and railroads centuries to achieve scale, but the airline accomplished the same feat in decades. The airline industry should be proud of breaking even with such rapid evolution. The next road ahead will be one of transformation. There are many possible routes to this goal. Three possible paths presented illustrate different distribution models capable of getting airlines to sustainable profitability.

## Notes

1  Tom Gregorson, "Evolution of Airline Pricing: Past, Present, and Future," in Nawal K. Taneja, *Transforming Airlines: A Flight Plan for Navigating Structural Change* (New York: Routledge, 2020).
2  Chris K. Anderson, Matt Davison, and H. Rasmussen, "Revenue Management: A Real Options Approach," *Naval Research Logistics*, 2004, vol. 51, issue 5, pp. 686–703. DOI: 10.1002/nav.20026

# Industry strategies for the new normal in air travel

*Eric Leopold*
Former Director, Industry Strategy Airline Capability, IATA

This thought leadership piece is based on the work I did at IATA in 2020 in my role of Director, Industry Strategy Airline Capability, where my task was creating the industry strategy for airline capability following the COVID-19 crisis.[1]

An industry strategy differs from a corporate strategy in the sense that it looks at what an entire industry should focus on to thrive. The industry strategy describes the rationale for the new priorities, while each priority will require a specific industry business case. Virtually any player in the marketplace may decide to tackle an industry priority.

## Could we have anticipated the crisis of the air travel industry?

The 2019 IATA vision paper identified drivers of change and defined scenarios based on possible outcomes. It highlighted "pandemics" as one of the top 13 drivers of change, based on their impact and the uncertainty of the impact, and the variance in impact and uncertainty. The paper clearly outlined a future where a potential outbreak would "limit people's desire and freedom to travel, as well as present significant economic challenges for the industry." Two years after the paper was released, this potential scenario has materialized.[2]

The vision paper made specific recommendations to mitigate the negative impacts of the changes. In Recommendation 7, the paper stresses the need to ensure that government responses are in line with international health regulations. The current COVID-19 situation confirms the need identified in the paper and shows that governments are unable to apply globally consistent sanitary measures.

Anticipation is not enough. Knowing that the existing reality is not sustainable does not create a sense of urgency, whether for future pandemics, for environment or any future threats. The only driver for change is a vision of a new model compelling enough for all parties to buy into. Making the current model obsolete is a consequence of the change, not a vision in itself.

## Strategic review

Strategies work better in times of certainty, whether growth or recession. Strategic reviews are more challenging in times of uncertainty and unprecedented changes, not only because of the number of unknowns in the future but also the lack of comparable previous situations to refer to when making decisions.

The solution is to build scenarios, to define a number of plausible futures depending on each variable, and to test the strategies against each scenario and plausible future. Collaboration is key in building the scenarios and in assessing the strategies.

The benefit of the strategic review is an anticipation of each plausible future, but in no circumstances can we predict what the future will be. We can learn from this exploration of the future, or as the *Harvard Business Review* (HBR) article says, we can "learn from the future."[3]

We are mindful that any strategy is useless unless it is followed by robust and determined execution, which is another uncertainty to anticipate.

Finally, this strategic review offers an exploration of a new normal, while most companies and people are focused on exploitation and mitigating the crisis. The challenge is to take a break from the crisis management and look three years down the road with a blank canvas.

### Industry sounding board

The strategic assessment initially covered the crisis, its roots, its consequences and the "new normal," then the industry solutions that will increase industry resilience and mitigate similar future shocks.

I personally interviewed 100 thought leaders who were selected to represent various parts of the airline industry and its ecosystem, among them, of course, the author of the book, Nawal Taneja. The sounding board itself and the interviews were kept informal to maximize openness and transparency.

The participants can be segmented into four groups:

- airline (and ex-airline) professionals in commercial, financial and digital roles,
- travel ecosystem professionals, working for travel agencies, airports, original equipment manufacturers (OEMs) and technology vendors,
- customers and observers, such as consultants, analysts and academics,
- IATA staff in roles covering airline capabilities and beyond.

### Impact of the crisis on the air travel industry

The first step of the strategic review consists in assessing and understanding the drivers of the crisis and its impact on the world and the air travel industry.

Safety is the airline industry's first priority. Until 2019 safety was related to all aircraft operations. Since 2020, safety also includes traveler health during the entire travel experience. Airlines and airports had to redesign the entire process to accommodate the rules mitigating the transmission of the virus, from social distancing to washing hands and wearing masks.

At the same time, the travel restrictions imposed by countries introduced many operational challenges to airlines, their pilots, crews and customers.

The travel restrictions, combined with new sanitary measures, resulted in lower passenger numbers in 2020 (about 55% compared to 2019, as estimated by IATA) which have severely impacted the industry profitability and caused its largest financial crisis ($200 billion lost revenue in 2020 estimated by IATA). The financial crisis not only meant loss of revenue for airlines, but also refunds to customers who had already paid for all the canceled flights. Credit card acquirers lost faith in airlines' ability to operate flights and held back the cash. For airlines having on average two months of cash available, liquidity became the key issue, requiring emergency financial state aid.

The lack of liquidity prevented many airlines from refunding their customers. The complexity in the ticketing processes created delays in the processing of the customer claims. The massive scale of the disruption caused delays in customer service. Overall, the crisis became the worst commercial crisis that airlines ever faced and ruined years of investment in building a trusted relationship with customers.

Finally, consumers were led to alternatives to flying, and, if continued, these alternatives may totally alter the size and shape of demand for air travel. Students may consider following classes online. Tourists may prefer to spend their vacation close to their home. Business colleagues may be requested to organize meetings online. Friends and families may prefer to commute by night train or coach or car. Environment-aware citizens may appreciate their new lifestyle without flying.

### Thriving as an ambition

Economists like Kate Raworth are proposing new economic models, like her famous "Doughnut," to rethink economic growth in the 21st century.[4] The focus of the new models is on "thriving" more than on growth. The doughnut defines an ideal area of development between a minimum requirement—the "foundation" or the inside of the doughnut—and a maximum growth—the "ceiling" or the outside of the doughnut. This paper will propose a doughnut for the future of air travel.

The city of Amsterdam is at the forefront of this new thinking, and its vision is a "thriving city" that is socially fair and ecologically safe. The foundations include the health, connectivity, enablement (education) and empowerment (justice) that citizens are entitled to expect. The ceiling includes the footprint of the city of air, land and water. Within these boundaries, the strategy of the city will help it find the optimum position, where it can thrive.

### A renewed purpose for the air travel industry

What does "thriving" mean for the world and for air transport? At a global level, the United Nations have defined Sustainable Development Goals (SDGs) to help guide and measure initiatives and business, ranging from "No poverty" to "Good health" and 15 other goals, to which air transport contributes with tourism and cargo as examples.[5]

In summary, air transport contributes mainly to SDG #8 "decent work and economic growth" via:

- well-being of people: from connecting families to delivering medical supplies,
- jobs: from direct jobs in the airline industry to indirect jobs in tourism,
- economic development: connecting markets for people and goods,
- profits: generating return on airline investments.

At the same time, air transport has a negative impact on SDG #1 "No poverty," SGD #3 "Good health and wellbeing" and SDG #13 "Climate action" via:

- use of taxpayer money: government bailout in case of airline bankruptcy,
- disease spread: infected travelers carry the virus with them,
- environment impact: $CO_2$ emission, noise.

A thriving air transport industry would contribute positively to all SDGs; that is, "connecting people in a safe and sustainable way."

### Sustainable purpose in the strategy

Where growth is the solution to increasing shareholder returns, companies usually pick one of the following strategies: conquer new markets, address broader customer needs or change rules of the market. Besides "growth as a strategy," this strategy paper proposes to put purpose at the core of the strategy, as suggested in a recent HBR article.[6]

Purpose in the strategy means addressing the liquidity issue, the virus spread and the environment footprint that impact the world negatively, while keeping the contribution to SDG #8 described above. The authenticity and value of this strategy will come from the ambition of the commitments.

Ambitious commitments for the purpose of air travel will drive new customers to fly, new employees to join airlines and new investors to bet on air travel. Purpose is the beginning of a virtuous cycle.

### Rebuilding after an earthquake

We saw in the introduction that it is impossible to predict what will happen in 3 years due to the uncertainty of the world. However, we can identify the drivers behind the uncertainty and observe the scenarios and how they vary. Ideally, we will identify a preferable scenario that our strategy will influence, while mitigating alternative scenarios.

The COVID-19 crisis felt like an earthquake, in the sense of a natural disaster causing hundreds of thousands of casualties. The world has more experience with earthquakes than with pandemics requiring the lockdown of half of the world population. Following previous earthquakes scientific labs implemented detection mechanisms and warning systems, while architects defined seismic design for structures to resist against earthquakes.

After the COVID-19 crisis, which we described as a safety, operational, financial and commercial crisis for airlines, there are two options:

- restart: rebuild with the same norms as before COVID-19, or
- define the new norms, equivalent of seismic design, to resist future pandemics and shocks.

The first approach has the benefit of restarting what used to work, something we know, and should still work as long as we don't have another earthquake with the magnitude of COVID-19. But, the hidden cost of this approach is the hundreds of billions of lost revenues and the dozens of billions of losses of another crisis.

The second approach requires more creativity to design new norms, and a dose of uncertainty in the success of the new norms; however, it is the only one which promises a future less uncertain and vulnerable to massive disruptions.

A recent study by McKinsey & Company shows that even if a COVID-19-scale pandemic is a 50-year event, preparedness investments (in billions of dollars for early warning systems, etc.) will vastly pay back to prevent future economic losses (in trillions of dollars for global cost of COVID-19).[7]

### Evolution of key crisis drivers

Scenario planning is a well-established practice, and consulting firms have developed their own models. For example:

- BCG scenarios based on two drivers: duration of flatten phase vs. depth of economic loss—ranging from 13 weeks of lockdown with 30% economic loss to 7 weeks of lockdown with 15% loss.
- McKinsey scenarios based on two drivers: virus spread vs. economic-policy response—ranging from pandemic escalation without economic recovery to virus contained with growth rebound.
- Accenture has four scenarios based on the growth of monthly travel demand, influenced by virus containment, societal response, consumer behavior and economic climate.

In this model, I propose three drivers related to the uncertainty of the crisis:

- Sanitary: How will the virus evolve? How effective will sanitary measures be?
- Social: How will governments react to the sanitary crisis? Lockdown? Travel restrictions?

- Economic: How will businesses perform given the sanitary and social impacts?

For each driver, the situation can evolve either positively or negatively, as illustrated below.

On the sanitary side, the situation can evolve in two opposite directions:

- Positively: protection (ubiquitous masks and hand washing), detection (massive testing), prevention (effective vaccine), control (COVID-19-tracing apps, medical passport).
- Negatively: failure of the above leading to a second wave, virus mutation leading to a "COVID-20."

On the social side, the situation can improve or worsen:

- Positively: governments prioritize freedom of movement, ease travel restrictions, become creative with laissez-passer or temporary travel bubbles, provide predictive criteria for future restrictions (e.g. threshold based on number of COVID-19 cases vs. number of tests).
- Negatively: uncoordinated and unpredictable government policies without clear criteria, unpractical solutions that maximize uncertainty such as test on arrival.

On the economic side, the situation can get better or deteriorate:

- Positively: governments provide financial stimulus packages, including incentives to travel and tourism (which contributes 10% of world GDP), changes to the payment of taxes and charges.
- Negatively: governments let unemployment and debt grow, global economy (measured by GDP) slows down, companies and individuals cannot afford to travel as much as before the crisis.

In summary, the drivers are clearly identified, as well as the uncertainty, but we ignore the timing and magnitude, and there may still be surprises. In other words, in some instances we know what we don't know, and in other instances we simply don't know that we don't know them.

### Scenario planning for air travel supply and demand

These drivers have an impact on the evolution of air travel supply and demand.

On the supply side (Figure 7.29)—the air travel product and experience— we can map the impact on two axes: sanitary, and social and economic:

- The best scenario (top-right quadrant) combines the positive measures listed in the previous section. In this case, travel restrictions are lifted, borders reopen, the travel experience becomes smooth and virus-free, bookings are flexible and include travel insurance.

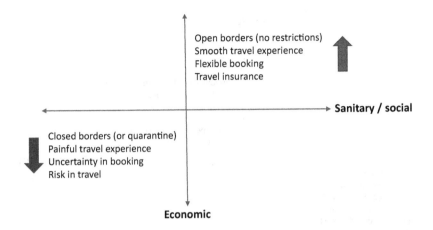

*Figure 7.29* Air travel supply (product and experience)

- The worst scenario (bottom-left quadrant) combines the negative measures, meaning borders remain closed or quarantine is required, the travel experience is an inconsistent hassle, booking and traveling represent a relatively high financial risk.

On the demand side (Figure 7.30)—the need of customers for air travel—we can identify two opposite scenarios based on sanitary, social and economic measures:

- The best scenario (top-right quadrant) sees corporate travelers valuing human interaction, as in-person meetings are more effective, and willing to travel despite the financial crisis and video conferencing tools, while leisure travelers value the physical presence of their family or friends and prioritize their discretionary spending into travel.
- The worst scenario (bottom-left quadrant) sees corporate travelers worried about their health and constrained by the new travel policies encouraging virtual meetings and by reduced budgets, while leisure travelers add environmental concerns to health concerns and struggle with lower disposable income.

### Plausible futures

As quoted in the introduction, learning from the future includes designing plausible futures based on various scenarios.

Following our analysis of the root causes of the crisis and its drivers, of the evolution of air travel supply and demand, and of the future size of the industry, let me suggest some plausible futures in terms of impact on air travel demand (by number of passengers) or supply (by available seats).

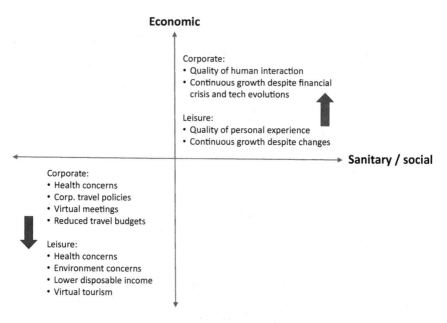

**Economic**

Corporate:
• Quality of human interaction
• Continuous growth despite financial
  crisis and tech evolutions

Leisure:
• Quality of personal experience
• Continuous growth despite changes

**Sanitary / social**

Corporate:
• Health concerns
• Corp. travel policies
• Virtual meetings
• Reduced travel budgets

Leisure:
• Health concerns
• Environment concerns
• Lower disposable income
• Virtual tourism

*Figure 7.30* Air travel demand (corporate/leisure customers)

As a reference, the growth without COVID-19 can be used, based on the trend of the past years, approx. 5% annual growth. As of September 2020, the passenger volumes have dropped compared to 2019 and started to recover. The industry is in the "restart" phase.

The end of the "restart" phase will lead to different phases and different futures, based on variables outside our control (virus, etc.) and other variables that we can influence (government policies for health and economy, airline implementation of enhanced processes, etc.). Each plausible future is the outcome of these mixed variables.

Three plausible futures are proposed for the air travel industry:

• Back-to-old industry: this future resembles the past; it assumes that we don't implement any new industry strategy. It's a future expected by people who "know well how conservative the air travel industry is," who "don't believe anyway that another pandemic will hit in the next 50 years" and who "don't believe that change is necessary and affordable right now."

• New resilient industry: this future has become resilient to shocks like pandemics by implementing solutions to mitigate the safety, operational, commercial and financial issues that arise from a crisis. This future is expected by people who believe that "we could not effectively prepare for this crisis, but we cannot afford to go through another one like this."

- Disruption: this future is expected by visionary people who believe that legacy processes are not relevant in the 21st century and that traditional business models will be disrupted by new entrants. These new business models and new players may change the paradigms of the air travel industry, making obsolete some dimensions of the current industry, in the same way that Uber and Airbnb pioneered new models after the global financial crisis that disrupted the hospitality and mobility sectors.

The industry strategy, described more specifically in the following sections, is designed to deliver this "new resilient industry" through a series of industry changes that will mitigate the commercial, financial and digital issues identified at the beginning of this paper. While we prepare for the changes that we know are required, we will monitor the potential changes that we don't know and that may come from the "disruption" scenario.

### *A proposed new industry strategy*

We've learnt the lessons that the COVID-19 crisis taught us about the vulnerabilities of our industry. Following the massive disruption, we've questioned the actual purpose of the industry. Aiming for a refreshed purpose, this paper mapped several scenarios leading to possible futures and picked one leading to a resilient industry. I articulated the vision and ambition for the industry, and let me now outline one strategy that can deliver them.

The strategy is based on three pillars corresponding to the scope of the strategy: commercial, financial and digital. The ambition of the commercial and financial pillars is to lead to resilience and to restore confidence. The ambition of the digital pillar is to enable the agility and to restore trust between stakeholders.

In the commercial pillar, the ambition will be achieved through three building blocks:

- Maintain connectivity and stimulate demand: this block addresses the supply of air travel services through solutions that will maintain connectivity during and after a crisis, and the demand for air travel services through new ways to identify and stimulate this demand. Eventually this block will enable airlines to dynamically match supply and demand, which is ideal in a volatile world driven by demand.
- Restore customer confidence: this block addresses the relationship between airlines and customers and intermediaries through solutions that will improve information to customers, flexibility in booking changes, and guarantees in payment. Eventually, this block will enable airlines to convert demand into loyal customers.
- Increase customer satisfaction: this block proposes to put customers in control of their data, of the processes to interact with airlines and the value chain, including a contactless experience. Eventually, customers who are treated well will be more satisfied with their travel experience.

In the financial pillar, the ambition will be achieved through the following three blocks:

- Secure cashflow from customer payments: this block proposes forms of payment that are alternative to credit cards, enabling airlines to predict cashflow based on their risk profile and with full transparency on payment methods. Eventually, the risk of card processors holding back airline cash will be reduced.
- De-risk cashflow from and to travel agents: this block addresses the opportunity of customer accounts, for leisure or corporate customers, enabling secure and seamless transfer of cash between parties. Eventually, this approach will reduce the friction where intermediaries are involved in transferring the cash from customers to airlines and potentially back, in case of refunds.
- Foreign investment and control: this activity proposes advocating for the liberalization of foreign investment which would increase airline liquidity, and of foreign control which would allow for the creation of global air travel operators. Eventually, well-funded global operators promise to be more resilient and sustainable, attracting confidence from customers and investors.

In the digital pillar, the ambition of agility and trust will be achieved through the following three blocks:

- Open and secure data exchange: this block proposes an open architecture, designed to maximize connectivity and inter-operability, and a secure framework; that is, security is included by design, as the backbone for the global air travel value chain. Eventually, all parties will securely exchange data using a common industry protocol, inspired by the Internet Protocol (IP) developed for the exchange of data between systems.
- Agility in implementing changes: this block focuses on agility as the key to resilience; that is, implementing changes quickly will accelerate adaptation and recovery. Open source allows us to leverage innovation and inter-operability, cloud-based architecture allows for scalability of new solutions. Eventually, an open-source community supporting the key modules of end-to-end travel operations will drive agility and sustainability of future developments.
- Ability to predict without history: this block addresses all the use cases where historical data is critical to forecasting and to optimizing processes, from revenues to maintenance. Using predictive analytics from various datasets will make up for the lack of history. Eventually, an industry repository of AI resources will enhance decision-making capabilities in times of uncertainty.

It should be noted that this strategy includes inter-dependencies; for example the customer account presented in the commercial pillar to restore customer confidence is also presented in the financial pillar to secure cash flow. It should also be noted that this strategy proposes solutions to improve the resilience of the industry; that is, to recover faster from crisis. The potential of the strategy needs to be measured in terms of financial returns. The industry business cases will follow the approval of the strategy and deliver the metrics. For example, after launching the digital retailing strategy in 2011, IATA assessed the benefits as up to $40 billion per year.

## Conclusion

This short paper represents a proposal for the air travel industry to learn from the future, to learn the consequences of inaction and to invest in its future resilience. COVID-19 will disappear one day, either because we find a vaccine or simply because it has infected a critical mass of people. When the next shock comes, whether it's a pandemic or something else, this resilient industry will be faster to react, more innovative in finding solutions, more impactful in implementing them, and more convincing in dealing with local stakeholders. It will minimize the impact of the shock and it will be quicker to recover.

## Notes

1 Prior to my role in strategy, I worked for 15 years at IATA, including 3 years as Director Passenger Services and 7 years as Director Transformation. I was accountable to the air travel industry, represented in advisory councils of senior airline commercial, financial and digital leaders, for the relevance of industry advocacy and standards supporting airline capabilities.
2 IATA, *Future of the Airline Industry 2035* www.iata.org/contentassets/690df4ddf39b4 7b5a075bb5dff30e1d8/iata-future-airline-industry-pdf.pdf
3 J. Peter Scoblic, "Learning from the Future," *Harvard Business Review*, 2020, July–August. https://hbr.org/2020/07/emerging-from-the-crisis#learning-from-the-future
4 Kate Raworth, *Doughnut Economics: 7 Ways to Think Like a 21st Century Economist* (White River Junction, VT: Chelsea Green Publishing, 2017).
5 United Nations, Sustainable Development Goals www.un.org/sustainable development/sustainable-development-goals/
6 Thomas W. Malnight, Ivy Buche, and Charles Dhanaraj, "Put Purpose at the Core of Your Strategy," *Harvard Business Review*, 2019, September–October. https://hbr.org/2019/09/put-purpose-at-the-core-of-your-strategy
7 McKinsey & Company, "COVID-19 and the Great Reset: Briefing note, July 16, 2020" www.mckinsey.com/~/media/mckinsey/business%20functions/risk/our%20 insights/covid%2019%20implications%20for%20business/covid%20july%2016/ covid-19-and-the-great-reset-briefing-note-july-16-2020.pdf

## The Hammer & Dance process based on Door-to-Door modelling

*Benedikt Mandel*
Managing Director, MKmetric GmbH

*Julian Mandel*
Economic Psychologist and Model Developer, MKmetric GmbH

### 1. Pandemic-sundown and the planning dilemma

Due to the threat of the pandemic crises it is almost impossible for airlines to keep operations running in an economically profitable way. The uncertainties evoked by a virus and its mutations where it is not clear how drugs and vaccines will help to eliminate the spread worldwide "force" politicians/administrations to impose restrictions on mobility, social and economic life. While safeguarding the health of the population and controlling the spread of the virus, the policy measures nail down air demand widely like a "Hammer", undermine travellers' confidence, redirect mobility behaviour and finally disrupt planned schedules at short notice. The aviation industry leaders have no other chance but to learn to "Dance" by enhancing flexibility and adjusting their network (frequency, capacity, destinations) quickly to keep air transport business alive. And the dance is not a smooth one like "the blues" it is more of a "Rock 'n' Roll" style.

While airlines have to fly to make money (and airports only make money if airlines are successful), their basic source of information for planning (internal direct bookings and Global Distribution Systems (GDS)) eroded dramatically. In addition, the established network planning tools of the aviation industry no longer work because the standard processes are based on historical travel flow (origin-destination (O&D)) data. Furthermore, the planning models neither reflect the current situation nor can these models handle the ongoing, multiple interdependent changes. Reliable network planning is essential for both the aviation industry and administrations. Regardless of whether a decision has to be made on an air transport portfolio, a fleet of aircraft, infrastructure needs or the levying of new taxes, the negotiation of bilateral air transport agreements and the enforcement of cohesion policy, the consequences must be quantified before a decision is made.

Indicators generated on the basis of clicks and social media statements can provide information and a kind of feeling about the actual consumer situation, which is better than having nothing at hand. But are they valid enough to make decisions for the future that involve millions of dollars in spending, at a time when liquidity and profits are stretched to the limit?

It should be mentioned also that governments are facing challenges too. They need to provide a framework addressing different targets which are in conflict with each other (economy, environment, connectivity, fundamental rights, etc.).

However, the aviation industry does not have sufficient instruments at its disposal. How can this dilemma be overcome? A forecast with average or trend-based standard models, equivalent to driving a car on the motorway at a speed of 200 km/h while looking in the rear-view mirror? Or the substitution of the O&D data backbone by new mobile or media data sources, which did not bring the expected success and, moreover, drive the aviation industry into dependency on the internet giants, running the risk of becoming their workbench?

## 2. Airport-to-Airport versus Door-to-Door

The static view of air transport must be transformed into a dynamic, consumer-oriented view. This will be achieved through a bottom-up, "Door-to-Door" approach that consistently reflects consumer behaviour. The following is a step-by-step derivation of how the consumer behaviour of the traveller is reflected in the model approach whilst comparing with the standard "Airport-to-Airport" approach.

### Step 1

We assume a simple air transport network of two airlines in a closed market at a fixed time, consisting of three routes and showing travel flows from A to B. For the planning of such a network and aircraft capacities, airlines use travel flow data, which are generated in separate processes, so-called O&D data. These combine sold tickets into passenger flows at airport level. This is represented symbolically by dotted lines in the left upper graph of Figure 7.31.

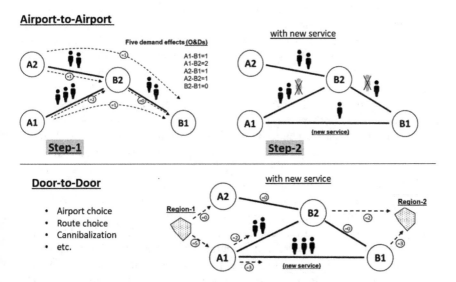

*Figure 7.31* Simplified example Airport-to-Airport vs. Door-to-Door

How many passengers appear on each flight of this network is depicted by the persons assigned to the links. Flight A1–B2 has three people on board, flight A2–B2 has two people on board and flight B2–B1 has two people on board.

*Step 2*

The route (A1–B1) will be added to this network in a further step as shown in the upper right graph of Figure 7.31. The addition of this new route (A1–B1) will create redistribution effects. In the following, the results of the O&D model ("Airport-to-Airport") approach are compared with the (realistic) "Door-to-Door" approach.

**The "Airport-to-Airport" O&D model approach** allocates the O&D data to the departure and arrival airports of the trip. This defines the origin and destination of the trip. If this were translated into the real world of travellers, they would live and work at airports, meet friends/relatives and spend their holidays at airports – because they would (only) depart from and travel to airports. This does not take into account the real sources and destinations of the journeys, nor the route to and from the airport. The influence of these factors on the choice of flights is therefore missing from the model. This example redistributes the existing demand quantity (of the five O&D data values) based on the modified flight offer. This means that flight B2–B1 will be thinned out (cannibalised) because the passenger of O&D A1–B1 will choose the new non-stop connection A1–B1. Hereby the number of people starting their trip from airport A1 (three) remains constant (leaving aside some generation effects added at the end of the computation).

**The "Door-to-Door" model approach** depicts the world realistically. On the one hand, the routes with passenger loss lose profitability. Capacity adjustments (frequency of service, aircraft size) can lead to the necessary abandonment of the route. On the other hand, the new route will deduct a significant number of passengers from the existing routes, as travellers have now chosen a new alternative to the old route. However, the O&D model approach does not show such changes. In our example, passengers change their departure airport (A2) and travel from A1 (see Figure 7.31). This effect is also known as cannibalisation. Both passengers choose the new nonstop connection A1–B1. In addition, a passenger departing from A1 who previously travelled via B2 to B1 will now (also) choose the nonstop flight A1–B1. All in all, these interrelationships (airport/route choice effects) can be explained if real mobility needs are depicted in the model. These effects appear out of the "Door-to-Door" perspective. The lower graph of Figure 7.31 describes these (complete) travel routes from Region-1 to Region-2.

Both effects lead to cannibalisation of existing routes; that is, the old existing routes lose passengers due to redistribution. However, the "Door-to-Door" approach (also) results in a change of departure point and a change of destination. The "Door-to-Door" approach thus realistically reflects mobility needs and the decision-making behaviour of passengers. In an open market a new route (A1-B1) could also attract more passengers (e.g. transfer passengers).

In the following, these relationships are described in a somewhat structured manner:

DEMAND GENERATION EFFECTS

The new route generates new demand. This is the case when a destination was previously not reachable but is now reachable. On the one hand, the new demand results from people's nature to discover new destinations. On the other hand, additional demand results from the possibility for business to establish new business relationships.[1] This is equivalent to satisfying subliminal mobility needs in the market, which is optimal for an airline.

DESTINATION CHOICE EFFECTS

There will be destination choice effects for which regional connectivity is crucial. Especially if the destination becomes directly accessible for the first time by a new route. Regional connectivity differs in principle from the connectivity indicators used in the aviation industry. The focus here is not on the airport hub, but on the source (e.g. Region-1 in Figure 7.31) and the destination (e.g. Region-2 in Figure 7.31) of travellers who use air transport services only as a means to an end.[2] The destination choice effects can be classified as follows:

- The new route will lead to a change of transport mode. This means that the new route induces traffic by attracting travellers who previously travelled by car or train to switch to air transport. This effect occurs mainly in the short-haul sector, where the journey by train or car takes more than 4 hours. Predominantly time-sensitive customer groups feel addressed.[3] Please note that the effect might reverse when surface modes (e.g. high speed trains or new techniques like hyperloop, maglev trains) offer attractive travel times (and costs) on short-haul destinations so that air passengers are attracted. As airlines can react faster by modifying their network than surface transport due to the necessity that land-based infrastructure need to fit to these services. The shift from air to rail is an issue of mid- and long-term scenarios unless there is a political will to suspend short-haul flights below a certain distance.
- The airline stimulates demand for the new route. This is the case when the airline promotes the new route through marketing campaigns. This is usually linked to introductory prices which appeal to very price-sensitive demand groups and thereby make travel possible. However, the stimulus is questionable for a sustainable network development, as most of this demand is lost when the network returns to normal price levels and the

profitability of the new route suffers considerably during the low price phase. Existing routes will also be affected, as low fares reinforce the effects described above and divert demand.

It has to be noted that the travel flow data (O&D data) reflect the fluctuations in demand described above, but do not capture their background. However, the standard "Airport-to-Airport" models use this data as a basis or for calibration. As a result, the distorting stimulation effects are incorporated into these models and no longer reflect the true travel desires; that is, the models incorrectly reflect the mobility needs of the population and the economy.

*Step 3*

The understanding of the real origins and destinations of the trips as well as the respective route to and from the airport are of huge relevance for modelling. The influence of these factors on the choice of flight services is missing in the O&D model approach ("Airport-to-Airport"). However, it is very important to depict this on the model side, as the route-specific catchment areas overlap (see Figure 7.32). It is illustrated that the origin of the travellers is crucial for the choice of the departure point. The same applies to the destination of the journey, as this can also be in the overlap area and thus influences the choice of destination airport. However, the static structure of the catchment area underlying an O&D model approach ("Airport-to-Airport") is dynamic in the real world. This dynamic behaviour of passengers changes in the context of the competitive situation respectively in relation to the air services offered at airports (destination portfolio).

So how can an airline or airport take the primary effects of cannibalisation into account at the planning stage?

As postulated at the beginning of the section, the static approach, oriented on the process of the air transport industry, is replaced by a consumer-oriented dynamic approach. To this end, the models reflect the "Door-to-Door" travel route of the travellers (see Figure 7.33). A traveller wishing to travel from origin Region-1 to destination Region-2 (travel relation Region-Region) chooses route A2-B3, while in the network with the new route (dotted line A1-B1) the traveller prefers this route A1-B1. Although the distance to A1 airport is longer than to A2, the traveller evaluates the benefits of the overall travel route (high speed train from Region-1 to A1, nonstop flight A1 to B1, taxi from B1 to Region-2) as being greater. For the sake of clarity, Figure 7.33 does not show the land-based rail and road network between the regions and to/from the airports.

If we apply this example to all relations between sources and destinations, a combinatorial growing number of possible travel routes is created depending on the network extension; for example, for all Spanish regions (approx. 60) to all German regions (approx. 400) approximately 24,000 relations would be calculated (without the diagonal). Furthermore, it should be noted that not all travellers between two regions choose the same travel route, so that, for example,

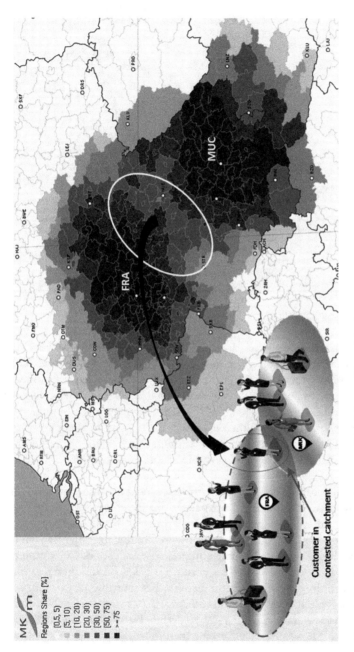

*Figure 7.32* Overlapping catchments of Frankfurt and Munich airports

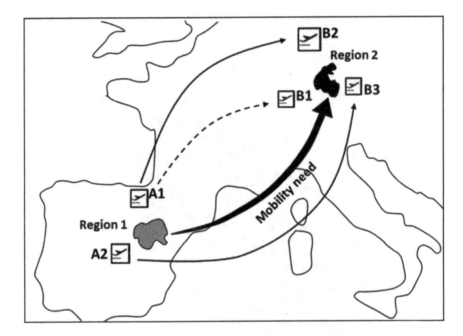

*Figure 7.33* Basic modelling problem for the simplified example

in the medium distance sector the first 20 travel route alternatives between two regions compete with each other. For the above example, this requires a consideration of 480,000 travel route combinations (including transfer connections), which must be evaluated in a differentiated manner for at least three travel purposes (business, visiting friend/relatives, holiday) (approx. 1.4 million).

In network planning, it is therefore essential to take into account passenger choice of airport and route when quantifying passengers on air services. In this way, the behaviour of passengers due to changing network conditions can be recorded and the success of a new route can be determined much more accurately. The cannibalisation and attraction effects caused by interdependencies must be determined and financially quantified before a route inauguration. Possible alternative intermodal travel routes of "Door-to-Door" are to be considered. The key here is to realistically predict the customer behaviour (see Figure 7.34). For the sake of clarity competing surface modes are not depicted.

The individual choice of the travel route is based on the preferences of the travellers according to the decision criteria. The purpose of the journey also plays a major role here, as private travellers attach less importance to the travel time than business travellers, for example, while business travellers attach more importance to the frequency of service than vacationists.

- A blueprint to set up a "Door-to-Door" model can be found in "Contemporary Airport Demand Forecasting: Choice Models and Air

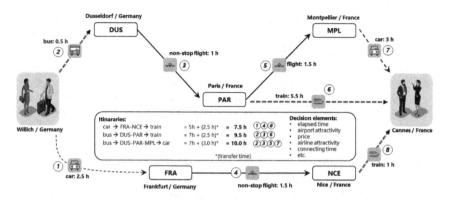

*Figure 7.34* Principal example of consumers' travel path choice set

Transport Forecasting" presented at the OECD/ITF Roundtable on Forecasting Airport Demand.[4] The paper provides a wrap-up of the model characteristics for the aviation stakeholders as well as for governments as a base to get started. Information about tools can be found at www.mkm.de

## 3. The power of Door-to-Door applications – Users benefit

This section presents three examples of practical applications. The benefits differ for each user group (airline, airport, policy/administration, manufacturer, intermodal operator).

Section 3.1 focuses on the challenges network planners face in finding, investigating and quantifying flight services to new destinations (route development). Based on two cases (intercontinental, continental), the daily work of planners is addressed.

Section 3.2 concentrates on a more complex problem, covering network strategy, infrastructure investments and air transport policy. The example reflects the challenges faced by airlines, airports and governments. For manufacturers the section is of interest due to the interdependencies explained, which also apply for the example raised in Section 3.3, and for intermodal service operators to quantify their demand potential in the context of the aviation system.

Section 3.3 focuses on the interaction with the decision-making process chain network strategy – aircraft rotation and crew scheduling – fleet strategy for airlines, which in their entirety are also of interest to manufacturers.

### 3.1. Planners challenge – Route development

**CASE 1:** INTERCONTINENTAL, SAN JOSE, CALIFORNIA, US (SJC)

A network planner is responsible for the development of the North Atlantic market and works with a network airline based at the Frankfurt/Main Airport

(FRA). Demand has (generally) increased in recent years and is proof that the airlines' presence in the market can be expanded. Therefore the planner is looking for new destinations. The analysis of macroeconomic data, local information (of the branch), existing and announced air services, as well as air traffic statistics and ticket data from global distribution systems (GDS) suggest that a new route from FRA to San Jose, California (SJC), around the corner from Silicon Valley, would work. In addition, the network planning tool used by the planner to validate the new destination shows the need for opening the route both now and in the future.

However, reality showed over several years that this service was not efficient and, at the same time, the demand for air services to San Francisco, California (SFO) declined. A lot of money was destroyed, no investment was made in another promising service and overall the airline's market position was weakened. This happened although the analyses were reviewed several times, the internal process was correct, the quality checks did not show any deviation from the airlines' standards and the management supported marketing campaigns for the new route. What went wrong?

According to the information available to the planner and the tool used, the decision was based on an O&D model approach ("Airport-to-Airport" view). As a result, the basis for the decision is per se limited, as only a limited number of competing travel alternatives could be considered and the impact on competition is therefore correspondingly limited. Overall, the analyses did not reflect the demand between the true origin and destination regions; from the traveller's point of view the true source (e.g. Fremont, California) and destination (e.g. Hannover Region, Germany), defined as "Door-to-Door" mobility. Moreover, consumer behaviour differs in terms of local situation and purpose of travel, as travel alternatives vary according to departure and destination airports and transfer possibilities, taking into account access and egress to and from airports.

The underlying planning model (O&D model approach – "Airport-to-Airport") cannot, by definition, reflect the competitive situation between travel routes that do not start and end at FRA and SJC. But a traveller has the choice and evaluates carefully. Travellers find out for themselves which travel path (including flight) around their location offers the maximum benefit for their purposes, taking into account all elements of the travel chain down to the last mile to the true destination of their journey. While business travellers want maximum flexibility and minimum transport time, leisure travellers prefer low ticket costs. When thresholds are exceeded, they reconsider their choice (if they are not bound by any agreements with commercial companies).

A "Door-to-Door" approach makes it possible to check the elasticity of consumer choice in relation to flight service characteristics across all travel routes of the real consumer choice set of travel paths. This means that travellers living in the Palo Alto/California region will make different choices than travellers from the Fremont/California region. Furthermore, mobility differs in level and spatial distribution. Attracting 100% of the demand from a region with 500 travellers makes a difference in the validation process, compared with a market (region) in which you attract 50% of 5,000 travellers. Furthermore, the diversification of destinations (spatial distribution of mobility) varies from region to region (e.g. there are only 100 travellers from Fremont with Hannover as a real destination, while there are 200 travellers from Palo Alto), and the same is true for Germany on the other side of the line.

The aggregation of the elasticity of travel paths on a regional basis results in route-specific catchment areas. The overlapping of the catchment areas shows the local competition. Further analyses identify cannibalisation effects that lead to a shift between the air services offered. In our case, the demand for FRA in the SJC catchment area is neither sufficient for the route nor beneficial for the network as a whole, as the SFO-FRA service loses passengers that cannot be compensated by supply-driven demand generation. This type of analysis will be equally important for airport marketing teams. This is because they would not see a net increase in passengers at the airport, while running the risk of losing a well-established route or even an airline.

In summary, in order to calculate the number of passengers attracted by a flight, the actual route chosen by the traveller, the level of local demand and the distribution of demand to the final destination are crucial. This implicitly increases the number of competing air services to be considered. The evaluation of a new flight is therefore based on a much wider range (decision-making space).

Another weak point is the analysis process itself. Apart from the review of announced new routes, there is no proactive assessment of competitors' activities. However, should another airline also identify SJC as a new destination, the choice of routes for consumers will be influenced. As a result, the demand attracted by a new service will change due to the additional competitor. If the other airline is located at an airport close to FRA, e.g. Düsseldorf in Germany (DUS), there are two effects. Firstly, DUS-SJC's catchment area will overlap with that of FRA-SJC, so that the latter route will attract fewer local passengers, for example from Bremen and Hannover. Secondly, options to transfer at DUS (let's assume this is achieved through code-sharing agreements) will divert transfer passengers from FRA to DUS and demand on the FRA-SJC route will be affected. If the other airline is not close to FRA (e.g. at London Heathrow, UK (LHR)), the effect is limited to the second case. In the present case, in reality, another LHR-SJC route has been opened in parallel to FRA-SJC. And LHR as a hub offers a lot of transfer options to the European continent so that rerouting effects are significant.

The situation outlined above cannot be examined with the standard instruments of network evaluation based on the O&D ("Airport-to-Airport") model approach. The planner therefore simply has no way of quantifying the risk of an incorrect assessment, as the planner does not have the right tool. Firstly, there is no network generation algorithm to identify new route options of competitors (or the airline the planner works with). Secondly, the mathematical model underlying the standard tool (O&D model approach) is not capable of reflecting the "Door-to-Door" mobility needs with their differentiated behaviour structure. In order to reduce the risk of disinvestment, development scenarios need to be simulated. These should quantify the deviations in results so that conclusions can be drawn from these deviations.

In conclusion, the assessment process of a new route needs to include alternative "Door-to-Door" travel routes and the activities of competitors in more detail. Scenarios must be simulated using network generation tools that use the "Door-to-Door" model world, otherwise information will be lacking. The risk of a disinvestment in inaugurating an air service would not be minimised. Instead, the information deficit described above will increase the risk of a wrong decision.

**CASE 2:** EUROPEAN CASE PAMPLONA, NAVARRA, SPAIN (PNA)

In this example, a network planner worked out new route options in the growing Spanish market to Europe. All analyses were initially conducted with tools based on the O&D ("Airport-to-Airport") model approach. The model calculations did not show sufficient demand for Pamplona (PNA), for example, to open a new route. Neither the O&D data (travel flow data) nor the analysis of social media and internet search data (clicks for hotels, travel, etc.) indicated a potential demand for a new route. These arguments were also shared by AENA[5] and airline representatives. In contrast, the results of the network analyses showed the strong position of Bilbao Airport, Spain (BIO), which is located close to PNA (approx. 160 km, 1.5 hours by car). From BIO, all European network carriers offer services to their home bases and in addition there is a portfolio of point-to-point services from other airlines (including low-cost carriers).

However, Pamplona, a beautiful city with industry, research and above-average per capita income, wanted to expand its further development and sought direct access to metropolitan areas. This is because the existing connection via the hub Madrid, Spain (MAD) is unattractive. The detour requires an unacceptable amount of time from travellers heading to a European metropolis or looking for a wider spectrum of intercontinental destinations. Investigations addressing the problem of Pamplona were executed with a "Door-to-Door" model. The first step was to analyse the spatial distribution of passengers flying from BIO. The analysis showed that about 43% of total demand for BIO came from the Bizkaia region, where BIO airport is located (Figure 7.35). Passenger demand from Navarra is spread over several airports, with BIO accounting for <10%. Furthermore, the economic strength of Navarra is about half that of the Bizkaia region. Taken together, this shows that the market of Navarra (Region of Navarra) is under-served.

The next planning step was to find a suitable target in Europe to which PNA could be linked. With the help of a network generator[6] a portfolio of possibilities was calculated, which could be analysed in more detail. In order to demonstrate the "Door-to-Door" procedure, the following section focuses further on a proposed route PNA-FRA, which can be served by DLH (Deutsche Lufthansa AG, Germany). DLH did not consider launching a PNA-FRA service because the airline, which carried more than 200,000 passengers each

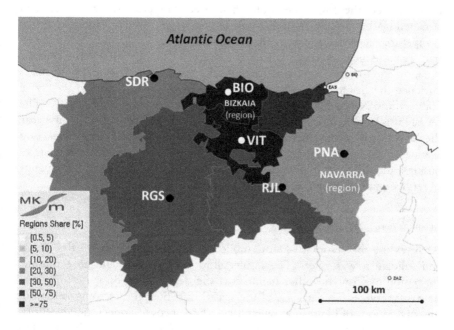

*Figure 7.35* Catchment of Bilbao Airport (BIO)

from BIO to FRA and Munich, Germany (MUC) at that time, did not want to cannibalise these services by a new one to PNA. Although the argument was valid, the airline did not have any tools and analysis to support or counter these expert assessments.

Here, the analyses based on the "Door-to-Door" approach assisted. This model approach integrates all travel routes into the considerations. Also the services from BIO to MUC and FRA are included in the comprehensive analysis and competing effects of these services on a regional basis with a possible PNA-FRA service are considered. For the implementation of the route, the optimal location of the service slots had to be found in the FRA hub system whilst considering the spatial distribution of mobility between regions (weighted connectivity). This way, besides the local demand, a maximum of behind, beyond and bridge passengers can be attracted. Using the results for the layout of the schedule a simulation run shows that apart from some intercontinental transfer passengers to the east and west, transfers to European destinations are mainly concentrated at airports in the UK and Central and Eastern Europe. The route-specific catchment area of PNA shows that two-thirds of the route demand comes from Navarra and only one-third from neighbouring regions.

Now the question is how many passengers DLH's routes lose with BIO. The simulation shows that the BIO-FRA and BIO-MUC routes have lost less than 8% of passengers, so that these (existing) routes are not at risk at all. Looking at the overall net effect on the demand attracted by a new PNA-FRA

DLH service, the losses are more than over-compensated by the demand attracted by the new PNA–FRA route. Furthermore, it is (also) interesting that competitors such as Air France/KLM and Iberia lose a significant number of transfer passengers travelling for business reasons. The regional macroeconomic situation and the argumentation based on the network analyses and simulations enriched the airline's information. DLH was convinced to set up an air service connecting PNA to FRA despite the sensitivity of its engagement at BIO. The service was launched on 17th November 2017 as a 7/7 service. In the first year, the load factor of this (new) service was between 62% and 75% (69.4% on average), with evenly distributed sales at both ends, a disproportionate share of business and still a significant transfer share. In the following year, the frequency of service doubled, while the load factor remained stable.

RELEVANCE FOR THE STAKEHOLDERS

**Airlines** use the "Door-to-Door" model in the traditional way to find, study and validate new services. The results allow on the one hand an economic evaluation and on the other hand show the dependence of routes on other network services. The analysis of the spatial distribution of a route is used to identify regions of high value where the airline needs to concentrate its efforts or where advertising needs to be intensified. The planners also use the model to evaluate the airlines' route network and to optimise the flight schedules. Flight plans are adjusted according to slot preferences based on the weighted regional connectivity analysis. Analyses such as the overlap of route-specific catchment areas show the degree of cannibalisation (for local and transfer passengers) and the extent to which overall demand in a region is attracted (as an example see Figure 7.32). As the model is sensitive to service characteristics (e.g. time, frequency of service, cost), a variation of these characteristics quantifies the impact on the demand for a route. It is thus possible to assess whether it is worthwhile to change the specific characteristics of a route or to adjust certain routes.

Scenarios can be used to analyse competitors' activities in their networks and future interests of competitors in the development of the networks. The results of the route finder (from the competitors' point of view) show their relevant markets/destinations. An overlap with the new destinations in focus makes the planner aware of the need to create scenarios that include the airline's own activities and potential activities of the competitors. This reduces the risk of investing in a new route. All findings of a planning team are finally cumulated to an overall scenario and an overall simulation of the network is carried out. The results are used for final adjustments to minimise cannibalisation effects. These market-driven results are then compared with the aircraft routing in respect to operational restrictions. In general, the model is used for conservative validation. The central question is whether the services are attractive enough for a sustainable economically viable performance in respect of the given competitive situation. Therefore, the model is not primarily used to quantify price-induced demand generation and stimulation effects.

**Airports** use the "Door-to-Door" model to develop their destination portfolio. In principle, they work in the same way as airline planners, although their focus may or may not be airline specific. The main objective is to attract new air services independently of the airline. They investigate the leakage of passengers from their catchment area who choose another airport. In doing so, they quantify the backlog in an airport's air service portfolio. For example, the sheaf analysis shows route demand and passenger mix, but the interpretation also focuses on identifying market potential for nonstop flights (see Figure 7.36). A high number of transfer passengers to BKK (Bangkok, Thailand) on an Emirates flight from HAM (Hamburg, Germany) to DXB (Dubai, VAE) indicate a market potential for a nonstop flight HAM-BKK. This requires further investigation and may be proposed to another airline, for example as seasonal service due to the nature of the demand. A simulation also shows whether the HAM-DXB flight would be endangered if HAM-BKK existed and whether the overall net demand of the airport would increase, as a nonstop flight to BKK attracts more passengers than the existing connecting flight. Analyses show the differences between the reference (status quo situation) and the scenario, and quantify gains and losses by route for the own and competing airport.

A further analysis concerns the "Door-to-Door" markets. This analysis of transport volumes between markets covers all transport volumes between two markets, including potential transfers at third locations. The airport planner therefore knows the market position of the airport and is aware of the underrepresentation that needs to be addressed.

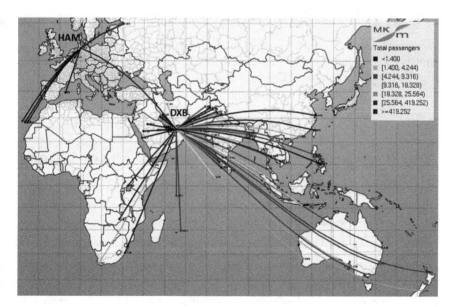

*Figure 7.36* Local and transfer passengers on the route Hamburg–Dubai

The weighted connectivity analysis is used by airports in the context of slot discussions. The analysis shows whether an exchange of slots between airlines (or within an airline) makes sense and creates a win-win-win situation for both airlines and the airport in relation to the passengers attracted.

The scenario technique is used to quantify demand effects if an airport wants to convince an airline to concentrate its services. The questions address profits and losses that arise from the relocation of services from a neighbouring airport to the airport itself. Other scenarios such as the bundling of flights of an airline to small hubs are also examined. In addition, activities at competing airports are explored to see how their own airport is affected.

Finally, the planners' findings are cumulated into a scenario and the results are processed for final adjustments. A consistent flight plan forecast is created. Aircraft types (landing fees), passenger volume (passenger fees, ground handling), transfer passenger mix (retail), local passengers (parking) are extracted and used for further planning.

**Administrations and policy decision makers** use the "Door-to-Door" model, for monitoring purposes, to evaluate policies such as air transport agreements or to foster regional development. The analyses provided by the tool are used in the context of competitiveness and cohesion analyses and to maximise the location advantage for the economy. The "Door-to-Door" approach can also be used to determine the regional dominance of air services or airports in order to verify monopolistic situations. The results of the analysis show whether an airport needs to be controlled in terms of charges and fees or whether air service agreements should be renegotiated to allow or restrict competition.

In terms of cohesion (policy aiming at an equal standard of living throughout the country) and location advantage, the analyses of accessibility and regional connectivity apply. An initial analysis makes it possible to identify regions with handicaps. Regional connectivity shows the quality of access to air services from a regional perspective. This indicator does not reflect the usual connectivity used by the aviation industry,[7] which is concentrated at one airport. On the contrary, the indicator reflects access to services regardless of which service is used at which airport. Indeed, a region with an airport "around the corner" may be less well qualified than a region located in the overlap of three airport catchment areas because of better access to more services. Such kinds of results provide this "Door-to-Door" application.

The scenario technique is used to analyse where policy can help to increase cohesion (e.g. by a public service obligation flight) and location advantage, where monopoly situations are reduced and where the aviation industry needs to be supported or regulated.

### 3.2. Strategy and politics – Network horizon

The example described in the following concentrates on requests of governments but addresses also the topics of network strategy of airlines and infrastructure investment at airports. These results are of interest for strategy units from airlines (network strategy, fleet structure and dimension) and airports (terminal, runway, airport acquisition investments).

The tasks requested by the governments concerned the computation of mid- and long-term scenarios under consideration of the following framework conditions:

- socio-economic development (low, most recent, high) for a 5, 10, 15 and 25-year horizon,
- infrastructure changes over time on rail and road networks,
- infrastructure changes on airports (capacity – runway/terminal, new airport),
- airline strategy (aggressive including transfer optimisation, business as usual, under dominant pressure of competitors),
- policy measures (taxation – flight/$CO_2$ emissions, kerosene blending by synthetic/$CO_2$ neutral fuel, air service agreements – protective/open sky, restrictions on airport subsidies, night ban, air traffic management (ATM) costs, social employment standards, and some other ones).

The forecast to perform concerned all national airports, the cross-border neighbouring airports and the competitive hub airports around the world (all together more than 60 airports). From the combinatorial possible scenarios a subset was chosen.

The questions to be answered on national, airport, airline and regional level concerned:

- demand figures (passengers, cargo) split by passenger mix/commodities,[8]
- air traffic movements split by aircraft classes,
- competitive situation between national airports,
- national leakage of transport volumes to extraterritorial airports,
- likelihood of success for the strategies of the airline in focus (including advice for adjustments),
- access/egress volumes split by surface modes rail and road,
- rationality of building a new airport (including investment steps over time),
- rationality of subsidies to airports,
- effects of policy measures upon air transport demand,
- cohesion and advantage of location concerning air transport.

Reviewing the questions and the scenario settings it is obvious that neither unimodal and airport specific models nor "Airport-to-Airport" approaches address the complexity of the problem. Furthermore the interdependencies between welfare/economic development, infrastructure capacity, airlines network strategy and policy measures require a consistent model approach where changes at one end trigger effects on the other end and vice versa. As key elements to answer the questions one can identify the regional focus and the air network. An intelligent network generation model based on a "Door-to-Door" approach is needed. Our product SONAR$_{NetGen}$[9] was used to execute the tasks.

The work sequence incorporated the following: The socio-economic forecasts were generated with input of governments, International Monetary Fund, Organisation for Economic Co-operation and Development (OECD), European Commission, and some banks. Accordingly the oil price varied under consideration of the forecast by OECD and the US government. Infrastructure master plans for road and rail were provided by governments. With the exception of the new airport all other investments were collected from the airports in focus. Airline strategies were discussed with the airlines and a consistent set of principles was derived. For the airline in focus three sets of rules were defined in cooperation. The rules allowed that airlines exit the market with exception of the airline in focus. The policy measures were outlined by the government but flexible in level and detail to fit the principal scenario (low, most recent, high). The policy measure excluded the closure of national airports while for extraterritorial airports economic thresholds (downgrading, closure) applied. Based on the information for each time horizon a set of framework data was created to feed the model. The network generation process was executed and validated for consistency and plausibility for each scenario along the time line. The set of analyses provided by the tool allowed us to extract the information required to answer the most questions. Some specific queries were executed to analyse the policy effects in detail.

The example illustrated combines three projects whereby all of them covered all framework conditions but in different granulation and intensity. The first one concerned a "national concept for a Central Airport of a European country" affecting the whole transport system of this country. The second was dedicated to a "basic evaluation for an air transport concept of a government" focusing on policy measures to reach certain targets. And the third project worked out a "development perspective of an airport hub" in respect of the competitive situation. The first two projects included additional tasks beside the transport forecast which were dedicated to project partners. Results of all studies have been published by the clients along with the political opportunities and necessities. For the first project the deviation of the forecasted demand for the first period (here 8 years) of the most recent scenario to reality was less than 1%. For the time being for the other projects one has to wait until the first forecasting horizon appears. All projects were executed before the pandemic crises occurred.

The example given does not deal with alternative traffic concepts, but the model used makes this possible. Current technological development is testing air taxis. There are many projects addressing regional air transport with smaller hybrid aircraft. They all focus on "Door-to-Door" mobility and require equivalent models to study and develop concepts offside and integrated into the overall transport system.

RELEVANCE FOR THE STAKEHOLDERS

For **airlines**, an intelligent network generation process combined with a "Door-to-Door" forecasting model is essential for strategic network development and fleet planning. The development of mobility needs determines the network options with regard to political, infrastructural and technical restrictions (or opportunities due to new aircraft technology). Setting the scene in accordance to the strategy in focus or just defining framework conditions giving the model the freedom to decide allows us to review the whole space of potential events with destinations where demand rises stays stable or are at risk. So strategies can be assessed, quantified and validated to minimise the risk of failure.

Beside the short-term seasonal and yearly network development where X-VIA can be used there is the continuous necessity to plan some years ahead. A realistic picture of network scenarios in 5 to 10 years produced by SONAR$_{NetGen}$ is the base to design the fleet portfolio and network dimension. Investments that commit airlines financially for a long time and define the aircraft performance related to the markets, are setting the scene whether the airline is economically successful or not. Once more, to minimise the risk scenarios incorporating competitors' strategy, socio-economic development, oil price variations and even changes by surface modes (e.g. services by high speed trains) are required. A wrong aircraft choice today causes performance losses for many years, giving advantage to competitors.

For airlines with hubs or multiple bases and a wide network, the interdependencies increase exponentially. It is not sufficient to define a growth rate for each market and to assume a representative destination to construct a future network manually which is the base to generate the future aircraft portfolio. This neglects the flexibility of the market on the consumer side and the competitors' side and does not consider the interdependencies between air services at different locations. Moreover it narrows the base on which decisions are taken by excluding obvious risk factors by definition. So the management and supervisory board decide based on suggestions provided by the fleet and network strategy unit while not knowing that existential risks are not considered due to methodological reasons of the applied analyses tools.

A standard scenario for an airline is described hereafter. For the generation of an air network the network generation algorithm will be processed, which develops for a user-defined set of airports in parallel the aviation network whilst considering the offers of all air services at competing airports and their catchment areas. The network generator finds and implements "White Spots" (including greenfield destinations) at each airport in the simulation system and integrates them into actual flight schedules whilst addressing the transfer potential in parallel. Thus cannibalisation is minimised. The new routes to be investigated are identified by a process addressing competitors' activities, catchment, leakage, indirect passengers, and the "Door-to-Door" air transport mobility. The network generation process can adapt to certain strategies. Thus a scenario can reflect different strategies and offers tactical advice and/or it simply investigates challenges arising from, for example, competitors, new air-craft types, partnerships, policy measures, rail services, road infrastructure or an airline merger respectively an airline market exit.

Finally using the same approach on the strategic level as on the planner level ensures a vertical consistency of information and drives transparency to avoid mistakes. Planners have other daily business from strategy units but being familiar with the network on a daily basis they can easily contribute to the val-idation of the assumptions and results of a strategy scenario. Making use of skills along the vertical line benefits the overall result and communication culture of the company. Employees learn from each other and the motivation to practic-ally achieve the strategy targets rises significantly.

For **airports** already the long-term horizon is of interest as infrastructure investments amortise over a long period. Furthermore a runway or terminal is dedicated to a specific purpose and the flexibility to use the assets differently is very limited. Therefore a long-term forecast should always incorporate the development of competitors. To ensure consistency a network generation process incorporating the "Door-to-Door" mobility is a prerequisite. Neglecting this instance leads to an overestimation of the demand and a wrong dimensioning of the infrastructure. This holds true especially for airports focusing on the transfer market (competitive transfer routes) and in case of a high density of airports with multiple intermodal opportunities (overlapping catchments).

The latter opens the question of the impact of rail and road accessibility. Obviously, railway stations in the immediate vicinity of an airport site have a major impact. The catchment of FRA (Figure 7.37), with its excellent hub of high-speed rail links and multiple highway connections, covers a wide hemi-sphere, drawing passengers directly from regions "around the corner" from competing airports. To depict such effects, the models must reflect the "Door-to-Door" perspective of the passengers. The same effect in a smaller dimension holds true for other intermodal connections with regional trains which is of more interest for smaller airports. In Europe less attractive but of increasing interest are coach connections. In consequence intermodal effects need to be considered in a forecast.

Finally, all airports wishing to invest in other airports or to divest an invest-ment should carry out a forecast to examine the competitive situation and the economic viability of these infrastructures. Scenarios of varying scope provide the basis for the risk assessment.

For **operators of intermodal services** the "Door-to-Door" approach provides the possibility to include their services as feeder system (rail, bus) to the aviation network checking out the demand effects by simulation runs. As the mobility is distributed in the regions (Figure 7.37) service lines can be planned accordingly. On the other hand large infrastructure investments like high speed rail or hyperloop tracks aiming for modal split effects can quantify their ability to attract air passengers.

For **administrations and policy decision makers** the example already shows the power evoked by "Door-to-Door" approaches. Otherwise such

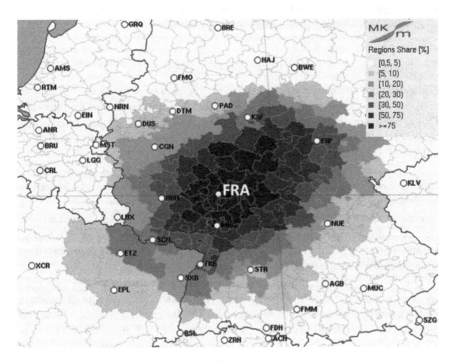

*Figure 7.37* Catchment of Frankfurt/Main Airport (FRA 2019)

complex scenarios can hardly be investigated due to the interdependencies and dimension of players to be considered. Especially policy measures imposed at a national scale and driving costs or limiting capacity at airports have effects on the selection of travel alternatives. Extraterritorial airports can be easily used to start the air trip or to use transfer connections. In consequence the policy target to reduce $CO_2$ emissions is failed; the national air industry faces an unbalanced competitive situation, earns less money and misses liquidity to invest in cleaner and less noisy aircrafts. Overall national-based airlines are urged to adjust their networks which affects cohesion and the advantage of the location resulting in wider economic consequences such as unemployment and welfare as well as less tax income for the government. On the other hand, the government has to contrast this with the saving of external costs (e.g. environment).

In the case of the environmental aspects, other policy measures can cause less distortion of competition and have a long-term positive impact. For example, a policy can drive technological developments and go hand in hand with research and industry to create economically competitive alternatives to conventional oil that can be used for blending or other measures to help airports become $CO_2$ neutral. Scenario simulations show the different effects of the policy measures. It is possible to focus on environmental aspects. The complexity of the interrelationships could be extended at will by considering air transport agreements, night flight bans, subsidies or ATM costs.

## 3.3. Network scenarios for fleet planning and optimisation

The development of network scenarios should also be seen in the context of decision chains that focus on company dimensions/infrastructure developments. This concerns the fleet planning/strategies of airlines, the development planning of airports, the support of manufacturers in the development of new aircraft, and governments to push infrastructure decisions.

For medium- and long-term planning, network scenarios are developed which reflect different strategies. These network scenarios are the basis for the development of the fleet planning/strategy. The scenarios are used to create a decision space which is underpinned by concrete forecasts. The scenarios include destination, frequencies, time slot and passenger demand (split as usual). Details on fleet planning/strategy based on these input variables are described in detail in the Leadership Piece by Dr Karl Echtermeyer.

The process of generating these network scenarios includes the potential behaviour of the competition. The different network strategies result in concrete fleet portfolios which, on the one hand, satisfy the airline's general conditions and, on the other hand, meet the mobility needs of the passengers. The network generation described above can be carried out for several airlines at the same time (e.g. for members of Star Alliance or members of oneworld, etc.). In coordinated working groups with manufacturers, these (coordinated) network scenarios of different airlines are incorporated into the evaluation processes when designing new aircraft models. In the final analysis, these networks serve to simulate the operational deployment of new aircraft models at the beginning of the design process.

In addition to technical parameters, the competitive situation and the development of demand are decisive factors for generating future airline network scenarios. The latter two in particular are subject to a high degree of uncertainty, but are of fundamental importance as they are the basic building blocks for determining corporate strategy in terms of market positioning through network development. When using average values, trends and network representatives for aircraft types as well as network planning based on "Airport-to-Airport" models, errors in the operational as well as economic calculation are knowingly accepted. A quantification of the errors is not possible afterwards for a correct interpretation of the results.

RELEVANCE FOR THE STAKEHOLDERS

For **airlines**, medium/long-term planning involves not only network development close to the market under competitive conditions and a coordinated fleet development, but also a quantification of their needs within the design process of an aircraft. For the near time horizon there is potential for optimisation between market skimming and operational deployment.

For **airports**, the scenarios are used to plan capacities (terminal, gate, apron, runway) and to acquire airlines (e.g. decentralised intercontinental traffic technically and economically feasible through high-performance narrow-bodies).

For **administrations and policy decision makers**, scenarios linked to political measures are important for shaping their air transport system and for political control of traffic.

For **manufacturers**, the large number of flight network scenarios for different airlines results in a decision-making space for the market-oriented development or optimisation of aircraft, so that disinvestments (airframe, engine) are avoided.

Common to all of them are the variables that can be derived from these scenarios for financial planning (revenue/taxes, capital requirements).

## 4. Flexibility and agility of Door-to-Door models in disruptive situations

In the previous section the benefits of the "Door-to-Door" approach were outlined prior to the pandemic crises. This section shows how the "Door-to-Door" model logic is used for planning purposes under the uncertainty of SARS-CoV-2 (or other disruptive situations) while models based on "Airport-to-Airport" approaches fail because they have no regional dynamics. Two aspects must be taken into account. First (4.1), pandemics with the consequences of reduced confidence in flying and changes in mobility must be addressed. Second (4.2), a policy response matrix must be included with regard to the further ups and downs of pandemic development. This will become part of the forecasting model. Embedding these two aspects in the "Door-to-Door" approach makes it possible to capture the mobility wishes of customers in the pandemic environment.

### 4.1. Pandemic model features of the Door-to-Door approach

The major characteristics and capabilities of a bottom-up "Door-to-Door"-based tool can be summarised by a mathematical expression reflecting the interdependencies between regional socio-economy, attractiveness, and connectivity on trip purpose level. This allows us to generate the mobility needs between regions. To cope with the pandemic challenge and the large disruption of the air transport market the model must be enriched by three additional features.

**First**, SARS-CoV-2, a new, hazardous experience, makes people feel insecure. Insecurity results in low confidence to travel which is part of human behaviour in general. The underlying assumption of the model part addressing "confidence to fly" is the fear of getting infected with SARS-CoV-2. However, fears are not based on rational evaluations of the respective situations. It's rather a strong feeling of general unpleasantness regarding the specific circumstances. To approximate the factors which are relevant contributors in constituting this fear, psychological research results of general loss aversion of humans were used. In principle humans try to avoid any course of action that makes their situation worse than their current one. With regards to air travel, we modelled this kind of behavioural tendency with the comparison of the SARS-CoV-2 situation in the origins and destinations. If the situation in the destination is worse than in the origin, the confidence to travel will be lowered significantly. Factors used concern the medical treatment in a foreign country, the health system, being forced into quarantine, likelihood of having COVID-19 on board the flight, and other local policy measures preventing the spread of the virus up to the risk that there is no possibility to return home because flights are suspended and borders are closed. To embed the psychological certainty effect non-linear formulations of the models were applied.

**Second**, even though the world around us is constantly changing, people are resistant to change. More often than not people stay in their comfort zone, take the default option when they don't know any better or do things the way they have always been done. Changes from these patterns are triggered when we are forced to leave said comfort zone and do things differently from before. Crises trigger such changes and the pandemic triggers security, disease and economic effects on a worldwide dimension resulting in less air travel. On top there is the immanent bounce back effect of the virus with even more dangerous mutations. The latter in particular forces everyone to adjust priorities and to adjust their comfortable daily life to rapidly changing circumstances caused either by the health situation or by the political measures imposed. The behavioural change concerns a massive change in terms of work by using virtual meetings and home offices; vacation trips were redirected to local activities or short distance destinations; and visiting friends and relatives (VFR) traffic was on hold wherever possible. Everyone was urged to leave the comfort zone and aviation faces a cut in business travel and a time lag for VFR and vacation demand. On top airlines and airports are forced to follow new guidelines, and policy measures are imposed pricing $CO_2$ emissions. The circumstances addressed result in a "change of mobility" and are translated into technical, economic and network constraints as well as regional competition reflected by model variables used on the demand side and the characteristics of the travel paths.

**Third**, a model mirroring the "pandemic situation" is needed. The spread of the virus has to be put into relationship to air, surface and community activities/mobility whereby policy measures in place have to be considered. This part also allows us to examine the future development of the COVID-19 situation to foresee policy actions and the necessities to adjust air services in capacity and destination. Clearly it has to be stated that this model component is no substitute for the pandemic models or the medical forecasts resulting from them. However, the findings to be drawn from the pandemic models are of great value in explaining interrelationships and generating the formation process of a flight network as an adaptation strategy.

The differentiation of characteristics is necessary to take into account the specific effects that influence mobility needs (by purpose of travel, business, VFR, vacation) or the demand for air travel. It is also a prerequisite for understanding the different aspects of travellers' behaviour and needs before making investments. Integration into the model system ensures that interdependencies are reflected and quantifiable.

Due to the rapidly changing environment of the pandemic situation, evocative policies and competitive responses, the tool needs to be designed in such a way that weekly forecasts can be made. This can be cumulated into a periodic four-week forecast to meet operational requirements.

### 4.2. The Hammer & Dance process with the Door-to-Door approach

Besides the characteristics of the pandemic, a "Hammer & Dance" process must be considered. The pandemic literature refers to the "Hammer" to contain the spread of the infection and the "Dance" to the dosage of relaxation measures so that social life returns to normal but the pandemic is kept under control.[10]

This "Hammer & Dance" approach can also be applied to the problem of air transport. Again, policies to limit the spread of the infection in the form of travel restrictions (e.g. travel warnings, closure of airports and borders, suspension of flights) are considered to be the "Hammer." In contrast, the "Dance" component has two functions. On the one hand, the search for and establishment of air services which are economically valid but which do not revive COVID-19 infections, and on the other hand, the rapid response to exogenous policy measures by adjusting air services in terms of capacity and destination in order to avoid losses or ensure a valid service portfolio. This allows the development of scenarios of a preventive and expansionary nature to be simulated in parallel.

The pandemic model features consider the policy measures imposed due to COVID-19 and they embed a forecast of the pandemic spread in respect of transport and the situation in the communities (respectively regions). In consequence one can set up a bounce back policy matrix reflecting the reaction of politicians/administrations to certain levels of SARS-CoV-2 situations.

Such a "Hammer & Dance" heuristic works in principle as follows: COVID-19 cases go down by a certain number and the policy will allow for trips, in reverse the policy will declare travel warnings in case the indicator becomes higher. Threshold values of the indicators subject to the process should be flexible to be defined user-specifically whereby indicators can be defined country-specifically. Alternatively, likelihoods of policy actions in relation to pandemic indicators can be derived and imposed. As the "Door-to-Door" model considers all regions including the interdependencies described in the previous sections the network generation process is dynamic to policy measures, COVID-19 and consumer behaviour.

Short-term forecasts can be carried out on a weekly basis, and the accumulation of a few weeks provides a necessary lead time buffer for operational requirements (aircraft scheduling, crew planning, etc.). For more complex tasks, for example demand and network forecasts (medium and long term) involving several airports or hubs in parallel, the tool must be equipped with a procedure for generating multiple airlines and airport networks. In principle, the process for examining a route is (just) extended to cover large multiple route changes. In addition, the network generation process must have the freedom to adjust existing networks to balance supply and demand.

### 4.3. Network development under the uncertainty of COVID-19

At the time of writing our tools X-VIA and SONAR are being enriched successively by the COVID-19 features outlined above, to finally allow the computation of the following scenarios.[11]

THE HAMMER & DANCE PROCESS TO DEFINE AN EXIT STRATEGY

In the context of the pandemic model features the network generation process is enriched by the indicators represented in the regional bounce back policy matrix so that they are embedded in the network generation processes as restrictions, whether it is allowed to implement a route for testing the passenger potential or not. This enhances planning security and allows airlines to build up an orderly exit strategy to successively ramp up flight business during the crises whilst reacting quickly and flexibly to rebound effects.

Based on the findings outlined in the previous sections one allows the system to generate a network following the "Hammer & Dance" philosophy, resulting in an exit strategy for, for example, the European Union or an airline.

Taking Europe as an example, for the sake of simplicity, it can be assumed that the EU (European Union) would have taken the lead: EU governments agreed to a common approach of policy measures concerning thresholds for the bounce back matrix keeping the spread of SARS-CoV-2 under control while restoring freedom of movement for citizens and businesses wherever possible. When the thresholds are reached, a set of policy measures will automatically be applied for the NUTS3 region[12] concerned. As soon as the regions show indicators below the threshold, the policy measures will be automatically released. For example, we can define the following two scenarios:

- The first one is very liberal with high thresholds and low policy actions. Here one can expect increasing SARS-CoV-2 cases with moderate limiting effects by policy actions.
- The second one is very conservative with low thresholds and high policy actions. This scenario will show a levelling curvature of SARS-CoV-2 cases with a lot of policy actions.

Of course a bounce back policy matrix can be defined for each country as well, such as the suggestion of the German Chancellor Angela Merkel to apply travel bans on regions which show more than 50 COVID-19 cases per 100,000 inhabitants within a week. Or the French idea to differentiate between green and red regions[13] whereby the former are allowed to travel and the latter have to stay in their region. Obviously a set of rules can be applied based on different indicators triggering various policy measures depending on the threshold imposed for the indicator (for low, medium, high risk or mutation regions, etc.). Important to note is just the flexibility of the system to develop different scenarios either to interact with the politicians about rule making or to be prepared having different exit strategies at hand.

Again analyses will show the effects upon demand at airports, airline networks and the COVID-19 spread. Of interest will also be the policy measures active once the forecasting horizon is met. Monitoring these results allow a fine tuning of the bounce back policy matrix.

ROUTE FORECASTS UNDER THE UNCERTAINTY OF SARS-COV-2

Once the model adaptation is completed the regional mobility is computed in respect of the consumers' confidence to fly and corrected by mobility changes. Thus the system is working as usual and to execute route forecasts one just edits the schedule of the implemented network. Whether one or many routes are implemented does not matter for the model. But this needs to be taken into account when interpreting the results. Effects displayed in the results are caused by all changes implemented. There are two ways to handle the scenarios:

- A ceteris paribus forecast for the actual week equals the assumption that nothing else changes with the exception of one or more routes of the air network. The advantage is a profound knowledge about the actual market situation and no assumptions or forecasting effects need to be considered while interpreting the results. The effects just reflect the consumer behaviour.
- In case there is a need to explore the coming weeks, the scenario settings of the model have to be adapted to the week in focus. This concerns the selection of the weekly demand slice and the adjustment of the policy matrix according to the users' expectation (if the planner has a clear indication about the release or instalment of a policy).

Despite the effects on the COVID-19 numbers and their spatial distribution, of more interest are the (local, behind, beyond, bridge) passengers attracted by the routes investigated and the cannibalisation caused to other routes. Other analyses such as route specific catchments will be of interest for the marketing department.

EVALUATION OF POLICY MEASURES DUE TO SARS-COV-2

To explore the effects of policy measures an ex post and ex ante forecast can be executed. In principle two questions can be addressed:

- What would have happened if one or more of the policies imposed had not been applied (ex post)?
- What will happen when, for example, all policies measures are released (ex ante)?

The analyses show the effects on the COVID-19 numbers and their spatial distribution as well as airport and network specific demand. It is also possible to explore what effects air service connectivity has on the spread of SARS-CoV-2. On the one hand one can look backwards and explore the correlation between air connectivity and the virus and on the other hand one can execute a simulation assuming a network connecting SARS-CoV-2 hot spots to investigate the spreading of the virus. The implications of air services upon SARS-CoV-2 can be identified as the regional air connectivity is used. This does not work with the set of air connectivity indicators used so far by the aviation industry as they are just linked to an airport.

## Notes

1 www.researchgate.net/publication/5182064_Introducing_Spatial_Competition_Through_an_Autoregressive_Continuous_Distributed_AR-C-D_Process_in_Intercity_Generation-Distribution_Models_within_a_Quasi-Direct_Format_QDF
2 www.researchgate.net/publication/313891821_Europe-wide_aviation_connectivity_measures_and_the_PATH_theorem
3 www.researchgate.net/publication/24053363_A_disaggregate_Box-Cox_Logit_mode_choice_model_of_intercity_passenger_travel_in_Germany_and_its_implications_for_high-speed_rail_demand_forecasts
4 www.researchgate.net/publication/271700707_Contemporary_Airport_Demand_Forecasting_Choice_Models_and_Air_Transport_Forecasting
5 AENA: the Spanish national airport management company.
6 The network generator is a procedure automated by MKmetric, which finds new and attractive destinations in the "Door-to-Door" mode. The mathematical philosophy underlying the "Airport-to-Airport" models does not allow such a procedure.
7 www.researchgate.net/publication/313891821_Europe-wide_aviation_connectivity_measures_and_the_PATH_theorem
8 For passenger transport X-VIA passenger was used, for air cargo X-VIA cargo.
9 SONAR$_{NetGen}$ is a tool developed by MKmetric which calculates complex mesh generation and analysis tasks according to the "Door-to-Door" model approach for aviation (www.mkm.de).
10 https://medium.com/@tomaspueyo/coronavirus-the-hammer-and-the-dance-be9337092b56
11 X-VIA becomes X-VIA-Covid and SONAR is extended to SONAR-Covid (www.mkm.de).
12 https://ec.europa.eu/eurostat/de/web/nuts/nuts-maps; NUTS3 reflects a county.
13 https://dobetter.esade.edu/en/green-zones-covid-19

## Consolidation and nationalisation on the North Atlantic

*Keith McMullan and James Halstead*
Managing Partners, Aviation Strategy Ltd

The North Atlantic was the largest and most mature long-haul air transport market in the world, until March 2020. Since then it has in effect been shut down, operating at around 20% of 2019 capacity. When it reopens what will the competitive landscape and regulatory framework look like?

The reopening date is simply unknown, but it is now clear that a V-shaped recovery pattern is highly unlikely. The CEOs of various airlines have been pushing back on the year when 2019 traffic volumes will be recaptured: 2023 or 2024 appears to be the consensus at the moment. And even if traffic does get back to the 2019 level by 2023/24, it will be 15–20% below that expected and planned for in the pre-COVID world.

Post-COVID, when most of the world's population has been vaccinated or when travellers have adjusted to the risks of the disease, the transatlantic airline industry could resemble the pre-deregulation world—dominated by a few large airlines, owned or controlled by their governments, subsidised by their states, with limited real competition.

This outlook is partly the culmination of a trend that long predates COVID-19. From 2009, the North Atlantic market has become increasingly consolidated and divided up among three multinational groups: the antitrust immunised joint ventures of Air France-KLM with Delta (having taken over Northwest); the Lufthansa Group with United (having taken over Continental) plus Air Canada; and British Airways, Iberia and Aer Lingus with American (having taken over US Airways). On the North Atlantic these groups, under the alliance brands of SkyTeam, Star and oneworld, became virtually merged entities, with the US and European partners making joint decisions on fares, schedules and capacity, sharing revenues and costs on a "metal-neutral" basis so that in theory there was no difference as to whose aircraft were operated, and producing their own consolidated (and confidential) financial accounts for the sector.

By the end of 2018 the three airline combinations had gained control of roughly 68% of the capacity on services between North America and Europe/ Middle East (see Figure 7.38), and their hub-to-hub routes across the Atlantic were in many cases completely monopolised. What once might have been seen as illegal collusion was protected through the antitrust immunity provisions of the joint ventures. However, all of the network carriers appeared commercially robust—the European carriers having gone through privatisations and rationalisations, and the US majors having restructured under Chapter 11 bankruptcy protection—and profitability on the North Atlantic appeared strong.

That robustness proved to be an illusion once COVID-19 struck. Collectively the six network carriers have absorbed some $45 billion in state aid in grants and loans, and another round of state funding of a similar amount is likely over

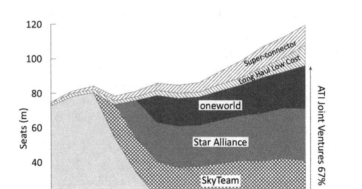

*Figure 7.38* North Atlantic market pre-COVID

the next 12 months. For comparison, the combined stockmarket value of the six carriers at the end of September 2020 was $44 billion.

The consolidation process on the Atlantic was predicated on an open skies regulatory regime—which would allow, hopefully, new entrants onto the North Atlantic, injecting competition into the market. COVID-19 has largely finished off that competition.

Long-haul, low-cost capacity, in various forms, had peaked at about 12% of the North Atlantic total. But Norwegian's operating model was being severely stressed before COVID-19, and survival prospects for the carrier, despite its own dose of state aid, look dim unless it too is nationalised. In which case it will join the myriad of small European flag-carriers now fully supported by their states—Alitalia, SAS, TAP, among others—which in the pre-COVID era had about 13% of the capacity on the Atlantic. The innovative Icelandic low-cost hub operation has collapsed and the charter-type carriers such as Thomas Cook either went out of business even before COVID-19 or have been left in limbo (Air Transat which was due to be merged into Air Canada).

It is somewhat ironic that the super-connectors—Emirates, Etihad and Qatar Airways—provoked such outrage in the US over state subsidies when they started to become a threat on the Atlantic, with about 9% of capacity. Their Middle East passenger hubs have been devastated by the pandemic, and recovery will be painfully slow. Funnelling huge volumes of passengers to/from 200-plus countries through a few terminals no longer appears to be an attractive prospect.

So after decades of extracting themselves from their national carriers, governments now find themselves as significant shareholders—20% at Lufthansa, 28% at Air France/KLM—again supporting their major airlines.

Under the US Coronavirus Aid, Relief, and Economic Security (CARES) Act, which allocated some $50 billion to US passenger airlines, the government will have the right to participate in "the gains of the eligible business or its security holders through the use of such instruments as warrants, stock options, common or preferred stock, or other appropriate equity instruments"—in other words, partial nationalisation. On the Atlantic, this means that effective government ownership and control of capacity may well be close to total when the industry emerges from COVID-19.

What role will governments play in this new world? Some of the conditions of the state aid reflect social aims—in Europe, the acceleration of carbon emission targets and the shifting of short-haul passengers from air to rail while in the US the priority is the protection of jobs through no-furlough conditions—but the governments' stated aim is to facilitate rapid turnaround strategies so their subsidised airlines can repay their loans or convert them into commercial debt. The terms of the loans incentivise this, for example Lufthansa's interest rate on some of its state loans escalates from 4% pa to 9.5% pa in 2027.

However, the challenges of restoring long-haul services to anything like pre-COVID operations are such that governments may find themselves enmeshed for the long term, in which case it is not difficult to envision long-haul international airlines once again assuming the role of national champions or chosen instruments. Aeropolitics necessarily reflect global trends in politics, and the political and economic *zeitgeist* has changed profoundly over the past five years—from a consensual belief in the benefits of globalisation and free competition to diverse nationalistic agendas, protecting and promoting narrower interests.

One issue that may well arise concerns conflicts of interests within alliances. The North Atlantic joint ventures may not be as solid as they appeared to be in the pre-COVID era; just as military alliances realign under the threat of war, so do commercial alliances under the stress of a lengthy recession or depression.

In the oneworld joint venture the two main participants have been diametrically opposed in their attitude to state aid; whereas American has taken the maximum available, $10.6 billion to date, IAG has minimised its exposure to what it sees as potential state interference. BA has taken just £300 million under a general industry support scheme, while Iberia and Vueling have received €1 billion in total of Spanish state funding. IAG is the strongest of the European carriers in terms of liquidity, having raised €2.5 billion through a rights issue (though about €500 million of that came from Qatar Airways, which has been hugely subsidised by its state). American is the weakest of the Big Four US carriers and is regarded as being the most likely candidate for Chapter 11. IAG had the strongest position on the North Atlantic in terms of overall capacity, twice that of Air France, and was dominant in the point-to-point markets (essentially London–New York) and in the premium travel market. American has been relatively weak in the north-east US but in July signed a strategic alliance with jetBlue, with jetBlue providing a domestic feed operation to

American's transatlantic flights. It will be intriguing to see how this tripartite arrangement plays out when jetBlue starts up its own transatlantic A321 LR service, still scheduled for 2021.

In the Star joint venture the Lufthansa Group has been Europe's most avid recipient of state aid—over €10 billion—while United has focused on raising funds through monetising its frequent flyer programme for $6.8 billion, and has received just $5.0 billion from the US government. Lufthansa's problem is that it has a low proportion of transatlantic and other long-haul point-to-point traffic at its Frankfurt hub and has relied on its hubbing expertise to collect feed traffic. Downsizing a hub operation, as Lufthansa is planning, is a complex exercise as culling seemingly unprofitable short-haul routes may damage the viability of certain long-haul routes. Rationalising the hub network by consolidating long-haul traffic flows at Frankfurt and downgrading Vienna or Zurich is fraught with political problems. The state aid that the Lufthansa Group has received has come from Austria, Switzerland and Belgium as well as Germany, and those countries understandably want to protect air transport connectivity at their capitals, as do the various *Länder* within Germany.

In the SkyTeam joint venture Air France/KLM has received €10.4 billion in state aid, two-thirds from France and one-third from the Netherlands, while Delta (which incidentally owns 9% of Air France/KLM) has taken $5.4 billion in US government funding. The problem is that the pandemic has exacerbated existing tensions between Air France and KLM. Put crudely KLM resents the fact that it has been the profit generator within the group while Air France is perceived to have made too many concessions to its unions. Despite assurances from the two governments that all is well between the two airlines, investors will have to be persuaded that the Air France/KLM Group is operating as a coherent entity before providing the funds necessary to replace the state loans (some of which rise to Euro LIBOR plus 7.75% in year six).

Indeed, relations between Air France and Delta seem to be closer than those between Air France and KLM. Paris represents the second most important origin and destination (O&D) point after London. Air France's new management might be considering whether, if the short-haul network can be rationalised, a downsized transatlantic operation, with a higher proportion of local traffic, emulating IAG's Heathrow model, might be the way forward. Where this would leave KLM's Amsterdam hub operation is unclear.

### Collapse of premium business

The North Atlantic market has been heavily reliant on premium travel for its profitability, but that sector has collapsed. At some point business travel will recover to pre-COVID levels but it is not going to be soon. The use of semi-efficient video technology such as Zoom is now universal; embattled corporations will continue to cut travel budgets; corporations have realised that they can use reduced business travel to meet their carbon reduction obligations; and super-elite passengers are much more likely to choose private jets.

This is particularly bad news for the transatlantic joint ventures where premium passengers have accounted for 30–40% of their revenues. In the post-COVID world a Boeing 787 configured with 60 first/business seats out of a total of 214 will still probably make sense on the key London–New York route, but on the thinner routes and hub-bypassing routes, smaller gauge equipment may well be the optimal solution—one that is being proposed by JetBlue with the launch of its Airbus A321 service featuring its MINT premium product.

It is not just premium volumes that have collapsed, premium class fares are down 70% year on year compared to a decline of around 30% for economy class, according to IATA. Pre-COVID the ratio of premium to economy fares was about 5:1 as a global average, higher on the main transatlantic routes. That type of ratio will not be achieved in the foreseeable future because to fill premium cabins premium fares will have to be moderated. Which means, for the revenue part of the profitability equation to get close to balancing the cost part, economy class fares will have to be raised. In turn, a rise in economy fares would threaten to choke off a substantial recovery in traffic volumes.

### *Fragility of feed networks*

Unlike US domestic hubs, European hubs are designed to feed traffic from short-haul to intercontinental long-haul. This exposes their short-haul operations to direct and indirect competition from the low-cost carriers (LCCs). Hubs with low proportions of local long-haul traffic, like Frankfurt or Amsterdam, are more vulnerable than those, like Heathrow and to a lesser extent Paris, that have strong local long-haul traffic demand.

It is perhaps surprising that in the intra-European market pre-COVID (i.e. 12 months ago) the big three network carriers (including their subsidiaries) accounted for nearly 40% of seat capacity. Add in the smaller flag-carriers—Alitalia, SAS, TAP, among others— and over 50% of intra-European capacity market is state subsidised and facing a fundamental restructuring, partly dictated by the conditions of state aid. The network carriers are being forced into addressing the reality of the economics of feed to their global hubs, abandoning unprofitable routes and airport bases. Non-hub flying is being rationalised nearly out of existence.

About 30% of the intra-European market is operated efficiently by the three well-capitalised and liquid LCCs—Ryanair, easyJet and Wizz Air—though each is differently positioned to deal with the post-COVID world. They are going to encroach further onto the routes that the network carriers rely on for feed.

How this will impact long-haul operations from the continental hubs is uncertain. Streamlining of short-haul operations at Air France is overdue and actions like shutting down Air France's domestic subsidiary Hop! and moving to an Airbus A220 fleet should be beneficial for the airline's finances; Lufthansa has perennially tried to defend unprofitable non-hub short-haul services as a marketing defence for its hub feed. Pre-COVID it had been in the process of trying to develop Eurowings as a low-cost, point-to-point solution, but has since cut back its plans.

Reducing short-haul services into hubs could undermine the viability of some long-haul services, and these in turn may have to be culled. If yields are depressed further on short-haul as the result of increased presence of LCCs, the only option may be to increase fares on the long-haul services—reinforcing the premium travel reduction effect described above.

For the moment the network carriers are able to retain their precious slots at their main hubs, as the European authorities have suspended the 80/20 use-or-lose rule, but there is no guarantee that this waiver will be renewed for summer 2021. If not, excess capacity at these hubs may be seized by new entrants, probably LCCs, intensifying the competitive pressures on the network carriers and the joint ventures.

### The new reality

Nothing is clear in the post-COVID world, other than the fact that the key, previously highly lucrative, North Atlantic market faces a major medium-term disruption. It seems that governments, having been obliged to subsidise their network carriers, are going to find it more difficult to extricate themselves as quickly as is officially expected. The structural changes in premium travel will probably push up economy fares which will slow the recovery in overall traffic volumes. The European hubs will have to been further rationalised and costs further reduced to protect streamlined feed operations. And new opportunities may be opening up on the North Atlantic for carriers with lower costs and the right equipment (perhaps A321 types) for the new market conditions.

# Having your head in the clouds while keeping your feet on the ground

*Simone van Neerven*
Founder, reBel.la and former Head of Innovation, Vueling Airlines

*Jirka Stradal*
Founder, TalkAir and Captain, KLM

## *A wake-up call for the world*

The COVID-19 pandemic has resulted in the most simultaneous shutdowns and lockdowns worldwide in history. By 26 March 2020, 1.7 billion people worldwide were under some form of lockdown, which increased to 3.9 billion people by the first week of April—more than half of the world's population.[1]

The skies were eerily empty, as thousands of grounded planes were parked wingtip to wingtip on runways and in storage facilities. At the peak of the crisis, more than 16,000 passenger jets were grounded, representing about 62% of the world's planes.[2]

## *Pressure is on*

The debate about whether this was a black swan or a grey rhino event is not that relevant. More important is to realise that every now and then, the world will be shaken-up by an impactful event such as a war, a meteor impact, a major hack, or a virus, to name some of the possible disruptive events. Also, many industries were already and are constantly under a lot of pressure. The aviation industry is no exception to that. This comes from a number of forces, from the economic, political, legal, competitive, technological, social, environmental, and global environments.

Only the countries and companies that either mitigated for or hedged against these risks are resilient and moving towards a healthy future. Moreover, as a company or country, the ongoing thriving state should be antifragile, rather than in a coping survival mode.

Furthermore, the belief introduced by Friedman in the 1970s that a business's sole responsibility is making profit and a focus on shareholder return is being questioned more and more. Research by Edelman shows that 73% of employees are saying that they want the opportunity to actively change society, and nearly two-thirds of consumers are identifying themselves as belief-driven buyers. Nearly half of respondents are even willing to accept a smaller salary to work for an environmentally and socially responsible company.[3]

This belief is even stronger for the younger generations: 64% will not take a job with a company that does not have strong corporate social responsibility (CSR) practices. Meaningful engagement around CSR is a business—and bottom line—imperative, impacting a company's ability to appeal to, retain and inspire younger talent.[4]

CEOs are beginning to realise that their mandate has changed. They are expected to lead from the front. Over nine in ten employees say CEOs should speak out on broader issues of the day, including retraining, the ethical use of technology and income inequality. Three-quarters of the general population believe CEOs should take the lead on change instead of waiting for the government to impose it.

### Shifting towards an infinite mindset

Organisations need to think differently to build a healthy organisation. Doing business is not about winning. Winning means there is an end to the game. The focus should be on how to keep playing. In finite games, like football or chess, the players are known, the rules are fixed, and the endpoint is clear. The winners and losers are easily identified. In infinite games, like business or politics or life itself, the players come and go, the rules are changeable, and there is no defined endpoint. There are no winners or losers in an infinite game; there is only ahead and behind. In these types of games you have to prove your worthiness to participate and to aim to stay ahead of other participants.

Many of the struggles that organisations face exist simply because their leaders are playing with a finite mindset in an infinite game. These organisations tend to lag behind in innovation, discretionary effort, morale and ultimately performance.[5,6]

### Reframe what you do

So the question should be, how to play to succeed in the game we are in? This requires you to begin reframing what you do. As Steven van Belleghem states, become a "partner in life" of your customers. "Every customer has dreams, fears and ambitions." You need to have continuous insight into the needs and emotions of your customers.

> To become a partner in life, it is necessary to understand the bigger issues that play a role in the customer's thinking. For example, as a bank it might be interesting to learn about people's dreams and ambitions—a new house, a trip around the world, etc.—so that you can see how the bank can help the customer achieve their realisation.
>
> (Steven van Belleghem)[7]

Two great examples of companies' purposes that have been formulated around becoming a partner in the life of the customer are "to make every part of people's life as easy as possible" (Google), and "to make it easy for everyone to discover the world" (AirBnB).

Typically, airlines are mainly focused on transporting people from airport to airport and providing a good experience to the customer. However, airlines should stop seeing only the physical customer journey, but rather start seeing it as a customer's *life* journey. This no longer has anything to do with the optimisation of the operational processes. Instead, it aims to reduce the frustrations and help realise the larger life dreams of your customer.

For an airline, this change of focus means to divert from terms such as aircrafts, airports, suitcases, baggage, air, network, carrier, and so on. Their restated purpose could be something like "to bring meaningful experiences and connections everywhere, everyday."

Looking at business with an infinite mindset will be a game changer and can open up the entire landscape of services an airline could offer, but it will mean that it will need to completely reinvent itself. Making the right choices is key, and understanding that there are a number of forces at work will be essential.

### May the force be with you

The world is constantly changing and developing. To maintain or build a successful business, it is crucial to gain a basic understanding of the drivers of humans and the trends and forces that are shaping the world. We distinguish three types of forces (see Figure 7.39):

- The human drivers that are more internally driven and based on the fundamental human needs or desires. We distinguish eight of them in Figure 7.39. Keen observation, research, and centuries of history show us that we are motivated by a desire to meet the fundamental human needs. That is, humans are motivated to do things by a desire to meet their intrinsic needs. These needs are not *wants* but *needs* that we all have by just being human.
- The current technology drivers, examples of current key technologies, that are foundational to shaping a number of trends. Examples are innovations in processing and computing architecture, advances in semiconductors and electronic systems, new kinds of batteries and electronics, machine vision and speech technologies, (general) artificial intelligence and machine learning, haptics, 5G, Internet of Things and robotics, and many more. These technologies are constantly under development and have profound enabling power, the differentiation they can create, and their potential to catalyse change, often without the final users having a direct interaction with these technologies.
- There are 12 trends or forces that will forever change the ways in which we live, work, learn and communicate (see Figure 7.39). The future will bring with it even more screens, tracking, and lack of privacy. These forces should not be thought of as separate boxes to deal with in isolation from each other. Instead, they are all mixed and interrelated.[8]

The last 20 years have been a relatively easy shift in digital transformation. "Easy" problems could be solved with "easy" solutions. The real challenges are starting now, where more complex problems need to be resolved. Today, we are

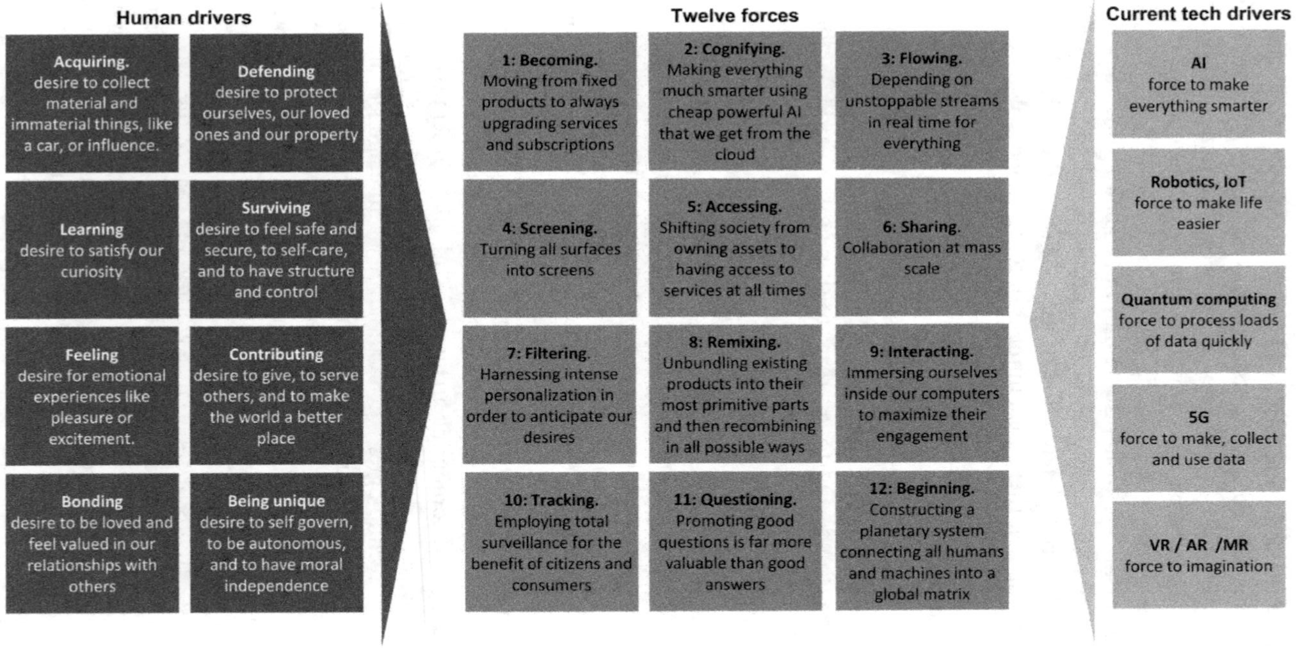

*Figure 7.39* Staying relevant today, tomorrow and the day after tomorrow

in the best possible time to start something or invent something. The opportunities open to us now are enormous. The forces give direction on how the world is going to change. Most likely most of the greatest products running the lives of people in 2050 will be invented after 2020.

However, most of us focus on today. On the meetings we will be having, the emails we will respond to, the price offers we need to send out while deadlines are breathing down our neck. And we should. Today is what pays our bills. We also think about tomorrow, about our future value, how we must adapt to an increasingly digital world, and how—or even if—our company will survive disruption. Fears about tomorrow are what keep us awake at night. But let's face it, most of us do not think (much) beyond that.[9] With an infinite mindset you start looking at the possibilities in business as a lifetime game, where no one wins or loses, and where you have to make sure you stay relevant to the infinite.

For that, we need to be aware (and not afraid) of the unrelenting pace of change of technology and the enhancement of human life and intelligence by these technologies. This will bring the imminent opportunities and threats for those businesses that choose to embrace or ignore them. The forces as identified in Figure 7.39 can be used as guiding principles in shaping the horizons and making the right decisions.

### Working in the three horizons at the same time

When talking about today, tomorrow and the day after tomorrow, this also refers to the well-known three horizons framework, originally conceived by McKinsey & Company (see Figure 7.40). It provides a method to distinguish how daily actions impact current, medium and long-term goals for

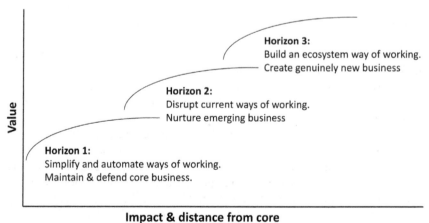

**Horizon 3:**
Build an ecosystem way of working.
Create genuinely new business

**Horizon 2:**
Disrupt current ways of working.
Nurture emerging business

**Horizon 1:**
Simplify and automate ways of working.
Maintain & defend core business.

Value

**Impact & distance from core**

*Figure 7.40* Three horizons: Impact and value

long-term success. It shows how to bucket today's actions into three distinct categories.

Horizon 1 is about subsistence. Horizon 1 activities have a short-term impact and are typically low-risk—there is a large degree of control over execution and results. So, they should be done as quickly as possible, but with consistency, reliability, and high-quality levels. Survival in this stage is made up of daily iteration of tasks, maintenance, and follow-up. Neglecting to execute each of these with consistency will, in turn, make you extremely vulnerable.

Bold, new initiatives—this is what horizon 2 is all about. Here you make moves into new markets, which can mean introducing a totally new product category or innovating your business model. For more established enterprises, mergers and acquisitions are also horizon 2. These activities always come with a significant risk—it is uncertain how the market will react and whether the organisation can pull it off.

Horizon 3 activities are designed for long-term impact. Think about conducting exploratory travel, meeting people in new fields of expertise, or investing time into wild ideas. These activities have a highly uncertain outcome and are categorised as low probability, so there is a realistic possibility of not happening.[10]

So how could this three horizons framework be applied to the aviation industry? We use the forces as ingredients to imagine the different horizons.

### Horizon 1: Can you offer transactional perfection?

*Ingredients: surviving, defending, tracking, screening, accessing, becoming, cognifying*

When thinking of horizon 1 for the airline industry, the major challenge (and opportunity) is to improve the current customer journey to an end-to-end frictionless travel journey. Reduce all the waste, get the basics right, and be able to anticipate quickly any changing customer behaviour, such as caused by the COVID-19 crisis where the centre of gravity shifted towards touchless and hygiene priorities.

Two major focus points are crucial. First, all too often, in the airline industry the focus is on planes and operations, whereas it should be much more on people: "We don't fly planes, we fly people."[11] Second, there is still far too much friction in the entire journey of a customer. This is also caused by the sole focus of an airline to transport people from airport to airport.

The near future is that the customer's entire travel journey will need to be smooth. Information and context flows directly to the customer through screens and gadgets. Existing touchpoints are optimised, and all transactions are perfectly and seamlessly connected, both digitally and physically. This journey starts from the customer choosing a destiny, to anticipation, planning, getting there by plane, receiving the latest contextual information on the destination, paperwork pain-relievers, arranged transport from airport to hotel, local travel, helping making meaningful experiences, all the way back to buying a ticket again.

**Horizon 2: Are you ready to flip the industry upside down?**

*Ingredients: feeling, learning, acquiring, flowing, remixing, filtering, sharing*

Many airlines are working towards the perfect customer experience. All focus is on transactional perfection as described in horizon 1. (Digital) frustrations and non-logical activities such as having to enter the same information several times or having to use multiple sources of information will no longer be there.

Horizon 2 is about becoming *truly* customer centred. "People will forget what you said, people will forget what you did, but people will never forget how you made them feel."[12] Real interaction, two-way information-flow and feedback will be key. Companies can surpass their peers in customer experience design by really listening to and observing the customer in the given context. The journey will be hyper personalised, acknowledging that needs differ per person and the context that person is in. For instance, recognising that when the same person is travelling alone or with friends or family, and whether the purpose of the trip is for work, to relax, or a combination of both.

Exploring new touchpoints and subsequently optimising existing and personal touchpoints by instant customer feedback, will give rise to a dynamic connected ecosystem. Tailored, personalised products, services and experiences are proactively provided to smoothen the entire journey from consideration of travel to journey back to reconsideration of travel. The ecosystem will keep expanding, and emerging businesses are constantly added.

This will not be limited to just making onboard reservations for transport to the final destination; booking all kinds of other activities and experiences on board have also become a normality. Technology will be used to ensure a frictionless experience, for instance by using facial recognition during the entire journey, from identification for the pickup transportation to the entrance of a hotel or a co-working space. The ecosystem of services keeps growing and will be based on expanded partnerships. By understanding the needs and desires of the customer in real time, products and services from the ecosystem can be offered to smoothen the journey even further, leading to a higher customer satisfaction and higher revenues at the same time.

And what if you push customer centricity even further?

Today, flight schedules are created months in advance. They are inflexible and airlines are not capable of changing schedules overnight. What would it take for an airline to anticipate real-time customer demand? This would require an airline to schedule on daily and maybe even hourly fluctuations. The entire airline operating model should be radically altered; all activities that nowadays depend on long-term planning require a dramatic makeover. The (re-)opening of a new destination or route should be done overnight. Deployment of aircraft, crew and maintenance needs to become hyper flexible, or just in time and demand driven. And of course the process of slot allocation and planning, a highly regulated process, will have to change. No longer will it be necessary to reward customers with lower prices the more in advance they book. It will be much more lucrative to promote certain flights at short notice, based on changing customer needs to optimise the fleet on the day of operations.

Only with very advanced algorithms can this be efficiently managed. Moreover, human behaviour needs to change. We are so used to the current entrenched airline model, that we are in the habit of booking all our trips well in advance to get the best price. And consequently, we plan everything around these dates. It will become extremely important to be able to identify and predict and meet the real and specific needs of the customers.

The benefit for an airline, besides becoming truly customer centric, is the flexibility it will bring. Nowadays, whenever there is a sudden change or disruption, it takes a lot of effort to anticipate and to reschedule. A lot of effort and energy is subsequently put into informing both customers and employees.

Even though this will be a rigorous and complete makeover of the airline industry, we still regard it as a horizon 2 topic since it is still about flying, whereas in horizon 3 we truly go beyond the core business of flying.

### *Horizon 3: Will you still be an airline in 10 years from now?*

*Ingredients: bonding, being unique, contributing, interacting, beginning, questioning*

In horizon 3 it is all about daring to ask provoking questions and really reframing what you do. This will lead to new business models and might even make you divert from the current core business of flying people around the globe.

During the COVID-19 crisis people were forced to radically change their behaviours. In a moment, the world changed and working from home became a normality, Zoom became a verb and the market cap value of Zoom exceeded the value of the seven largest American airlines. Microsoft reported that they saw two years' worth of digital transformation in two months: from remote teamwork and learning, to sales and customer service, to critical cloud infrastructure and security. Ever since, Microsoft has been working alongside customers to help them adapt and stay open for business in a world of remote everything.

Another interesting development was seen with virtual reality. In 2019, 14 million people visited the Louvre in Paris. The museum was closed due to the lockdown. The museum offered an alternative to visit the museum virtually. Within the first two months of the lockdown, already almost 12 million people had virtually visited the museum on the digital platform!

The question that arises from this is will it become a normality for people to enjoy a "micro-experience" whenever they have 15 to 30 spare minutes by virtually travelling to Venice or visiting the van Gogh museum in Amsterdam for a quick recharge? This might not be a very radical thought. When people started to use smartphones, our behaviour changed. What used to be our predictable, daily sessions online have been replaced by many fragmented interactions that now occur instantaneously. There are hundreds of these moments every day—watching something, buying something, learning or discovering something new, texting a spouse, chatting with friends on social media. Google calls these "micro-moments."[13]

Our human behaviour is constantly provoking and adjusting to changes. People are now used to meeting in the virtual space. The human needs such as feeling, bonding, learning, and being unique are still fulfilled, and technology helps us to do so in different ways. Virtual reality is a great example of this, and is therefore becoming a realistic alternative to physical travel.

Looking at your business by following future trends, originated from developments in technology and human needs, will open up and can bring tremendous opportunities. A great way to start is by immersing yourself into the customer's life and thinking about becoming their partner in life. It is crucial to understand why they are flying (or why not) and identify the possible alternatives.

The future will probably not be that people will never travel again. But there will be many alternatives to choose from. Could the train be a really good alternative to air travel? And if not yet, are there developments going on that might change this in the future, such as a high-speed train or a hyperloop? Will VTOL (vertical take-off and landing) or self-driving electric cars become realistic alternatives? And will the experience to meet in virtual reality become so realistic, that more often people will decide to opt for this? By defining the airline's purpose as "to bring meaningful experiences and connections everywhere, everyday", these become interesting options to create genuinely new business models.

### Open up to new perspectives and embrace polarities

We live in the *never* normal, a time when nothing but uncertainty is certain. How you react as a company—and *how quickly*—will make the difference between success and failure. The world is getting far too complex for linear or binary thinking.

The three horizons model is an excellent tool to support leaders to hold a bold vision *and* deliver short-term results. To have their head in the clouds *and* their feet on the ground. But this is not the only polarity a leader has to deal with. Polarities are everywhere. Leaders also need to be able to maintain stability *and* galvanise change. To honour what is working *and* seek the freedom to create something new. We need to strive for excellence *and* be willing to fail. To gain trust *and* be willing to disappoint.

The challenge is that choosing between these opposing goals is not a problem to be solved. A problem is linear and can have a "right", or at least a "best" answer. Instead, these opposing goals are ongoing polarities to be managed. One pole is not better than the other, or truer or more worthy to be chosen over the other. The poles are interdependent and complementary, and they work together as part of a system.[14]

Once we begin to embrace the concept of dealing with polarities, and acknowledge that this is an important developmental opportunity, it prevents binary or linear thinking and it will be easier to open up to new perspectives.

### Demographic diversity is not sufficient

It is a divisive and polarising time in which we respond by constantly seeking like-mindedness. We have a growing number of ways to meet up with people similar to ourselves: we are drawn to people with the same interests, same tastes, and same politics. Every time we buy something online, we are told what other people like us also bought.[15]

It is human nature to find people we recognise to be "like me." Ironically, the wider our social options, the less likely we are to seek diverse friendship groups. Although it is human tendency to interact with people of the same interests and values, it shows that we are at risk of being in an echo chamber. Echo chambers occur when our own beliefs are regularly repeated by the people that surround us, whether in person or online. And, surprisingly, if contradictory beliefs find their way into our echo chamber, they do not allow us to question our own positions; they essentially oppose and polarise us more.

This kind of behaviour forms collective blindness and hinders the success of a team, a nation and global humanity. Even if a team consists of extremely intelligent people, if they all think alike, they won't know their blind spots, what they are not seeing. So dealing with complex problems needs more than only intelligence and skill. It needs a deliberate seeking of diversity. This diversity should not be restricted to demographic features, like gender, race, age, sexual orientation or religion. It needs to be a diversity of the mind, or cognitive diversity.[16]

### Tapping into the wisdom of the group

To be really innovative, a diverse team needs to consist of people who are diverse within themselves (see Figure 7.41). Our thinking can be diversified by making sure that we do not turn into a slave to one area of interest, crossing conceptual borders if not geographical borders. This was a routine Charles Darwin used. Switching his research between botany, zoology, geology, and psychology provided him a new perspective and enabled him to bring ideas together across fields.

When we form a team that is cognitively diverse, we expand our expertise in order to make our blind spots disappear. We increase what is called group wisdom; that is, the extensive range of views in the team gives it full coverage. But this collective intelligence does not only occur from academic knowledge. True group wisdom needs a profound knowledge of human behaviour.

If we truly want to improve our collective intelligence, the combined intelligence of a group, we need to defeat bias. When we need to make a decision with imperfect information, we unknowingly rely on our prejudices or biases,

**A non-diverse thinking team**

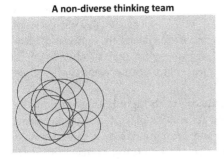

**A diverse thinking team**

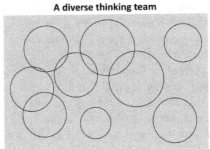

*Figure 7.41* Non-diverse and diverse thinking

for example we trust someone more if they are an authority figure than if they're not, or we assume someone's gender based on their profession. When we set our biases apart and surround ourselves in the midst of minds that have understanding and experience that is different from our own, we form a team with wider and deeper understanding.

Another way to minimise the effect of biases can come from technology. Algorithms are less affected by these kinds of biases when the models are trained well. Complex emergent properties from human–AI interactions will challenge our binary and linear thinking. This is a great example of where AI can help to enhance human intelligence.

Regularly engaging with diverse ideas and people working in different fields enhances our brains, which helps us to come up with better solutions and ideas. A leader should encourage people to get out of their comfort zones every now and then. People that are not regularly outside their comfort zones are less likely to feel these surges of inspiration since their minds have developed into what they are used to.

### Getting comfortable with being uncomfortable

Many airlines are constrained by their incrementalism, protecting existing lines of business, silo thinking, old hierarchies and thinking small. The airline industry is under a lot of pressure, even more so due to the impact of COVID-19. Surviving and thriving asks for a different kind of mindset. It is not about *what* we know, but *how* we know. We do not need more skills or information. We need transformation. Transformation is not about adding more to our minds, it is about changing the very mode or operating system of our minds.

The ability to step away from binary thinking and to embrace polarities will help to deal with the growing complexity of our world. But changing the way you have dealt with challenges for a long time and opening up to new perspectives can feel uncomfortable.

If leaders are able to create psychological safety in their teams, the advantages of cognitive diversity can be fully exploited. The environment forms the basis for non-leaders to voice their opinions, it will support the sharing of ideas and encourage open communication to prevent brilliant thoughts and ideas from being lost. The key for this lies in working with one another to open up through empathy and trust to create meaningful connections with people regardless of being different.

At this time of change and reflection, the call to thought leaders is to understand that doing business is not linear, but rather like playing an infinite game, where you have your head in the clouds and keep your feet on the ground at the same time. This requires us all to see that the emerging human and technical forces that are shaping the world are a positive opportunity to build a sustainable business, rather than a threat. The forces at play create a landscape of new and unfamiliar possibilities in the traveller's journey and beyond, as well as tearing down previously segmented markets. Defining a bold and inspiring purpose as a leader will help to mobilise the organisation, and working with polarity and communication with the three horizons is a pragmatic way to connect the future with the here and now.

## Notes

1 https://en.wikipedia.org/wiki/National_responses_to_the_COVID-19_pandemic
2 www.bloomberg.com/news/features/2020-04-16/coronavirus-travel-what-happens-to-planes-grounded-by-covid-19
3 www.edelman.com/news-awards/2020-edelman-trust-barometer
4 https://sustainablebrands.com/read/organizational-change/3-4-of-millennials-would-take-a-pay-cut-to-work-for-a-socially-responsible-company
5 J.P. Carse, *Finite and Infinite Games* (London: Simon & Schuster, 2013).
6 Simon Sinek, *The Infinite Game* (London: Penguin Business, 2019).
7 www.stevenvanbelleghem.com/blog/three-steps-to-define-your-partner-in-life-strategy/
8 www.whatyouwilllearn.com/book/the-inevitable/
9 Peter Hinssen, *The Day After Tomorrow* (Amsterdam: Lannoo, 2017).
10 www.thnk.org/insights/the-three-horizons/
11 Quote by Guido Woska, Lufthansa Group.
12 Attributed to Maya Angelou.
13 www.thinkwithgoogle.com/marketing-strategies/app-and-mobile/how-micromoments-are-changing-rules/
14 www.thnk.org/blog/innovation-and-inner-polarities-why-innovation-is-the-ultimate-place-for-growth/
15 Adam Kahane, *Collaborating with the Enemy* (Oakland, CA: Berrett-Koehler Inc, 2017).
16 Matthew Syed, *Rebel Ideas* (London: John Murray, 2020).

# How brand experience drives revenue and loyalty

*Moé Weisensee*
Customer Experience and Digital Marketing, Airbus

Good branding and brand experiences can drive the loyalty of customers and thereby the revenue of airlines. Let us examine, for a moment, why a brand is something that is worthy of an investment in time, reflection and various other resources. Is the return on investment worthwhile? The author of this book, Nawal Taneja, has been advocating for many years about changes in passenger decision making. Nawal specifies that there used to be three key aspects that influenced the decision: itinerary, fare, and loyalty programmes. However, going forward, will there be a fourth factor that may even overshadow loyalty programmes, the brand?

The importance of branding will not only increase due to the changes in passenger decision patterns, but will also prove itself as a safe means to navigate future times of crisis. When looking further into the future than the current inflection point and its challenges, this book also points out that environmental disruptions will become more commonplace. As such, a growing number of passengers will become increasingly aware and invested in taking measures to live more sustainably and with a reduced impact on our planet and expect the companies they select to do the same. As discussed later in this piece branding is, at its core, about listening to the customers' needs and values and providing them with solutions. It is therefore a powerful tool to assemble customers who adhere to the brands' values and enables the company to navigate times of crisis with more stability.

On the horizon is also a challenge that the rapid transportation from point A to point B is becoming more of a replaceable commodity each year. In order to stay differentiated and sustainably escape the commoditisation, airlines will need to take action. A few options are available to the airline's top management. Increasing passenger satisfaction by installing new and differentiated assets (e.g. latest generation seats and inflight entertainment systems) is one of them, but it can be very costly in terms of capital expenditure. In order to protect their market share, some airlines may be tempted to offer more competitive pricing or promotions instead. This will not only accelerate the commoditisation, but is also unsustainable as it drains profit margins.

For these various types of challenges, truthful branding and innovative tailored brand experiences that fulfil the specific needs and align with the views and values of customers is an excellent way to navigate an uncertain world and secure sustainable success.

Brands that have a clear and well-communicated personality will significantly outperform others and continue to thrive even in tougher times. When airlines might have to compete against Uber Air and Amazon Travel or others, having people who truly adhere to what the brand stands for and go to great lengths to be customers will be an invaluable asset reserved to those airlines that master creating and maintaining an attractive brand for their audience.

Branding is more than simply a logo, colour scheme, livery and a trademarked name. A good brand is unique and stands out from the competitors while being true and authentic to its values. It aims to solve its customer segment's specific needs with tailored brand experiences. Thereby it creates positive feelings towards the airline, which is indispensable for a successful brand. Furthermore, experiences are a key decision factor on spending for millennial and Gen Z populations, who are about to become the majority in many countries in the coming decades, which will elevate the importance of great brand experiences even further.

From a scientific perspective, airlines and airports need to create and evolve their brands so that people can understand them. Human beings like to personify all that surrounds them. An interesting anecdote proving this is found in a study by Professor Ann McGill of Chicago Booth as well as Jan Landwehr and Andreas Herrmann of the University of St Gallen.[1] They found that people attributed character traits to cars depending on whether their appearance resembled a smile or a frown. This phenomenon is called anthropomorphism. Therefore one should ask: If this brand was an actual person, would customers be good friends with the brand? Would the target customers have the same views, values, priorities and needs to be solved and therefore be drawn to it?

Another common misconception is that the company decides what the brand shall be. In reality one can define it and attempt to communicate it as best as one can, but the brand perception is defined by the cumulated opinions that the public holds about the brand. Although money can buy lots of advertising and publicity, changing the public perception can be expensive, difficult and time-consuming. Therefore it is a constant and long-term exercise that must not change its direction and message every few years. Self-evidently, the designs and style in which the brand appears and communicates can evolve over time and be made to stay relevant, but the core should always remain stable. This also means that in order to inform the public's cumulated opinion, they must be involved and informed. While there are various means to do so, one that should not be ignored is to make sure the employees understand, accept and adhere to the brand image first. They are ambassadors of the brand and must be clear on what they represent in order to be able to communicate and embody it clearly towards the public and customers.

The brands' deep connection with customers is the most valuable and sought-after outcome. An anecdote that perfectly showcases such a successful connection took place during a previous time of crisis, in the aftermath of 9/11. Southwest Airlines was surprised to receive unsolicited cheques from loyal customers. There were many cheques with varying smaller sums, but also some above US$1,000. It is remarkable to see that individuals decided to help a big corporation like Southwest and were willing to make a personal sacrifice for this brand that they feel so strongly connected to. These cheques are a testament to the incredible brand loyalty of some people who feel heard by and connected to the airline. These customers are invaluable assets to any company, as loyal customers and even ambassadors, who secure revenue and provide a competitive advantage.

## *The hidden brand in airlines*

If the brand is not just a logo and a colour scheme with a trademarked name, what are the actual other parts of the brand then? Especially those hidden parts of the brand at airlines? In this case hidden means small details that are part of the brand experience, but are generally not the first thing one thinks of when talking about branding.

It is crucial to stay away from benchmarking one's peers with the intention to offer the same level of user experience and branding. This often leads to a behaviour where competitors become indistinguishable. Instead, starting with ideas based on values from within and learning from customers is the more promising way. A few examples of unique branding and brand experiences follow that precisely fit the values and styles of the related airlines:

- Something expected by most customers when they fly is to get a bag of free pretzels or peanuts. JetBlue does this with a slight but important twist. They tried something different and unexpected, which is not very costly or extremely innovative either. Yet, they made an impact, because all of the competition was undistinguishable in this field. JetBlue started distributing blue potato chips instead of peanuts. Customers noticed this and started to cherish those blue chips. The chips fit perfectly with the brand of jetBlue as, on a superficial level, they are blue and, further, they are challenging the status quo, as is the airline.
- Another airline that often does unexpected things is Southwest in the US and similarly Kulula in South Africa. They are both taking a different path from many others, who perform standard announcements. In most cases the crew announces the weather forecast, flight time or local time in a serious and neutral tone before take-off or landing. Instead they both rely on their core brand values of fun and include humour and do not take themselves too seriously, while of course still respecting all necessary security protocols.
- A final example comes from Bangkok Airways. In general passengers would be expecting to have the usual airport waiting experience with a standard waiting area with the well-known benches and neon lighting. Instead, what they offer their passengers at Koh Samui Airport is an open-air facility, fully taking advantage of their tropical location. A roof, but no walls, surrounded by a lush landscape with palm trees and flowers between the gates and runway. Additionally they provide free popcorn and local sweets wrapped in banana leaves to all waiting passengers, including economy class.

It is evident that not all airlines should be doing these three things, but all airlines should be thinking about personalising even these types of minor details. These examples showcase situations in which a brand clearly understood what they represent and implemented that message in parts of the customer's experience. They are examples of the hidden areas where airlines are actually strengthening their brand and the perception of it by the customers.

### IKEA: A customer journey case study

Benchmarking is most effective when not solely done within one's own industry and region. This is when innovative solutions can be found, rather than a standardisation of competitors. It is best to do so broadly across different industries, countries and cultures as opposed to solely within airlines in the region. In order to do so and to benchmark and aim to rival the top brands in the world, this paper will take a detailed look at what airlines can learn from a completely unrelated industry.

The brand selected for the following case study is not one of the famous German car brands, or one of the French luxury designers, neither is it a Chinese trading giant or an American tech company. The brand to be examined was founded in 1943 and revolutionised its industry through creative solutions that make customers' lives easier. It is a brand that is recognisable even in the most minor details of their products and brand experience. This brand is a great benchmark for all types of airlines, as it is based mainly on personality in all aspects of their activities and is therefore as relevant for flag carriers, full-service airlines, low cost or value airlines, startup airlines, business airlines, commuter airlines and all hybrid forms. Incidentally it will be especially interesting to observe how more and more low-cost airlines will grow out of the main message of price in branding and find new additional values and personality to enrich their branding. Startup airlines emerging currently have the immense opportunity to start with a completely clean sheet and have the chance to revolutionise airline branding in new ways. One could expect the first airlines to also soon reevaluate their purpose and become a mobility as a service provider, not only providing flights, but also offering various options and combinations with partners, such as trains, buses, taxis and autonomous vehicles. No matter their product, every airline should and can have a delighting and unique personality.

From its humble beginnings in Älmhult, Sweden, IKEA is nowadays in living rooms all over the planet and rated the 25th most valuable brand in the world with a brand value of US$18 billion according to Interbrand.[2] Unfortunately this same list of the top 100 most valuable brands of 2019 does not include a single airline brand. However, there have been immense improvements in airline branding since about 40 years ago, when only Singapore Airlines, Southwest and Virgin could be seen as truly branded airlines, which is of course not the case today, as many other airlines have caught up and the context of branding has much evolved since then. It will now be intriguing to observe which will be the first airlines to make it into the top 100 in the coming years.

IKEA's brand is recognised for its authenticity and consistency. In order to understand how this is perceived in terms of customer experience, which is an important part of branding especially for airlines, a typical IKEA customer journey shall be explored. The following user journey is described through the perspective of a persona representing a young family. The following short description of the situation will later serve as a basis for the customer experience analysis regarding the fulfilment of detailed customer needs. It is common practice to give personas names to make them appear more real and relatable. In this case, they will be named Mark and Sheela with their 4-year-old Kyle. They are in their early 30s, work in engineering and education and earn the national median salary in the United Kingdom. The family just moved and need furniture but do not want to break the bank. They have several options of furniture stores in town and decide to try IKEA, because they know the brand from family and friends (ambassadors) and are aware that they have options adapted to their budget. Right at the entrance, they find "Småland" where they can leave Kyle to play with other kids supervised by the Småland team, free of charge. Mark and Sheela then head into the furniture showroom. After a tour of the showroom they take a quick break at the restaurant for some Swedish "Kanelbullar" cinnamon buns and a coffee. Since their family car can't hold the new table they bought, they arrange a delivery by IKEA. Reunited with Kyle, at home they build their new table with a quirky Swedish name and the typical assembly instruction illustration that does not need any words and can be instantly recognised by most people.

With this user story we shall now analyse IKEA's value proposition, which means how they recognise and address their customers' jobs (tasks), pains (unpleasant issues) and gains (delights) and simultaneously strengthen their brand. The job or task Mark and Sheela want to fulfil is to purchase furniture for their new home.

Their needs with regards to this are:

- They don't want to break the bank buying furniture.
  - IKEA addresses this by offering well-designed contemporary furniture starting at low price points.
- Their 4-year-old must be supervised.
  - IKEA has understood that investing in and offering a free service, such as the "Småland" childcare, enables the company to generate more revenue. This is because otherwise either Mark or Sheela would have had to stay at home to watch their child, thereby making an immediate purchase decision in the store much less likely without consulting their partner. Or they could have hired a babysitter for the time, costing them money that could have otherwise been spent on furniture. And finally they could have brought their child with them to the store,

making them much more prone to distraction and having a less smooth shopping experience.
- They are not interior designers, but still want a nicely decorated home.
  - The showroom is an opportunity for IKEA to upsell their customers. It gives them ideas, for example, combining the sofa they came for with the matching cushions displayed on it.
  - All of the items are named in line with IKEA's quirky style and Swedish origin, strengthening the brand perception.
- They get tired and hungry from selecting interiors.
  - Hungry customers simply want to get out of the store as quickly as possible. The restaurant included in IKEA stores satisfies people's need to replenish their energy, creates an additional revenue source for IKEA and keeps people engaged and shopping for longer amounts of time.
  - The brand identity is also clearly implemented here, as the offering is affordable, the self-service represents IKEA's philosophy and the menu options are inspired by Swedish cuisine.
- Their car is not large enough for transporting large furniture.
  - IKEA's initial breakthrough innovation was to offer disassembled furniture that was cheaper to ship and store that customers were able to transport on their own.
  - Delivering very large and bulky items to customers or lending them large vehicles for a fee is a natural addition to this.
  - Even for those without a car, in some locations IKEA offers free shuttle buses to their stores.

By observing their customers' jobs, pains and gains, IKEA has found various ways to offer more value to their customers and has been rewarded in return with growing revenues and great brand loyalty.

They are removing barriers one by one that people used to face when buying furniture. How can airlines remove all of the barriers that still exist for travellers?

The following section will look at how to apply this mindset to create more value for passengers and strengthen the airline brand.

### *Applying IKEA branding principles on airlines*

The same principles that IKEA uses to create such an attractive brand experience can be equally applied in the aviation industry by airlines, airports and all other customer-facing companies. Simply copying the Småland solution will obviously not work in all situations. Instead the brand must reflect on what their customers' common jobs, pains and gains are and then ideate solutions for those customers, which will then provide them with an excellent brand experience. In order to illustrate this, a few examples can be found below, which each take into account one customer job, pain or gain and one of the many possible solutions that the brand could provide.

- Customer **job**/pain/gain: The customer travelling to a touristic destination needs to research places of interest and is unsure about their itinerary choices.
  - Possible solution: Where IKEA offers a convenient service to parents with Småland, a tourist-focused airline can instead offer an adapted service that is of value to their leisure passengers.

One of many possibilities is to train one of the flight attendants on board as a local specialist about the destination of the flight and provide travel tips to curious passengers. Creating a tailored digital guide for the destination sent via email can be another one.

- Customer job/**pain/gain:** Sustainability in terms of a minimised environmental impact is of key importance for a considerable number of people and this number can only increase over time with the availability of scientific findings and rising awareness.
  - Possible solution: Transparency is one of the key first steps towards sustainability. This trend can already be observed in many sectors, such as nutrition and fashion. Some brands choose to be fully transparent on the impact of the produced goods, giving the consumer a clear vision and replacing the guessing. Many customers would value an airline which can clearly and transparently calculate the impact of a specific flight based on the distance, but also aircraft and engine model, load factor on the specific day and so on. The first step is not to be perfect, but to be fully transparent here to gain the trust and partnership of customers with an open dialogue with those who care deeply about the planet's future. While this may sound scary to many airlines, the ones who manage to be open and transparent about and committed to improving their flight's impact will gain loyalty from this rapidly growing segment of people feeling a personal responsibility to live sustainably, which will become mainstream in many societies in the near future.

- Customer job/**pain**/gain: Customers dislike having to read uninteresting documents.
  - Possible solution: Airlines can take a page out of IKEA's book with regards to IKEA's uniquely recognisable assembly manuals. While there is nothing to be assembled, there is still plenty of paperwork most don't like to go through.

This might sound like a detail, but do your terms and conditions represent your airline well?

If you are able to put a smile on the face of someone reading the tedious small print, that is unexpected and extraordinary. It is not only the big brand stunts that make a great brand, it is the accumulation of many details.

- Customer job/**pain/gain:** Certain customers dislike having to bother staff in order to ask for something they desire.

- Possible solution: What impact will it have to be the first airline to have a possibility to order snacks onboard on your phone, which will be futuristically delivered by a robot driving down the aisle?
- Customer job/**pain**/gain: Airlines seem impersonal and call centres or staff unable to solve certain problems or be flexible. Passengers therefore feel helpless and uncertain or stressed about changes and unexpected situations.
  - Possible solution: An airline that empowers their staff in the call centres, airports or on board to make a passenger's day with a small gesture, may win a passenger's loyalty.

Another possibility is to empower passengers directly to make their own changes easily online and without hidden costs. And most importantly, when talking about trust, the passengers will feel confident that if an unexpected issue were to occur, the airline will take care of them. More specifically, they will know that if they are stuck in a foreign airport because of a volcano erupting or a pandemic, the airline will make sure that they will be taken care of.

### Next steps

First, one must remember that a brand is more than just a name or a logo; using the term brand experience can make this clearer when discussing it. A journey back to the origins of the airline can refocus what the brand stands for. It is crucial to understand what the personality, vision and values of the brand are. These must not solely be defined, but also accepted and proudly adhered to by all of the employees, which is why involving them in an ongoing dialogue is crucial. This is the basis for making any further steps towards creating a brand experience that drives customer loyalty and therefore revenue.

Second, it is necessary to apply the same principle of understanding and solving your specific customer's jobs, pains and gains. To begin with, a clear understanding of the customer is needed. Most airlines have an existing clearly defined set of personas, which are helpful here. It is important that the team looking at offering a next level brand experience fully agrees with those personas. Borrowing a concept from the Lean Startup methodology formed by Eric Ries in Silicon Valley, which applies to early startups and large corporations equally, this requires that those employees get out of the headquarters building and talk to real customers. Quantitative surveys sent to customers give valuable insights as well, but for the employee to truly understand the customers' deepest needs and emotions, they will have to have open, unstructured, in-person discussions with passengers regularly. This will add an invaluable new personal dimension and many learnings to the personas. It can be very simple to do so and also important to get these insights continuously and not simply once every year or less. Employees needing those insights can simply go to the airports' check-in, or gate area and offer passengers a small coffee shop or onboard catering gift card in exchange for a chat of 10 to 20 minutes. It is then essential to ask questions about the passenger's needs, struggles and delights. The airline must stay away from asking simple yes or no questions and instead focus on understanding why the customer chooses or does certain things. Be careful to only listen to them and not promote or teach them about existing services or features of the airline. One must also stay away from "Would you like …" questions, as most people will agree to those without considering it further. Instead focus on listening to what they mention about their jobs, pains and gains when travelling. This then allows the team to create solutions for their customer segments, as IKEA has done. Customers will slowly become aware of the fact that your airline's brand experience solves more of their jobs, pains and gains than others and will prefer this experience over others. The reward is clearly a more loyal customer base, which leads to increased and more reliable revenues.

## Notes

1 www.researchgate.net/publication/261942206_It%27s_Got_the_Look_The_Effect_of_Friendly_and_Aggressive_Facial_Expressions_on_Product_Liking_and_Sales
2 www.interbrand.com/best-global-brands/ikea/

# About the author

Nawal Taneja, whose experience in the aviation industry spans five decades (starting with TWA at its headquarters in New York City), has worked for and advised major airlines and related aviation businesses worldwide. His experience also includes the presidency of a small airline that provided schedule and charter services with jet aircraft and the presidency of a research organization that provided consulting services to the air transportation community throughout the world. On the government side, he has advised worldwide departments of civil aviation on matters relating to the role of government-owned or government-controlled airlines, and their management. Within the academic community, he has served on the faculties of the Massachusetts Institute of Technology (as an associate professor) and at the Ohio State University (first as a professor, later as the chair of the Department of Aviation, and finally, as the chair of the Department of Aerospace Engineering). Currently, he serves as an Executive-In-Residence at the Fisher College of Business, at the Ohio State University.

He has served on the advisory boards of both public and private organizations. He continues to be invited to provide presentations at industry conferences worldwide, moderate panel discussions, and develop and discuss "what if" scenarios for individual aviation businesses. He advises senior executives in airlines and related aviation businesses, as well as senior government policy makers, on the impact of powerful forces that are converging and intersecting, such as the:

- profoundly changing behavior and expectations of connected, empowered, and increasingly divergent passengers in the on-demand and sharing economies;
- proliferation of smart technologies that facilitate the development of business intelligence and consumer intelligence to support end-to-end journeys with consistent and seamless customer experience;
- emergence of new forms of air and ground transportation systems; and
- rapidly evolving aviation regulatory policies, making the market more dynamic and more unpredictable, but also more environmentally acceptable.

He has authored an aviation management series that includes 13 books, written at the encouragement of, and for, practitioners in the global airline industry. This series attempts to move the arc of thinking about the airline business to develop and capture real strategic advantage by pursuing creativity and collaboration to drive change. The ambitious objective throughout the series is to stimulate visionary leaders to not only think out-of-the-box, but to think out-of-different-boxes to explore multiple perspectives and to think laterally to shield against challenges and to sense and seize opportunities. The series also presents best practices from other business sectors for creating, capturing, and delivering value, given that the rules of customer centricity and competition are changing continuously. Moreover, at the suggestion of some readers, the series has begun to include a portfolio of thought leadership pieces that touch upon a broad spectrum of topics, such as game-changing digital technologies, customer-centric platforms, state-of-the-art retailing strategies, and new transportation processes and systems. These pieces, contributed by experienced practitioners with diverse backgrounds, provide real-world examples of challenges and opportunities facing different sectors of the aviation industry.

Nawal Taneja holds a Bachelor's degree in Aeronautical Engineering (First Class Honors) from the University of London, a Master's degree in Flight Transportation from MIT, a Master's degree in Business Administration from MIT's Sloan School of Management, and a Doctorate in Air Transportation from the University of London. He is a Fellow of the Royal Aeronautical Society of Great Britain.

# Index

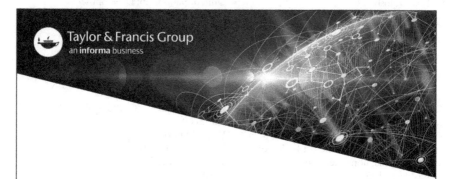